Healthy Living Centres

Contents

A list of case studies and their architects

Foreword

As someone who always wanted to be an architect, a book like this is always welcome. It is set in the context of changing patterns of health care, and this is especially relevant as the role of primary care become more evident. The development of primary care trusts sets a new direction in the delivery of health and health care and, as the Trusts take over a wide range of services, the premises used by the team, become even more relevant.

As the primary care team develops so facilities need to be available for dieticians, psychologists, physiotherapists and many others in addition to doctors and nurses. The increasing link to social services will also need to be taken into account. The patient is at the heart of the process and thus the environment within which they are cared for is critical. If, as is emphasised in this book, quality of life is important, then the whole atmosphere of the building can make a difference. As someone who has visited many premises over the years, the variations across the country are significant. Some are welcoming, bright, open, and have a sense of being designed for the purpose. Others seem to be designed to make it difficult to see the doctor or the nurse, lack confidentiality in the consultation and certainly do not support a team approach. Patients coming to see the doctor are likely to be anxious and worried. They will be concerned about the possible diagnosis and the treatment that might be suggested. They need an environment which reduces anxiety and provides a source of care and helpfulness.

The buildings, of course, are only part of this. The staff need to share the same vision and to be able to listen and communicate with patients and their families and to be able to provide information and support. Primary care facilities also provide a social context for the patient. They meet other patients as well as staff and can share problems and solutions. The premises are part of the community and provide a focus for services and information.

I have used the word 'design' already in this preface. It is crucial to the whole concept. It is partly about the finish and the materials used but also about the planning and use of space. The circulation of staff and patients, the provision of waiting areas, quiet spaces, and facilities for children, are all relevant. Of particular interest is the role of art in the design of primary care premises. Paintings, sculpture, and music all have a part to play in providing an atmosphere which is as relaxed, and welcoming, as it can be. In addition, where it is possible, the introduction of plants and greenery are also relevant. The ability to look out of a window onto a garden can add to the quality of life.

Finally let me emphasise again the importance of the relationships between staff, patients, the community and the buildings. Each component should add to the quality of life of the patient and staff. Patients come to a primary care setting with anxiety and concerns, and seeking help and care. The premises within which the advice and care are given can add to, and support, the work of the staff. This book gives a wealth of ideas on how such improvements can come about.

Kenneth C. Calman
University of Durham

Acknowledgements

The book began as research for a PhD, growing out of the collection of data that I had accumulated during the design of over 50 primary health care buildings during the past 20 years. My supervisor at Newcastle University, Dr Peter Kellett has offered many helpful comments on the structure of the book and also my thesis which is developing in parallel, although I remain responsible for all of the opinions and conclusions.

An architect, of course, always needs a client, and I am appreciative of the trust and responsibility given to me, and my colleagues in my practice (the Geoffrey Purves Partnership) by the many clients for these buildings, some of which are illustrated in this book. An architects' office is a team effort, and over the years many members of staff have contributed to the architectural process flowing out of clients' instructions. In particular, I would like to thank my former partner, the late Peter Thorneycroft who was personally involved in many of the doctors' surgeries we designed. This work has also led to my appointment as an Honorary Research Associate in the Centre for Arts and Humanities in Health and Medicine (CAHHM) at Durham University under the direction of Dr Jane Macnaughton. This is an initiative by Professor Sir Ken Calman and I am very pleased that he kindly agreed to write the foreword for this book.

My views have been influenced by the many people I have interviewed, especially those I have referred to and quoted in the book. I have received generous and unstinting assistance from a wide range of people involved in the case studies, particularly the architects for the projects illustrated who have provided drawings, photographs and descriptions of their work.

The production of the book would not have been possible without the encouragement and support of the staff at my publishers, Architectural Press. I could not have completed the text without the secretarial help from Val French who has willingly coped with endless revisions to the text and to Sharon Brown who has helped to co-ordinate and check all the illustrations and copyright issues. Every effort has been made to contact the copyright holders for their permission to reproduce material in this book. However, I would be grateful to hear from any copyright holder who is not acknowledged so that any errors or omissions can be corrected in any future editions of this book.

I would like to thank everyone who has helped me with this book, and I have tried to ensure that credit has been given throughout the text not only for their opinions and views but also for the material which they have kindly agreed can be reproduced.

Finally, I would like to thank my wife, Ann, for her support, tolerance and patience during the many long evenings when I wrote most of the words for this book.

Preface

Having been involved in the design of doctors' surgeries for the past 20 years I became interested in the relationship between client and designer (usually doctor and architect) and the factors which govern the briefing process. The wider debate about the way primary health care buildings are conceived and procured, the interaction between the medical and architectural professions and the management of those issues all have an impact on the quality of the completed buildings. These buildings affect the lives of those who use the environment which has been created – patients, doctors, staff and visitors alike. Change is in the air – procurement methods, funding arrangements, ownership and management systems are all under review – the challenge is for the architect to marshal these events, to put patients first in high quality buildings, and to design healing environments.

The book has evolved from the need to emphasis the importance of the briefing process in designing primary health care buildings. Of course, a good brief is a pre-requisite for the design of any successful building but this is particularly true in the health sector. It also seeks to capture the sense and pace of change sweeping through the National Health Service (NHS) and to highlight the importance of good environmental design and the therapeutic benefits which can accrue in the healing environment. A sense of well-being is important for good health and buildings have an important part to play in creating a comfortable environment. The quality of life is a holistic concept that has been overlooked in recent years. The procurement process which evolved had concentrated on cost and technical matters but this is changing: the quality of design for primary health care buildings is now firmly back on the agenda.

During the life of the NHS buildings have not played a key role in the formulation of the nation's Health Policy despite the substantial investment made in the fixed assets of property. New ideas on the strategic delivery of health care as set out in the NHS Plan 2000 provides on opportunity to re-examine the design of buildings to be used for primary health care in the future. The book brings together current ideas and explores the opportunities for the medical and architectural professions to work together in the twenty-first century so that building standards can improve.

Primary care, once again, is refocusing on the care of the patient as an individual. The view of patients as consumers, linked with the concept of customer care is bringing about many attitudinal changes to how medical services are delivered. Similarly, the architectural profession must respond to environmental design challenges so that buildings offer comfortable, pleasant spaces and are more than the provision of areas of accommodation within prescribed cost limits.

An exciting time for innovation lies ahead. Opportunities to look at new funding arrangements, new management structures, and new strategic health policies will need to be built into the briefing process. The ethos of the building will become an important starting point to achieve environmentally well designed buildings that can offer therapeutic benefits to patients, as well as all of the users of the buildings, and that are flexible and efficient. The buildings need to be flexible and efficient, and reach out to form linkages with their community and to acknowledge the need to be sustainable.

The pattern of health care delivery is set to change in future. As the information age develops there will be the easier transfer of specialist knowledge to community based services.

The pattern of health care now and in the future:

Now	Future
home	home
primary	primary
secondary	community
tertiary	specialist

(Source: based on work done by Susan Francis of MARU.)

Finally, these changes are related to the trend in international primary health care, originally established by the World Health Organisation (WHO) in 1978 as the attainment by all citizens of the world by the year 2000 of a level of health that would permit them to lead socially and economically productive lives. Rich countries now have policies that poor countries that can both ascribe to and aspire to. This should encourage a global flowering of preventative primary care identified as desirable in the 1920s in the UK by the Dawson report. The briefing process provides an opportunity to allow architects to provide primary health care buildings in the future from which this patient centred health strategy can be effectively delivered.

Healthy living centres will provide community based multifunctional centres from which a wide range of medical and related services will be provided.

The following diagram identifies the position of Healthy Living Centres in the broader sweep of patient centred care as envisaged in 'Building a 2020 vision: future health care environments' (Nuffield Trust, 2001).

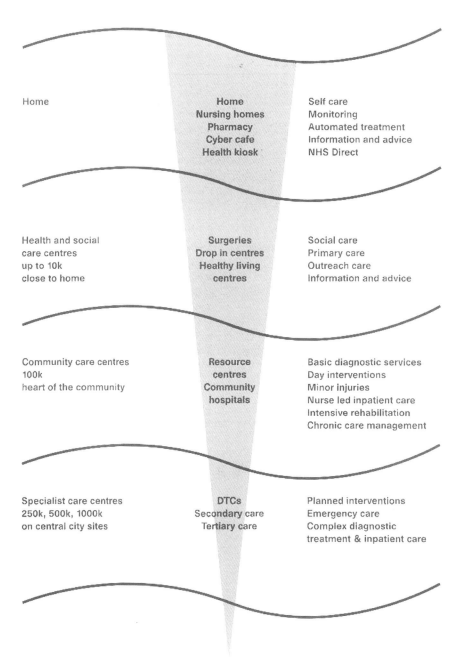

Home	**Home** **Nursing homes** **Pharmacy** **Cyber cafe** **Health kiosk**	Self care Monitoring Automated treatment Information and advice NHS Direct
Health and social care centres up to 10k close to home	**Surgeries** **Drop in centres** **Healthy living** **centres**	Social care Primary care Outreach care Information and advice
Community care centres 100k heart of the community	**Resource** **centres** **Community** **hospitals**	Basic diagnostic services Day interventions Minor injuries Nurse led inpatient care Intensive rehabilitation Chronic care management
Specialist care centres 250k, 500k, 1000k on central city sites	**DTCs** **Secondary care** **Tertiary care**	Planned interventions Emergency care Complex diagnostic treatment & inpatient care

Introduction

Quotations

'Architecture, of all the arts, is the one which acts the most slowly, but the most surely, on the soul.'

Ernst Dimnet, French priest and writer
What We Live By, 1932

'Health depends on a state of equilibrium among the various factors that govern the operation of the body and the mind; this equilibrium in turn is reached only when man lives in harmony with his external environment.'

Hippocrates

'Beauty has a healing power.'

Claude Monet

'We have seen that all great art is the work of the whole living creature, body and soul, and chiefly of the soul.'

John Ruskin, *The Stones of Venice*, 2001

The aim of the book: for both the medical and architectural professions

Better briefing brings benefits

This is a book for both doctors and architects (and indeed I hope it will be of interest to all users of primary care facilities). It sets out to explore the briefing process for primary health care facilities, and the beneficial effect that a good brief can bring to the environmental quality of buildings from which health care is dispensed. It aims to help the understanding of the briefing process which is one part in the larger web of relationships which govern the interaction of medicine and architecture.

The book's title, *Healthy Living Centres*, is intended to convey a broad concept of well-being. Not only does it embrace the building type of the same name used by the Government as part of its drive to develop primary health care services in the UK but it also considers other building concepts such as one-stop primary care centres, walk-in centres, polyclinics, superclinics, health kiosks, drop-in facilities, local health care resource centres, and other community based health facilities.

The main theme focuses on the briefing process as a starting point to raise standards of design for primary health care facilities, and thereby raise the quality of health provision in the community.

Audience

The scope of the book is to explore the inter-relationship between the architectural and medical professions and to see how the briefing process can contribute to the improvement of design quality. The consequence of raising the design standards for primary health care buildings will be to raise their environmental quality and help to release the inherent therapeutic benefits which will flow from these improved standards. This will improve the health of patients, their recover rates and show cost benefits with greater efficiency in delivering health services.

Investment

The Government has embarked on a major investment programme which will bring £1 billion's worth of refurbishment, improvement and new building work to primary care facilities. Working jointly with the private sector NHS LIFT (local Improvement Finance Trust) will be set up as a limited company. It will invest £175 million over four years, overseen by Partnerships UK, the Government-backed public–private partnership investment bank. Together with further funds sought from other private companies the Secretary of State for Health, Alan Milburn said that this would amount to £1 billion of investment over four years and that 'Primary care is the first port of call for patients' (Hawkes, 2000).

Patient-centred Care

The NHS Plan places patient centred care at the heart of its objectives. Primary care will be the focus of the Government's plans for the future of the NHS and this will be reflected in the desire to achieve cost benefits from higher environmental design standards for individual patient service. Patients will be seen as customers and the concept of customer care will become paramount to future standards of medical service.

Approach

After reviewing the historical approach to primary health care and outlining some of the key issues the book reviews a matrix of relationships which influence the design of a primary health care building. Looking at four main criteria; policy, design, financial, and briefing issues the factors which impact on the decision making process are examined.

Future opportunities

Following an analysis of the problems and challenges future opportunities are examined under the following main headings:

- The building's location in the community, and does it contribute to the urban fabric of the locality.
- Is it welcoming and accessible to all?
- Is it convenient to transportation linkages (by car, public transport, by foot, etc.)?
- Is the building easy to use? (functional).
- Is the building efficient? (clean, comfortable and pleasant to use).
- Is the building flexible?
- Is the building sustainable?

Case studies – United Kingdom and internationally

Finally, a selection of recent good examples illustrate the potential which can be delivered by dedicated and forward looking clients appointing imaginative and innovative designers to produce architecture of a high standard. Buildings which convey civic pride, are popular, efficient, and effective in providing an essential service. In short, buildings which are a joy to use by patients, and staff alike.

The standard of health care is important internationally and although the book primarily examines what happens in the UK I hope the ideas which are explored and the conclusions drawn will have a wider audience and be of interest to both medical and architectural professionals in other countries. The strategic aim of improving therapeutic care in a healthy and sustainable environment is valid wherever in the world it is applied. This is reflected by the WHO slogan 'Health for all by the year 2000' which was first adopted in 1978. It is inextricably linked to the quality of life, and all that is understood by that phrase.

International centre for life (Architect: Terry Farrell & Partners)

Writing this book in Newcastle upon Tyne it is a fascinating coincidence that a major millennium project, The Centre for Life, has been built in the city centre, which captures the connection between architecture and medicine. Designed by Sir Terry Farrell, who grew up in the city and is a graduate of the

Department of Architecture, Newcastle University (or King's College, University of Durham as it was when he qualified) the plan reflects the form of a human embryo in a building for generic research and education. The International Centre for Life sits adjacent to Newcastle's central railway station and offers a mixture of educational and research facilities, in particular into genetics and DNA. The *Architectural Review* (April 2000) says that 'the Centre curves embryonically around a central square, its north south spine traced by a public footpath through the site ... the scheme, curving north-south around the easterly edge of the site, is characterised by separation of parts and articulated links. Visually the buildings are given distinguishing colours taken from DNA codings: green (global garden roof), yellow (bioscience and genetics), blue (genetics) and red (internal wall, global garden).'

The buildings epitomise the intertwining strands between the quality of 'place', the sense of well-being, the natural curiosity of children, and the search for knowledge which are all inherent in the quest for better, standards of design in health architecture. DNA, the building block for humanity seems a fitting start for thinking about the design of primary health care buildings, wherever you are in the world. For Farrell, The Centre for Life is a celebration of the diversity of life. It is a group of buildings which you can enjoy, and which contribute to the quality of the urban environment, with a mixture of uses.

Figure 0.1 The Centre for Life, Newcastle upon Tyne: External View. Architect: Terry Farrell & Partners

Figure 0.2   The Centre for Life, Newcastle upon Tyne: aerial view. Photographed by Sean Gallagher (also in colour section)

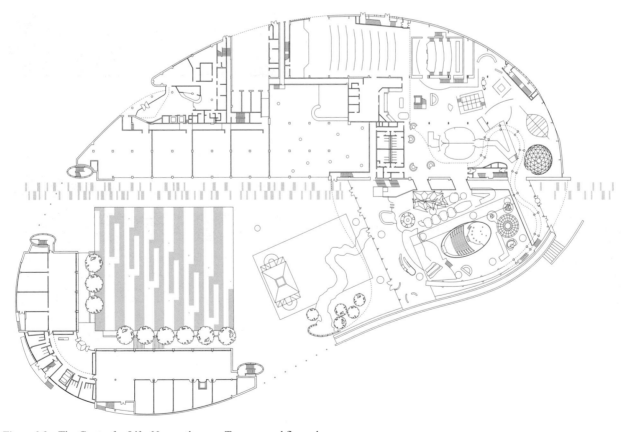

Figure 0.3   The Centre for Life, Newcastle upon Tyne: ground floor plan

Although outside of the main theme of this book, the Centre for Life encapsulates many of the qualitative aspirations that Architects set out to achieve when they are designing health buildings. For example, compare this building with the Glasgow Homeopathic Hospital (case study 2), Maggie Centre (case study 4) and the Centre for Clinical Research at Stanford University (case study 19).

Changing attitudes to good design

During the preparation of this book there has been a sea-change in the attitude towards good design for public buildings including primary health care facilities. In the UK the Treasury has moved away from lowest cost procurement policies and now says that good design can actually save money (Treasury Taskforce, technical note no. 7).

From a position not many years ago of seeing design quality largely the responsibility of others, NHS Estates has moved centre-stage to promote the Government policy of 'best value' so that this country once again has great public buildings. Who could have imagined only two or three years ago that CABE (Commission for Architecture and the Built Environment) would host a conference in February 2001 promoting the benefits of good design, including buildings in the health sector, with several Government ministers advocating from the same platform on the same day the importance of this approach?

Therefore, the opportunities for architecture and medicine in the future are exciting, as words such as delight and joy are on the lips of those responsible for the next wave of primary health care buildings.

We are experiencing a massive change in the operation of the National Health Service, created by Nye Beavan, Minister of Health in the Labour administration in Government in 1948. We are seeing a fundamental shift in how health care buildings are planned. Primary focus will be on the patient, not on the procedure, and this is part of a greater focus on the provision of primary health care services. There is a departure from conventional planning principles and buildings are likely to be less specific in functional requirements and will need to accommodate greater changes of use and adaptability during their lifetime.

The NHS is in the spotlight on the political stage. Attention is focused on the performance of consultants, the shortage of nursing staff, and the quality of medical services. To the construction industry, and architects in particular, the NHS is one of the largest clients in the UK with an annual capital procurement budget of nearly £3 billion. The NHS employs 1 in 20 of the working population in the UK. Consequently, great attention is being given to the NHS's response to the Egan Report which has set out ambitious targets for a reduction of construction time of 30%, and a massive reduction in faults on completion of a building. At first sight, it is easy to assume that these targets will be met at the expense of design quality, but fortunately the Government is rapidly moving architecture to the top of its agenda. From the Prime Minister downwards, Government Departments are being urged to achieve high standards in building design.

This is particularly relevant to the medical sector where the architect should always have in mind factors that make a building emotionally and spiritually uplifting as well as functionally efficient.

There has been little overlap between the literature of medicine and architecture and the two professions have followed, historically, relatively independent paths of research and investigation. Sadly, it would seem that even today, in the midst of a major upheaval of NHS policy, scant attention has been given by the politicians to the physical fabric from which the nation's health is to be dispensed during future generations. It has been alleged that in the committee rooms of Richmond House, the Department of Health Headquarters in Westminster, what the buildings look like is the last thing that is mentioned when reviewing future policy issues.

This gap must be closed, and the briefing process provides the opportunity to bring doctors and architects together to discuss and review how the health buildings of the future should be procured and designed. Clearly, the scale of this task must not be underestimated and it is exacerbated by the tension between the analytical approaches of a scientifically focused medical profession when compared with an intuitively stimulated architectural profession. These two opposing forces are well represented by the classical intellectual debate between scientists and philosophers which have raged down the ages from the commencement of civilisation.

The quality of life and environment design

The quality of life is difficult to define but it should be fun and enjoyable in addition to helping people to live longer.

However, this raises a dichotomy between empirically based science research and the qualitative methodologies of social science research. Why? – because there is insufficient evidence-based research to show the cost benefits of good design. The business case for a medical building must inevitably demonstrate the tangible economic realities of cost and time parameters but it must also embrace the intangible qualities that each of us recognises plays a part in the quality of our lives. Essentially it relates to the gap between what an individual or a community wants and what is available to them; the differences between dreams and aspirations and the reality.

Fortunately, we are beginning to understand that good design embraces a more holistic approach to life, and goes beyond the cost of technological brilliance. We can see these issues at work in our hospitals and health buildings as we begin to understand the contribution that the humanities can play in improving the speed of recovery. The measurement of therapeutic benefits is in its infancy, but the soothing effects of music, and the calming effects of a view of nature from a bedroom window has physiological benefits such as reducing blood pressure and lowering the heart rate.

At the heart of this debate is the concept of the quality of life. Lying at the crossroads of these interacting forces (see Figure 0.4) are all the diverse factors which impinge on our the health of the nation and this has been a trigger to adopt a more holistic approach to health care and to acknowledge the importance that a healing environment can contribute to our health.

Another illustration attempts to show some of the forces at work. Perhaps the balance of power is shifting as we show greater concern for sustainability and the balance of global systems on which we all ultimately depend. These tensions will continue to stimulate the debate between the theory and practice of both medicine and architecture. (See Figure 0.5.)

This suggests a more open and receptive attitude for inter-professional discussions to flourish, and an attitude that buildings should be more flexible, accessible, and convey an expression of diversity. Rather than being pillars or icons of an era, buildings should be responsive to human needs and provide a framework for the activities which will go on within them. This is especially relevant for our future health buildings and therefore the brief for these buildings must reflect this and be people centred. The cliché that an investment in buildings should be depreciated whereas an investment in people leads to an enhancement in value is perhaps an over-simplification of the Keynesian economic theory that we must leave behind in the twentieth century.

The way forward

Hence, returning to the central theme of this book, the brief-

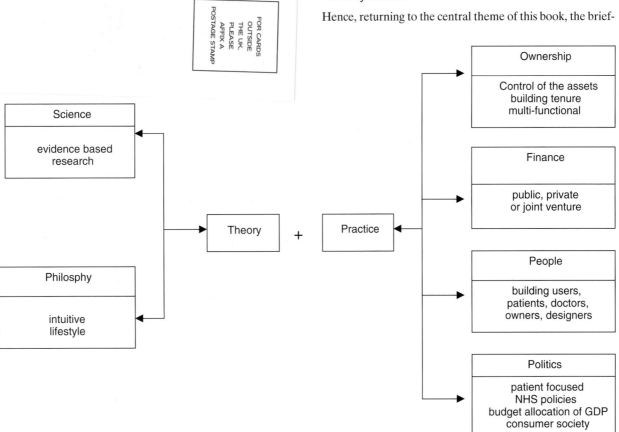

Figure 0.5 Theory and practice

ing process for future health buildings will be less about space standards and room areas and more about environmental standards, flexibility, and 'quality of life' issues.

There is a growing recognition that the introduction of the arts and humanities into the process of health care have a beneficial effect. The arts are not just an aid to medicine, they are important in their own right and need to be integrated into life. Alan Howarth, MP, in a recent ministerial speech with regard to what the Government can do said, 'I would start with the field of architecture'. The quality of the environment directly effects the quality of our lives and it is this challenge where architects are well placed to provide new solutions for future buildings. Good design really does mean healthy living.

The role of primary care through the ages (in the UK)

- *Ancient/early civilisations*: care in the home and community, hospices (e.g. Roman guesthouses for healing/recuperation).
- *Medieval*: care in the home and community, almshouses, hospices, leper hospitals, lay and monastic houses for healing.
- *Renaissance*: care in the home, development of monastic foundations based on early medical knowledge.
- *Georgian*: development of a hospital building programme in London to cater for the expanding medical knowledge and discoveries about how the body works

- *1800–1948 (birth of NHS)*: network of hospitals (becoming more specialised) for medical training, cottage hospitals, spas, workhouse, infirmaries, philanthropist foundations – a variety of facilities (note: 1858 was the year of the introduction of Florence Nightingale's ward design).
- *1948–2000*: rapid expansion of NHS, technology based science medicine centred on hospitals. Professional interests dominate service provision. Primary, secondary and tertiary levels of care.
- *2000–onwards*: primary care, patient focused. Specialist skills dispensed world-wide, utilising local community resources, the service going to the patient. Concern for sustainability, environmentally friendly, holistic medicine embracing alternative therapies. Consumer-orientated service.

Until late Georgian times medical assistance of any kind outside of the home or immediate community was rare, and usually only available to the wealthy. With the development of medical knowledge in the seventeenth and eighteenth centuries a wider range of institutions sprang up. The nineteenth and twentieth centuries saw the advancement of institutional medicine associated with a rise in the power of professional bodies. The twenty-first century will see a decline of professional control over patient focused provision of medical services.

1

An outline review of the issues

Changes and developments in the NHS

The growth of the National Health Service (NHS) over the first 50 years of its life has resulted in it becoming a victim of its own success. During the 1990s there was an accelerating rate of change as Governments and society began to recognise the financial and social limits which were necessary to constrain the NHS. Outdated philosophies of 'doctor knows best' are being challenged by patients who have become used to the higher standards of service and respect offered by other consumer-orientated industries.

On the technological front it has become apparent that the research-driven clinical approach promoted by medical scientists became increasingly isolated from the traditional patient-focused healing environment of the home and community where 90% of the nation's health treatment is administered. A balance needs to be struck between clean, modern, professionally competent surgeries and friendly, humane environments. Recognition that primary health care should be the main focus of a health policy of the future has taken hold in the past few years and is powerfully promoted in the NHS Plan published by the Labour Government in July 2000.

By 1995 the Royal Institute of British Architects (RIBA) had published its strategic study of the health system, conceived as an aid to architects for reshaping their marketing strategy to secure future commissions in the health sector. It was recognised that there would be a sea change in the type of buildings that would be required for future health care. These would be buildings designed for flexibility over their life span. Working patterns would need to change and the buildings would be used 24 hours each day as the emphasis of health care moves towards primary care. Private finance would become influential in the determination of future building types and their location. Terms used at that time included polyclinic and resource centres and these multi-purpose flexible buildings remain the corner stone of the NHS Plan looking forward from the year 2000.

The NHS Plan

The executive summary of the NHS Plan states:

'This is a plan for investment in the NHS with sustained increases in funding. This is a plan for reform with far reaching changes across the NHS. The purpose and vision of the NHS Plan is to give the people of Britain a health service fit for the twenty-first century: a health service designed around the patient. The NHS has delivered major improvements in health but it falls short of the standards patients expect and staff want to provide. Public consultation for the Plan showed that the public wanted to see:
* more and better paid staff using new ways of working
* reduced waiting times and high quality care centred on patients
* improvements in local hospitals and surgeries.'

It goes on to say that the extra funding provided by the March 2000 budget will fund additional investment including:

* 500 new one-stop primary care centres
* over 3000 general practitioner (GP) premises modernised and 250 new scanners
* modern information technology (IT) systems in every GP surgery.

Alan Milburn, the Secretary of State for Health, stated in the introduction to the plan that 'At its heart the problem for today's NHS is that it is not sufficiently designed around the convenience and concerns of the patient.'

Therefore, the Government has given very high priority to reorganising the NHS, allocating substantial additional resources, and committing itself to providing a significant number of new and improved facilities, particularly at the primary health care level. Interestingly, however, the main vehicle for procuring these physical assets in the future seems to hinge on successfully implementing a series of private finance initiative (PFI) projects.

'As well as new hospitals there will be a range of other new buildings developed between 2000 and 2010. As a result of the NHS Plan there will be:

1

- £7 billion of new capital investment through an extended role for PFI by 2010
- 40% of the total value of the NHS Estate will be less than 15 years old by 2010
- The NHS will have cleared up at least a quarter of its £3.1 billion maintenance backlog accumulated through two decades of under investment by 2004
- Up to £600 million realised through a one off auction of empty and surplus NHS property to reinvest in new NHS premises.
- The new buildings will be provided through a mixture of public capital and an extended role for the PFI.'

The NHS will enter into a new Public Private Partnership within a new equity Stake Company – the NHS Local Improvement Finance Trust (NHS LIFT) – to improve Primary Care premises in England. The priority will be investment in those parts of the country, such as the inner cities, where primary care services are in most need of expansion. As a result of this NHS Plan:

- up to £1 billion will be invested in primary care facilities
- up to 3000 family doctors' premises will be substantially refurbished or replaced by 2004.

This record level of investment will allow for a range of brand new NHS facilities, bringing primary and community services – and where possible social services – together under one roof to make access more convenient for patients. new one stop primary care centres will include GPs, dentists, opticians, health visitors, pharmacists and social workers.

NHS Estates: procurement strategies

NHS Estates, the Government agency responsible for the maintenance and provision of the health service's physical assets have responded to this series of initiatives by a newly created procurement system known as Procure 21. Initially envisaged to include projects from £1 million to £25 million in value this has been revised upwards to a range of £2.5 million to £25 million, as a result of pressure from the construction industry.

However, a very large percentage of the NHS Estates property portfolio consists of small buildings and it remains to be seen if the procurement methodologies can be designed to provide sufficient flexibility for the creative provision of new smaller facilities to provide the patient-focused primary care facilities.

This challenge has been recognised by the development of LIFT (Local Improvement Finance Trust) as another initiative to stimulate private investment in local community-based health facilities.

The World Health Organisation: primary care policies globally

The Times reported on the World Health Organisation's (WHO) *The World Health Report 2000* that lists Britain as eighteenth in a world league table in terms of the effectiveness of the care it delivers for every pound spent and twenty-sixth in its responsiveness to patients and in its ability to treat them professionally and with dignity (25 June 2000). The same leading article goes on to say, 'By any measure, the National Health Service is failing in its purpose. Cancer survival rates are appalling for a wealthy nation and well below the rest of Europe, America and Japan'. WHO's experience suggests that throwing money at the problem does not produce a good health system for a country. The world's best health system, in France, has succeeded on a mixture of public and private financing, where patients pay for their GP appointments.

There is danger, also, in shifting policy towards lifestyle diseases such as high blood pressure, cancer, heart disease and depression. Treatable diseases in the developing world should remain the priority of WHO to the millions of young people in undeveloped countries who continue to die from these diseases.

Sustainable and holistic principles: all of this leads to a greater awareness of a more traditional healing environment and raises many of the issues which the Prince of Wales continues to raise in his speeches. In his Reith lecture (Wednesday, 17 May 2000) Prince Charles said:

'I believe that if we are to achieve genuinely sustainable development, we will first have to rediscover, or reacknowledge, a sense of the sacred in our dealings with the natural world, and with each other ... part of the problem is the prevailing approach that seeks to reduce the natural world, including ourselves, to the level of nothing more than a mechanical process ... in this technology driven age it is all too easy for us to forget that mankind is a part of nature and not apart from it ... above all, we should show greater respect for the genius of nature's designs, rigorously tested and refined over millions of years. This means being careful to use science to understand how nature works not to change what nature is.'

Prince Charles' argument that we should follow 'the grain of nature' underpins his architectural opinions. But leaving aside any comment on the heir to the throne's stylistic ideas, he does bring together the strands of an all-embracing philosophy that buildings are designed for people, and should be people centred. This seems to be entirely compatible with the holistic and quality-of-life concepts fundamental to the future well-being of the medical profession.

Bringing the medical and architectural professions together

Bringing together the medical and architectural professions seems to be a fundamental necessity if the patient-focused primary care development plans envisaged by the Government are to succeed.

The primary care buildings of the future need to be multifunctional, flexible, long-life buildings that are easily accessible by the community in the broadest possible sense. Not only accessible from a physical point of view, embodying the latest requirements for the Disability Act, but also accessible in a social sense; friendly, welcoming, human in scale, obviously offering dignity and privacy to the sick and disadvantaged in society, and are transparent and inclusive offering opportunity for everyone's well-being.

Historical overview: a holistic approach

Early knowledge of health care goes back to at least Egyptian times, when faith and healing were the basis of the relationship between patient and carer. The Hippocratic Oath has survived from its Greek origins when health care was viewed within a natural and totally holistic framework. A hospital was a place of hospitality, which in today's terms would be seen more as a health resort. With almost no technical knowledge as we know it today (but a long tradition of faith, wisdom, and experience by practise and observation), health care was also associated with religion, music, poetry, the arts and good food. The lack of scientific knowledge put reliance on the natural healing process which is today receiving greater attention than ever before as an alternative approach to modern, high-technology medicine.

Perhaps this return to studying alternative forms of medicine is part of the process of a return to care in the community beginning to take precedence again over the institutionalised treatment of the ill which has been prevalent during the past 200 years.

'It is only comparatively recently that the focus has returned to care in the community. As medical invention and technology become further sophisticated so technology itself can begin to break away from hospital buildings and move into the community. Therefore the hospital no longer needs to be the focus of health care.

This is also reflected the world-wide economic crisis in the funding of large hospital programmes and the enormous expense of hospital technology which encourages providers towards the low tech form of treatment. Have we therefore come full circle?' (Valins and Salter, 1996.)

Valins and Salter suggest a chronological split for the nature of caring in the western world as follows:

0–1800	care takes place at home or in the community
1800–2000	care takes place in medical institutions
2000 and beyond	care takes place at home or in the community.

Although valid in the Western world, this analysis would not be representative of many developing countries where home and community care may be all that is available to the great majority. Hospitals are likely to be a great distance away and often offer very limited medical skills and facilities.

These trends will provide new opportunities for the design of specialist buildings, to provide sophisticated day care treatment located within the localities they serve, thereby reducing the demand for highly expensive capital intensive hospitals (although some will continue to be required for research and complex medical conditions).

'Health for all'

Health care is of great concern to all nations; this is reflected by the existence of the WHO. At the World Health Assembly in 1977 a commitment was made to '... the attainment by all citizens of the world by the year 2000 of a level of health that will permit them to lead a socially, useful and economically productive life' (WHO, 1979). At a joint WHO/UNICEF conference at Alma-Ata in 1978 it was declared that primary health care was the most promising vehicle for '... attaining the target of health for all by the year 2000 as part of overall development and in the spirit of social justice' (WHO, 1978).

This new approach will certainly have its impact on the planning, building, and operation of health care facilities. It is therefore imperative, in order to avoid costly mistakes, to consider carefully what should be the place of these activities in a health system based on primary health care and what are the constraints to be overcome.

This is further developed by Kleczkowski and Pibouleau, the editors of a 1983 WHO document (Kleczkowski and Pibouleau, 1983). They identify that the role of the hospital in the primary health care context will inevitably change, and argue that it is difficult to predict the full extent of that change until the primary health care programmes have become more firmly established. Many developing countries are staking large investments in vast national networks of health care facilities, and the success or failure of their planning, building, and operation is a priority issue.

They state that architects are frequently not involved in formulating the building brief '... when decision require relating to the size and scope of facilities and to their general standard of construction and equipment are being made'. At the design and production stage, an excess of project loads lead to a general lowering of professional standards and the easy adoption of *ad hoc* designs as standard solutions. In achieving the 'goal of health for all' through the medium of health systems orientated towards primary health care, there needs to be a fundamental re-arrangement of building and equipment priorities involving completely new building types, design approaches, methods of construction, uses of material, and modes of implementation.

USA: the early days for primary health care

In the USA more literature is available on the evolution of the primary health care facility and its development over the last 50 years. During the 1950s there was considerable development of the concept of a health centre. Under the Hill Burton Programme the development took place of providing a range of medical services from the same building. Health centres ranged in area from 1000 to 20,000 sq ft, with the national median at about 5000 sq ft, although a greater number of about 3000 sq ft were built, which was deemed capable of serving a rural population of up to 35,000 people.

The general background of this programme is set out in Hunt's (1960) work. The overall planning concepts were much the same then as they are today in the UK, and the list of accommodation which was recommended would be familiar to an architect designing a doctor's surgery under the requirements of the current 'Red Book' procedures (NHS, 1996). They include:

- waiting areas, including the main entrance
- administration, including offices and record space
- clinic, including sub-waiting, examination, treatment and consultation rooms
- service, including heating, storage and maintenance rooms.

The importance of flexibility in the use of rooms was also recognised and '... multi-use of clinic space should be exploited in the interest of economy, not only of expensive space but of valuable personnel'. It was also recognised that benefits would accrue from incorporating additional medical facilities such as dental and X-ray facilities. The idea of grouping examination and consulting rooms in groups of two or more which interconnect closely follows the design of treatment suites in GP surgeries which have been designed during the 1990s in the UK. The importance of using a doctor's time as efficiently as possible has been recognised, therefore, for 40 years or more.

Other facilities that were considered included nutritional advice, and a mental health clinic. It was estimated that one full-time mental health clinic per 50,000 people should be provided as a minimum. However, it was acknowledged that the provision of mental health facilities was at an early stage of development and that the required standards were not fully understood.

Development work in the USA continued during the 1960s and 1970s and the design of primary health care facilities continued to advance. During this period the emphasis also shifted from the treatment of disease to keeping people healthy.

'The trend is to prevent disease; to keep people out of the hospital through health education programmes and holistic ideology, making persons responsible for their own health. Raising the general public's knowledge about the importance of proper nutrition, exercise and the risks associated with alcoholism, drug abuse, and smoking is perhaps the most effective weapon in the battle against disease. Health education centres as agents to hospitals and other health service agencies have sprung up recently in store fronts and shopping centres, making sound information accessible to the community. Future social, economic, and political considerations will change the character of health delivery systems considerably. Good medical care

is now considered the right of all citizens, rather than the privilege of a few. In addition, we have increased longevity, so more elderly persons will be around to need medical care. These two factors demand a comprehensive health planning system co-ordinated on a nation-wide basis.

From the stand point of economics, *prevention* of illness is more economical than disability and disease.' (Malkin, 1982.)

United Kingdom

During the past 15–20 years there has been a large development programme in the UK in upgrading doctor's surgeries, providing architects and interior designers with considerable opportunities to explore a wide range of design solutions. The advantageous financial arrangements made available to all GPs has resulted in over 600 architectural practices listing primary health care facilities as an area of expertise with the RIBA's Client Advisory Service. A very large database of statistical information is therefore available.

Relationships between environmental design factors and therapeutic benefits

As we start the new millennium the climate of opinion – certainly within the UK, and probably in many other parts of the developed world – is more receptive to the influence of design quality in the built environment than probably at any other time. During the past 10 years there has been an increasing interest in the influence of good design on the comfort of human beings living in an urban environment and this has manifested itself in wider press publicity, and a diversity of architectural responses in a wide cross-section of buildings, but especially health buildings.

At one level, this interest in design is represented by three recent publications published by client bodies in the major public building sectors of health, higher education and commerce:

- *Better by Design: Pursuit of Excellence in Health Care Buildings* (NHS Estates, 1994)
- *Design Quality in Higher Education Buildings* (Thomas Telford, 1995)
- *Time for Design: Good Practice in Building, Landscape and Urban Design* (English Partnerships, 1997).

Lord Palumbo, in his keynote address at the Royal Fine Art Commission Seminar in November 1995, powerfully underlined the part played by the art of architecture on the effect buildings have on an individual. It is interesting to note that he used hospital design as an example of how a building

'designed in a thoughtful way, combining good design, attention to detail and a subtly ordered and embellished character, often with artwork, landscape and lighting ...

[can] ... have a positive effect upon the healing process.' (Palumbo, 1995.)

The NHS Estates publication, *Better by Design* sets out clearly the parameters and advantages of seeking good design in the creation of health care environments. The concern of the Government is noted by the then Parliamentary Undersecretary of State for Health, Tom Sackville, and is followed by a series of cogent and snappy summaries of many key objectives which should form the basis of design in the health sector. Also included are a number of appendices including a checklist of design pointers. Unfortunately, although aimed at senior personnel in the health service responsible for the procurement of health buildings, and their professional advisers, the document remains only advisory rather than mandatory. There is no requirement, beyond exhortation to incorporate the advice that is so persuasively advocated. During the design process for a new primary health care facility there is no necessity to undertake any checking or auditing procedures to measure or evaluate if any of the desired design qualities have been incorporated and achieved.

The third document, *Time for Design*, published by English Partnerships catches the mood in the UK in 1997/98 that design is 'a good thing'. It sets out a series of design aspirations, with a forward by Sir Richard Rogers announcing English Partnership's desire

'to support projects of quality and long-term value'. Sir Richard says '... but regeneration is not simply about economics. It is about health and happiness too. English Partnerships has a real opportunity to take a longer view of people's needs. Restoring density to the urban scene will surely help repopulate cities, especially at night. This in turn will help to make for successful commercial centres as well as places in which it is enjoyable to live'.

The document reiterates a series of common threads being advocated by a number of clients and sets aspirations such as:

• To design an attractive and safe environment. Commercial sense – it repeats the point made by Peter Yorke (Yorke, 1995) as part of his presentation to the Royal Fine Art Commission seminar in November 1995: 'that if the lifetime cost of a building is assumed to be 100%, its capital cost is only 10% of this. Its design cost generally represents only a mere 1%. But this small percentage can determine a building's lifetime usefulness and its overall artistic merit' (Coonan, 1996).
• Making time for design.
• Design and the community.
• Design and disability.
• Site assessment and environmental impact.
• Energy efficiency and building in safety.

The author of the English Partnerships' publication is Rory Coonan who was Head of the Architecture Unit of the Arts Council of England from 1992 1995. He was responsible for raising the profile of good design in architecture within the Arts Council at the critical period when the National Lottery was launched introducing large sums of capital to five 'good' causes; the Arts Council, the Sports Council, National Heritage, the Millennium Commission and the Charities Fund. He assisted in the establishment of architectural panels, to seek to evaluate design quality in applications made to the Arts Council for capital funding. Others have attempted to rationalise the influence of good design in terms of architectural quality. The North-West Regional Health Authority, working with MARU (Medical Architecture Research Unit) have prepared a resource book to be used as a manual and to assist and support particular aspects of the design of primary health care facilities. In a guidance note on using the book it says that 'it offers an introduction to key ideas and methodologies with suggestions of how to access other existing documentation which may inform the process'. Included is a section called 'Ambience' that seeks to identify factors in the design of health buildings that contribute to 'well-being'.

The benefits of high quality environments in the health sector are also promoted in *Environments for Quality Care; Health Buildings in the Community* (NHS Estates, 1994). However, although this booklet sets out a series of exemplar projects, it only sets out aspirations, and provides a checklist against which to test other designs. The then Secretary of State, Virginia Bottomley said:

'The Government is committed to developing care in the community, and places great emphasis on the provision of an integrated community service. A poor environment can work against the high quality and dedicated care delivered by individual teams. Much of our experience in developing quality in the NHS shows that patients are generally more at ease in a human scale environment which is well designed and maintained'.

I suggest, therefore, that there are two key issues that will form the backbone of this book.

First, although there is an awareness in the health sector that high-quality design has a beneficial effect on the quality of the environment, there is no requirement to attempt to evaluate this aspect of design in the building procurement process, nor are there any mechanisms to seek to quantify, or measure, the effectiveness of quality in the working environment.

Second, the huge changes to the health service, and in particular the provision of primary care services, instigated by the Labour Government elected in 1997 appears to have given little consideration to the effect on the building fabric which will result from the proposed policy changes. Buildings are essentially a long-term investment that deserve to be well designed, but policy changes are demanding a more flexible usage than previously allowed for. The current thinking in the design of office space may offer an approach that will lead to greater flexibility in the use of health sector buildings.

This latter point was touched on by Francis Duffy of DEGW International at a seminar in 1997 in Trondheim, Norway during a conference on human centred design for health care buildings. Peter Scher reporting on his presentation noted that Dr Duffy anticipated a totally client-focused design demanded by the ferociously competitive world of international financial conglomerates for new buildings with a grim message for architects that this concept had to be embraced or they would run the risk of being discarded (Scher, 1997). Peter Scher has also undertaken a study on patient-focused architecture for health care. He attempts to describe and explain in very simple terms the advantages to be gained by approaching health care design in a patient-focused manner. He also identifies the gap between patient's personal experiences, and the professional criteria set out in such documents as *Environments for Quality Care* (NHS Estates, 1994).

Preventative medicine is increasingly being recognised as consisting of more than technological solutions to medical problems. As has already been noted, early medical practitioners operated more as faith healers, recognising the beneficial effects of calm, relaxing spaces, and environments conducive to a feeling of spiritual fulfilment. The well-being of the human condition is once again being examined more closely by academics both in a general sense as well as in buildings provided for primary health care. At the macro-scale, Sir Richard Rogers devoted his Reith lectures in 1996 to a discussion about the quality of urban life, and in the post-technological age greater adherence is being given to arguments urging a return to urban spaces that relate to the human scale. There is a rich history of architectural references that can be quoted to sustain the validity of these arguments, many of them springing from the Renaissance period and the cities of central Europe in particular. Although beyond the scope of this book, a range of factors including climatic variations, seasonal changes, geographic influences, urban and rural influences, and the effect of social stability, all have influences on the mind.

At the micro-scale, there is a paucity of research recognised by NHS Estates, who have identified the need to undertake further research work into the effect on the well-being of patients who receive their primary health care treatment in well-designed buildings.

The healing environment is considered by Albert Bush-Brown and he highlights the complex relationships between the physical relationships of spaces and the effect architecture plays on the mind. He defines the will to live as follows, 'a spiritual reason to live is the most precious and delicate motivation the critically ill or ageing adult can sustain'. Although the spiritual influence is regarded today as a less important influence than in many previous eras, the influence of the mind on the healing power of spiritual belief cannot be lightly dismissed (Bush-Brown, 1996).

The architectural dimension for this spirituality is reflected in the tranquillity of a design that can banish anxiety. During the 'high-tech' 1950s and 1960s, hospital design often resulted in clinical spaces which could be very intimidating to patients. They represented fear in an unknown environment, often when individuals are at their most vulnerable. The same senses are invaded when primary care facilities were designed with an ethos of clinical efficiency. The confidence of technical skill, instead of raising confidence with the patient created anxiety from someone ill at ease in their surroundings.

One of the first areas of health care design to recognise these dilemmas between efficiency and comfortableness was perhaps examined during the emergence of hospices. A building type once thought of as being unnecessary has emerged over the past two decades to represent the very best standards of a caring environment for the seriously ill. Many of the best seek to emulate the reflective, comfortable and relaxed atmosphere of a private home, usually incorporating a direct relationship between the spaces inside the building with nature. The conflicts highlighted by these issues touch all aspects of ethical philosophy in a culture emerging from a period of intense materialism where the marketplace has been considered pre-eminent. 'Our emotional life, including spiritual life, depends on that dual context, privacy and community, self and membership' (Bush-Brown, 1996).

David Kuffner takes a more pragmatic view of the recent history of primary health care design and provides a short historical review of patient-focused design (Kuffner, 1996). Looking back over the past 30 years he identifies four models of approach as follows:

- *team nursing*: an administration-focused system (early 1960s)
- *the Frezen concept*: a clinical technician-focused approach (late 1960s)
- *primary care*: a consumer-focused approach (1970s)
- *patient focused*: an operational policy linking patient benefits to those of the institution and the community as a whole.

The harshness referred to by Dr Duffy at the conference in Norway reflects the dangers of adopting a commercial and managerial focus on patient care. Seeking higher standards of efficiency, new ways of tempering the cost benefit demands made by the financial regimes established by NHS Estates for the provision and procurement of primary health care buildings need to be examined and tested in practice.

These issues were, perhaps, at the heart of the symposium held at the RIBA on in April 1996 to discuss future premises for Primary Health Care. The Chairman, John Wells-Thorpe, an architect as well as Chairman of the South Downs Health NHS Trust opened the proceedings by declaring that 'the delivery of Primary Health Care has changed significantly as a result of the government's initiative to move towards a Primary Care lead NHS' (RIBA, 1997). The proceedings of the symposium carefully record the comprehensive discussions identifying the issues faced by the architect when designing new primary health care facilities. The importance of people rather than places was highlighted as well as the need to strive for high standards of design within a stringent cost framework. The change in use patterns of a building used for primary health care were also considered, including the possible move towards buildings which might be open 24 hours a day.

The conclusions of the working groups conducted during the symposium were broad ranging, and great emphasis was placed on the importance of good design. Checklists for what represented a well designed primary health care centre were advanced, that design is a process rather than the fixed interpretation of an individual design.

The most important attributes, according to participants of the second focus group were:

- *Value for money.* If value for money was achieved, then the design would be tailored to the health budget and allow more money to be invested elsewhere. Good design would also reduce running and maintenance costs and would ensure efficient functioning.
- *Flexibility for future use.* Participants felt it was important that a building be designed for expansion, but it should be flexible and adaptable and that it should be able to accommodate new technology.
- *Client/architect rapport.* If client and architect worked in close collaboration the doctor would benefit from a better building; it would capitalise the design team's previous experience and be able to tap into creative and imaginative solutions to problems. The end result would be a building that more successfully projected the GP practice's image, and maximised the collective professional skills of both medical and architectural teams.
- *Attractive to patients.* An attractive building would be welcoming and relaxing as well as reducing stress and apprehension about entering. It could also provide a focus for the whole community.
- *Improve staff morale.* A well-designed building could also do much for staff, reducing stress, providing a pleasant and comfortable working environment, and helping to cut absenteeism and staff turnover.

As I have previously identified, the aspirations of these investigations are readily agreed to by the leading components of health care design work in the UK at the present time. However, there are two main issues that require closer examination: (1) further research is required to test the benefits that flow from a well-designed building (as compared to a building that is efficiently designed) and (2) mechanisms need to be considered to evaluate and test the design performance of a primary health care building before the project is built.

The shifting philosophy of the approach to health care design is summarised in the following statement that encapsulates the high-tech or high-touch dilemma:

'As post-industrial society continues to unravel, we must again recognize the need for centers of health to become places of healing. We need to reintroduce a sense of poetry, rhythm, peace and serenity in our inner souls and redis-

cover the healing powers of techniques such as yoga, aromatherapy or reflexology which can provide an alternative, or perhaps even a complement, to our high-tech future care. The health practitioners of the future, with their technical abilities now largely undertaken by computers, may need to return to the role of healer as portrayed in pre-industrialized society. That is, a healer who relies upon care, the good spirit and the touch and smile of an understanding and sensitive professional. The challenge of technology raises in turn this equally important challenge and reminder of our spiritual needs'. (Wylde and Valins, 1996.)

The quality of life

In the *Potential for Health* (Calman, 1998) a strong case is made for the importance of the quality of life. In the introduction it states that: 'being healthy is a positive concept and should be valued. That is the challenge, central to which will be the theme of quality of life, of fun and of enjoyment.' Calman continues 'the overall objective is to improve health, health care, and quality of life … . The aim is to make people feel better and enjoy life in addition to living longer. Being healthy is a good thing to be, and should not be associated with negative images of what not to do.'

Calman goes on to argue that 'quality of life is a concept which is generally understood, but is very difficult to define.' This establishes a dichotomy between empirically based science research and the qualitative methodologies of social science research. This is a recurring theme throughout the book. Government policy, and its examination of the procurement system for health buildings wishes to base its decisions on evidence based scientific research whereas many of the human aspects of the quality of life revolve around surreal and spiritual concepts of hope, aspirations and dreams.

'Essentially it relates to the gap between what an individual or community wants and what is available to them, to the differences between dreams and aspirations and the reality. It is clearly subjective and linked to past experiences, future hopes, and the culture of the group or the community. No matter how difficult it is to define quality of life, it should be the end point by which health programmes are judged. It should cover all aspects of life – physical health being only one of a whole range of issues (physical, emotional, psychological, social, and spiritual) which can affect or influence the quality of life. People who are ill or disabled can be happy; people who are physically well may not be. Quality of life is therefore the summation of many factors synthesised to give an overall feeling of well-being.'

Calman's approach provides many useful pointers for the objectives of this book; that is an exploration of the relationship between architects and doctors when focused on the provision of primary health care facilities and the quality of the environment they provide. It is useful to list the factors important for the development of the NHS as identified by a former chief medical officer. This interchange of ideas is always the basis for a good brief, and as all architects will tell you a good brief is the cornerstone of a well-designed building. This implies a commitment by the client, and no matter how talented the architect, a building will not succeed without the support and commitment from the client.

Calman provides a helpful list of key factors to consider:

• the importance of quality of life, not just longevity
• the need for a knowledge base in medicine and science
• the importance of social and economic factors
• the need for environmental factors to be considered
• the centre role of education
• the role of women
• the importance of our health service being based in primary care
• the need for resource allocation to be based on outcomes and effectiveness.

Similarly, links are made, to which I will return to later, between health care objectives for both countries and individuals.

An overall improvement in the nation's health will improve the quality of life for the individual and the community. The aims are stated as:

• holistic, in that it covers physical, psychological, social and spiritual aspects of life; it puts the patient in the community first
• ecological, in that it puts human health in the context of the world as a whole, and relates human activity to animal and plant life, and the wider environment
• inter-sectoral, in that it acknowledges that a wide range of agencies and individuals need to be involved in achieving the potential
• equitable, in that it recognises that the variations in health which exist must be tackled.

There is a growing body of evidence and support for the view that the introduction of the arts and humanities into the process of health care has a beneficial effect. Lord Attenburgh, President for Arts for Health has said that 'I know that the arts can and do inspire happiness a sense of well-being in those who, for reasons of ill health, are also those who need them most.' The arts are not just an aid to medicine; they are important in their own right and need to be integrated into life.

Presentations at two conferences held in 2000 attempted to illustrate graphically quality of life factors that influence the way medicine and architecture responds to the challenge to improve primary health care services.

At the launch of the research group CAHHM (Centre for Arts and Humanities in Health and Medicine) at Durham University the Vice Chancellor referred to the coalescence of architecture and medicine as an idea whose time has come. The arts are important in their own right and they are not just an aid to medicine. Architecture and the arts need to be integrated into

life and their evaluation must be sensitive and sophisticated. However the key factor is quality of life and this relies on professional education, and community development. To illustrate his concept of the quality of life he used a series of diagrams. Figure 1.1 shows that over a period of time individual's ambitions and dreams often exceed reality and the gap between these two positions is the shortfall in the quality of life that might be achievable. One way to close this gap is to reduce our personal expectations and also to attempt to improve our quality of life (Figure 1.2). However, how successful we are at achieving this goal may be influenced by events outside of our control (Figure 1.3). Our ability to cope may be significantly effected by whether or not we are on a 'personal high' or 'low'.

The aim, therefore, is to narrow the gap, and this may be achieved by introducing extra energy, either self-generated, or from other sources. Intuitively, we all know that the quality of life is important, and therefore this extra energy can be stimulated by subjectively pleasurable environmental factors. This might include architecture, music, light, colour, and a variety of others sensual stimuli (Figure 1.4).

Roger Ulrich, speaking at the Second International Conference for Health Care in Stockholm (June 2000) presented an approach to the therapeutic benefits that can be gained from a well-designed environment. He argued that it provides a key starting point for understanding how design effects medical outcomes. Three components to consider are:

• *psychological*: such as anxiety, depression, or anger
• *physiological*: elevated blood pressure, decreased immune functions
• *behavioural*: sleeplessness, hostility.

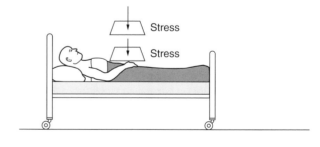

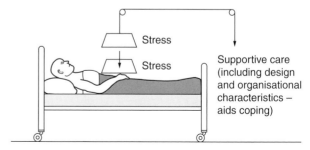

Figure 1.1 Based on Roger Ulrich's diagrams

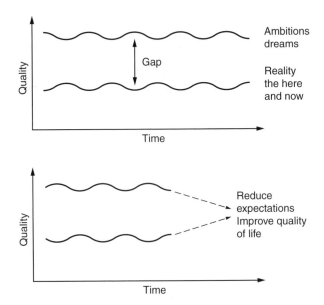

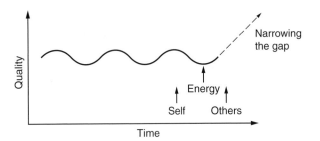

Figure 1.4

down bed in a patient room where a close personal friend or relative can stay overnight with a patient has a very beneficial effect on a reduction of stress.

Access to positive distractions can provide immediate benefits in 3–4 minutes. Laughter and looking at nature can both have very rapid benefits in reducing blood pressure, for example.

Therapeutic benefits

Until very recently the Government has taken the view that the quality of the environment in the health care sector would remain in second place to the top priority of medical treatment and clinical care. 'In response to a bald choice between providing cancer treatment and supporting arts projects, then of course the arts will come second' (speech by Alan Howarth, 14 April 2000). Much of this thinking has been based on the belief that the introduction of environmental improvements to the quality of health buildings could only be determined by a fully researched cost benefit analyse in other words, good architecture had to be demonstrated as necessary in the business case. Perhaps this is why so many of our health buildings over the past 50 years have failed to provide the delight and feeling of spiritual uplifting that a good building can provide and strikes at the heart of the dilemma between the quantitative approach of scientific methodologies and the qualitative methodologies used by social science researchers. How these two positions can be brought together for the benefit of health buildings is another theme that runs throughout this book.

The challenge is to demonstrate the tangible benefits, and although research work is surprisingly limited, a large body of opinion is now rapidly moving towards the challenge of providing answers to the relationship between patient medical outcomes and therapeutic environmental issues. This can take many forms, and stretches across the arts field including music, drama, literature, and all the visual arts embracing a light, colour, tactile responses, and the whole panoply of responses that go to make up architecture.

The American researcher, Roger Ulrich, based at Texas A&M University is perhaps pre-eminent in the field of developing research methods to demonstrate the linkages between environmental quality and medical care. In his early

Figure 1.2   Based on Sir Kenneth Calman's diagrams

If the design of a building increases stress, patient outcomes will be poorer and if the design achieves lower stress levels then there will be an improvement in patient outcomes.

Ulrich illustrated this by two diagrams in each case representing stress as weights on a patient lying on a hospital bed. There are two components to this stress; stress from the environment (for example, noise, loss of privacy, etc.) and stress from the organisational culture of the institution. With supportive care the level of stress can be reduced. This supportive care can come from both organisational characteristics, but significantly also from the design of the environment. He advocates a theory of support with designs based on ideas including the creation of a sense of control, access to social support systems, and access to positive distractions. Sense of control: uncontrolled conditions are stressful and therefore personal control of a patient's privacy, and for example lighting levels will be welcomed. This also would include control of televisions and to have the opportunity not to watch or listen.

Access to social support, strong connections with caring, an emotionally supportive staff will reduce stress and improve health. Any design factors that foster this feeling of support will improve patient outcomes. For example, a fold-

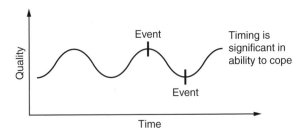

Figure 1.3

work looking at the recovery rates of patients who had undergone gall bladder operations he demonstrated faster recoveries for those who looked onto a natural environment than those who looked at a brick wall (Ulrich, 1984).

Intuitively, most people readily relate to this more holistic approach to medical care. By embracing the whole body, and a sense of well being, it is easy to understand the calming effects that come about from listening to soothing music. Physiological changes such as lower blood pressure and pulse rate can be measured, and conversely, stress levels are raised when looking at the strident and discordant geometry of some contemporary art. Or again, patients enjoy, and feel better, when looking at visual representations of nature such as impressionist paintings depicting sunlit romantic garden images.

As the Government is moving rapidly towards a greater concern for raising design quality in the procurement system we are at a fascinating crossroads of how design quality is measured. The Lottery funding bodies, such as The Millennium Commission, and other public sector bodies including the funding councils for educational buildings have been grappling with the concepts of how to evaluate design quality and measure design efficiency. The PFI procurement methods are incorporating much greater emphases on design quality and NHS Estates are similarly shifting towards a much greater recognition of design factors in their recently launched Procure21 system for building procurement. So there is a complex matrix of evolving techniques as we move from a cold and calculating cost benefit regime to a more rounded and holistic approach to running the economy. The Treasury now talks about non-measurable quality issues, and CABE offers advice to Government on the quality of architecture for public buildings.

Humankind has rediscovered that physical and mental well-being go hand in hand, a theme that has challenged scientists and philosophers throughout the ages. We have at last realised at the beginning of the twenty-first century that sustainability is a global issue for everyone and that the pursuit of technical excellence at any cost must be matched by the philosophical concepts which embrace the mental well-being of everyone.

The Hippocratic Oath

The Hippocratic Oath sets out the need for an equilibrium between mind and body to establish a state of good health. As architects probably seldom see the text in full it is reproduced below:

I swear by Apollo the physician, and Aesculapius, and Health, and All-heal, and all the gods and goddesses, that, according to my ability and judgement, I will keep this Oath and this stipulation – to reckon him who taught me this Art equally dear to me as my parents, to share my substance with him, and relieve his necessities if required; to look upon his offspring on the same footing as my own

brothers, and to teach them this art, if they shall wish to learn it, without fee or stipulation; and that by precept, lecture, and every other mode of instruction. I will impart a knowledge of the Art to my sons, and those of my teachers, but to none others. I will follow that system or regimen which, according to my ability and judgement, I consider for the benefit of my patients, and abstain from whatever is deleterious and mischievous. I will give no deadly medicine to any one if asked, nor suggest any such counsel; and in like manner I will not give a woman a pessary to produce abortion. With purity and with holiness I will pass my life and practise my Art. I will not cut persons labouring under the stone, but will leave this to be done by men who are practitioners of this work.

Into whatever houses I enter, I will go into them for the benefit of the sick, and will abstain from every voluntary act of mischief and corruption; and, further, from the seduction of females or males, of freemen and slaves. Whatever, in connection with my professional practice or not in connection with it, I see or hear in the life of men, which ought not to be spoken of abroad, I will not divulge, as reckoning that all such should be kept secret. While I continue to keep this Oath unviolated, may it be grated to me to enjoy life and the practice of the Art, respected by all men, in all times! But should I trespass and violate this Oath, may the reverse be my lot!

Therapeutic benefits of music

The emotional and healing benefits of music have been known about for over 2000 years.

In the Middle Ages the spiritually uplifting benefits of chanting were understood not only by Christians, but by other religions. For example, Buddhist chanting as a process of healing can be traced back for 2500 years. Also 'The chant was the heartbeat of religious devotion in England in the year 1000' (Lacey, 1999).

'The chant uplifted people spiritually – and it provided physical uplift as well. The decades following the year 1000 saw a significant growth in the building of monastic infirmaries which were medical institutions in the modern sense of the word, but also offered refuge to the old and dying, as well as accommodation for travellers and pilgrims ... Many of these infirmaries were built on deeply symbolic thoroughfares, beside bridges or rivers, or much travelled road, and though they could offer rest and seclusion and simple herbal remedies to those who were sick, the main constituent of their healing regime was the primeval resonance of the mass and the deeply effecting rhythms of the chant.' (Lacey, 1999.)

The Renaissance provided a period of experimentation as the theoretical relationships between architecture, mathematics, and music were explored. Classical principles were analysed as mathematical proportions and ratios and comparisons made with musical intervals. As medical technology began to take precedence during the last 100 years the link between the healing process and the humanities has been lost. However, there has been a reawakening of interest in the holistic approach to medicine during the last decade. Interestingly, the launch in October 2000 of the 'National Network for the Arts in Health' used a flyer which included the following paragraph:

' "Spital" is Old English for "hospital". A medieval priory located in Spitalfields was a physical healing centre as well as a spiritual healing centre. A choir sang 24 hours a day because of the healing effects of music. Further, Christ Church itself was built by architect Nicholas Hawksmoor, who also designed Greenwich Hospital. This venue provides a perfect historical and architectural backdrop for the launch of the National Network for the Arts in Health.'

During the past few years there has been new research undertaken and interesting results have been published. One doctoral thesis (Menin, 1997) undertaken at Newcastle upon Tyne University explores the emotional differences between the buildings of Alvar Aalto and the music of Sibelius.

Professor Paul Robertson is at the forefront of research in this field and produced a series of programmes for the Channel 4 television broadcaster 'Music and the Mind' which explored our emotional responses to music and included a consideration of the healing benefits which can be demonstrated (Roberston, 1996). Robertson reported on the work of Dr Ralph Spintge, a German surgeon who has demonstrated a reduction of pain thresholds by the use of music. At the Chelsea and Westminster Hospital further research work is being undertaken by Dr Rosalia Staricoff looking at the therapeutic benefits of music in the Oncology Department during outpatient treatment clinics. By using music with a beat which is synchronised with a patient's heartbeat it can be demonstrated that after a time, by slowing the tempo of the music, a patient's heartbeat will similarly respond by slowing.

'In a more active role Spintge and his team have composed musical pieces which induce the optimum condition, mentally and physically, for specific medical procedures. 15 minutes of soothing music lulls the patient into such a state of wellbeing that only 50% of recommended doses of sedatives and anaesthetic drugs are needed to perform otherwise very painful operations. Indeed some procedures are now undertaken without any anaesthetic, which was previously unthinkable.' (Robertson, 1996.)

Table 1.1 The emotional music scale

Emotion	Tempo	Instrument	Mood
calming	slow	quiet	funereal
		bells harp cello guitar trumpet drum	
energising	fast	loud	celebratory

Based on the emotional music scale (Boyce Tillman, 2000).

Research is in progress to investigate the neurological patterns created by listening to music. For example, researchers have discovered that listening to Mozart raises spatial IQ. Their investigations were based on a mathematical modelling of brain function (Robertson, 1996, 2000a). Another interesting correlation relates to the natural rhythm of the heard. 'Rhythm in all societies – from primitive drumbeats to the patterns heart in the symphonies of music – tends never to deviate from the rate variability of the human heart, which lies in a range from around 60 to 150 beats per minute' (Persaud, 2000.)

Musical experience and emotion spans many events and some of these are shown on a range of scales in Table 1.1.

Professor Paul Robertson (2000b) in a lecture at the Second International Design Conference in Stockholm expanded on his views and explained how he believes that music and spirituality can come together very effectively. He believes that music acts as a beautiful mediator between the inner and the outer worlds and that mind, body and soul are brought together. A great deal of music stems from a strong emotional event and one only has to look at the work of Beethoven or Shostikovich to understand the power of this medium. Finally, perhaps it is significant that music is the last sense to leave us before death. The ability of most people to hear to the very end of their lives is perhaps a poignant reminder of the part it plays in our emotional and spiritual well-being – in turn, a sense that should not be underestimated in the beneficial effect of designing therapeutic environments to improve healing.

2

Architecture and medicine: is it art and science or illusion and reality?

Many theories of design have been promulgated by architects and a number of systematic approaches are set out in a later chapter. Architecture is regularly described as both an art and a science and in academia architects are frequently criticised for having insufficient research evidence to back up judgmental decisions. Medicine is looking towards a widening of its scientific framework to embrace a more holistic philosophy. The juxtaposition of these two great professions sets new challenges in the way primary care buildings are to be designed in the future for the provision of health services. The measurement of therapeutic benefits asks new questions about illusion and reality. Can sensory perception be scientifically controlled? What are the differences between the tangible and intangible characteristics of people, and the buildings they occupy?

Art and science in medicine

The relationship between medicine and architecture requires greater study but there are many parallels that can be drawn between the theory and practice of the two professions. A doctor, as well as having technical knowledge based on scientific principles must also make clinical judgements and these issues are discussed in a recent book (Downie and MacNaughton, 2000). They use a diagram reproduced in Figure 2.1 to illustrate the main relationships.

Doctors who are in the middle of their careers (i.e. the 40–50 year olds) were trained as clinical scientists and this has led many leaders in the medical profession to begin to question training methods. With the Government increasing expenditure to encourage greater numbers of medical students to commence their training, developments are taking place in the design of curricula to include non-medical subjects. Special Study Modules (SSMs) are being proposed that would deal with not only 'ancillary medical subjects such as mathematics, physics, the social sciences, and philosophy' but also non-medical subjects particularly in the arts and humanities (Downie and MacNaughton, 2000).

These traditional values have also pointed to the next generation of primary health care buildings being more akin to a cottage hospital than a 'high-tech' building. Such scientifically based buildings represented the intellectual high ground of both professions in the 1980s and 1990s and which are now increasingly being questioned by those advocating a more rounded and broadly based philosophy of life. Cottage hospitals are to be created from GP surgeries as part of a drive to cut NHS waiting lists for operations:

> '... family doctors will be encourage to earn extra fees by training to perform procedures such as cataract removal in their own mini operating theatres. There are thousands of people waiting for the 12 minute procedure to restore their sight. Moving this and similar non-complex operations into a new generation of the cottage hospitals that used to feature in small towns and villages will do much to meet an ambitious 6 month maximum waiting time target for all operations.' (Rogers and Prescott, 2000.)

It is this challenge that architects need to meet to satisfy the demand for new facilities that can accommodate the new services in a caring and humane environment. New policies are unfolding to encompass a comprehensive re-examination of primary care policies, management and required facilities.

A philosophical shift to holistic care

The changing attitudes and policies, representing a shift from scientific theory has been further reinforced by a plea from Dr George Carey, the Archbishop of Canterbury, saying that religion is being replaced by therapy. 'Western culture today is obsessed with three alternative saviours – therapy, education and wealth, among many others – none of which can provide lasting healing for our broken world'. He went on to say 'Our society is fascinated with the healing of the body and mind. Its unspoken assumption is that if we can but keep in tune with

13

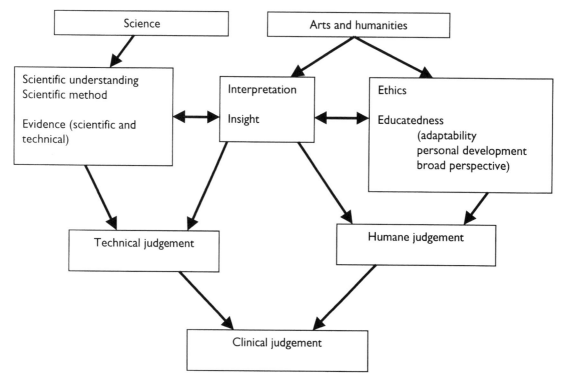

Figure 2.1 Clinical judgement: a diagrammatic summary (Downie and MacNaughton, 2000)

the well being of our inner selves, all will be well' (Gledhill, 2000a). His encouragement for the importance of faith to be reconsidered encourages a return to traditional values.

The emotional and uplifting benefits from a pleasurable environment have been recognised from early civilisations. Knowledge and interest in health goes back to at least Egyptian times, when faith and healing were the basis of the relationship between patient and carer. The Hippocratic Oath has survived from its Greek origins when health care was viewed within a natural and totally holistic framework. The hospital was a place of hospitality, which in today's terms would be seen more as a health resort. With almost no technical knowledge health care was also associated with music, poetry, the arts and good food. The lack of scientific knowledge put reliance on a natural healing process which is today, once again, receiving greater attention than ever before as an alternative approach to modern high-technology medicine (Valins and Slater, 1996). Perhaps this return to studying alternative forms of medicine is part of the process of a return to care in community. It is beginning to take precedence again over the institutionalised treatment of the ill which has been prevalent during the past 200 years. Put simply, it could be argued that it is a policy to 'do less and achieve more'.

Architectural illusions

This leads towards the requirement for definitions and therefore generalisations. Conversely, the attractive egalitarian

flavour of subjectivist theories pre-supposes that the view of every individual is as valid as the next. The scientific basis of the objective view requires discrimination and a rational judgement and in aesthetic terms is likely to appeal only to a minority. In a visual sense appearance can be considered as either cognitive (subjective) or optical (objective) (Vesey and Foulkes, 1990). We may well have pre-conceived ideas of how an object should look which belies the scientific analysis of facts. For example, the length of the lines AB and BC appear dissimilar (AB looks shorter than BC) although geometrically, and in fact, they are equal in length (Figure 2.2). The shape also illustrated generates confusion – is it a duck or is it a rabbit? (Figure 2.3). Similarly, the black and white square can be seen as two objects. Is it a vase or two profiles nose to nose? (Figure 2.4).

Illusions abound in architecture and we progress through a building using the background of experience accumulated from our spatial awareness developed from childhood sensations. This argument is explored by Kant in his *Critique of Pure Reason* that all our awareness is grounded in spatial

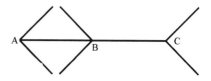

Figure 2.2 AB = BC?

Figure 2.3 Duck or rabbit?

Figure 2.4 Vase or two faces?

Figure 2.5 Perpetual waterfall by Maurits Cornelis Escher

experience. At a more light-hearted level the graphic artist Maurits Cornelis Escher (1898–1972) is well known for his visual tricks (Figure 2.5) and yet they have a disturbing and unsettling effect on the mind. The eye is not comfortable with the mind's interpretation of what is drawn. It searches across the drawing looking for visual footholds because what is seen can not be real.

Classical architecture is based in seeking to find art within geometry. However, we are familiar with the distortion of Ionic and Corinthian columns (by the introduction of subtle curves in the vertical axis) to create the illusion of perpendicularity. The search for simplicity and elegance in a mathematical statement becomes increasingly complex to accommodate the subtlety of design necessary to satisfy the eye. Many mathematical ratios were devised such as the Golden Section (Figure 2.6). The Renaissance period further refined these attempts to reduce art to mathematical formulae, and further complexities were introduced by making comparisons with poetry and music (Read, 1949). These comparisons continue today and a current Open University television programme for its arts foundation course uses musical notation to analyse and explain the American artist Pollock's 17-foot long abstract landscape 'Summertime' which is the centrepiece in the Tate Gallery's recent extension designed by James Stirling.

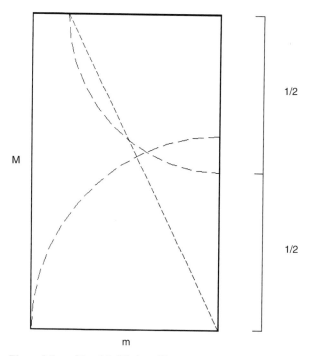

Figure 2.6 $m:M = M: (Mm) \rightarrow (2)$

The advertising industry goes further: it seeks to influence our mind by allusion. By implanting concepts in our mind we associate emotions with the desirable attributes of products which are being promoted. Architectural illusion, therefore, is a powerful influence that we associate with intangible emotions. We are gradually understanding how to measure intangibility in architectural design. Questions of scale and sensory perception are beginning to be measured, increasingly blurring the boundaries between quantitative and qualitative methodologies.

All these attempts to rationalise and explain the basis for art represent a convenient shorthand which fits within the cultural sensibilities of the relevant era. We now know that Newton's laws are not the full explanation for the laws of nature and scientists continue their relentless pursuit of knowledge. Another attempt to provide a framework on which to build an architectural set of rules of thumb, or an everyman's guide to good design was given in a series of lectures at the RIBA in 1959 by Rasmussen. He reduced the explanation of architecture to a series of observations based on his observations from the modern movement. Perhaps they are a more fluid and complex set of inter-relationships than set down by geometrical ratios but nevertheless they remain an analysis of proportions, light and dark, rhythm, colour, and texture (Rasmussen, 1959).

Architecture: art or science?

Once again, it is necessary to return to the question of is architecture art or science? Is science a source of social stability or instability? The philosophical substance verses the sociological function of science demonstrates the unanswerable tension between reason and feeling (Fuller, 1997). The relentless pursuit of a scientific model, searching only for questions and answers is bound to fail. The development of professionalism in science, and the creation of scientists has been mirrored in the development of architecture. The Royal Charter of RIBA was only granted in 1834. The order and discipline and rationalisation of procedures that took 150 years to develop reached their height perhaps 20 years ago. Since that time, post-modernism has questioned the rationale of a scientific profession as we tumble towards a global complexity of innovation, flexibility, and a new humility to the cosmic scale of our existence. Charles Jencks describes it thus: 'In the mid 1970s however, realization dawned among a few scientists and philosophers that the cosmos had more *non-linearity*" in it than linearity gathered strength. It became clear that the universe was more like a cloud than a clock, more like a growing fern than a Euclidean structure. Even the eminent rationalist philosopher Popper started to write pregnantly of clouds.'

In architectural terms, new ideas about the importance of complexity in the urban built environment were being propounded by Jane Jacobs in her important book *The Death and Life of Great American Cities* (1961) whereas previously city planning had been based largely on grids and zones according to use including the 'scientific' work of Le Corbusier. She unravels the complexity of urban life and identifies it as an essential ingredient of a successful city. She argues that the real vitality of cities lies in their human diversity and architectural variety. She identifies that cities that people want to live in are more akin to the natural world (Jacob, 1961). Research is examining the natural healing process and the classical connections between architecture and music. More recently the harmony of the natural world has been compared to the work of Alvar Aalto and Sibelius (Menin, 1997). She describes her fascination with the organic nature of Aalto's work and was struck by something similarly organic in Sibelius' music. Her thesis explores the phenomena of the Finnish forest, which was a core influence on the creativity of both men, and demonstrates that the common tools which were requisitioned for this were experience and knowledge of nature's growth process, knowledge of vernacular culture, and inspiration from the Greek notion of creating harmony. A quotation from Alvar Aalto reinforces this point: 'After all, nature is a symbol of freedom. Sometimes nature actually gives rise to and maintains the idea of freedom. If we base our technical plans primarily on nature we have a chance to ensure that the course of development is once again in a direction in which our everyday work and all its forms will increase rather than decrease it' (Weston, 1995).

Complexity and flexibility

Modern theories of architecture are emerging from the hands of Charles Jencks (*The Architecture of the Jumping Universe*) and Sir Colin St. John Wilson (*Architectural Reflections*). They come from very different backgrounds. Sir Colin St. John Wilson as Professor of Architecture at Cambridge, worked under Sir Leslie Martin and was influenced considerably by Ludwig Wittgenstein who was professor of philosophy at Cambridge from 1939 to 1947. Charles Jencks, by way of contrast, has been credited with anticipating the post-modernist movement. Paul Davies, Professor of Natural Philosophy at the University of Adelaide offers the following comment. 'A new paradigm is sweeping through science, changing both our view of the universe and of mankind. Charles Jencks is one

Figure 2.7 Concert Hall, Los Angeles. Architect: Frank Gehry.

Figure 2.8 Wideopen Medical Centre, Newcastle upon Tyne. Architect: Geoffrey Purves Partnership (also in colour section)

of a handful of thinkers with the courage to embrace the emerging paradigm and interpret it architecturally. This inspired synthesis of art design, science and philosophy, charts a bold new course not only for architecture but for post-modern thought.' He recognises the richness, and diversity, and sheer eclecticism of architectural theory as we move into the twenty-first century.

So in conclusion, how are we to reconcile this diversity of choice? The freedom it offers, allows architecture to respond to local conditions with flexibility, richness, and diversity. We can see that the rigorous application of rules can produce a harmonious architecture but the scientific test fails modern architecture when exposed to the rigours of professionalism, engineering and the market economy. The NHS is currently going through the biggest transformation it has experienced since it was founded because it has been unable to devise an effective economic model. The banality of its physical state is ample evidence of the failure of a scientific approach to procuring buildings. A system that has created a whole bureaucracy to control budgets and programming has failed entirely to offer any framework to assess quality.

A series of booklets is now emerging not only in the health sector, but also in higher education, and industry to promote

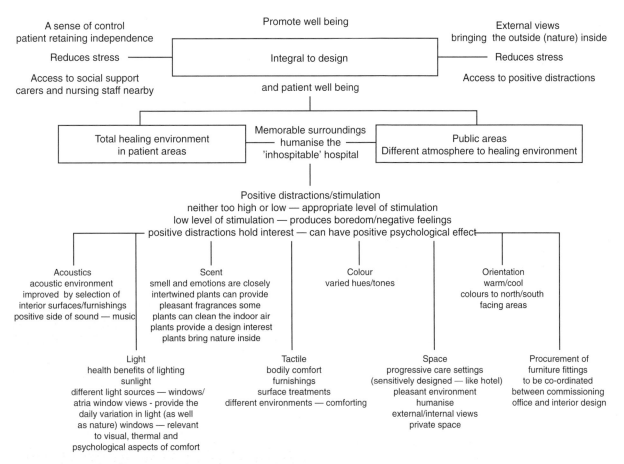

Figure 2.9 The art and science of creating environments that prevent illness, seed healing and promote well-being. An extract from the briefing document for South Tees Hospital prepared by HLM Design International Limited.

the benefits of good design. The new Lottery Funding bodies responsible for distributing money to the five good causes (The Arts Council, The Sports Council, National Heritage, The Millennium Commission and the Charities Fund) are attempting to evaluate and appraise architectural quality by the establishment of architectural panels. There are proposals in the health service in the new NHS Plan, to undertake a series of pilot studies. These recognise the need for diversity in local requirements.

A healing environment

What has emerged from a diversity of architectural theory is a rapidly growing awareness of the need to create healing environments in our health care buildings for the future.

Medical schools are introducing courses on the arts and humanities so that the next generation of doctors have a more rounded and broader education. Architectural research is pursuing new avenues to provide the evidence demanded by politicians; this is necessary to justify the funding decisions consequential to policy changes which embrace quality.

The promotion of a feeling of well-being is now central to the design of many new health facilities, including primary care community buildings. Many of these ideas are included in a diagram prepared by HLM a firm of architects responsible for the design of several new hospitals being built under the new PFI (private finance initiative) scheme (Figure 2.9).

The art and science of creating environments that prevent illness, speed healing and promote well-being defines the challenge which both the medical and architectural professions must address in seeking to advance the theory of health care.

3

Policy issues

Introduction to Chapters 3–6

The next four chapters bring together a range of views and opinions about:

- policy issues – Chapter 3
- design issues – Chapter 4
- financial issues – Chapter 5
- briefing issues – Chapter 6.

Many of the points referred to are interconnected, but the approach adopted is intended to allow the cross-fertilisation of ideas and concepts and to encourage consideration of how they impact on each other.

Any briefing process is complex and ultimately depends on the clarity and vision of the client to identify the ethos of the project. Of course, a successful building also requires a good architect who is able to interpret this mission statement, and balance the inevitably conflicting requirements to create an architectural solution that adds to its urban context and provides (in the case of primary health care buildings) a healing environment.

Figure 3.1 and Table 3.1 sets out a framework and will allow the reader to dip into issues of particular interest. By looking at the case studies in Chapter 11 the reader can judge how successfully, or otherwise, the examples illustrated have answered the difficult problems presented by the design of a primary health building. Of even greater interest is to look at how some of the schemes have attempted to meet the future aspirations for primary care – especially with regard to flexibility, community focused patient care, and environmental performance to create a sense of well-being. In addition, by solving the more practical problems of coping with the restraints of a site, meeting the funding criteria, organising a building contract, and overseeing its construction, the architects are translating the visions into reality. If the ethos of the client is preserved through that process, and embodied in the finished building everybody involved in the briefing process should be congratulated. Medicine, architecture, and the humanities become 'joined-up' thinking to use current political rhetoric.

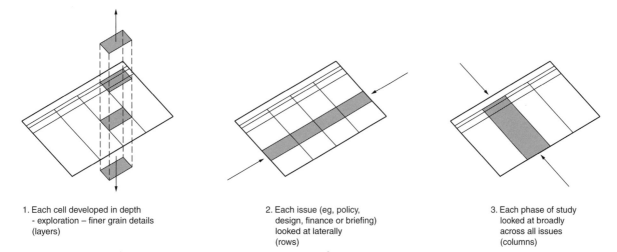

1. Each cell developed in depth
   - exploration – finer grain details
   (layers)

2. Each issue (eg, policy, design, finance or briefing) looked at laterally (rows)

3. Each phase of study looked at broadly across all issues (columns)

Figure 3.1   Three-dimensional expansion and exploration of data

Table 3.1 A matrix exploring how the architectural briefing process can raise quality standards in primary health care facilities

	Criteria		Question		Approach		Consequences and Outcomes
Chapter 3	**Policy Issues**						
3.1.1	Health policy is shifting to preventative care in the primary sector	3.1.2	What are the design and policy consequences of preventative medical care?	3.1.3	Consider GP policy aspirations.	3.1.4	Design consequences.
3.2.1	Quality thresholds have not been identified	3.2.2	How do you evaluate quality thresholds?	3.2.3	Review literature	3.2.4	The development of design guide recommendations
3.3.1	Design quality should have a higher profile	3.3.2	What is future Government policy for primary health care design quality and what should it be?	3.3.3	Review Government policy documents and technical journals for comment	3.3.4	Assess influence on design of alternative policy stances
3.4.1	New concepts for buildings will form a key component of primary health care	3.4.2	What are the design and policy consequences of these new building types	3.4.3	A short profile of Adelaide Terrace Centre based on an interview with Dr Chris Drinkwater	3.4.4	Collect views from 'leading edge' doctors and architects
Chapter 4	**Design Issues**						
4.1.1	No design standards have been set (for quality issues)	4.1.2	What design process should be adopted?	4.1.3	Comparison with other building types	4.1.4	Highlight variations and/or particular requirements
4.2.1	Primary care buildings need to be more flexible	4.2.2	How do you incorporate flexibility (long life, loose fit)?	4.2.3	Comparison with design criteria in the commercial sector for work environments	4.2.4	Review space standards, building life and future trends
4.3.1	Architecture has a poor track record in post occupancy evaluations	4.3.2	Should post-occupancy evaluations (POEs) be the architect's responsibility?	4.3.3	Review literature and analyse design process in projects	4.3.4	Development of design guide recommendations
4.4.1	NHS has no data on results of questionnaire issued to GPs	4.4.2	What does the 'Environments for Quality Care' questionnaire demonstrate about existing facilities?	4.4.3	Analyse questionnaire results from GPP designs – extend analysis to other surgeries	4.4.4	Expand on results. Identify successes and failures. Review with NHS Estates (Leeds)
4.5.1	Patients' views should be equal to other users (e.g. doctors and other staff)	4.5.2	How do you evaluate user satisfaction?	4.5.3	User questionnaires	4.5.4	Establish 'best practice' criteria and identify objectives
4.6.1	There should be a high level of user expectation with building design	4.6.2	What is the level of design expectation (patients, doctors, staff)?	4.6.3	Questionnaire	4.6.4	Assess results and make recommendations
4.7.1	Buildings should be enjoyed and include works of art	4.7.2	What are the benefits of 'art works' in design?	4.7.3	A Summary	4.7.4	Develop design guide recommendations

Table 3.1 (*Continued*)

Criteria		Question		Approach		Consequences and Outcomes	
Chapter 5	**Financial Issues**						
5.1.1	NHS has historically used cost parameters as a benchmark for design evaluation	5.1.2	Why has NHS concentrated on time and cost parameters for health building procurement?	5.1.3	Review historical bureaucracy and procedures for building procurement	5.1.4	Identify benchmark minimum criteria. Seek to demonstrate inadequacy of this approach
5.2.1	Life cycle costs are not fully considered (only initial capital costs)	5.2.2	How do you evaluate best value?	5.2.3	Comparison with 'Red Book'	5.2.4	Evaluate and compare with other building types
Chapter 6	**Briefing issues**						
6.1.1	Quality standards should be higher	6.1.2	How should an architect be briefed for primary health care buildings?	6.1.3	Analyse MARU Primer	6.1.4	Develop design guide recommendations
6.2.1	There is no qualitative methodology to evaluate building design	6.2.2	What element should be covered by a design brief – what is the process?	6.2.3	Review standard Architect Job Book with particular reference to GPP process	6.2.4	Comment and expand on existing procedures
6.3.1	Building design should lift the spirit (there should be a 'feel good' factor)	6.3.2	How important is therapeutic well-being?	6.3.3	Review literature	6.3.4	Develop design guide recommendations
6.4.1	New briefing documentation is required	6.4.2	How do you identify (prioritise) the key decision making processes?	6.4.3	Interviews	6.4.4	Establish briefing process recommendations

3.1.1 Criteria: health policy is shifting to preventative care in the primary sector

Not only in the UK, but also in many other parts of the world, health policies are focusing on the importance of preventative care in the primary health sector. The WHO declaration of Alma Ata in 1978 remains as valid today as when it was adopted.

WHO – health for all

The objectives were:

- To promote the concept of primary health care in all countries.
- To exchange experience and information on the development of primary health care within the framework of comprehensive national health systems and services.
- To evaluate the present health care situation throughout the world as it relates to, and can be improved by, primary health care.
- To define the principles of primary health care as well as the operational means of overcoming practical problems in the development of primary health care.
- To define government's role in national and international organisations in technical co-operation and support for the development of primary health care.
- To formulate recommendations for the development of primary health care. (WHO, 1978.)

The declaration goes on to provide a definition:

'Primary Health Care is essential health care made universally accessible to individuals and families in the community by means acceptable to them, through their full participation and at a cost that the community and country can afford. It forms an integral part both of the countries health system of which it is the nucleus and the overall social and economic development of the community.

Primary Health Care addresses the main health problems in the community, providing promotive, preventive, curative and rehabilitative services accordingly. In order to make primary health care universally accessible in the community as quickly as possible, maximum community and individual self-reliance for health development are essential. To attain such self-reliance requires full community participation in the planning, organisation and management of primary health care.'

The policies are enlarged on in Chapter 10.

Trends in UK health policy

These statements remain a central and crucial element of the health policy of most countries and provide the underlying objectives that health care should seek first of all to be preventive. So far as the UK is concerned there has been a reawakening of the importance of primary health care and that the real gains are to be made in economic terms by reducing illness rather than treating disease. These issues are recognised and promoted in the new contract for health promoted by the Government in the late 1990s (*Our Healthier Nation*, 1998). See Table 3.2.

Table 3.2 A contract for health

Government and national players can:	Local players and communities can:	People can:
Provide national co-ordination and leadership.	Provide leadership for local health strategies by developing and implementing Health Improvement Programmes.	Take responsibility for their own health and make healthier choices about their lifestyle.
Ensure that policy making across Government takes full account of health and is well informed by research and the best expertise available.	Work in partnerships to improve the health of local people and tackle the root causes of ill health.	Ensure their own actions do not harm the health of others.
Work with other countries for international co-operation to improve health.	Plan and provide high quality services to everyone who needs them.	Take opportunities to better their lives and their families' lives, through education, training and employment.
Assess risks and communicate those risks clearly to the public.		
Ensure that the public and others have the information they need to improve their health.		
Regulate and legislate where necessary.		
Tackle the root causes of ill health.		

Our Healthier Nation identifies two key aims: (1) to improve the health of the population as a whole by increasing the length of people's lives and the number of years people spend free from illness and (2) to improve the health of the worst off in society and to narrow the health gap.

These policies were further reinforced in the NHS Plan which lays down the criteria for a patient-focused health service, and increases further the emphasis placed on primary care and the preventive nature of those services. A list of proposals includes more routine screening tests, and guidance to patients on how to minimise or reduce risks to their health. In essence, it is a policy about encouraging communities to adopt healthier life styles.

As 90% of all health care is undertaken at the primary level, there are obvious cost benefits to aim for in a service that costs the country over £40 billion each year. The introduction of NHS Direct, which allows people to make direct contact by telephone to health professionals will encourage individuals to regard the NHS as a resource from which they can seek assistance to develop a healthier life style, and look after themselves in their own homes.

3.1.2 Question: what are the design and policy consequences of preventive medical care?

There has been a fundamental reorganisation of the way in which primary care is organised in the UK. The introduction of primary care groups has changed the landscape of GP services and the effects of these changes will snowball as the primary care groups assume the status of Trusts, with the attendant responsibilities of self-administration and control of substantial resources begin to become effective.

The integration of social services within these primary care trusts will provide a comprehensive range of services covering primary care, mental health, and social services, thereby creating a wide-ranging resource. In part, these changes are, perhaps, a result of the recognition that patients are consumers, and the medical profession has been slow to recognise the higher standards of service that a market economy has provided for the consumers of most other service providers. Therefore, there is a very rapid learning curve in process whereby the medical profession understands that the patient is a customer who will have all the usual questions of efficiency, cost effectiveness, and quality of service uppermost in their minds when seeking health advice in the future. The medical professions should see this as an opportunity, particularly with regard to health care facilities where the physical assets can be designed with quality as a key factor in the briefing process.

The brief will recognise that buildings of the future should be designed to provide a healing environment. The aim will be to achieve therapeutic benefits by the use of good design to provide flexibility, long life, and visually satisfying environments.

Even the Treasury is recognising that intangible benefits should be taken account of when looking at private finance initiative projects (PFI). Not that PFI is an appropriate vehicle for the design of small primary care health facilities (see also Chapter 8).

Therefore, the history of primary care health facilities is set to embark on another phase of development. Following the first health centres designed in the 1930s, for example the Finsbury Health Centre designed in 1938 by Leubetkin, through the generation of health centres designed in the 1950s (not a success because they were unpopular with GPs) and moving away from the 'Red Book' generated GP surgeries of the 1980s and 1990s. This last group of buildings produced many very well designed projects arising from the close working relationship between GPs and architects. It provided an example of health buildings which were procured relatively quickly, and avoided the bureaucratic and extended delivery period of the hospital building programme of the same period. Unfortunately, the financial constraints encapsulated in the 'Red Book' still frustrated the fluidity of much innovative design and both doctors and architects were constrained in their aspirations. For example, the cost allowances only allowed for fixed furniture. How does a doctor provide sofas in a consulting room? A doctor may not wish to tell a distressed patient that cancer has been diagnosed, or deal with a serious mental anxiety, across the corner of a desk sitting on upright chairs more appropriate to an office. Few doctors have been prepared to supplement the 'Red Book' allowances to fund additional equipment and furniture to personalise their surgeries. Stereotyped room data requirements have stultified innovative solutions within consulting rooms.

The next generation of health care buildings for the primary sector will be flexible long-life buildings, based on a comprehensive briefing document where design quality plays a major part in establishing the design philosophy.

3.1.3 Approach: consider GP policy aspirations

Many doctors do not wish to be building owners. Many doctors also wish to be salaried employees, rather than self-employed contractors to the NHS, providing a service where their remuneration is based on the quality of care they provide, rather than accountancy rules using patient lists, and number of visits and consultations as the basis for pay.

Professional demarcations have also become outdated, and we will see developments in the integration of social service personnel, mental health practitioners and greater specialisation for routine procedures to be part of the GP's future contract of employment. Technology will develop and telemedicine will offer more rapid diagnostic services from the laboratory back to the consulting room.

The aspirations for future doctors will be more rounded, less clinical, and integrated with the community in an accessible building. The next generation of doctors will have a much broader based education involving the humanities as well as the traditional clinical and technical basis for their studies. Already being introduced by Durham University at the Stockton campus, there will be a programme of humanity modules including literature, the arts, and architecture to encourage a holistic approach to the complete healing environment. Similar courses are also being introduced in London and Wales (University of Wales, Swansea).[1] Far better to have a community thriving with a high-quality of life rather than doctors fighting a rear-guard action to treat diseases which are often the result of poor environmental standards. Perhaps doctors may even prescribe environmental conditions. We already understand some of these issues, for example:

- safer driving reduces accidents
- no smoking in offices and restaurants reduces the risks of cancers
- fitness and diet are promoted as health policy.

The provision of new facilities will embrace a new partnership between public and private finance.

3.1.4 Consequences and outcomes: design consequences

The design consequences for a design policy focused on preventive care in the primary sector must reflect the policy aspirations for the medical GPs of the future. Buildings will need to be flexible and some will be open 24 hours per day, 7 days per week.

The buildings will relate to other functions where the emphasis is on self-help and prevention. Examples of other activities in a flexible building of the future might include:

- a pharmacy
- a fruit and vegetable stall
- keep-fit gymnasium
- a coffee shop/community meeting room
- social services office (e.g. housing and unemployment benefits payment office)
- citizen's advice centre
- a hairdresser, chiropodist, dentist, optician, pharmacy.

Work by others (MARU, 1996) have already identified that these buildings will not be space standard led nor cost led. There is much to learn from understanding the briefing process used by the commercial and office sectors of the property industry to achieve flexibility and cost effective design.

The buildings must create a sense of space, be friendly and accessible and on a human scale.

These changes offer new opportunities for architects and doctors and the consumer (patients) to work together. There must be an acknowledgement that the health service now operates in a consumer society within a market economy. The performance of buildings will be measured and there will be greater measurement of patient experiences and patient satisfaction levels.

We can look to the USA for good examples of private care and to France for good examples of public and private finance

working together to achieve high standards of health care.

The healthy cities programme (WHO/OMS, 1999) seeks to establish the relationship between the improvement of health by modification of the living conditions, the physical environment, social and economic factors that influence or determine 'our health'. The home, the school, the village, the work place, the city are the 'places or settings' where people live and work. The health status is often determined more by the conditions in these settings then by the provision of health care facilities.

A large proportion of diseases and accidents are preventable by improving the physical environment and social and economic conditions of everyday life. Management of the built environment is critical as environmental exposure that effect health occur in places where people live and work.

The consequences and outcomes of this shift towards preventive care in the primary sector is therefore seemed to be that health is central to a community's social and economic development.

3.2.1 Criteria: quality thresholds have not been identified

Architecture is essentially a practical art, rather than a fine art. Critics argue that neither a study of aesthetics nor of basic functionalism provides satisfactory answers to understand architecture. Is architecture composition or function? – pure art or pure pragmatism? – illusion of reality? – art or science?

> Because we all experience architecture on a daily basis the practical reality of being inside a building, outside a building, or on the threshold is always with us and cannot be detached as a pure study of aesthetics. This persistent dichotomy places architecture permanently in a state of tension between simple explanation (the practical) and the perception of space (aesthetics). 'What I wish to register here is the persistent presence (in our consciousness) of architectural experience whose very medium of sensation is at the same time the filter of our common experience 24 hours of the day ... From the very nature of its medium therefore architecture is rooted in our everyday experience and can never enjoy the "detachment" that is so dear to the aesthetes' (Wilson, 1992).

The healing environment was seen as a natural phenomenon, and only replaced with a scientific or technological approach which has come to the fore during the last 150 years. The perceived shortcomings of the scientific approach has grown out of the recognition that the market economy system of the 1980s has not provided the answers promised by this policy. The drive to complete buildings on time and within budget but with no measure of quality became an essential tenet of the procurement process developed so avidly by the NHS, among others. A term which is currently much in use – patient focused – recognises the importance of understanding the direct personal experiences of patients. Dr Roger Ulrich, Professor of Architectural Research at the Texas A&M University is referred to regularly in discussions about the beneficial effects that the environment can have on the improvement rate of patient recovery. In 1984 he studied the case notes of two dozen patients who had all had their gallstones removed. Half of the patients had a view from their window of open countryside, and the other half had looked on to a brick wall. Those with a view of nature had recovered more quickly with better clinical recovery rates. It remains the starting point for most researchers working in this field.

The 'high-tech' building period of the late twentieth century was represented in the health sector by a programme to construct an infrastructure of hospitals full of expensive equipment. Health budgets needed to continually expand as patients' expectations were raised.

The freedom of expression and technical brilliance of this period led into the fashionable phase of post-modernism during the 1970s and 1980s. This provided an opportunity to abandon stylistic convention for a global audience eager to explore innovation, and increasingly, complexity but with echoes of a classical and harmonious background. With the world becoming a smaller place the same triggers have enabled global objectives to be interpreted with solutions appropriate to local conditions. With a new interest in natural solutions generalised political policies can be embraced by a wide variety of local solutions. For example, primary health care, and the buildings and facilities required to attend to the well-being of the world's population is now embodied in an objective of the WHO. The ambitious aim was that all citizens of the world by the year 2000 would have a level of health that would permit them to lead a socially useful and economically productive life.

There are other powerful arguments, which look to the future and discuss the merits of complexity and the theory of chaos (Jencks, 1995). They are reflected in the new wave of eclectic approaches now being proposed for primary health care facilities around the world. At one extreme, we are moving towards the edge of architectural confusion – aesthetic autonomy – which will be reflected in a diversity of solutions seeking to respond to local requirements. There would appear to be a recognition that a bureaucratic approach to producing buildings according to theories of time and cost do not result in environments which are comfortable to the mind and spirit. The richness of solutions, and diversity of approaches underlines the inability of architecture to be resolved within a simple set of rules contained in a guidebook with a schedule of room areas and building cost limits.

There is considerable debate in the current medical and architectural technical press about the quality of building design in the health sector in the UK. A recent Junior Health Minister, Tom Sackville, addressing delegates at a conference said 'buildings with architecture and design that lift the spirits of patients need be no more costly than the depressing austere buildings so familiar to many who use and work in the NHS'. What is needed however is formal research from which a basis can be devised for measuring therapeutic advantage.

It should be of no surprise to us that there has been only limited success in this direction. Objectivity has been defined as 'conclusions rationally, reasonably and rigorously reached by the scientific method' (Harvey, 1997). Parsimony is described where the most useful explanation is the one which produces both the greatest number and most reliable predictions (has larger scope) from the fewest argumentative or unprovable assertions or axioms (from the 'simplest' theory). To meet that test, if aesthetics could be objective what specific features would we be looking for? How would one person defend their choice against that of another?

3.2.2 Question: how do you evaluate quality thresholds?

Without the pre-set rules of a design school, such as the Gothic style or the modern movement, architectural theory is today either infinitely variable or confused depending on whether you take an optimistic or pessimistic view of the opportunities which are presented by the lack of design guidelines. On the one hand, Charles Jencks advocates the advantages emanating from chaos theory, resulting in a fractured and segmental architecture of great variety or more negatively the philosopher Ludwig Wittgenstein is reported to have said 'you think philosophy is difficult enough, but I tell you it is nothing to the difficulty of being a good architect' (Lawson 1994).

In his book *Design in Mind*, Brian Lawson identifies four techniques we can employ to understand the designing process:

- We can analyse the task and propose logical structures and processes that we imagine must or should take place.
- We can observe designers at work.
- We can conduct laboratory experiments on designers.
- We can ask designers to tell us what they do.

He concludes the review of these approaches by favouring dialogues with architects, and inviting them to describe their working methods. However, the subjective appraisal of his choice of architects interviewed relies on the arbitrary appraisal of what represents high quality. Can high quality be justified solely by those architects who are held in highest esteem by their peer group at any particular point in time?

An interview with Richard Burton recorded the following points as being most important:

- interaction between members of a design team
- relationship with client is critical
- interactive nature of brief making
- briefing is an absolutely crucial element
- the higher the level of client contact is in the client organisation, the better the process works
- obtain feedback
- importance of drawing as part of the design process.

Other architects identified their own crucial factors, for example:

- *Hertzberger*: human relationships are fundamental
- *Michael Wilford*: sees himself as an editor waiting for copy to come forward from his staff
- *Eva Jiricna*: design is a generic process, map out the range of alternatives
- *Richard McCormac*: sees his role as making a series of interventions at different stages of the design process.

Another explanation of the design process is made by using an analogy with the conductor of an orchestra. Working from a brief (the score) the conductor co-ordinates and welds together a variety of contributions (individual musicians) each interpreting their line of the score, sometimes brilliantly, sometimes less so to orchestrate a performance. The component parts may vary in skill and flair but sometimes are brought together for a memorable concert.

3.2.3 Approach: review literature

There have been many attempts to analyse the design process and to map out systematic patterns to guide the intellectual methods of design. Design education in universities has, until fairly recent times, followed a historical route, taking each time period as a subject of analysis. In the final quarter of the twentieth century, more complex studies have been undertaken about the nature of design and studies have compared the design process between different fields of study, for instance comparing the differences between how fashion designers create their ideas and how civil engineers develop a structure (Lawson, 1997).

With architecture, the design process is influenced by two main characteristics, namely the design problem and the design approach. The following examination of various design systems considers how these two aspects are brought together by different people in the increasingly complex field of how an architect develops the brief and processes the information to produce a design product.

Design is now taught as a skill as well as an art. Computer graphics involve manipulative skills which can be learned and developed by teaching students, and this will enhance their ability to convey their imaginative and innovative ideas into reality.

'A bee puts to shame many an architect in the construction of her hive but what distinguishes the worst of architects from the best of bees is this, that the architect raises his structure in imagination before he erects it in reality. At the end of every labour process we get a result that already existed in the imagination of the labourer at its beginning'. (Karl Marx, *Das Capital* – from Lawson, 1997.)

The design process has been formalised over the past 100 years by the development of professional organisations, not least by the RIBA, founded in 1834. The development of respect for the professions gave their members social status and for a while the division of labour between those who

design and those who make was a keystone of our technological society (Lawson, 1997).

Royal Institute of British Architects

The process of brief and design development has long fascinated architects. The model advocated by the profession for the architectural design process is set out in the *Architect's Job Book* (sixth edition, 1995) published by the RIBA and this remains the basic approach adopted by most architectural practices when commissioned to design a new building. It is essentially a linear process and the Foreword to the document states that 'Architects are those who organise themselves to systematically translate their imagination and design flair into a building that meets their clients needs'. It is a systematic approach to the design and construction process which has survived from the first edition published in 1969. The foreword boldly concludes by saying 'The *Architect's Job Book* provides a framework for this systematic approach, which can be applied to any building or procurement method'.

The diagram of the process highlights the progressive linear path (see Figure 3.2). Although there are feedback loops which anticipate a dialogue developing between the written components of the brief and the evolving design proposals there is no reference to post-occupancy evaluations and feedback is only briefly mentioned at the end of the document.

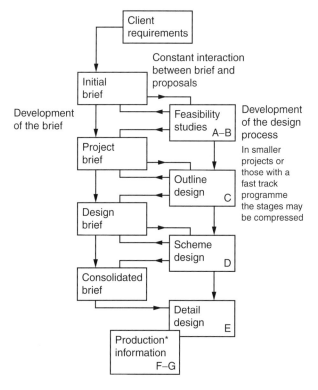

Figure 3.2 Source: RIBA, *Architect's Job Book* 6th edition, 1995

Debriefing is not referred to in the plan of work and most importantly not covered by the normal fee agreement entered into under the standard terms and conditions of appointment. Indeed, the *Job Book* states that 'both in-house appraisals and debriefing are exercises not normally listed in the services provided by the architect and are unlikely to be funded by the client ... a full feedback study can be costly, and if the client wishes this to be undertaken, it will probably have to be the subject of a separate commission.' The lack of provision for fees for post-occupancy work in an architect's normal appointment is probably at the heart of poor appraisal and analysis of complete projects. Each architectural commission is often viewed as a unique opportunity to start with 'a clean sheet of paper' to create an individualistic solution to a client's requirements.

However, it goes further in almost discouraging the debriefing process. It states 'it is a sensitive area, and confrontation should be avoided at all costs. It will not therefore be a productive exercise in all cases and great care needs to be taken in deciding whether or not it will be worthwhile for a particular project'.

It seems remarkable that in a document published in 1995 there should still be such a negative attitude towards post-occupancy evaluation techniques, and the benefits of cyclical learning which is considered a pre-requisite in other professional disciplines. Two obvious examples are the law and medicine. English law is developed on the principal of case law, or learning from previous experience, and likewise medicine is a developmental profession which in the past 100 years has relied on the development of technical expertise. Elsewhere, I comment on the changing philosophy of health care from a medical point of view, which is moving towards a holistic approach not entirely based on scientific methodology. My interviews with, for example Professor Sir Kenneth Calman have highlighted how leading members of the medical profession are beginning to advocate the introduction of artistic considerations to their work and have recognised the therapeutic benefits that can result from such combinations.

The attempt by the RIBA to distil the design process to a simplistic linear pattern would appear not to do justice to the complex inter-relationships, sometimes intangible, which build up the design process.

3.2.4 Consequences and outcomes: the development of design guide recommendations

Over the past few years the NHS has become increasingly aware of the importance of design quality and is seeking ways to introduce this in the briefing and procurement process.

This process is rapidly developing as this book is being written but it may be helpful to state the position at the start of the new millennium.

The principal client for health buildings in the UK is NHS Estates with an annual budget approaching £2 billion per annum.

The health service has lost many people with experience of design quality over the last few years.[2] Efficiency and competition were the key factors in NHS Estates' procurement methodology and they want to make their assets 'sweat'. This policy had been represented by the internal market in the hospital environment, represented by many business case studies being undertaken for new projects. In the primary care sector it was represented by fundholding, which the present Government is now dismantling as a policy and replacing it with PCGs (primary care groups) and PCTs (primary care trusts).

The new Government's philosophy is that we are all partners – the NHS family – and that rather than having a culture of competition the policy should be one of benchmarking best practice. This was being initiated with a number of pilot or beacon projects.

The present NHS Estates procurement policy is based on the *Capital Investment Manual* which requires a business case approach to justify new investment. This has led to a position where design quality is understood to be represented by functionality. Design quality is assessed by its functional suitability. This methodology is enshrined in their *Estate Code* document that sets out a five-facet analysis process.

- space utilisation
- functional suitability
- energy efficiency
- statutory standards (compliance)
- physical condition.

These factors are used as a basis for design quality evaluation. This is done by subdividing each category into four sections from fully compliant (e.g. new building) to below an acceptable standard. With this background an assessment of design quality can miss the point. Design quality had to be based on quantifiable data.

However, the Government is keen to promote good design, and is a strong advocate of the Egan initiatives. Architects are in a good position to influence NHS Estates' design strategy. However health care design policy needs to be evidence based. For example, to demonstrate the link between physical surroundings and the therapeutic benefits. This was helpful research because it enabled quality design to be quantified in terms that health professionals could accept. This was much more important in influencing health building policy than the subjective approach of commodity firmness and delight.

The Treasury is seeking to establish best value rather than lowest price as the key criteria for building procurement. Discussions are taking place within NHS Estates between professionals about the quantification of design quality. Typical areas of concern are:

- fit for purpose
- functional suitability
- form
- best value
- environment
- safety.

There must also be mechanisms for cost benefit analysis. There is concern that the RIBA were giving awards to health schemes that had been criticised by health professionals. It was important for health professionals and architects to agree on what they understood to be 'good'. NHS Estates has produced a CD-ROM illustrating their interpretation of best practice. Design is more than aesthetics. It is not about luxury but necessity.

Many architectural practitioners have attempted to codify design methodologies to provide design guide recommendations. As examples of this process several techniques are given below.

Example 1: MARU (Medical Architecture Research Unit)

A resource book prepared by the Medical Architecture Research Unit (MARU, 1996) takes a more focused look at the relationship between GPs and their architects and how a dialogue can be promoted between the two parties 'in order to secure the effective planning and development of Primary Care Resource Centres, including GP surgeries'. Fundamentally, the document recognises a more interactive relationship between the parties than implied by the RIBA model. This iterative process of development (Figure 3.3) suggests a more circular and interactive development of key areas of the design process. 'Developing a vision' immediately recognises the need to stimulate innovative ideas and evaluating 'buildings in use' also begins to understand the need to learn from previous experience.

A route map illustrated by Figure 3.4 sets out a list of key stages in the development of a project for medical facilities. This list indicates in diagrammatic form a direct link between 'evaluation' and 'strategic vision'. It is an essential part of the procurement of a medical facility.

These ideas were developed by Susan Francis, a research architect with MARU when she gave an address to a seminar entitled capturing design quality (Francis, 2000).

Francis commenced her talk by saying that as a research architect it was difficult to define quality. Quality is a result of both the process and the product of building and that design is a 'value generator'. What is research, she asked? She outlined three research realms that in her view influence design:

- process
- product
- value systems.

Construction research concentrated on value management techniques and looked at issues such as 'lifecycle' costs but paid little attention to 'added value' or 'quality' issues. There was much to gain from looking at urban design issues and

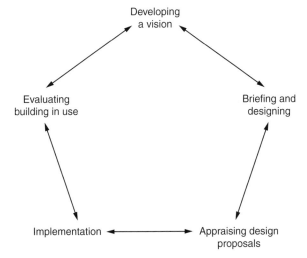

Figure 3.3 The iterative process of development. Extract taken from Resource book prepared by MARU 1996

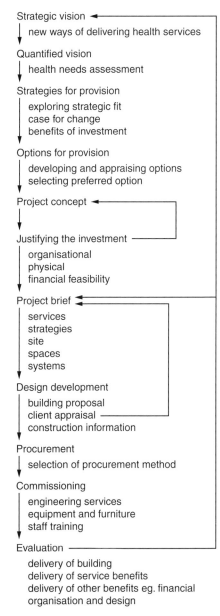

Figure 3.4 Procurement of the building. Extract taken from Resource book prepared by MARU 1996

she thought this applied particularly in the health and housing sectors.

Design quality was difficult to pin down. Figure 3.4 illustrates a sliding scale of variables between the least tangible factors (the intellectual and aesthetic qualities of architecture) compared to the most measurable aspects of a building (the adequacy of a building's functionality and its physiological characteristics). Architecture is illustrated at the top of a pyramid with a broad base of functional construction factors (Figure 3.5).

Design quality has three key factors, according to Francis:

- function
- sustainability
- perception.

Function was knowledge based and generated the commodity of construction. Sustainability was an awareness of the available resources including social, economic, and environmental issues. Perception also offers delight, which is dependent on the therapeutic outcomes of a building design and the level of user satisfaction. Perception also provides the personal interpretation of beauty and aesthetics. These three factors are all interconnected (Figure 3.6).

In conclusion, she reiterated the well understood relationship of qualitative methodologies being associated with the social sciences and quantitative methodologies being scientifically based. However, she went on to suggest that design expertise was a separate skill and that valuing design is a difficult task. She used the analogy that design expertise was rather like navigation when you could work out your latitude but not your longitude.

Example 2: Tony Jones – NHS Estates (Jones, 2000)

Tony Jones' presentation set out to describe the NHS approach for improving the quality and design of health

Table 3.3 Model of care from the brief

		Criteria
Good building	Meeting requirements	
Design quality	Creating an appropriate environment	Enhancing therapeutic
Architecture	Raising the spirits	

buildings. His central theme was that architecture should be accessible. Accessibility was his key word.

You cannot legislate for design quality, but it was important to create the right conditions for design quality. Table 3.3 demonstrates Jones' main criteria.

He also showed a diagram, not dissimilar to that used by Susan Francis, which was a triangle with good architecture at the peak and issues of efficiency and functionality at the base (Figure 3.7).

Jones suggested that the design team can use words to define requirements such as the following. More easily defined issues (hard edged) include: efficiency, functionality and economy and sustainability. (Not all of these factors are easily measurable.)

More difficult to define issues (softer edged) include the following:

- Architectural aspirations
  - social/civic
  - spiritual
  - aesthetic
  - life enhancing
  - therapeutic
  - comfort.
- Conceptual
  - creating a composition
  - context
  - scale
  - harmony
  - stimulation
  - coherence.
- Expression
  - the raw materials
  - line
  - form
  - space
  - light and shape
  - materials
  - colour, texture.

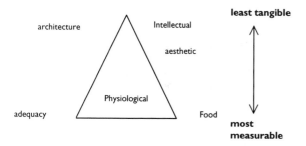

Figure 3.5 Extract taken from Resource book prepared by MARU 1996

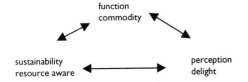

Figure 3.6 Extract taken from Resource book prepared by MARU 1996

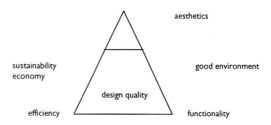

Figure 3.7 Extract taken from Resource book prepared by MARU 1996

Table 3.4 A design quality profiling method

	Criteria	Weighting	Scoring 1–10	
Economy				Good building
Efficiency				} Design quality
Functionality				
Aesthetics				Architecture

It is also possible to establish criteria for user satisfaction analysis:

- functional
- efficiency
- easy access
- flexibility
- economic
- a safe and secure environment
- appropriate health standards.

Jones referred to Herbert Read's *The Meaning of Art* (1931) for more understanding of these issues.

There are also methods of evaluating design and Table 3.4 shows a design quality profiling method.

Tony Jones offers an analytical approach to search for design quality analysis. Published with the permission of NHS Estates from Environments for Quality Healthcare: Health Buildings in the Community 1994, a Crown Copyright publication.

Example 3: John Cole – DOH, Northern Ireland (Cole, 2000)

Cole offered a personal view of how he procured good design for the NHS in Northern Ireland: good design needs good people and good design needs adequate resources.

Architects were often their own worst enemy in this regard, and he was very critical of architectural practices who offered extremely low fee bids such that he knew that they could not provide the level of service demanded by the job for the fees being charged.

Design quality was influenced by a number of problems in the public sector including:

- design champions were needed
- there was a lack of architects in positions of influence
- there was little investment in structured research and the sharing of knowledge

- patronage was needed
- there was an undue focus on time cost and process issues, all of which can be audited
- good design is not fully appreciated
- often there was a requirement for evidence-based design solutions.

To procure design of quality it was important to look for design quality with the right attitude and that architects should be properly remunerated and resourced.

With regard to the delivery of buildings the following problems were identified:

- adequate time on conceptual design was needed
- PFI processes often understate design issues
- there was no research (or too little) and little innovation.

To improve standard in Northern Ireland Cole used two techniques:

- Organising a design competition (for a pre-determined fee). The Royal Belfast Hospital for Sick Children designed by Todd in conjunction with Watkins Gray was an example of this approach.
- Competitive design interview (for a pre-determined fee).

In conclusion, Cole offered the following key points to help ensure the procurement of design quality when commissioning buildings:

- there should be project champions (and intelligent customers)
- there should be a desire for excellence in design
- there must be appropriate fees and adequate resources
- there must be an on-going commitment.

Example 4: Richard Foque – Antwerp (Foque, 2000)

Richard Foque – an architect based in Antwerp and specialising in health buildings – believes that 'the starting point ... is an interdisciplinary approach based on an holistic perception of man and environment'.

In a lecture given at the RIBA in May 1999 Foque reiterated the traditional and linear process of design which is irreversible in time (Figure 3.8).

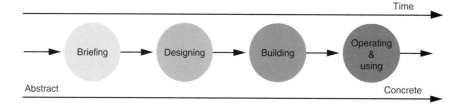

Figure 3.8

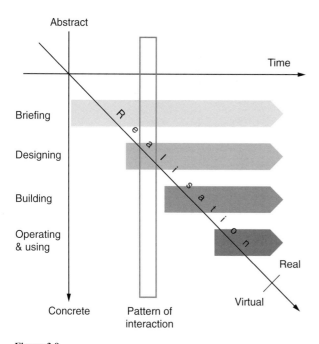

Figure 3.9

This linear pattern is developed to include concepts of abstract and concrete status and virtual and real states depending upon the passage of time. This is illustrated in Figure 3.9.

Each of the four important domains are further developed in a series of diagrams and in the case of the briefing process form, function, and context are identified as the key domains (Figures 3.10 and 3.11).

Example 5: Approaches to design – Frank Duffy

A particular approach to design has been developed by Frank Duffy, founding partner of DEGW, an international firm of architects, who has worked throughout his career in the field of commercial office buildings. He has concentrated on the changing patterns of office work and developed a series of techniques to analyse the requirements for the working environment. This work has been published in a series of books including *The Responsible Workplace* (1993) and *The New Office* (1997).

Duffy states that the reasons for these changes are many and complex but include:

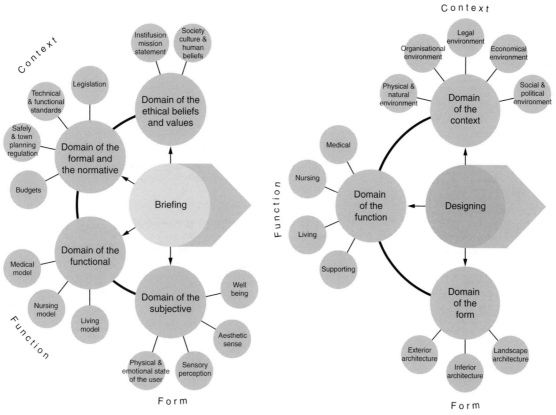

Figure 3.10

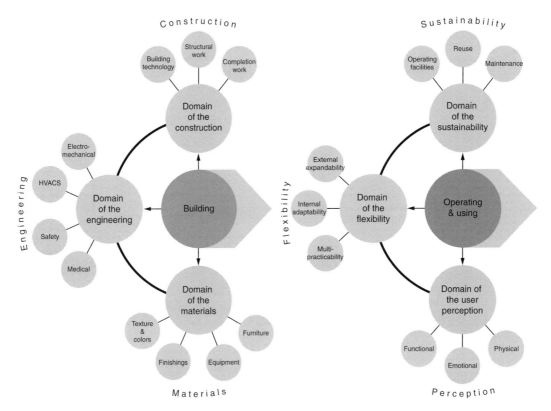

Figure 3.11

- the increasing pressures for businesses to become more customer focused and therefore more dynamic and responsive to change
- the opportunities offered by information and communications technologies that are reducing the importance of time and location to the modern business
- social and demographic pressures as workers adapt to the need for flexibility but wish to establish an acceptable balance between work and home.

Although directed at the implications for the design of office buildings and work places, these comments are equally valid when considering the design of primary health care facilities. Doctors' surgeries involve many complex relationships, and historically the design of medical buildings, be they hospitals, clinics, or doctors' surgeries have been largely based on the historic pattern of analysing room requirements as specific functional parameters with little thought being given to flexibility either of activities to take place within that space, or of how a space might function over a period of time.

Are there lessons to be learnt, therefore, from this work in its transfer to primary health care facilities?

The work has developed a categorisation of working methods and these are summarised as: dens, clubs, hives, or cells (see Figure 3.12).

This research which has looked at developing the design process for commercial buildings has also highlighted a num-

ber of measuring techniques to assess efficiency and effectiveness. Obviously, clearly focused on commercial productivity you would expect the design methodology to highlight the financial consequences and a series of techniques are advocated including:

- workplace envisioning (WE)
- time utilisation studies (TUS)
- workplace performance survey (WPS)
- post-occupancy evaluation (POE).

Although these measuring techniques are designed to measure business efficiency there is an underlying assumption that the financial performance of the workplace will be more successful if individuals are comfortable and effective within their environment, and consequently are performing better. Again, the transfer of these philosophies has validity for other building types and the intensive utilisation of medical facilities justifies closer attention to the performance of the buildings in which these services are provided.

3.3.1 Criteria: design quality should have a higher profile

Previous sections have approached design in a systematic and logical manner. They represent analytical and mathematical

Den

We believe this model will become increasingly important as team processes become more common in the office. The *den* worker is interactive but not necessarily highly autonomous, carrying out tasks that are typically of short duration and team-based.

The space is designed for group working, with a range of simple settings in the open plan or group room that encourage interaction. There is also access to some shared facilities.

Typical den organisations
Design, insurance, media and advertising.

Club

This model is likely to become increasingly common as IT and organisational theory develop. It challenges the simplistic assumptions upon which most North American and North European office design is based. The *club* is for knowledge work: both autonomous and interactive. The pattern of occupancy is intermittent and over an extended working day. A wide variety of shared task based settings serve both concentrated individual and group interactive work.

Individuals and teams occupy space on an as-needed basis, moving around the space to take advantage of a wide range of facilities.

Typical club organisations
Advertising or management consultancies, IT companies, and other high-value-adding knowledge workers in many sectors.

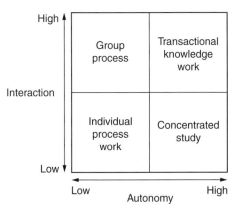

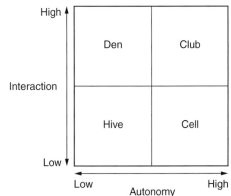

Hive

This model describes the vast majority of office buildings and office environmental systems. The *hive* is associated with individual process work, little interaction and low levels of individual autonomy.

Staff sit at simple workstations for continuous periods of time on a regular schedule. The settings are typically uniform, open planned, screened and impersonal.

Typical hive organisations
Telesales, call centres, routine banking, financial, and administrative operations and information services.

Cell

This is the model upon which many Northern European offices have been designed since the 1980s. The *cell* is for individuals involved in concentrated work with little interaction. Highly autonomous individuals occupy the office in an intermittent and irregular pattern with extended working hours. They spend many hours working away from the office.

Each individual uses either an enclosed *cell* or a highly screened workstation for a wide variety of tasks. This working space may be shared.

Typical cell organisations
Law, some parts of accountancy, academic offices and some research and consultancy organisations.

Figure 3.12   The hive, cell, den and club models

attempts to provide a scientific or quantitative explanation for design which I have attempted to explain is an inadequate, or, or at least, an incomplete solution.

Are there other approaches? A central hypothesis of this book is that a holistic lifestyle brings with it therapeutic benefits. Historically, there are numerous quotations that highlight this long held view of the relationship between medicine and the environment.

'Health depends on a state of equilibrium among the various factors governing the operation of the body and the mind; this equilibrium in turn in reached only when man lives in harmony with his external environment'. (Hypocrites.)

A more modern example of the same philosophy is set out in the briefing document for the Glasgow Homoeopathic Hospital which was held in 1999.

'We aim to help people self-heal – if possible from their disease, but always from their suffering. We wish to create a space, a place, an atmosphere, an approach and an experience that helps this healing happen. We strive to treat each patient as a unique, individual, and whole person, recognising that their inner and outer life can have a significant impact on the processes of disease and healing.

We seek to discover what is of value within traditional and complementary care, and integrate this with the best of orthodox care, blending the arts and sciences of healing. We recognise that our work as carers requires us to address our own understanding, health and well being. We aim to share this knowledge and experience with our individual patients, and with the community'. (Reilly, 1995.)

These ideas are gaining ground in medical education and Professor Sir Kenneth Calman has been instrumental in initiating lecture courses in the humanities in the medical schools of Glasgow and Durham.

'There is an old adage that medicine is both a science and an art. We try to give a detailed explanation of what that means, and to show how the evidence-based medicine movement can be integrated with the arts or humanities in medical education movement. This integration provides the basis for the sound clinical judgements which are evidence in practice.' (Downie and MacNaughton, 2000.)

However, there remains a problem of how to sustain a design methodology based on qualitative evaluations. Arts for Health is a movement that has been gaining support and offers a convenient and easy route for NHS Hospital Trusts to acknowledge the importance of works of art in medical environments. However, the more fundamental challenge, and one which is infinitely more complex and difficult, is to integrate the whole design process for the building fabric within a design framework striving for a high quality environment. Good design is about the quality of the spaces; about creating a place; about providing a caring environment that lifts the spirit. We have all experienced the joy of being inside this kind of space but we cannot measure it in scientific terms.

Of course, these holistic concepts are not limited to the visual arts, but include music, dance and drama.

'In a civilised society, where the importance of culture is recognised, the value of such a policy would be self-evident. In the UK, where culture is all too often seen as separate from life itself, we badly need to get away from the surgeon/barber institutionalised vision of health care, and acknowledge the potential of the holistic approach. There is an urgent need to develop far-sighted cultural policies for health. Such a policy ties in with the growing interest in and use of complimentary medicine, and the holistic approach which aims to cure the whole person, rather than simply deal with their physical symptoms.' (Senior and Croall, 1993.)

A shortage of research is limiting the introduction of such philosophies into the NHS system. This must change. Unfortunately, in our current accountancy led, market driven economy there is an expectation that a financial cost benefit analysis is necessary to justify any capital expenditure. As has been previously explained, a non-scientific with no evidence base system for an arts programme is an inadequate and defenceless criterion for a capital-spending programme.

Many of these arguments were touched on when the Prince of Wales formed his Institute of Architecture and he wrote in 1995:

'... there is a need for great recognition that mental and physical health are not simply about medical repairs. We are not just machines, whatever modern science may claim is the case on the basis of evidence provided by what is purely visible and tangible. Health also has a spiritual base, a foundation in the individual's sense of personal wholeness and in his relation to the other wholes in which we all live: our families, our communities, our nations, our world ... Is it not time that we began to escape from a stereotyped and bureaucratic approach to hospital design?'

Prince Charles returned to this subject when he delivered the Reith Lectures in 2000. He attacked the dangers of unrestrained scientific research and the perils of tampering with what he calls 'the grain of nature'. Written following a pilgrimage to a Greek Monastery he went on to argue that in this technology driven age, it is all to easy for us to forget that mankind is part of nature and not apart from it and that this is why we should seek to work with the grain of nature in everything we do.

3.3.2 Question: what is future government policy for primary health care design quality and what should it be?

Government policy over the past few years has moved rapidly towards strongly supporting better quality in the design of buildings. As reported in *Building Magazine* (20 April 2000):

'Tony Blair this week launched a crusade to improve the design and quality of public buildings so that they recall the Edwardian Era of civic pride. In his first speech about the industry as Prime Minister, Blair revealed that he has ordered Cabinet Office Minister, Mo Mowlam and Treasury Chief Secretary, Andrew Smith to find ways to 'improve the quality and design of Public Sector buildings and to modernise the procurement process.

In the most impassioned part of his speech Blair harked back to the beginning of the last century when schools and town halls were built that the community was proud of. He added, "I would like to return to that sense of civic pride when we construct our public buildings". Linking the quality of buildings to the services they provided, Blair said: "Children learn better in schools that are well designed. Patients can be treated better – indeed recover more quickly – in hospitals that have been built to the highest standards."

Blair said that the UK had "Some of the world's most respected and best known architects, world class contractors, suppliers and material manufacturers".' (Barrack, 2000.)

The two reports prepared by Sir Michael Latham and Sir John Egan have stimulated the construction industry to examine its performance. The industry has been challenged to aim for sustained improvement and to put in place methods of measuring progress towards its objectives and targets, including indicators such as capital costs, construction time, predictability, defects, accidents, productivity, and turn over in profits.

When looking at these issues are we confuse the definition of quality with that of quality control? It is tempting to suggest that Sir John Egan, coming from an industrial background, lays greatest emphasis in the report of the Construction Task Force, *Rethinking Construction* on raising the standards of quality control in the construction industry. Looking at the dictionary definition of 'quality' (*Collins English Dictionary*) we see 'Degree or standard of excellence, especially a high standard, ... having or showing excellence or superiority: a quality product.' The same dictionary describes quality control as 'Control of the relative quality of a manufactured product, usually by statistical sampling techniques'. The quality assurance accreditation standards now common throughout the construction (and other) industries sets out an assurance of consistency of performance: an ability to repeat performance standards regularly. However, architects use the term quality to imply excellence and imbue in the term a cultural significance.

The juxtaposition of medicine and architecture in this book highlights the divergence of definitions when the term quality is used by different groups of people. Architects and doctors talk about the quality of life and the cultural benefits that can be enjoyed from the built environment. The construction industry is being asked to address issues of efficiency in a market driven economy to provide consistently high standards of quality control. The industry is looking at quality control of the process. Designers look at the quality of the product.

The design of primary health care facilities epitomises the dilemma of these two opposing views perhaps better than almost any other building type. Small in nature, local to a community, sensitive to being in the right place, and the need to be open, accessible, and welcoming to people living in their immediate vicinity, health care buildings offering primary care seem unlikely to offer large contractors the ability to provide standardised solutions within a PFI procurement envelope.

3.3.3 Approach: review government policy documents and technical journals for comment

The Treasury, previously an advocate of lowest cost procurement methods, is now promoting best value and recognises the importance that design quality must play in these procedures.

Despite this development in policy, which is to be welcomed, there remains concern that design quality is established at the commencement of a large project and that the ensuing construction process is dominated by project managers and production engineering. Sir John Egan's interest lies in pre-fabrication, minimising defects to ensure consistently high standards of building, and the benefits that accrue through economy of scale by batching smaller projects into large contracts. Yet primary care buildings are about relationships with people at a local level, buildings being in the right place, and the constraints of local conditions being recognised and taken account of in the design solution. The Government appears to be on the horns of a dilemma – *Rethinking Construction* focuses on the process and yet the prime ministerial objectives of civic pride in the buildings in a community is a statement of intent about the product. Is not the PFI procurement methodology as a Trojan horse? – a proud symbol of good intentions but full of dangers from the worst consequences of PFI being unleashed upon us as a result of not fully understanding the intellectual or cultural value of design to society and the communities that make up that society – that applies not only in the UK but in any other country also.

To its credit, CABE (Commission for Architecture in the Built Environment) has embarked on an ambitious programme of negotiations with all Government departments and is urging them to appoint individual ministers to accept responsibility for improving the design quality of Government buildings. CABE is also looking to establish benchmarks and the Chairman, Sir Stuart Lipton, is promoting the view that good design in health buildings achieves a quicker patient turnaround in hospitals and that a more active and healthy population reduces our dependence on GPs.

Already, criticisms are emerging about the design quality of recently completed hospitals built under the PFI rules. A programme manager for Government, Stephen King[3], said: 'Functionality has improved a great deal, and there is better consultation with doctors. But it is at concept design where we are still failing. We want to get in at the earlier stages, and make sure design is considered.' The King's Fund says, 'As far as the buildings themselves are concerned, the contribution for the PFI to better hospital design is very limited' (Long and Lewis, 2000).

In conclusion, there would appear to be confusion between the terms being used – quality or quality control and product or process.

3.3.4 Consequences and outcomes: assess influence on design of alternative policy stances

Rapid changes are taking place within the construction industry as the Government reappraises its stance on the procurement of public sector buildings. The NHS is one of the largest estates in the UK, and a very large client. Procure21, the NHS Estates response to implementing the objectives of the Latham and Egan reports targets projects between £1 million up to £20 million. Projects above £1 million will use PFI procedures. However, a very large percentage of NHS Estates' projects (approximately 60% in value and an even great percentage in numbers) fall below the £1 million threshold and consequently will be commissioned by local health authorities and trusts. This will have the advantage of using the pool of resources and skills developed by regionally based architects and contractors working within the health sector.

However, we can expect the Government to urge these smaller projects to consider the development of:

- new forms of procurement
- post-occupancy evaluation
- issues of measurement and design and user satisfaction
- better understanding of capital/running/occupier costs.

Ultimately, health buildings must pass the test of whether or not they enhance the quality of life. A health building for the local community will ultimately be assessed on its ability to be admired by those people who use it. It will be about lifestyle issues, and whether or not the building joins with the needs and aspirations of the community it is serving. NHS Estates must encourage this diversity of response, without prejudicing its drive for value for money.

Many of these issues are recognised in *The Development of a Policy on Architecture for Scotland*. It is worth quoting a number of extracts:

- There is a fundamental interdependence between buildings and the lives of people.

- Buildings are not given, they are consciously made and how they are made profoundly effects the quality of all our lives. How buildings are made, the quality of their design and of the built environments they help shape should, then, be a matter of concern for us all.

The objectives of such a policy will be:

- To promote the social, cultural, environmental and economic benefits of good architecture and foster a wider understanding of its role in national and local life.
- To encourage informed debate on architecture and promote greater interest and community involvement in the design of the built environment.
- To foster excellence in architecture and seek improvements in design practice and the procurement of buildings.
- To develop an agenda for action for the promotion of architecture.

Good architecture brings benefits to people both as individuals and as communities. These benefits are both practical and cultural and have value for our present and our future. Good, well-designed buildings enhance and enrich their occupants' activities and lives and promote their well-being and health. (The Scottish Executive, 2000).[4]

3.4.1 Criteria: new concepts for buildings will form a key component of primary health care

The NHS Plan 2000 sets out bold objectives for primary care services including targets to refurbish GP premises and build new facilities. There will also be new community care centres, likely to group together existing GP practices as well as providing specialist services and care beds to support minor operating suites and the elderly (see the case studies in Chapter 11 for examples).

The National Primary Care Research and Development Centre have published a pamphlet *New models of Primary Care: Developing the Future (a Development and Research Programme)* (Wilkin *et al.*, 1997). This document summarises the recommendations coming out of the Government papers prepared by the Department of Health (*Primary Care: The Future, A Green Paper* published in 1966 followed by two White Papers also published in 1966 entitled *Primary Care: The Future – Choice and Opportunity* and *Primary Care: Delivering the Future*, followed by the Primary Care Bill 1997) picks up the proposals to undertake a series of demonstration or pilot projects based on five principles:

- *Quality* including professional knowledge, better team working, good premises, communications and linking professionals from different settings.
- *Fairness* to ensure that services are more consistent in providing access to good quality services including the use of audit and the equitable distribution of resources.

- *Accessibility* of services is important in terms of location and time including emergency services. Accessibility regardless of age, sex, ethnicity or health status is a fundamental tenet of the NHS.
- *Responsiveness* of services should reflect the needs and preferences of the individuals using them and to exercise such choice, patients need to have comprehensive information. Services also need to reflect the demographic and social needs of the area they serve and local flexibility and diversity are important.
- *Efficiency* is required to ensure that the highest quality and volume of services should be sought from all resources in Primary Care and to achieve this, services and quality should be based on evidence. To achieve these objectives the regulatory arrangements governing professionals need to be changed.

It offers a policy framework for new types of primary care provider organisations. It also highlights the new types of contract which are likely to develop between the health authorities and primary care providers and although it recognises the importance that buildings will play in this relationship it is only one issue of several.

At a time of rapid change in the concepts under consideration for the delivery of primary care services, GPs are being asked to identify their requirements – much of it known as an approach called 'prescription for fitness'. This is part of defining the strategic shift from secondary to primary care and identifying which services can be transferred from hospital to clinic or surgery.

Over the past few years a range of models have been examined include:

- healthy living centres
- health action zones
- walk-in centres
- NHS Direct
- one-stop primary care centres.

The last one, conceived as a multi-functional facility, is mentioned in the NHS Plan with a target of 500 to be built by 2004. The NHS Plan refers to 'a range of brand new types of NHS facilities, bringing primary and community services – and where possible social services – together under one roof to make access more convenient to patients'.

3.4.2 Question: what are the design and policy consequences of these new building types

The National Primary Care Research and Development Centre (NPCRDC) have published a book that examined 10 case studies. These provided a convenient test-bed to analyse the influences of new policies on funding arrangements and spatial requirements when compared to the historical model of projects designed using the 'Red Book' space standards adopted under the cost rent scheme. Such is the present rate of change, policies are changing and developing very rapidly.

The book commences by setting out the changes in Government policy saying that 'new developments in primary health services will place new demands on premises'. It identifies 'the twin challenges of developing new patterns of primary and community-based health services and funding and designing appropriate buildings in which these services can be housed'. Although GPs are expected to remain at the centre of the provision of primary health care the authors anticipate an ever-increasing complexity between local communities, health authorities, private financiers, and the building procurement sector including architects and contractors.

A fundamental difficulty may emerge in that buildings are essentially long-life (with a typical life expectancy of between say 25–60 years) but accommodate activities with a policy framework, which is very fluid, developing rapidly, and subject to close political attention. It immediately suggests a long-life loose fit approach to building design and this, in turn, may suggest a radical re-examination of budgetary control because the present system is heavily reliant on tightly prescribed space standards for specific uses and activities.

'Primary Care is no longer restricted just to GP, dental, optician and community pharmacy services or even those provided by an expanded practice based team. Rather, it encompasses a broad network of community health services provided in or near to patient's homes which together enables 90% of all health care in the UK to be managed outside hospitals'.

A number of key issues are identified:

- *Changes in the scope of primary health services* – this includes references to the GP fundholding scheme, and the purchasing of secondary services. More clinical accommodation will be required to accommodate new equipment and some spaces will be multifunctional. The traditional design of a doctor's consulting room is changing with the introduction of new technology. Space standards will need to be reassessed to accommodate fax machines, computer terminals, and possibly other specialist diagnostic equipment with direct links to the major hospitals for direct advice from consultants.
- *Changes in the primary care workforce* – at present most doctors in the primary care sector are self-employed GP's under contract to the National Health Service. Service contracts will have to become more flexible, to reflect the increase in the number of female GP's, a move to more flexible working arrangements, sometimes part-time, and also doctors who wish to be employees of a health centre rather than individually self-employed.
- *The strategic shift from secondary to primary care* – provision will need to be made for minor surgical procedures to be undertaken locally, with routine consultant clinics being held close to the community they serve.
- *Intermediate care* – the medical profession is debating the provision of intermediate hospitals for local outpatient's treatment and therapy services such as respite care and care of the frail and elderly. (Cottage hospitals or community facilities).

- *Changes in medical training* – more doctors will be trained in the community than at present.
- *Changes in the organisation of out-of-hour services* – the historical requirement of GPs to provide 24-hour emergency cover is moving towards specialist services and there are embryonic group services available in some major conurbations. This trend is likely to increase with an attendant requirement for purpose-built accommodation.
- *Widening definitions of health* – the interagency agenda – this introduces the concept of leisure facilities and the prevention of illness together with alternative therapies such as acupuncture and aromatherapy.
- The 10 test cases cover a broad range of funding arrangements using one or more of the following financial routes:
  - cost rent scheme
  - notional rent reimbursement
  - actual rent reimbursement
  - improvement grants
  - fundholder savings
  - NHS Trusts
  - NHS Executive Regional Offices and Health Authorities
  - London initiative zone
  - private finance including GP's own resources or private borrowings
  - private finance initiative
  - single regeneration budget
  - European sources
  - rural challenge programme
  - Mental Health Challenge Fund
  - Charitable trusts and foundations.

The Government set aside an additional £65 million in general medical services cash limited funds for 1997/98 to enable health authorities 'To develop primary care throughout existing mechanisms and take advantage of the additional flexibilities and initiatives in this White Paper' (Department of Health, 1996)

The book concludes by identifying the need for good working relationships with a commitment from key individuals. However, it does not give much attention to the briefing process for the design team. It does not show the test schemes in architectural terms, or discuss the quality of the proposals in environmental terms. It does not explore costs in use, qualitative responses or whether the patients were involved in any consultation process to arrive at preferred design options. It is these issues that I wish to enlarge and develop.

3.4.3 Approach: a short profile of Adelaide Terrace Centre based on an interview with Dr Chris Drinkwater

An example of some innovative work that has helped to stimulate and shape the new health policies in the NHS Plan is the Adelaide Terrace Centre in Benwell, Newcastle upon Tyne masterminded by Dr Chris Drinkwater. Known as a Health Resource Centre these ideas and policies were being shaped several years ago. As background information the following notes record an interview from November 1997.

Interview held 10 November 1997 at 4.30–5.15pm

I began by outlining my ideas for greater flexibility in the provision of primary health care facilities, the provision of which appeared to be restricted by the present 'Red Book' procedures which are very prescriptive. I wished to speak to Dr Drinkwater because of his involvement in the West End Health Resource Centre in Newcastle, a project I was aware of, and also one of the 10 pilot study schemes described in the National Primary Care Research and Development Centre publication '*Better Buildings for Better Services* (Bailey *et al.*, 1997).

Dr Drinkwater described the National Locality Commissioning Pilot project which is a National Initiative consisting of 22 pilot projects. This includes, for example, the Newcastle and North Tyneside area which is split into five localities, as part of a Tyneside Initiative covering Sunderland, Gateshead, Newcastle and North Tyneside.

We moved on to discuss the main pressures facing GPs at present and he particularly highlighted chronic disease control as an area of major expense to the health service. His concern was long-term illness and the increasing burden this places on the NHS as the population ages. He described that greater support may be needed from the community and that early identification of problems was crucial requiring better co-ordination between health services and social services. For example he commented on the design of bathrooms and the particular concerns of the elderly as bathing becomes more difficult. Rather than high-tech solutions which the health service tends to consider as necessary (e.g. bath lifts, alarms, grab rails and other complicated equipment) he wondered if a better solution would be to have a simple social network of carers who were able to be in the house when an elderly person was having a bath to offer re-assurance and help should difficulties arise.

He agreed with me that there was a lack of flexibility in the provision of space within new GP surgery facilities, and I asked him about the results of the West End Health Resource Centre in Benwell, Newcastle. He said that 'it had been more successful than anticipated and was run as a charitable trust'. Revenue streams came from a number of sources including:

- practice income from the GPs using the building (e.g. rent)
- provision of Resource Centre facilities (for several local practices)
- health and fitness facilities (currently generating £45,000 per annum)
- City Health Trust funds for the provision of chiropody, speech therapy and physiotherapy specialisms
- community coronary care services.

We moved on to discuss Healthy Living Centres, a new Lottery Initiative set out in the White Paper (July 1997) known as the 'People's Lottery'. Examples are being proposed in Liverpool, Glasgow, and Newcastle.

Central to the idea is the health action zone (HAZ). The aim is to free-up regulations in areas of social disadvantage and to create closer working conditions between the social services and the health services. The example on Tyneside would encompass a population of approximately 1.3 million people and would seek to provide better co-ordination of hospital resources. The HAZ would be broken down into 13 localities (each locality serving a population of approximately 100,000) as follows:

- five; Newcastle and North Tyneside
- five; Gateshead
- three; Wearside.

A Health Care Resource Centre would be provided for each locality, and it would be possible to build up a planning brief for such a facility. He said that approximately £300 million of Lottery money was allocated to be spent on this project. This would require close co-ordination between local authorities and health authorities and would be a stimulus for urban regeneration.

The new build option is attractive with urban regeneration proposals but it would also be possible to consider refurbishment of existing building stock. He said that bids for the Newcastle HAZ had to be with the Department of Health by mid-January and they were hoping to get additional leverage from Lottery money and European money (ERDF). Therefore it is anticipated that there would be three sources of money:

- Department of Health
- Lottery (New Opportunities Fund)
- ERDF (European Regional Development Fund).

Dr Drinkwater referred to the White Paper published in July 1997 known as the 'People's Lottery' and referred to Healthy Living Centres, a concept proposed in this document. The new Lottery Fund, New Opportunities, should be up and running by mid-1998. The proposed HAZ, subdivided into localities would enable a discussion to develop on the type of buildings and facilities required in addition to GP services in these areas.

Already there has been considerable investment in GP surgeries over the past 10 years, and the desire for GPs to extend their services is putting enormous strains on their existing buildings. This is not a very cost-effective way of providing these additional services, e.g. chiropody, speech therapy and physiotherapy services which all require special equipment. The proposal, which Chris Drinkwater supports would be to create a purpose built resource centre (see Figure 3.13) which would serve a population of approximately 100,000. The Tyneside and Wearside HAZ would contain 13 localities each serving approximately 100,000 population for a total population of 1.3 million.

3.4.4 Consequences and outcomes: collect views from 'leading edge' doctors and architects

It is almost self-evident to state that there is general acceptance of the policy set out in the NHS Plan to provide high quality care centres for patients. There appears to be no resistance to the proposals to concentrate services on patients within their community.

However, the dilemmas, such as they are, stem from a divergence of views as to how the facilities for primary care should be procured – what balance should there be between private and public finance for the physical assets.

Interviews across a broad range of architects and doctors found remarkable unanimity with the objectives of improving facilities at a local level, and of the important that these building should be well designed.

There is some divergence between those who believe that all 'quality factors' need to be found in evidence based scientific study while others accepted the intangible qualities that bring a high quality of life are immeasurable.

The strategy of the policy was without exception accepted but the tactics of achieving results were more divergent. There is a mis-match between the policy advocated by government of pursuing PFI initiatives even for the provision of Primary Health Care facilities, while GP's at a local level, and within the discussion groups of the new primary care groups, seem to be keen to exploit the advantages of local knowledge, and to mesh into the network of local community facilities. There is a natural tendency to believe that this approach will more sympathetic to the increasingly broad range of alternative therapies being embraced by doctors, when combined with the imaginative resources and design skills when used by architects to exploit the best characteristics of the uniqueness of any site within any given area.

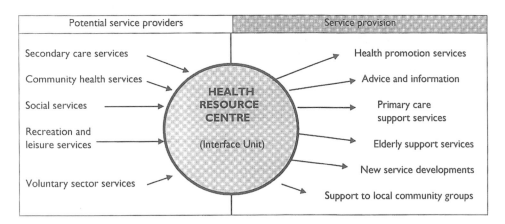

Figure 3.13 Co-ordination of locally based commissioning in response to local needs. The West End Health Resource Centre concept (adapted from *West End Health Resource Centre Annual Report 1995–96*). The Inner West locality at Benwell at present serves a population of 84,000 which will increase to 120,000. This is providing additional services for 13 GP practices at present which will increase to 18.

Notes

1. These issues are more fully discussed in *Medical Humanities: A Practical Introduction*, edited by Deborah Kirklin and Ruth Richardson published by the Royal College of Physicians, 2001. It includes schemes of modules for the MA (Wales) in Medical Humanities and the BSc in Medical Sciences and Humanities.

2. Over several years the employment of design professionals in the NHS Regional offices has contracted and the skills base has concentrated on management expertise. Few architects are now employed within the NHS and this dilution must inevitably be reflected in the way policy directives and advice was developed over the last decade. As discussed elsewhere there has been a dramatic swing towards recognising the importance of good design by the Government and many current policies are directed towards this aim. This represents a major shift in Government policy.

3. Stephen King, at the time of publication, is now Director of Public Affairs for CABE.

4. The Scottish Executive (Architecture Policy Client) published in October 2001 'A Policy on Architecture for Scotland'. Its objective 'is to seek improvements in the quality of Scotland's buildings ... the key to achieving this lies in a recognition of the importance and value of good design. Raising awareness of good design is, therefore, a fundamental aim of policy' (covering letter accompanying the document from John Gibbons, Chief Architect). The policy joins architecture policies already adopted by Norway, Denmark, Holland and Finland, all of which are regarded as countries of high architectural attainment.

4

Design issues

4.1.1 Criteria: no design standards have been set (for quality issues)

There is a growing weight of opinion being expressed about the need to pay greater attention to design quality in the procurement of primary health buildings. Although still unfocused, and a little unsure about what importance to place on the demands of conventional procurement methodology (i.e. the need for cost-effective evidenced-based research) there is an expanding number of highly respected and internationally acclaimed architects and designers who are beginning to make inroads into a wider acceptance of the health benefits of high-quality design. (See also the case studies in Chapter 11.)

The best evidence, of course, would be to allow the results to speak for themselves, but in the real commercial world that presents the usual chicken and egg dilemma, which is exceedingly difficult to bypass. There is no difficulty in canvassing support for the idea that good design is desirable but the caveat always remains that it is necessary to demonstrate tangible benefits. In time, the trick will be to turn good design into a strategic advantage.

These issues were extensively debated at the international conference, Design and Care in Hospital Planning held in Stockholm in June 2000 and the wide range of presentations suggests that the clinicians are at least beginning to listen to the designers.

In the UK, NHS Estates have identified design quality as one of four main themes in their Procure21 programme and define it as follows:

'Our programme aims to deliver design quality in NHS buildings. Good design creates the best atmosphere for the patients, staff and visitors, promoting more effective services and a speedier recovery. We propose to build on our existing programme, working with the NHS and other colleagues. This focuses on identifying and sharing best practice, anticipating development so that designs can reflect future clinical needs as well as design competitions, awards

and fora with NHS and Private Sector colleagues.' (NHS Estates, 2000.)

At a national level, the British Government is also strongly promoting the importance of design quality in public buildings. However, as has already been noted, early results from the PFI programme raise serious doubts about the effectiveness of good design intentions to survive the rigorous value engineering processes. These concentrate on extracting the best 'value for money' by focusing on quality control of the process rather than design quality of the product.

Health Building Notes 36 and 46 published by NHS Estates set out their advice on the briefing and design implications of departmental policy. Health Building Note 46 'focuses on general medical practice premises and is intended to assist GPs and their architects in understanding the problems and principles involved in building new premises for general practice, or in converting or refurbishing existing premises. It seeks to help GPs and all those concerned in a project through the various processes of a building scheme from inception to completion.' The document concentrates on functional and practical issues of design and typifies the historical approach to health buildings briefing which has concentrated on defining spatial requirements and setting cost limits, in the belief that the appointed architect would transform this data into a well designed building (NHS Estates, 1991).

To its credit, Health Building Note 36, Local Health Care Facilities, does include a statement that:

'Primary Health Care Centres and Local Health Care Resource Centres should be planned and designed to provide patients and their escorts with high quality facilities which will be as easy as possible for staff to manage and operate. The layout of these Centres should be simple and straightforward: long corridors, awkward corners, and changes in level should be avoided. The design should help to assure patients that they are receiving a high quality service. To this end, particular attention should be paid to the visual aspects of Centres as well as to functional and environmental needs. Patients and escorts may be anxious; the building design should help to alleviate patient's stress. Particular care should be taken with the most public spaces, especially waiting areas.' (NHS Estates, 1995.)

However, there are no qualitative components to this design guide, and therefore the architect is given no guidance on the expected environmental qualities of these buildings. It is this lack of qualitative definitions which provides a major opportunity to improve the briefing process for future primary health care buildings.

4.1.2 Question: what design process should be adopted?

The objective of the design process should be to convince the clinicians that good design can be cost effective.

Peter Scher argued that the basis of bringing together health care and architecture is understanding. He identified a list of 10 experiences and argued that by observing these factors there will be a greater understanding of patient-focused architecture (Scher, 1996):

(1) Space for health care: i.e. for curing, healing and caring.
(2) Suitability (functional fit): this also includes safety, security and the condition and maintenance of the facility.
(3) Privacy: for all users.
(4) Social support: for patients especially, but for all users.
(5) Comfort: for all users.
(6) Choice and control: for all patients and staff.
(7) Access to outdoors: for all users.
(8) Variety of experience: for all users.
(9) Access and wayfinding.
(10) Communication and information.

In simple terms, there should be less emphasis on the rigorous adherence to cost and space standards and more time spent in discussing the intangible qualities that the client expects the new facility to display. The problem that this approach presents is that there are no easily measurable techniques to judge whether the objectives of the brief have been met. Cost and area are straightforward numerical facts and are either greater or less than the declared target. The rules of accountancy reign supreme.

This approach must be changed and architects should not be embarrassed or afraid to argue on aesthetic grounds. If the quality of life is a key factor in the definition of good health it is certainly valid to promote the intangible benefits of aesthetics. Also, there should be greater emphasis on identifying and responding to the requirements of all users of the building. Perhaps this can be done by considering layers of need, starting with the basic physical constraints of space but adding concepts of flexibility, emotion and sensory perception to define the performance standards expected from a building. In the same way as a performance standard can be written for heating and ventilation systems we should be attempting to define the environmental standards in qualitative language as well as the traditional quantitative parameters.

4.1.3 Approach: comparison with other building types

More work has been done in the UK in the commercial office sector and there are lessons to be learnt in transferring the methodology from this building type to primary health care buildings. Primary health care buildings have complex functional requirements and accommodate human responses over a wide emotional range from casual routine visits to coping with life threatening conditions.

For primary health care buildings a considerable body of research has been conducted in the USA. In particular the Center for Health Design (www.healthdesign.org) has brought together many research papers that have been presented at an annual conference. The proceedings are available on CD-ROM and cover a wide range of topics.

An attempt has been made by the then Department of Environment Transport and Regions (DETR) in conjunction with the Housing Corporation to formulate a series of housing quality indicators (DETR, 1999). A key requirement of the system was for the Housing Corporation to be able to assess quality differences between schemes. It is based on a scoring system that examines a number of factors. A similar approach is being adopted by NHS Estates who are developing a quantitative methodology for evaluating design quality in the health sector and this work has been submitted to the prime minister's office as part of the background work in the Government's drive to raise design quality in public buildings. The development of a set of primary care quality indicators would similarly allow them to be used to audit the progress of a design and may be a more effective test of value for money than current PFI procedures. They would also be appropriate for reviewing the design quality of small projects without having to resort to batching a large number of projects to achieve the critical financial mass to fit the PFI model.

Table 4.1 seeks to illustrate those areas of the design process where more work is required to develop a critical understanding of the healing environment. By acknowledging these issues the briefing process will become more comprehensive and meaningful in helping to achieve high-quality buildings. The introduction of design ethos concepts will enable the quality of the building (e.g. the product) to be raised as well as ensuring high quality of construction (e.g. the process).

The Center for Health Design have undertaken an extensive literature search and having looked at 78,761 articles have identified only 84 articles published within the past 30 years that contain relevant data concerning health care environment. They conclude that many of the 'studies have sig-

Table 4.1 Checklist of areas of the design process where more work is required to develop a critical understanding

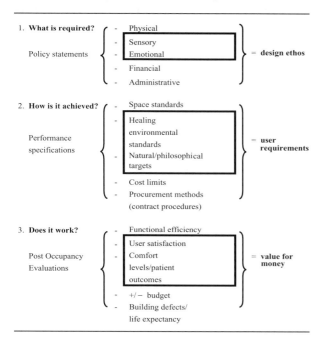

nificant methodological flaws that render their conclusions suspect or cast doubt on the generalizability of their findings. Future research into the effects of their health care environment on patient outcomes should be more carefully design and performed with greater methodological rigor' (Rubin *et al.*, 1998).

4.1.4 Consequences and outcomes: highlight variations and/or particular requirements

A fundamental shift is required in the design objectives for primary health care buildings. Pre-conceived ideas of form and function should be dissolved in a more free-flowing solution of philosophical objectives. This includes the concept that design should respond to all five senses (smell, taste, touch, sight and hearing) (Wells-Thorpe, 2000). There should be a concentration on the human scale. A naturalistic, human-centred design approach should permeate the briefing document.

Lord Robert Winston, a renowned doctor, is an advocate for the healing environment:

'I was on the island of Kos in Greece. At dawn the deserted Temple of Apollo, with a gentle breeze through the ancient olive trees and the smell of resin and honey, produced an astonishing feeling of complete tranquillity.

Perhaps this is what it was like during the time of Hippocrates. He was born on Kos and during his life people

came to him by the thousands. They were medical pilgrims seeking cures and what they found was this healing temple dedicated to the god Asclepius.

In those days there was little more a healer could do than give the body a chance to save itself. Hippocrates made little use of drugs, relying upon fomentations, bathing and diet. The diet was very simple and included vinegar and honey. Above all, he did not try to interfere with nature. He knew that most diseases had a natural tendency to cure themselves.

We doctors must take a more holistic approach. We need to be less authoritarian and more open-minded. This is not a plea for so-called 'alternative medicine'. Rather our treatments must be based on sound science and the recognition of the power of genetics. We doctors also must have the humility to accept that our bodies may well know what is in their own best interests. (Winston, 2000.)

Architects must similarly embrace the natural world and embody in their designs, especially for the design of primary health care facilities, humility for the natural world; to create buildings that put people first and which contribute to their quality of life.

4.2.1 Criteria: primary care buildings need to be more flexible

There is nothing new in the concept that buildings used for primary care should be adaptable. But like many ideas, a new generation sees new ways of interpreting similar objectives. Buildings now need to be adaptable to accommodate a knowledge-based professionalism with electronic technology playing a rapidly increasing and important part in the communication strategy between patient, doctor and specialist. One surprising spin off from an increasing use of computer technology is that the number of physical journeys does not appear to be declining – rather the reverse, in fact – with traffic congestion continuing to play an important part in the distribution of services in both urban and rural communities. This will influence the siting of future primary care facilities, such as 'one stop shops' and walk in centres, as new systems are developed to enable patient records to be no longer physically retained as a paper file in one location.

Buildings will need to reflect this diversity of functional requirements and we can anticipate that they will become more flexible and adaptable both in the pattern of their daily use as well as in the longer term, as policies and technologies evolve.

During the life of the NHS over the past 50 years flexibility and adaptability has been a recurring theme in the design of doctors' surgeries. In the 1960s there were proposals for adaptable buildings that were attractive to patients, in the sense that they were neither frightening to children nor intimidating for depressed people to enter. At the same time, the use of pre-fabricated buildings was thought to provide appropriate solutions for the major housing difficulties being experienced by the UK at that time, and parallel attempts were made to apply the same pre-fabricated technology to doctors' surgeries. Mobile surgeries, based on converted vans were one solution tried out to improve services in rural areas as the demand for better quality medical facilities expanded in the NHS (Thompson, 1964).

By the 1980s more research had been done on the ergonomic requirements for primary health care buildings (Cammock, 1981) and the design of buildings at that time was seen as an analysis of requirements to produce a schedule of accommodation which was then interpreted by the architect to produce a workable plan. It was a process of determining what was needed and how it should be achieved.

A more recent response to the demands for flexibility advocates a system of mobile docking stations. Achieving change in an organisation the size of the NHS is never going to be easy. However NHS Estates have funded a research project to examine new concepts for community health care facilities. The aim was to look for benefits in the following service areas:

- flexible use of any services
- services to local areas provided on a planned basis
- locality access for PCGs and Trusts
- health action zones to establish comprehensive local services
- economical and standardised building solutions
- higher levels of utilisation.

The core of the idea was to see if mobile units, used in conjunction with fixed terminal points could provide a more flexible alternative to individually design permanent buildings. The study looked at the opportunity for this approach to exploit the advantages of telemedicine, as well as opening up a range of new procurement methods with independent specialist companies providing supply, servicing and maintenance contracts. The study team also intends to investigate the concept for providing primary care and community services in developing countries (Bristow, *et al*., 2000).

4.2.2 Question: how do you incorporate flexibility (longlife, loose fit)?

Flexibility is going to effect almost every aspect of the provision of primary health care services in the future, as we move towards a knowledge-based profession. Doctors will need to respond to the easier access of information by changing work methods. This will mean not only great flexibility in the timing and programming of when surgeries are open but it will also mean that the buildings themselves will need to be more flexible. In the short term furniture and decoration may change frequently, and be seen as a stage set or fashion statement. Working practices will require workspaces to be more easily changed with partitioning, building services, and functional uses changing several times within the lifespan of the building shell. Finally, the building shell itself must be

able to accommodate these changes within its longer term lifespan of say 40–60 years.

The buildings themselves might even be seen as transient shells for a virtual surgery as a doctor moves around his territory accessing patient information from a variety of electronic sources and exploiting the potential of telemedicine. This science fiction view of the future should not be interpreted as a high-technology scientific approach to medicine but rather by exploiting everybody's accessibility to knowledge it will allow doctors and patients to return to a human centred medicine where consultation periods are longer and the interpersonal skills of the professionals will become increasingly important. The quality of medicine will be less dependent on technical information (because it will be readily available to all) but will be a reflection of a more caring, focused, patient centred concern for individual well-being. The buildings should reflect this by offering a comfortable set of outer clothes (the building shell) with a clean modern internal environment that acknowledges and reflects local environmental conditions. This suggests the return to vernacular architecture and a procurement methodology which is at the other end of the spectrum to large scale PFI procurement methods.

Primary health buildings and medical practices need to become more customer focused, and as the retail marketplace has demonstrated to us, the health service sector will become more dynamic and responsive to change. The importance of time and location of future facilities will become less important than they have been in the past as information and communication technologies develop. Patients (the customers) will influence these decisions to a greater extent than in the past as demographic pressures are allowed to influence the marketplace between where people live and where they work.

It is impossible to foresee accurately the influences of these changes as walk in centres develop, individual choice expands, technology provides greater accessibility to knowledge and diversity of choice will force future primary care facilities to be transformed in their approach to flexibility.

4.2.3 Approach: comparison with design criteria in the commercial sector for work environments

The concepts of change, working patterns, and the way buildings need to change to accommodate these requirements have been developed in the office sector of the property market.

For over 20 years Frank Duffy has been leading his firm, DEGW, through an exhaustive series of experiments and research projects looking at the way office accommodation must change to cater for new working practices. This research work needs to be transferred to the health sector, and indeed 'other workplaces'.

> '... I should mention what I mean by "office". I do not mean only prestige office buildings housing large corporations.

I mean all places where professional, administrative, recording, accounting activities are carried out, whether they be factories, surgeries, shop windows or prestige blocks – any place in which people who used to be called white collar workers work.' (Duffy, 1992.)

Duffy argues that applied research should be the basis for the development of this design work and should be based on an analysis of the way people use buildings. 'Buildings provide a framework for behaviour. They exist only to allow people to do what they want to do.'

These arguments are summarised in a neat list of variables.

- Organisation of work – *the job*: whatever is directly to do with getting the work done, e.g. the task to be completed, the line of authority and responsibility, work communication channels, management style, equipment used, numbers of visitors, etc.
- Behaviour at work – *the worker*: the social consequences of getting work done, e.g. display and prestige, work expectations, visitor communications, sex, age, income, education of the workers, secrecy required, etc.
- Building form – *the building*: the physical consequences of job and worker, e.g. location, space and equipment standards, disposition of groups and workers in plan, arrangement of equipment, size of room, use of partitions, screens, room dividers, etc.

Duffy's more recent work described in *New Environments for Working* (Laing *et al.*, 1998) develops these issues and sets out a framework for describing working patterns and the differing types of environmental systems required to support these. Much of this research work needs to be urgently transferred to the health sector and transform the way in which primary health care facilities are conceived. It is essential to break the mould of the briefing document being based on static physical requirements so that future projects embody the human ethos and quality of life issues begin to take precedence over traditional space standard and cost factors.

4.2.4 Consequences and outcomes: review space standards, building life and future trends

The health service of the future is returning to focusing attention on the patient. It will be a whole body approach, in a healing environment, where technology assists this process rather than being central to it. The consultation between doctor and patient will become more important. The patient will assert greater power as a consumer, and will become more challenging of doctors' opinions, be better informed, and be more willing to ask for a second or third opinion.

The health business will respond to these demands by providing:

- More comprehensive services involving both traditional and alternative therapies of care.

- Facilities which are more diverse, flexible, responsive to local conditions, and provided by a mixture of public and private finance.

Hence, the traditional 'Red Book' will become redundant, and the brief will become a looser framework of targets and objectives – not merely a schedule of areas with cost limits and a prescriptive schedule of maximum professional design fees. By integrating other services new models of primary care will emerge, probably with a significant proportion of funding coming from the private sector and ownership of the building possibly being owned by a specialist developer. New methods of measurement need to be devised to allow a proper assessment of whole life costs. Many of these parameters need to be determined by asking patients what they require. Sometimes by posing simple questions.

Freed from the financial restraints of running a traditional GP surgery, dynamic reactions can be allowed to flourish by the doctors which will result in patients being much more involved in influencing and shaping their own community resource.

4.3.1 Criteria: architecture has a poor track record in post-occupancy evaluations

Architectural education has been based, predominantly, on stimulating innovation and design originality. As already pointed out, this approach is diametrically opposed to a tradition of scientific analysis and developmental and sequential methodologies, which more typically form the stepping stones of progress in medicine and the law. The need for more evidence based research work in the architectural world has become accepted only more recently; it is only in the last decade, or so, that meaningful research data have begun to accumulate across a range of building types.

Design has traditionally built on precedent rather than the evidence base of a more thorough analysis of earlier work. Historical antecedents have been used intuitively rather than systematically developed in a scientific sense.

Not surprisingly, therefore, post-occupancy evaluations and other assessment techniques, have played only a small part in influencing the design development of buildings, and have played only a small part (if at all) as a tool to be used by architects in the design process. However, architects need to recognise that there is a range of analytical methods available to them to help them improve the performance and efficiency of their buildings. These tools should be used to assist originality, and not to stifle creativity, and assist in ensuring that the performance specification set out in the brief is achieved to a high standard. It is the establishment of performance specification standards which is bringing in a new rigour to the design process and the best examples are to be found in the commercial office sector.

The development of an architect's skills in these analytical fields has not been helped by the fee structure used by the profession. Only recently, has the importance of writing the brief become more widely accepted, and some large corporate clients now recognise that writing a brief for a building project is a separate process which needs to be paid for as a separate item. However, in many building types there is limited research available to provide adequate quantitative data to establish clear design parameters and this is perhaps a reflection of the limited research tradition in university departments of architecture. As a vocational profession young architects are encouraged to learn their skills in practice and we do not have a network of research centres focusing on particular building types such as secondary schools, police stations, housing for the elderly, or primary health facilities. Would it not be useful to have such centres of excellence rather than the more generalised arrangements (albeit frequently of exemplary quality) which are often a reflection of the random specialities of members of staff?

The development of an evidence-based body of data should shape the brief and drive the design process. It should establish the questions to be answered, allow the results to be tested, and an assessment to be made as to whether the original objectives have been met. Fundamentally, there should be a cycle of learning so that future buildings can be seen to acknowledge the work of previous good examples.

These issues once again highlight the opposing intellectual approaches of a scientific or philosophical solution. What is important, is that the rapid expansion of knowledge, available through improved technologies, is made available and is used by the designer to give added authority to artistic originality. To some extent, the NHS has been at the forefront of the analytical study of its building stock. Indeed, the *Capital Investment Manual* requires a post-project evaluation plan to be included in business case submissions and architects are required to measure a building's performance against the criteria set out in the original brief. Unfortunately, this exercise concentrates on an evaluation of whether the building was provided on time and within cost and does not seek to monitor building quality, which is a reflection of the approach to health building design over the past 50 years.

4.3.2 Question: should post-occupancy evaluations be the architect's responsibility?

Architects should certainly contribute to the preparation of post-occupancy evaluations, but there is room for widespread collaboration with clients, user groups, building owners, financial institutions, and indeed anybody interested in the value and performance of the built environment. The main requirement is for more work to be done in this field, the information to be made more widely available and for architects and all those interested in a building to include these data in the development of the brief for the next building.

Social scientists have developed a range of methodologies which are also used in architecture including:

- questionnaires
- *in situ* surveys
- user groups and focus groups
- participant observation studies.

Once again, it is necessary to note that the systematic analysis of data has been best developed in the commercial office sector. A range of measuring techniques are utilised and these are discussed in *The New Office* (Duffy, 1997) within the generic term 'post-occupancy evaluations' and includes:

- building appraisals
- workplace envisioning (WE)
- time utilisation studies (TUS)
- workplace performance surveys (WPS)
- post-occupancy evaluation (POE).

Duffy notes the resistance of architects to undertake post-occupancy evaluations, but concludes that if done they are always beneficial to clients and building users generally. The increase in the body of knowledge is emphasised as the main benefit arising from studies of this nature and which would improve the design of future buildings.

The use of case studies can benefit architects, clients and building users and forms the basis of much of the work done on office buildings. Interestingly, although the NHS has invested large resources in the development of room data and ergonomic requirements, together with cost parameters there has been little analysis of results. In the primary care field, perhaps this is as much to do with the ownership of GP surgeries, where the NHS sets minimum criteria and the GPs themselves are left to control, as clients, the design process as ultimate building owners. For a variety of reasons, this has led to mixed results, but has also produced a surprisingly fertile and imaginative range of responses, with some excellent small buildings.

Using the case study model, the Center for Health Design has carried out a design evaluation of six primary care facilities for the purpose of 'informing future design decisions' (Kantrowitz *et al.*, 1993). This report identifies a series of critical design issues arising from the data collected from the case studies. These are:

- design process
- humanistic design
- functional factors
- technical factors
- aesthetic factors
- cost factors
- materials and furnishings
- primary care practice.

The conclusions are hopeful:

'the research finds that although the definition of primary care varies among the six organisations, these groups have taken the initiative to custom fit the mix of primary care services to meet the needs of the population and communities they serve.

These organisations are finding ways to lessen the sterile, clinical image of medical settings of yesterday and instead, are designing more comfortable, welcoming space in primary care facilities.

There appears to be shift from large scale to smaller scale facilities and facility components that maintain a manageable yet effective size. Several of the six facilities attempted to decentralise a number of main functions in an effort to enhance the reality and the perception of personal attention in individual care.'

4.3.3 Approach: analyse design process in projects

The RIBA *Job Book* lays out a systematic approach to the design and construction process. It is presented as an *aide-mémoire* to assist architects with the design of all building types.

The sequential and systematic framework advocated is with 'feedback' at the end of this process and identifies three possible areas for examination:

- an analysis of the project records
- an inspection of the fabric of the completed building
- studies of the building in use.

It recognises that a full feedback study may be expensive and suggests that it may be necessary to negotiate a separate commission with the client should this work be deemed to be necessary. This highlights the failure of the profession to grasp the enormous value to be gained by constantly reviewing all available knowledge about the design problem in hand. As often as not, this feedback process suffers from the day-to-day pressures of dealing with the next job in hand. It always seems to be more important to press on with the excitement of the next design challenge, and even if there was time available there never seems to be the right moment to ask a client to spend more money on a project which as often as not will be stretching financial limits to the brink of acceptability. How easy it is to gloss over a few rough edges, not question a few embarrassing oversights in meeting the brief or open up old discussions about compromises on the quality of finishes due to cost limitations. All architects are familiar with this scenario and the most important issue on their minds may well be ensuring that their last fee instalment is paid on time. The culture of sharing knowledge and the benefits that might accrue if the same design team is commissioned to build a second or third building of the same type is a luxury rarely shared in the construction industry. Of course, the Egan and Latham Reports seek to address these issues but unfortunately they concentrate on improving the quality of the process rather than the quality of the product (see Chapter 3).

NHS Estates, until recently, considered that their involvement in primary health care was primarily to provide mechanisms for reimbursing the costs of providing premises for GPs, who, as independent contractors to the NHS, have the responsibility of providing premises for the delivery of services to their patients. They were not overly prescriptive in this, preferring to delegate responsibility for managing the process to the local health authorities who, in conjunction with local GPs, are considered best placed to make decisions which meet local needs and are within the resources available to them. This policy was reflected in *General Medical Practice Premises – A Commentary* (1998) which included a section entitled 'Environment'. It says:

'the control of the internal environment should be considered at the brief stage when opportunities to minimise maintenance and running costs can be addressed successfully.

The performance of the building services will be a major determinant of the comfort and perception of the premises by both patients and staff. Draughts, smells, poor ventilation and noise should be avoided.'

There follows a series of sections about lighting, heating, ventilation, hot and cold water, power, security, communications, patient call system, acoustics, fire safety, and lifts.

In 1996, MARU published a review of primary health care buildings including a helpful section about evaluating buildings in use. It recognises the circular process of reassessing design decisions and suggests three types of evaluation:

(1) Audit – measurement of certain criteria against an implied standard, in a defined location, to establish a range of values and indicate relative position.
(2) Case study – investigation of selected examples to learn lessons.
(3) Evaluation – assessment of the success in terms of specific criteria.

However, a more thorough review of post occupancy evaluation techniques is described by Mardelle McCuskey Shepley (Shepley, 1997). This comprehensive review of methodologies includes a list of references at the end of her chapter in 'Healthcare Design' edited by Sarah O'Marberry.

A more specific publication is *The Exeter Evaluation* (Scher and Senior, 1999). This report sets out the detailed results of an intensive research project undertaken at the new Royal Devon and Exeter Hospital. The report ends with five conclusions concerning:

(1) Awareness and communications (a programme to inform all staff about the benefits of art in the healing process)
(2) Displaying visual arts (careful consideration of location in both public spaces and in close proximity to patients)
(3) Staff participation (using staff skills in music, photography and writing for example)
(4) Resources (establish a budget heading)
(5) The value of arts in health care (increase knowledge).

Although not directly relevant to primary care facilities this work represents an excellent example of the systematic evidence-based research work that will become increasingly necessary to justify design quality decisions. The intuitive and artistic responses of the architect will in future require justification and substantiation to ensure design approval.

The design approach of my practice, the Geoffrey Purves Partnership, for GP surgeries is as much about people and understanding human relationships as architecture. The briefing process sets out to understand the interaction between doctor and patient, and to explore with the doctor (or doctors) their attitude towards treating patients through the eyes of the patient. The basis of the design process is to encourage our client to think of the building not just as a means to an end, but as a major contributor to the frame of mind of a patient when they arrive for that crucial interface between patient and doctor; the consultation.

The NHS among many advantages has the disadvantage of not having a commercial relationship between doctor and patient which is almost unique in our transaction based consumer-focused culture. The concept of our health service as a facility equally available to everyone is open to debate: is it not more available if you are articulate, demanding, persuasive, and intelligent? My observation is that the lack of financial incentive means that some doctors see themselves as distinct from, and unfortunately sometimes perceived as more important than, their patients. Doctors frequently assume that their time is more important than that of the patient. How efficient is their appointment system? Perhaps the concept of a waiting room is fundamentally flawed. Why should you need to wait if you have an appointment time? Therefore, terminologies need to be reappraised and the entrance areas seen as reception spaces with an accent on personal service.

Design should be approached by looking at the architectural issues from the convenience of the patient. Analogies are made elsewhere in the book to hotel receptions – is there a coffee machine, and a range of the morning's newspapers rather than dog-eared copies of out-of-date *National Geographic* magazines, along-side noticeboards with worrying information about cancer, smoking, and sexually transmitted diseases. Presentation needs much greater attention and this includes easy access to printed documentation.

In many of the poorer parts of our cities GP surgeries have developed a fortress mentality, and this needs to be completely reversed towards a respect for buildings achieved from higher standards of design based on encouraging friendly personal relationships. Clearly there are practical issues like the security of drugs and addicts know that a doctor's surgery may contain what they are looking for. However, banks have understood these issues of security and have found design solutions for their high street branches which places customer services at the forefront of their requirements. Bank robbers know that banks still hand over cash, but modern technology has provided solutions that largely has done away with glass screens and puts the staff of a bank in direct face-to-face contact with their customers. The personal interface has driven the design solutions and GP surgeries need to follow suit.

Patients need to be more assertive in demanding this level of service, and for too long the traditional relationships between themselves and their doctor has made little process from the low status and deference of patients which is no longer tolerated in almost all other activities of our society.

Therefore, our briefing meetings attempt to achieve acceptance of these personal relationships. They need to be open, friendly and accessible and the respect shown to the physical fabric of a building will grow in the local community. Another example of breaking down fortress mentalities can be illustrated by the change in policy with regard to security of churches. The insurance company responsible for the majority of church buildings, Ecclesiastical, no longer advocates locking churches to prevent theft. They have demonstrated that an open-door policy actually reduces the risk of theft, partly because if the door is open a thief is likely to wrongly assume that there is lesser value to steal than if the door was locked. Secondly, an open door policy means that a thief is more likely to be surprised by the entrance of an unexpected visitor.

The briefing document sets out to establish the criteria to ensure that the GP surgery will function with the requirements of a patient as a first priority, setting high standards which encourage respect, openness to encourage a relaxed attitude, and accessible to encourage appropriate use when necessary. It is a design approach viewed from the needs of the customer, and where the doctor does not assume that a patient's needs are subservient or secondary to his own operational preferences.

Functionality and cost effectiveness necessarily must be accurately and properly addressed, and therefore detailed room data sheets are a core feature of the brief, but subservient to the philosophical objectives. (A typical room data sheet is shown below.)

Geoffrey Purves Partnership: guidance notes for room data sheets

Purpose
To give guidance on completion of the room data sheets.

Sheet 1
Activities: The purpose of this section is to list the functions that are carried out in the identified room. Examples would be desk work for one person, storing files and records, displaying staff notices, information and messages, conferring with clinical staff colleagues, supervising, etc.

Personnel: The purpose of this section is to identify numbers of staff using the particular room and identifying whether their use is permanent day use or intermittent partial use. For example 2 × staff permanent and 1 × staff intermittent.

Planning relationships: The purpose of this section is to identify other key activity rooms that should be closely related to the room under consideration.

Additional notes: Any other factors that would influence the design of the room are to be indicated here

Sheet 2
Fittings, furniture and equipment: The purpose of this section is to identify the items which are to be included within the room.

This list should include 'built in' fittings (sinks, storage units, etc.), loose furniture (desks, chairs, couch) and equipment.

Building elements: The purpose of this section is to identify the materials that are required on the walls, ceilings, windows, doors etc. For example walls to be painted plaster, ceilings to be suspended tiles, windows to be flush with wall with no ledges, floors to be vinyl or carpet, doors to have any special requirements for example locks, special seals, etc.

Mechanical services: This section is for identifying specific requirements to do with mechanical services. For example filtration grade and temperature control of air, etc., provision of any medical gases or distilled water etc.

Electrical services: This section is designed for noting any special requirements, for example sealed light fittings, number of sockets listed under power and any specific telephone requirements (intercoms, outside lines, internal lines, etc.).

Signs: Any particular signage other than for statutory purposes (means of escape, etc.) which you think is necessary.

Special features and risks: Any other factors that need noting.

GEOFFREY PURVES PARTNERSHIP		
Room Data Sheet No:		
Hospital/Surgery:		
Scheme:		
Department:	Room No. & Title:	Area:
Built in Fittings	Furniture	Equipment
QTY	QTY	QTY
BUILDING ELEMENTS SERVICES	**MECHANICAL SERVICES**	**ELECTRICAL**
Walls	Heating	Lighting
Ceilings	Domestic Services	Power/Sockets
Windows	Ventilation	Clocks
Floors	Medical Gases/Suction	Telephones
Doors	Steam & Condense	Computer Points
	Other Mechanical Services	
SIGNS	SPECIAL FEATURES & RISKS	

Sheet 2

4.3.4 Consequences and outcomes: development of design guide recommendations

Fortunately, with enthusiastic support from the prime minister, CABE is vigorously promoting the importance of good design in new public buildings (Department for Culture, Media and Sport, 2000). The short document that is reproduced below highlights the value of good design in health buildings.

Three examples of design guide recommendations are worth noting:

(1) Why good design matters.
(2) A guide to devising an evaluation study.
(3) Is design working for you?

An example of an elementary post-occupancy audit

Used as part of a quality accreditation scheme, this could be included in an architect's office manual.

The Geoffrey Purves Partnership has also introduced an elementary post-occupancy evaluation process that the job architect reviews on completion of each project. This is reproduced below. The important part of this exercise is to develop an awareness for learning from previous experience so that the intellectual knowledge of the practice is enhanced,

GEOFFREY PURVES PARTNERSHIP		
Room Data Sheet No:		
Hospital/Surgery:		
Scheme:		
Department:	Room No. & Title:	Area:
ACTIVITIES		
PERSONNEL		
PLANNING RELATIONSHIPS		
ADDITIONAL NOTES		

Sheet 1

and this information is used for the benefit of future clients. It instils a cultural attitude that the body of knowledge in the firm as a whole is greater than that of any individual member of staff. Hopefully, this corporate skill becomes a valuable asset and enhances the value of the work of the practice.

Why good design matters Better Public Buildings

Good design of public buildings can and should:

- respect and enhance the location, the environment and the community
- add value and reduce whole-life costs
- create flexible, durable, sustainable and ecologically sound development for the community
- minimise waste of materials and energy, in construction and in use
- provide functional, efficient, adaptable spaces for home, work and recreation
- be attractive and healthy for users and public
- contribute to construction which is quick, safe and efficient
- use space, materials and resources with imagination and efficiency
- produce buildings which are safer to construct and easier to clean and maintain.

Good design enhances people's lives, transforming how they feel and how they behave; it can:

- revitalise neighbourhoods and cities
- transform derelict sites and neglected buildings, reducing pressure on the countryside
- uplift and bring hope to neglected communities
- reduce crime, illness, truancy
- help public services perform better: hospitals, schools, housing, transport.

Good design in the public sector is achievable and affordable.

Good design delivers functional buildings and civilised places while retaining a human dimension.

Good design is worth investing in. It is the key to giving the client maximum value for money through the whole life of a building.

Good design is a commitment to a better quality of life for all.

Table 4.2 A guide to devising an evaluation study. This checklist should be used as a tool in devising a project specific study. It lists some of the different possibilities that can emerge when setting up an evaluation study – these are in the right hand column of each table.

Purpose of evaluation – setting up the study	
Who is it for?	Service managers
	Service users – local community
	Project owners
	Other planning teams

Which questions need to be answered?	
Business objectives	Investment decisions
	Capital costs
	Delivery of project on time
	Market position/share
	Customer satisfaction
	Staff satisfaction
	Recruitment and retention of staff
Health service outcomes	Improving health status
	Meeting needs
	Quality of care
	Location and access for patients
	Activity levels
	Improved uptake of services
Operational effectiveness	How is it working?
	Match between design and service intentions
	How did design meet brief
	Meeting the needs of the community
	Assessing degree of management and organisational change
	Revenue savings
Building effectiveness	Improved environment
	Functional suitability
	Functional relationships
	Utilisation levels
	Running costs
	Energy use
	Ambience

What information will be required?	
What measures will be used	For business objectives
	For health service outcomes
	For operational objectives
	For building performance
What analyses will be required?	Quantitative
	Qualitative
How will the results be used?	To improve management of new building
	To improve organisation and use of new building
	To improve organisation and use of an existing building to feed into next project

How will the study be managed by the client?	
Who will undertake the study?	In-house team
	Outside agency
What skills will be required on the team?	Finance
	Management
	Clinical: medical, nursing, therapy
	Planning
	Voluntary sector
	Community representatives
	Facilities management
	Design and construction
	Technical
	Research

Who will be on the steering group?	Service manager
	Building manager
	Building owner
Who will be the study co-ordinator?	Service manager
	Building manager
	Building owner

Dissemination of results

Who will receive study results?	Building users: staff
	Building users: community
	Building owners
	Purchasing authority
Will there be a summary report?	For whom?
Will results be published?	When?
	Where?
	For whom?

Feasibility, cost and timing

What is the cost?	Is there a budget?
	Secondment?
When should the study take place?	When will the data be available?
What is the timescale of the study?	6, 12, 18, 24 months
How soon is the information needed?	Who needs it?
	When?

Is it worth doing?

Is design working for you?

This checklist is an extract from 'Better Public Buildings – a proud legacy for the future' (Department of Culture, Media and Sport) and can be used by local planning authorities as the basis for selecting priorities.

Design policies
- Does the development plan contain design policies?
- Do the policies include general, area-specific and topic-based design policies?
- Are the design policies expressed at the right level of specificity?

Supplementary planning guidance
- Is the development plan supported by supplementary planning guidance:
    urban design frameworks?
    development briefs?
    design guides?
- Does the council need internal guidance notes on preparing supplementary planning guidance?

Urban design frameworks
- Does the council need urban design frameworks as a means of creating confidence, unlocking potential, managing change, providing a strategy for implementation, and expressing design and planning concepts and proposals in two- and three-dimensions?

Development briefs
- Does the council produce development briefs as a means of implementing its design and planning policies?
- Does the council produce development briefs jointly with other organisations where appropriate?
- Does the council set out its expectations for any development briefs it does not prepare itself and the procedure for preparing them?
- Does the council have sufficient design expertise to manage consultants effectively or to assess the design element of a developer's brief, in cases where the council itself does not prepare a development brief?

Design guides
- Does the council need a more comprehensive series of design guides?
- Are design guides prepared in collaboration with all relevant departments of the local authority (and other local authorities if appropriate) and with other relevant organisations?
- Are the public and potential users consulted effectively when design guides are being prepared?
- Are design guides sent out with planning application forms?
- Do design guides have the status of supplementary planning guidance?
- Does the council hold internal seminars with elected members and officers to share experience and ensure commitment to implement the guides?
- Does the council hold seminars with potential users of its design guides?
- Are design guides promoted through other publications and visits to show how they can lead to higher standards of design?
- Do staff have the necessary negotiation skills to ensure that development complies with the principles of the design guide?

Design statements
- Does the council insist on design statements being submitted with planning applications to help in evaluating development proposals against its own design policies and Government guidance?
- Does the council use design statements to structure the design and planning process in relation to sites which are not the subject of development briefs?

Design assessments
- Does the council commission independent assessments of development proposals, where it does not have adequate design skills itself (in view of the scale or sensitivity of the proposed development)?

Collaboration
- Is the council making the most of collaboration and public participation as a means of resolving conflicts early in the design and development process and avoiding unnecessary confrontation, polarised attitudes and delay?

Skills
- Does the council employ staff with appropriate design skills?
- Does the council have a training and education programme to ensure that everyone involved in design and planning has the necessary skills and knowledge of design appropriate to their role?

Design initiatives
- Is the council active in promoting awareness of design, highlighting good practice and facilitating joint working though design initiatives?

Quality audits
- Does the council conduct quality audits to assess how it is managing the design and planning process and the effectiveness of its design policies and guidance?

An example of an elementary post-occupancy audit

Used as part of a quality accreditation scheme. This document could be included in an architects office manual

The Geoffrey Purves Partnership has also introduced an elementary post-occupancy evaluation process (see Sheet 3) which the job architect reviews on completion of each project. The important part of this exercise is to develop an awareness for learning from previous experiences so that the intellectual knowledge of the practice is enhanced, and this information is used for the benefit of future clients. It instils a cultural attitude that the body of knowledge in the firm as a whole is greater than that of any individual member of staff. Hopefully, this corporate skill becomes a valuable asset and enhances the value of the work of the practice.

GEOFFREY PURVES PARTNERSHIP

POST OCCUPANCY EVALUATION

Checklist to be completed by Design Team

Project completed...
Review carried out ....

1. Did the design meet the brief?

    - strengths
    - weaknesses

2. Was it completed on time?

3. Was it completed on budget?

4. Was it completed within office management programming schedules?

5. Was it profitable./are fees paid?

6. Partner to arrange meeting with Client 3 months after completion to review

    - satisfaction with design
    - satisfaction with design team performance
    - satisfaction with build quality
    - satisfaction with cost
    - satisfaction with contractor
    - satisfaction with construction programming
      (eg was it built on time)

7. Partner to arrange meeting with client at first appropriate time to discuss ongoing responsibility and involvement with the building
    eg • annual maintenance review
       • regular review of running costs
       • interior decoration/space planning reviews

8. Is the project suitable for publicity or an award?
    - agree action to be taken

9. Have photographs been taken?

10. Are office records in order/filing/dead storage?

11. Has publicity text been written?

Sheet 3

4.4.1 Criteria: NHS has no data on results questionnaire issued to GPs

With the publication of *Environments for Quality Care – 'Health Buildings in the Community'* (NHS Estates, 1994) doctors were invited to complete a self-appraisal questionnaire about their own premises. It provided a comprehensive review of topics to allow doctors to examine the day-to-day running of their practice and to gauge its performance against patient satisfaction.

The questionnaire (reproduced later in the chapter) sets out a series of questions covering the following topics:

- first impressions
- assess
- reception and waiting area
- consulting, examination and treatment rooms
- circulation spaces
- staff areas
- building efficiency.

The last question invited doctors to ask themselves 'Does the building convey a message of well-being?'. Obviously, this questionnaire does not gather information about the views of other users of the building such as patients or members of staff, although some doctors may have canvassed views from other people before completing the forms. Also, some of the questions only invite a self-assessment of policies which will have been established by the doctors themselves.

In addition, the National Primary Care Research and Development Centre has carried out a survey of 10 innovative projects where the processes of service development and premises development have been interactive (Bailey, 1997). This has led to the resultant buildings developing individual facilities particular to their locality.

The NHS Estates questionnaire is the potential source of a great deal of valuable data, but there has been no process to collect or collate the results. An opportunity has been lost to invite doctors to return the forms so that an analysis of their views could be undertaken.

4.4.2 Question: what does the 'environments for quality care' questionnaire demonstrate about existing facilities?

The questionnaire was an imaginative initiative by NHS Estates and sought to look beyond the traditional assessment criteria of functionality and cost effectiveness for primary health care facilities.

The questions reflect the philosophies that were common currency a decade ago. As a self-appraisal system designed to give doctors a quick review of how their surgery performed, in their eyes, it served a valuable purpose. However, it is disappointing that NHS Estates did not collate any of the information and therefore no statistical results have been published. The results of the surveys on a group of surgeries designed by the Geoffrey Purves Partnership are described more fully in the next section.

The same questionnaire could have been made available to a randomly selected cross-section of patients and staff and the results compared with the judgements scored by the doctors. Therefore, the questionnaire is not an assessment of patient satisfaction and more probing questions might have been asked about patient needs and facilities not included in the designs. It would have been useful to go back to the briefing process to see if appropriate challenges had been set for the design team and the quality thresholds set out as a requirement for approving the design.

Lessons might be learned from the commercial world of marketing and public relations, where customer requirements are reviewed and analysed by focus groups and other surveys conducted from the point of view of the customer. Fortunately, these issues are now better understood and acknowledged by the NHS and the annual patients' survey has begun to tackle these issues. More work remains to be done as priority shifts from meeting the requirements of the service provider to satisfying the services expected by patients.

4.4.3 Approach: analyse questionnaire results from GPP designs – extend analysis to other surgeries

Of the primary care centres designed by the Geoffrey Purves Partnership 14 have completed the questionnaire and the results are shown in Table 4.4.

An analysis of the results highlights some interesting points. The overall response to section 1, first impressions, shows a high level of satisfaction (88.9%). The main criticism from this group of questions arises at 1.03 which indicates that there is dissatisfaction with the level of parking for patients and staff. All of the respondents said that their building appeared welcoming and that there was easy access for disabled people and parents with prams.

However, question 2 on access showed the lowest level of satisfaction of all the sections with less than half (46.4%) considering that all parts of the building were accessible to everyone, and that adequate provision had been made for people with mobility, hearing and sight difficulties. This immediately suggests that the briefing requirements to the architect are either inadequate, or that the architect has failed to respond adequately to the needs of patients and staff with disabilities.

Although there was a high level of satisfaction with the questions regarding reception and waiting areas the design and structure of the questionnaire itself is suspect in that doctors were scoring against their own requirements for the brief. For example, question 3.17 shows that all surgeries were satisfied with their patient call system. This should not be surprising because the patient call system in every case is that which was requested by the doctors themselves. Following a more limited participant observation exercise involving two waiting areas it was apparent that there were many deficiencies in the detailed functioning of the reception and waiting areas which would not necessarily be apparent to the doctors or staff of the surgery in question. However, there were significant shortcomings when seen from the patient's perspective. The patient call system does, of course, touch upon the very essence of the patient/ doctor relationship. Should a doctor come out of his waiting room and greet a patient personally, which is time consuming, or call a patient to the consulting room by the use of indicator boards, Tannoy systems, or simply by reception staff calling out names? In many cases, the patient feels disadvantaged, and immediately less equal than the doctor. An apprehensive patient, feeling unwell, waiting to be called by the doctor conjures up the mental image of a child being called into the headmaster's study, or in an adult scenario, someone seeking a job being called in to present themselves to an interview panel.

A visit to a private hospital, for example the Nuffield Hospital in Newcastle upon Tyne, illustrates the different approach taken where consultants come to the waiting area personally to greet their patient on neutral territory. How do you measure the cost of these alternative approaches?

High levels of satisfaction were expressed for the consulting, examination and treatment rooms. These space are the subject of detailed briefs within the NHS procurement system and doctors have a significant control over the detailed layout of their working environment. However there was a significant level of dissatisfaction (21%) of the confidentiality ensured in terms of both sight and sound (question 4.04).

Generally, circulation spaces were not criticised although 64% of the respondents said that staff could not circulate without going through the waiting room. Although not stated, the implication of this question is that it was disadvantageous for staff to use the waiting room as a circulation route. This, of course, may not necessarily be so.

Lighting in the staff areas was not considered to have been designed to meet flexible working needs by 29% of respondents.

The highest levels of negative answers to the questionnaire was in the building efficiency section. Overall, only 61.3% answered yes to the questions in this section and only 36% thought that there was flexibility in relation to future needs. The question regarding telephone systems is flawed, in that it asks two questions (i.e. is the telephone system adequate and is a telephone provided for patient use?).

4.4.4 Consequences and outcomes: expand on results. Identify successes and failures review with NHS Estates (Leeds)

This survey has therefore highlighted three principle areas of concern:

(1) Internal accessibility, particularly for people with mobility, hearing and sight difficulties.
(2) Issues of building efficiency, such as sound confidentiality between consulting rooms and circulation spaces, energy conservation, and heating and ventilation systems.
(3) Flexibility for future requirements.

Overall, despite the shortcomings, all 14 primary care practices said that their buildings (externally and internally) conveyed a message of wellbeing. It is immediately apparent, that the shortcomings, within the three broad categories identified, are issues arising from the briefing process, rather than from the fundamental ability of architects to design appropriate buildings that please their clients.

Surprisingly, correspondence with NHS Estates has revealed some interesting comments. For example:

'I am not aware of any other surveys carried out using the questionnaire contained in our publication "Environments for Quality Care". Certainly there have been none carried out centrally. As you are aware the questionnaire was intended for use at practice level for self-assessing the need for improvement to premises.

As you will be aware, GP's, as independent contractors to the NHS, have the responsibility of providing premises for the delivery of services to their patients. Historically the involvement of the department was primarily to provide mechanisms for reimbursing the costs of doing so. More recently we have also been keen to encourage the development of purpose built Primary Care premises for delivering the modern NHS and we have and will continue to issue guidance accordingly. Nonetheless, we are not overly prescriptive in this, preferring to delegate responsibility for managing the process to Local Health Authorities who, in conjunction with local GP's, are best placed to make decisions which meet local needs and are within the resources available to them.' (Letter from the Policy Manager – Primary Care, NHS Estates 30 September 1998.)

A later letter (25 May 1999) comments:

'... I have also enclosed for your information two recent documents issued by NHS Estates, i.e. an augmented version of the previously issued "General Medical Practice Premises – a Commentary" and "A Guide to the provision of Leasehold Premises for GP Occupation".

'... These documents do not cover design issues but do further inform the process of Primary Care premises provision ...'

Interestingly, the revised issue of the *General Medical Practice Premises – A Commentary* is subtitled *A Guide to the Size, Design and Construction of GP Premises*. This appears to contradict a letter to me dated 4 August 1998 which said:

'When planning the new cost rent schedule, issued with effect from 1 November 1997, the Department's purpose was to move away from what was, under the old schedule, and outdated and overly prescribed model of premises provision. The desire was to encourage GP's, other Primary Care staff and users of the premises, Health Authorities and professional advisors, to develop innovative designs for good quality premises. In this way premises would be provided which would best meet the current needs of the Practice but allow planning for future additional facility space, internal restructuring and change of space usage. Durability, energy efficiency, appearance, environment, access and security, where amongst the many factors taken into consideration. However, there is a requirement for the department to ensure value for money and, therefore, a need to set both cost and space maxima within the schedule. Those maxima, generally regarded as generous, were established with a clear understanding of the above criteria and other quality issues ... .

... It was intended that the commentary and cost rent schedule should together constitute a benchmark against which to judge all Primary Care premises, however provided. It has since been acknowledged that the existing commentary may not sufficiently have addressed all of the quality issues involved. For that reason we should shortly be issuing Health Authorities with a revised and expanded version of the commentary. This will provide further guidance on construction parameters and specifications for good quality premises from which to deliver a modern and responsive primary care service ... .'

In telephone conversations with the department, it has become apparent that NHS Estates believes that it is on the horns of a dilemma on the questions of quality. In the commentary referred to above, the section on design principles consists of a series of statements which could be interpreted as good intentions, for example:

Para 2.1.5 – wherever practicable premises proposals should also allow flexibility in the medium to longer term to accommodate for example anticipated changes to list size and methods of working by practitioners and services development by the Primary Health Care teams.

Or

Para 2.3.2 – the exterior design will be influenced by many factors including the location, site shape, preferences of the practitioners, influences of the Planning Department and not least the design skills of the Architect. Where co-ordinated well, a rich variety of premises that are effective, attractive and comforting to patients should be the result.

The failure to comment on design until recently, or include any process of design evaluation in the assessment process for new premises, highlights the reluctance the Government had to involve itself in the subjective assessment of quality factors. Fortunately this position is changing rapidly – more details can be found at www.nhsestates.gov.uk (see postscript at end of Chapter 12).

This apparent reluctance to benchmark quality standards, admitted in 'off the record' conversations is also illustrated by the publication *Better by Design* (NHS Estates, 1994). In the forward, written by Tom Sackville, parliamentary Undersecretary of State for Health at the time, and responsible for commissioning the document which was written by Mike Nightingale he says:

'... Much of the estate and the NHS have suffered by poor design and bad planning ... I am glad to say that things are changing ... quality buildings need good designers, prepared if necessary to turn conventional thinking on its head ... .'

The document sets out cogent arguments for good brief writing, and helpful advice on commissioning a quality building. There is a checklist of design pointers but the process continues to revolve around an assessment of cost schedules and space standards. Despite encouraging statements, the government remains hesitant and non-committal in its interpretation of what a quality building represents. It seems unable to make any judgements about what good quality represents. It encourages good design but is unable to define it. This methodology attempts to provide some pointers towards answering that question.

Doctors' surgeries designed by the Geoffrey Purves Partnership that have answered the questionnaire

(1) Lintonville Medical Centre, Old Lane, Ashington, Northumberland.
(2) Monkseaton Medical Centre, Cauldwell Avenue, Monkseaton, Whitley Bay.
(3) The Grove Medical Centre, 1 The Grove, Gosforth, Newcastle upon Tyne.
(4) Dr S Vis-Nathan, Medical Centre, Wear Street, Jarrow, Tyne & Wear.
(5) Bewicke medical Centre, Tynemouth Road, Wallsend, Tyne & Wear.
(6) Trinity Medical Centre, New George Street, Laygate, South Shields.
(7) Oxford Terrace Medical Group, 1 Oxford Terrace, Gateshead.
(8) Westerhope Medical Group, 377 Stamfordham Road, Newcastle upon Tyne.
(9) Gosforth Memorial Medical Centre.
(10) Denton Turret Medical Centre, Kenton Road, Denton Dene, Newcastle upon Tyne.
(11) Parkway Medical Centre, 2 Frenton Close, Chapel House Estate, Newcastle upon Tyne.
(12) Forest Hall Medical Group, Medical Centre, Station Road, Forest Hall, Newcastle upon Tyne.
(13) West Road Medical Centre, 170 West Road, Newcastle upon Tyne.
(14) Wideopen Medical Centre, Great North Road, Gosforth, Newcastle upon Tyne.

Checklist

This checklist reproduced in Table 4.3 is designed to help members of primary health care teams assess the quality of their environment. It highlights a series of points following a journey through a hypothetical surgery or health centre. It could also apply to a small community hospital. The list is not exhaustive, and is seen as a starting point for discussion.

Sometimes it is more effective, and more fun, for three or four members of a team of staff to carry out the check together. Each of the 60 questions has a box for the answer – yes, no, or a question mark for an indeterminate answer. If the answer is not clear, it suggests some improvement could be made. If the answer is no, and especially if there are many negative answers, it may be helpful to begin discussion of an improvement plan.

Table 4.3 Checklist

First impressions	Yes	No	?
Is the entrance easy to see and easy to use for everyone?	❑	❑	❑
Is there good access by public transport?	❑	❑	❑
Is there adequate and secure parking for patients and staff (including parking for disabled people)?	❑	❑	❑
Is there easy access for disabled people and parents with prams?	❑	❑	❑
Does the building appear welcoming?	❑	❑	❑
Does its appearance convey both its purpose and a relation to its setting?	❑	❑	❑
Are the external areas suitably planted and attractive?	❑	❑	❑
Is there a porch or lobby with space for prams?	❑	❑	❑
Does the entrance give a clear view to the interior?	❑	❑	❑
Access			
Is the whole building accessible to everyone?	❑	❑	❑
Is provision made for people with mobility, hearing or sight difficulties?	❑	❑	❑
Reception and waiting area			
Is the desk open and comfortable for patients, and easy to see on entry?	❑	❑	❑
Is it comfortable for staff?	❑	❑	❑
Does it combine the needs of security and confidentiality?	❑	❑	❑
Is there a section for wheelchair users?	❑	❑	❑
Is there a section which provides additional privacy?	❑	❑	❑
Are there good sight-lines from behind the desk to the entrance and waiting area?	❑	❑	❑
Does the design facilitate communication between receptionists and other staff?	❑	❑	❑
Is the whole area free of clutter?	❑	❑	❑
Is there natural light and is lighting sympathetic to patients and staff?	❑	❑	❑
Are seats comfortable and co-ordinated with the design of the interior?	❑	❑	❑
Are colour schemes restful?	❑	❑	❑
Is flooring appropriate to use and as quiet as possible?	❑	❑	❑
Is there a view, or are there pictures to look at, or visible evidence of links to the community?	❑	❑	❑
Is there a designated space equipped for children's play?	❑	❑	❑
Does the play area have good visibility from the main waiting area?	❑	❑	❑
Is it screened to mask sound?	❑	❑	❑
Is the system by which people are called for a consultation user-friendly?	❑	❑	❑
Is health information given in a way which meets individual needs?	❑	❑	❑
Consulting examination and treatment rooms	**Yes**	**No**	**?**
Are these designed to help people be comfortable?	❑	❑	❑
Is there enough space for all users?	❑	❑	❑
Do consulting rooms have natural light?	❑	❑	❑
Is confidentiality ensured in terms of both sight and sound?	❑	❑	❑
Is equipment designed in a patient-friendly way (or masked from view if not in use)?	❑	❑	❑
Circulation spaces			
Are they free of clutter?	❑	❑	❑
Are signs, if used, simple and user-friendly, and in a 'house style'?	❑	❑	❑
Are routes taken by patients as short as possible?	❑	❑	❑
Can staff circulate without going through the waiting room?	❑	❑	❑
Are there appropriate seats (and places for informal meetings in larger buildings)?	❑	❑	❑
Staff areas			
Do they have natural light and adequate ventilation?	❑	❑	❑
Is a comfortable common room or seminar room provided?	❑	❑	❑
Are training needs met?	❑	❑	❑
Is effective use made of computer technologies?	❑	❑	❑

Is lighting designed to meet flexible working needs?	❏	❏	❏
Is furniture co-ordinated with the design of the interior?	❏	❏	❏
Does the design facilitate communication between staff?	❏	❏	❏

Building efficiency

Are you happy with heating and ventilation systems?	❏	❏	❏
Are heating and ventilation systems integral to the design of the building?	❏	❏	❏
Do you know how they work?	❏	❏	❏
Are safety and security needs met?	❏	❏	❏
Is the building likely to be economical to maintain?	❏	❏	❏
Are materials and fittings chosen to be durable and easy to maintain?	❏	❏	❏
Is the interior easy to keep clean?	❏	❏	❏
Is there adequate storage space to prevent clutter?	❏	❏	❏
Is there flexibility in relation to future needs?	❏	❏	❏
Are needs for information technology met for today and tomorrow?	❏	❏	❏
Is the telephone system adequate, and is a phone provided for patient use?	❏	❏	❏

Finally

Does the building (externally and internally) convey a message of well-being?	❏	❏	❏

Table 4.4 Questionnaire results

Question	Yes Number	%	No Number	%	Don't know Number	%
First impressions						
1.01	14	100	0	0	0	0
1.02	14	100	0	0	0	0
1.03	8	57	3	21	3	21
1.04	14	100	0	0	0	0
1.05	14	100	0	0	0	0
1.06	14	100	0	0	0	0
1.07	12	86	2	14	0	0
1.08	12	86	1	7	1	7
1.09	11	79	3	21	0	0
Access						
2.01	4	29	10	71	0	0
2.02	9	64	4	29	1	7
Reception and waiting area						
3.01	13	93	1	7	0	0
3.02	13	93	1	7	0	0
3.03	6	43	7	50	1	7
3.04	7	50	7	50	0	0
3.05	7	50	7	50	0	0
3.06	12	86	2	14	0	0
3.07	13	93	1	7	0	0
3.08	11	79	3	21	0	0
3.09	13	93	1	7	0	0
3.10	13	93	1	7	0	0
3.11	14	100	0	0	0	0
3.12	13	93	1	7	0	0
3.13	13	93	0	0	1	7
3.14	10	71	3	21	1	7
3.15	10	71	1	7	2	14*
3.16	1	7	11	79	1	7*
3.17	14	100	0	0	0	0
3.18	14	100	0	0	0	0
Consulting, examination and treatment room						
4.01	13	91	0	0	1	7

Question	Yes Number	%	No Number	%	Don't know Number	%
4.02	12	86	2	14	0	0
4.03	14	100	0	0	0	0
4.04	10	71	3	21	1	7
4.05	13	93	0	0	1	7
Circulation spaces						
5.01	13	93	1	7	0	0
5.02	13	93	0	0	1	7
5.03	14	100	0	0	0	0
5.04	9	64	4	29	1	7
5.05	13	93	1	7	0	0
Staff area						
6.01	12	86	2	14	0	0
6.02	13	93	1	7	0	0
6.03	11	79	1	7	1	7*
6.04	13	93	1	7	0	0
6.05	8	57	4	29	1	7*
6.06	10	71	2	14	2	14
6.07	10	71	0	0	3	21*
Building efficiency						
7.01	6	43	6	43	2	14
7.02	7	50	3	21	4	29
7.03	12	86	2	14	0	0
7.04	12	86	1	7	1	7
7.05	8	57	3	21	3	21
7.06	7	50	4	29	3	21
7.07	10	71	4	29	0	0
7.08	12	86	1	7	1	7
7.09	8	57	6	43	0	0
7.10	5	36	4	29	5	36
7.11	8	57	1	7	4	29*
7.12	8	57	7	50	1	7*
Finally						
8.01	14	100	0	0	0	0

* date incomplete or 2 answers given

Table 4.5 Summary

Question	Yes		No		Don't know	
	Number	%	Number	%	Number	%
First impressions Q1 (126)	112	88.9	9	7.1	5	4.0
Access Q2 (28)	13	46.4	14	50	1	3.6
Reception and waiting area Q3 (252)	197	78.1	47	18.7	8	3.2
Consulting, examination and treatment room Q4 (70)	62	88.6	5	7.1	3	4.3
Circulation spaces Q5 (70)	62	88.6	6	8.6	2	2.8
Staff area Q6 (98)	77	78.6	11	11.2	10	10.2
Building efficiency Q7 (168)	103	61.3	40	23.8	25	14.9
Finally Q8 (1)	1	100	0	0	0	0

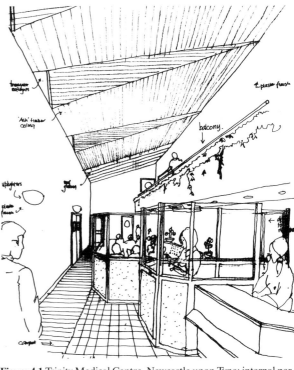

Figure 4.1 Trinity Medical Centre, Newcastle upon Tyne: internal perspective of reception. Architect: Geoffrey Purves Partnership

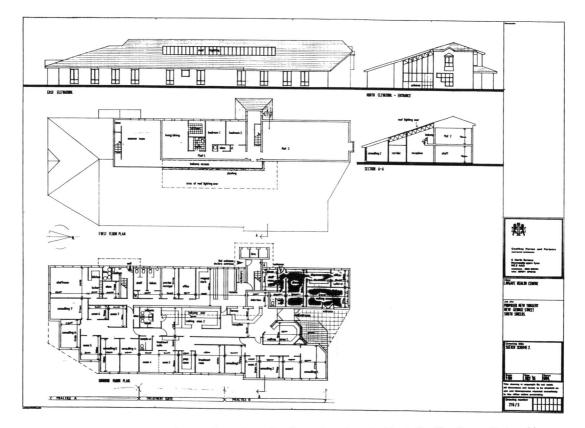

Figure 4.2 Trinity Medical Centre, Newcastle upon Tyne: plans, elevation and sections. Architect: Geoffrey Purves Partnership

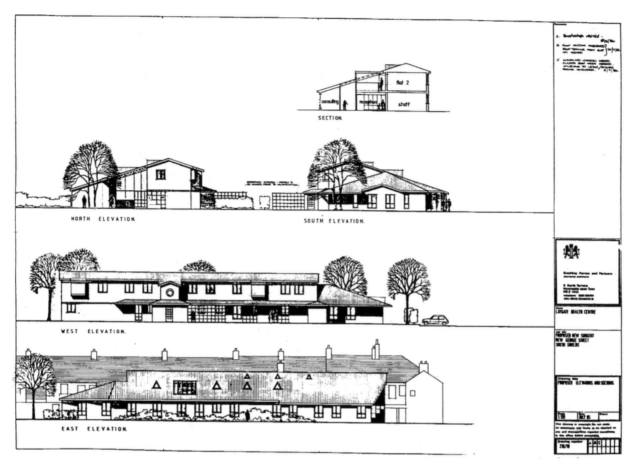

Figure 4.3 Trinity Medical Centre, Newcastle upon Tyne: elevations and section. Architect: Geoffrey Purves Partnership

4.5.1 Criteria: patients' views should be equal to other users (e.g. doctors and other staff)

The NHS Plan (NHS, 2000) sets out in the first paragraph of the Executive Summary that: 'The purpose and vision of this NHS Plan is to give the people of Britain a health service fit for the 21st century: a health service designed around the patient.' The document goes further; the chapter 'Our Vision: A Health Service Designed Around the Patient' says that the vision of the NHS Plans to offer people fast and convenient care delivered to a consistently high standard. Services are to be available when people require them, tailored to their individual needs. The objectives, therefore, could not be more clearly stated.

However, this vision will require changes in attitudes not only towards the physical fabric of the buildings from which the services will be provided but also by the professional staff working in the health field.

Architecture was exposed to this customer care environment, or consumerism, in the 1980s. At that time the concept of community architecture became fashionable and the architectural profession was exposed to the full force of Government legislation which strengthen the rights of individuals and removed some of the traditional aspects of professional life such as the RIBA fee scale for professional charges. Architects were allowed to become directors of building companies but at the same time found themselves pitching for work on a competitive basis from clients who readily began to exploit the market economy for procuring professional services. At the same time, public opinion was seen as just as important as the professional view and a turning point for the profession was the famous 'carbuncle' speech by Prince Charles which he delivered at the 150th celebrations of the RIBA at Hampton Court in 1984. He advocated a return to an interest in ornament, decoration, and old buildings, and to take account of the views of ordinary people – views which were not universally endorsed, but they formed the basis for a debate which continues today. Architectural confidence has regained its poise and architects in practice are learning new techniques to work in a consumer orientated economy, assisted, in no small measure, by the Government's recent adoption of the importance of good design as a key element in the procurement of the next wave of public buildings, including those in the health sector. 'The best designed hospitals help patients recover their spirits and health' (DCMS, 2000)

Figure 4.4 Lintonville Medical Centre, Newcastle upon Tyne: internal corridor. Architect: Geoffrey Purves Partnership (also in colour section)

Some two decades later, the medical profession now finds itself exposed to similar pressures on its working practices as a result of consumerism. Patient focused care reflects this trend in the health field, none more so than in primary care. Increasingly, doctors are being questioned about their decisions, and job demarcations are breaking down. Society offered doctors a very special position in the community; a protected commercial environment in return for the dedicated and skilful care of those most in need in our communities. However, the advent of the knowledge revolution has

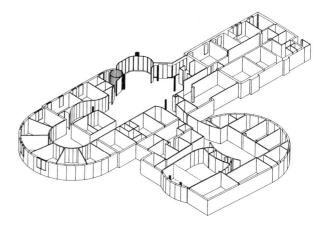

Figure 4.5 Lintonville Medical Centre: isometric view. Architect: Geoffrey Purves Partnership

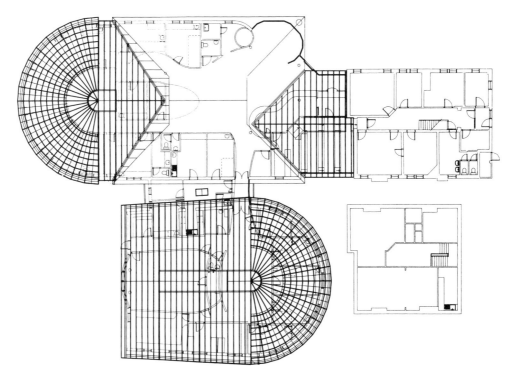

Figure 4.6 Lintonville Medical Centre: plans. Architect: Geoffrey Purves Partnership

initiated a wide range of challenges to traditional medical practice. Nursing technicians are to be trained to assist with coronary care operations which will enable routine aspects of the procedure to be undertaken in less than half an hour rather than taking up to two hours when carried out by trainee surgeons, who are 'learning on the job', working under the supervision of more experienced colleagues. The Archbishop of Canterbury, Dr George Carey, picked up this theme in his sermon at St Paul's Cathedral in celebration of the 200th anniversary of the Royal College of Surgeons. Addressing a congregation which included top surgeons, Dr Carey said that for many centuries until 1775, the Archbishop of Canterbury had been the principle medical licensing authority in England:

'It is precisely because the vocation of the surgeon that we celebrate here is such a great calling that it is so painful when there is a falling short'.

Surgeons working at the frontiers of human existence, at the boundaries between life and death and at the limits of what humans know and can achieve, 'but that makes the gift of humility all the more vital. And there have been well publicised vocations in recent times when it seems to have been lacking. At such times, public confidence can drain away and professional morale can plummet.'

The Archbishop went on:

'It must be recognised that we live in a society where people are no longer prepared to doff their cap towards authority in any walk of life – including, I may say, my own. Anything that smacks of arrogance or high-handedness is unlikely to be productive.' (Gledhill, 2000b.)

Architects and doctors, therefore, need to recognise the essential need to serve the individual. Perhaps it is no coincidence that the year 2000 saw the introduction of the new Human Rights Act which focused on the protection of all citizens against the actions of the State, and other Public Authorities.

The Human Rights Act 1998 which came into force on 2 October 2000 is widely regarded as the most significant pieces of constitutional legislation introduced this century, and probably much longer. The European Convention for the Protection of Human Rights and Fundamental Freedoms (The Convention) was drafted, mainly by British lawyers, and set out to guarantee the citizens of Europe basic human rights and freedoms. The objective of The Convention has been identified as the protection of individual human rights, and the maintenance and promotion of the ideals and values of the democratic society. These values are pluralism, tolerance and broad-mindedness (Gibson, 1999.)

The Convention rights can be put into categories:

- Rights:
  - right to life
  - right to liberty and security
  - right to a fair trial
  - right to marry
  - right to respect for private and family life.
- Prohibitions
  - prohibition of torture
  - prohibition of slavery and forced labour
  - no punishment without law
  - prohibition of discrimination.
- Freedoms
  - freedom of thought, conscience and religion
  - freedom of expression
  - freedom of assembly and association.

These new powers underpin the importance of the individual and directly challenge the concepts of professionalism developed in the mid-nineteenth century. The learned societies in exchange for meeting entry requirements offered their members status and security in the community. However they were open to the criticism that they managed the policing of poor or inadequate provision of professional services weakly and ineffectively. Against this background of a transformation of individual rights it is not surprising that architects and doctors are experiencing a huge change in the way in which their professions are viewed by the public. One may ponder if the pendulum will swing too far towards individual rights without the checks and balances of personal responsibility. There is a danger of moving towards a society that has forgotten that accidents can happen, and that human beings make mistakes. A healthy society does not encourage a litigious response to every personal misfortune.

4.5.2 Question: how do you evaluate user satisfaction?

Building users are frequently categorised as clients (in the sense of being the building owner) and, this is often the case. But in the health sector building users consist of a more diverse group of people. It is immediately apparent that effective consultation with future patients will be more difficult to achieve during the design process than with a group of GPs even if they are the tenants of a building which is being procured by others. This poses considerable difficulties for the architect because a successful building must be a response to the needs of the future users of a building, and the design must be informed and influenced by those considerations. As the new NHS Plan makes clear 'Too many patients feel talked at rather than listened to' (NHS, 2000).

The architect's task is further compounded by the need for future buildings to accommodate the rapidly changing treatment regimes. These are a consequence of the explosive rate which information is becoming available to all together with the shift to a patient-centred approach to primary care. Therefore, historical evaluations of existing buildings are likely to be of limited value and great leaps of imagination will be required to design the new buildings from which these new services will be administered. Perhaps it will take time for

Figure 4.7 Wideopen Medical Centre, Newcastle upon Tyne: external view. Architect: Geoffrey Purves Partnership (also in colour section)

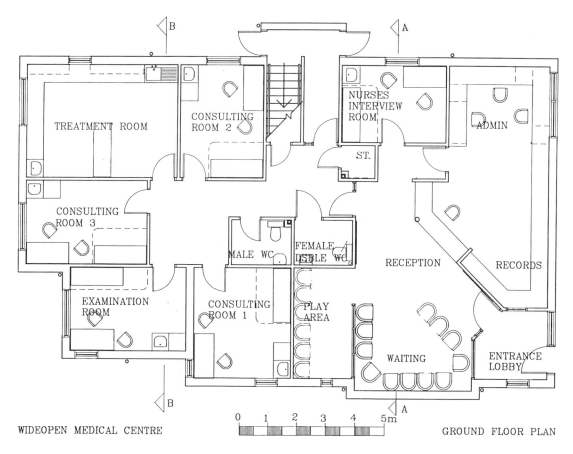

Figure 4.8 Wideopen Medical Centre: ground floor plan. Architect: Geoffrey Purves Partnership

patients to understand the new power within their grasp to influence the shape of future facilities. However the influences of supply and demand in the market economy will inevitably challenge the providers of buildings to meet the new requirements.

The following two examples illustrate short participant observation exercises conducted in surgeries designed to the standards of the 'Red Book' during the 1990s.

A short participant observation project conducted at the Gosforth Memorial Medical Centre, Newcastle upon Tyne – an examination of how the waiting room functions

Background

As architect for many GP surgeries (both new and refurbishment projects) I thought that it would be interesting to examine the operation of a waiting room during a typical mid-week morning surgery session. My architectural practice (the Geoffrey Purves Partnership) carried out improvements to

the Gosforth Memorial Medical Centre, Church Road, Gosforth, Newcastle upon Tyne in 1992/93 for Doctors Ian and Sandra Winterton, a two-doctor (husband and wife) practice who had increased their number of patients and required additional space to improve their facilities. A central requirement of the alteration works was to improve the waiting area, and create a more welcoming and pleasant entrance to the building. This involved forming a new footpath to the street, building a new canopy, and organising an obvious place for patients to enter the building, giving shelter from the elements, followed by a pram space, leading into a reception area. The reception desk is immediately obvious, and three sub-waiting areas are immediately adjacent to the reception desk offering a choice to patients. Two are used by patients waiting to see a doctor and one (on the left when entering the building) is used by patients waiting for a treatment clinic.

Preparation for observation period

Because I have worked with the doctors for several years, and I am one of their patients, there was no difficulty in discussing

Figure 4.9 Gosforth Memorial Centre, Newcastle upon Tyne: reception/waiting area as built. Architect: Geoffrey Purves Partnership (also in colour section)

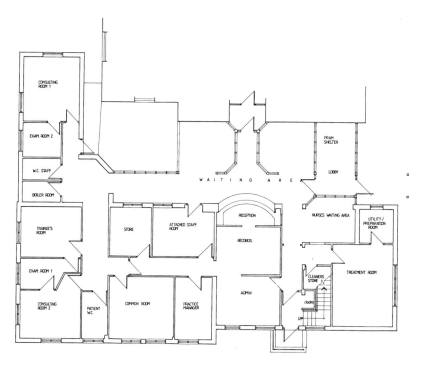

Figure 4.10 Gosforth Memorial Health Centre, Newcastle upon Tyne: ground floor plan. Architect: Geoffrey Purves Partnership

my proposed observation of the operation of the waiting room. They were happy to allow me to sit 'as a patient whose turn never arrived'! Before undertaking the observation period I also arranged to have a short discussion with the administrative staff and completed the questionnaire (which forms part of the Environments for Quality Care document). This is offered as a checklist to GPs who are considering improving their facilities as part of the booklet of exemplar projects published by NHS Estates (1994).

I am pleased to say that the surgery scored highly on the questionnaire, and the staff were generally very happy with the improvements which had occurred following the building works. It was thought to be 'much better', and that privacy was improved. Criticisms that were raised included a comment that '... the bell on the reception desk was not used very often, and some patients on arrival seemed a little reluctant to draw attention to themselves by using it'. Other criticisms that were mentioned included an observation that the pram space at the entrance was larger than necessary, and that the signs for the doctors' surgeries and the patients' toilets could have been clearer.

Wheelchair access is difficult to one of the doctor's surgeries (Dr Winterton) and it was observed that there is no lower section of the reception desk to enable a wheelchair user to have an easy line of sight to reception staff behind the reception desk. There is no separate children's play area, although children's toys were provided and there were mixed views as to whether a separate play space would have been preferable. Generally, I gained the impression that the staff were well disposed towards the building, and were a friend-

ly and cheerful group who enjoyed their work with a smile. One comment made by the receptionists about the paintings hung in the reception area was 'why do we need pictures when they have us'!

Participant observation

All patient names have been changed to ensure confidentiality. I arrived as a prospective patient at 8.45am on Tuesday 10 March 1998 and announced my pre-arranged arrival at reception. I took a seat in the waiting area and quietly observed the proceedings for the next 45 minutes.

08.45   Two sub-waiting areas – some patients waiting already – father and son – reading from book – no particular children's play space – child asks – What is crooked? – father replies – not particularly straight – children's books available neatly displayed with selection of magazines on low table.

08.50   Single women arrived – ringing bell for attention – some noise – warm/bright atmosphere – outside views possible to look at the weather.
Small groups – two parents + children (five in total).
'Alistair don't do that, pick them up' – partly overhead conversation.
Small table – generally quiet/relaxed – a wall display unit for pamphlets – copies of practice pamphlets freely available from the reception

counter – a larger report, also on the reception desk gave more details of the practice philosophy, including brief details of the doctor's qualifications and experience (including specialisms).

08.55   Two women arrived – one filling in form/one quietly reading.

Child left on his own reading a book while father called to surgery and mother waits in adjoining waiting area – on fathers return child asks – What's happening? – father replies – I've just got my note – family group left, father, mother and son.

One woman, form now completed rang bell for attention – then left.

Very quiet – two women waiting.

08.57   Mother and child arrived – sat in other sub-waiting area. No discussion between patients – both reading magazines – body language – independent/no eye contact – relationships as if in a coffee shop.

09.00   Male patient arrived and also Dr Winterton through main entrance. Male patient waited at reception – then mother and child (son) arrived – Male patient appeared to know one of the women.

Small talk – not feeling well. General chit-chat about winter bugs – moved closer together to engage in more conversation.

Mother reading to son in other sub-waiting area. Conversation in hushed tones. would some background music have helped to provide 'white noise'? – overheard conversation about teaching/schools/staff problems – again, thinking of body language – similarities to friends meeting in a hotel lounge.

09.05   Grandfather (I assume) arrives with child in pushchair.

Call for James Fisher (son/small boy).

Older woman picks up prescription/examines it and rings bell for attention.

Man has heavy cold/blowing his nose, etc. Some sighing (minor irritation by delay?) – from single women who is still waiting – now six people waiting (four adults and grandfather and son).

Miss ? called for Sandra Winterton at 9.11.

09.12   Young woman arrives at reception, asks for directions to clinic next door – and leaves.

Call for David Leigh: 'he's just got a bag full that he's dishing out' – an aside by David Leigh to his friend as he leaves (referring to his quick consultation and receipt of a prescription) – next patient arrives/Sandra West – picks up magazine to read – grandfather and child called to surgery.

Now three patients waiting.

09.17   Now two women at reception – aural privacy could be a problem – can overhear some conversation.

Mrs Gerrard called to doctor.

Patient at counter has discussion and leaves.

Man arrives (55ish?) and mother and child.

09.20   Mother and child arrives – child lifted to ring bell (very loudly) – picks up prescription or form and sit in front waiting area.

Generally no crush/adequate space/relaxed, comfortable feeling – planting/views out possible to street and internal courtyard.

Child making funny faces through glass from one waiting area to another – enjoying this!

Sub-waiting one or two mothers + children.

Sub-waiting two men.

Next patient arrives at counter – asks for prescription and leaves.

Cyril Taylor called to surgery.

09.25   Next woman patient arrives – any chance of an appointment today?

Engages in conversation with two reception staff – chatting animatedly.

Older man now slightly restless/doesn't look well – looks absent-mindedly at a couple of magazines – full of cold or flu?

Next woman patient arrives at reception.

Mother and child.

Mr Telfer called.

Matthew Newton called – doesn't appear to be present in waiting areas.

09.30   Woman still chatting at reception.

Sub-waiting on left of entrance not being used (because no clinic is being held).

Conclusions

I arrived at the surgery intending to find appropriate moments to engage in conversation with some of the patients. However, in the event, there never seemed to be the right moment to naturally engage in conversation. Had I done so, the advantages of observing as if 'a fly on the wall' would have been lost and the exercise would have been changed into a user-questionnaire type relationship. I concluded that the advantages of merely observing outweighed the potential disadvantages of disturbing natural behaviour.

Having been involved in the design of the building, I arrived with a number of pre-conceptions as to how the space would function. After this short exercise I have changed my opinion. In general, the spatial relationships between approaching the building, entering the main doors, passing the pram parking space, registering at reception and waiting until called by a doctor functioned more smoothly and quietly than I expected. The relatively sophisticated but relaxed manner slightly surprised me. I was anticipating a space which would be rather more chaotic, more noisy, and less structured than was the case during my visit. I am unsure of the reasons for this atmosphere – is it a result of good architectural design or efficient management of the practice? Perhaps it is a combination of both.

Figure 4.11 Gosforth Memorial Health Centre, Newcastle upon Tyne: sketch proposals for new reception/waiting area. Architect Geoffrey Purves Partnership

Although a number of young children came into the building to visit a doctor they made no undue noise, and there was no crying whatsoever. Assuming that the children were not well, or even if they were well and coming for say an inoculation, there was no perceivable level of stress. Quite the reverse, in fact, with a relaxed atmosphere and several parents quietly reading to the children. Another parent accompanied an inquisitive child around the sub-waiting areas in a cheerful and contented manner.

The waiting areas were less crushed than I expected, with room for comfortable spacing between waiting patients, although I was assured by the reception staff that it was a typical morning clinic. Patients treated the building with respect, appeared to be comfortable in pleasant surroundings, and quietly waited until called by loudspeaker to go to the doctor's surgery. Shelving units adjacent to the reception counter offered a supply of health leaflets and a brochure about the practice. As you would expect, patients tended to be either young adults accompanying children or older people.

This practice serves approximately 6000 patients, and after the observation session I asked the reception staff a number of further questions. The pictures which were hung on display were for sale and I asked if any sales were achieved. I was advised that pictures were sold from the waiting room and that the doctors periodically received a commission cheque which was donated to the Yellow Brick Road Children's Cancer Charity. The problems highlighted earlier with regard to limitations on disabled access was not a serious problem because usually a disabled person was accompanied by another able-bodied person. Although snippets of conversation were occasionally overheard a separate interview room is available and I was assured that on occasions this was used when individual patients requested a private discussion or where patients became distressed. An example given was when a patient was referred immediately to a hospital by one of the doctors which could give cause for considerable dis-

tress. I asked if they had considered playing background music and although this had been considered it had been decided as inappropriate.

My overall impression was that the space performed more successfully than I had anticipated. Although some relatively minor criticisms were raised (as already mentioned) one of the reception staff joked with me that on more than one occasion a patient had arrived and asked to book a room – the favourable comparison of the entrance area to a hotel foyer was regarded as a compliment.

A short participant observation project conducted at the West Road Surgery, Newcastle upon Tyne – an examination of how the waiting room functions

Background

Following a similar exercise that I carried out at the Gosforth Memorial Medical Centre I visited the West Road Surgery to observe a typical Friday morning surgery session on 19 June 1998. I had previously discussed this exercise with Dr Tony Francis who was happy for me to observe the way their waiting room functioned.

The Geoffrey Purves Partnership had acted as architects for a refurbishment and extension of this medical practice which is located in a tough inner-city environment (designed and constructed between November 1995 and May 1997). It is located on a corner site in a parade of shops on the West Road, Newcastle upon Tyne within the Benwell area of the city, renowned as having a number of serious social problems such as high rates of unemployment, and crime. The existing building had presented a fortress mentality with the premises guarded by a high brick wall perimeter fence topped with barbed wire.

Figure 4.12 West Road Surgery, Newcastle: external view. Architect: Geoffrey Purves Partnership (also in colour section)

Our instructions were to increase space, improve the facilities, and re-organise the entrance, which was an unsupervised lobby opening off the main shopping street. This space was frequently trespassed by unruly local school children during their lunch breaks and was a constant source of management difficulties to the practice manager and doctors.

As at the Gosforth Memorial Medical Centre I sat in the waiting room as if 'a fly on the wall' and observed the behaviour of patients and reception staff. The same questionnaire used by the Gosforth Memorial Medical Centre which forms part of the document *Environments for Quality Care* (NHS Estates, 1994) had also been previously completed by Dr Francis which records a high level of satisfaction with the refurbished building.

Participant observation

All patient names have been changed to ensure confidentiality.

08.30   Busy entrance – introductions to Mrs Muriel Cowans and Dr Tony Francis – somebody has locked the front door – telephone ringing continuously in reception – five people waiting – mother and child (playing noisily with toys) – phone stops ringing (unanswered). Mother, daughter and child arrive at reception – phone

starts ringing again. 'if you want to wait until a doctor is free' – phones continuing to ring – 'doctors surgery – a visit?'

08.35   Another patient (women) arrives – asks for patient toilet.
'Ten to ten on Monday (09.50)' – phone conversation overheard 'When would you like to come, this morning or this afternoon?' '5.30 with Dr Heardman'.
Intrusive ringing of phones.
Patients' attention seems to be held by the activity behind the reception desk.
Magazines piled untidily on small table.

08.40   Patient arrives at reception desk to see Dr Dixon – directed to first floor waiting room.
Child in pram starts to cry. Mother takes small son to the toilet.
First patient leaves.
Sheila Moore – misunderstanding at reception – walks briskly to desk – 'I'm waiting' – *sotto voce* – 'O God!' – paces into consulting room with child.

08.45   Next patient called.
One patient now remaining in waiting room.
Mother and child leave consulting room and leave.
Mrs Chapman – arrives at reception – known to staff who chat to her – 'it all happens at half past

67

eight – that's it for the minute' – discussion behind reception desk can be overheard – phone rings – 'doctors surgery' – 'sorry what number – what is the problem' – another phone rings – it was Gillian Oats.

Patient leaves consulting room.

Next patient arrives for Dr Dixon – directed to first floor waiting room.

Dr Dyer speaks to reception on intercom – advised that nobody is waiting.

Conversation behind reception' – 'how do they expect to speak to a doctor at 8.30, Dr Dixon, Dr Heardman, Dr Francis ...!' Arrangements on phone being discussed.

8.50   Small talk by reception staff clearly audible. Two other members of staff arrive and go into reception.

Two patients waiting.

Family group leave consulting room (mother, daughter and small son).

'5.20, Dr Francis' – telephone appointment confirmed.

General impression – hard surfaces, poor acoustic privacy.

Teenage girl arrives drinking carton of juice.

'Betty Watson – surgery 2 – on your right'.

'Wednesday – 9.30 Thursday?'

8.55   'What kind of injections – holiday injections – OK – 12.30 Tuesday'.

Two more patients (arrive – mother and daughter) browse through heap of magazines.

Internal location of waiting room limits views to outside.

'Sharon Davies' – called by doctor.

'Christine Muse' – called by doctor.

No response to either name.

'Which vaccines?' – telephone conversation easily overhead.

Well illuminated, cool colours, hard surfaces but carpeted – yet sound reverberates around.

'Surgery 4 is free – upstairs'.

9.00   Patient leaves consulting room.

Once again telephone conversations clearly overhead.

'Valerie Watson – surgery 2 – on your right'.

A quiet moment – but conversation soon starts again in reception.

Looking around there is a rack of pamphlets and a noticeboard. No other pictures – would flowers or planting or a fish tank provide visual interest?

'Judith Chapman' – called by doctor (after receptionist takes in mug of coffee to doctor).

Older woman patient arrives.

Three women now waiting in ground floor reception area. Teenage girl returns from consulting room and leaves with her mother (I assume).

9.07   'Mrs Crawford – surgery 2' – patients not clear which surgery to enter – numbers on doors not easily seen – but on moving seat I see that name plates on surgery doors do have numbers.

9.10   Mother and small daughter arrive in waiting room.

High noise level.

Next patient called.

Next patient arrives at reception desk.

Woman stands and goes over to rack of leaflets – picks a selection and returns to seat.

One patient with child now in waiting room – child exploring and playing with toys.

Mother and child leave from first floor.

9.15   Quiet spell.

Little happening.

Doctor leaves surgery, door ajar, disappears into reception.

Nurse comes along from treatment room with plastic bag of items to restock surgery 2.

Doctor returns to surgery 2.

Woman at reception – some discussion – then leaves.

Another discussion on the phone making an appointment – suggested times offered for appointment clearly audible.

Another woman arrives to wait in ground floor waiting area.

Women and child leave with friend who now has seen a doctor.

Indian lady at reception – some language difficulties.

9.20   Woman arrives – directed upstairs – 'just knock on the door'.

9.22   No patients now in waiting room on ground floor.

Computer printer heard (from surgery 2?) 'Its gone very quiet' – overheard from reception.

Phone rings – not quickly answered.

Man at reception – 'you need to get those from DSS' – phone still ringing.

Young woman in sari arrives in reception – 'what is your family name?' – language problems and misunderstandings – 'S-I-N-G-H?' – the computer is off – family registration queries – 'have a seat upstairs – when you make an appointment that's the name you must use'.

9.27   Man arrives and leaves reception desk.

'I've a medical – Offshore Medical?'

'Mr Smith – that's right – just come round'.

Patient leaves surgery 1.

Member of staff arrives and enters reception area.

9.30   Mr Smith – sitting in reception area filling in medical form.

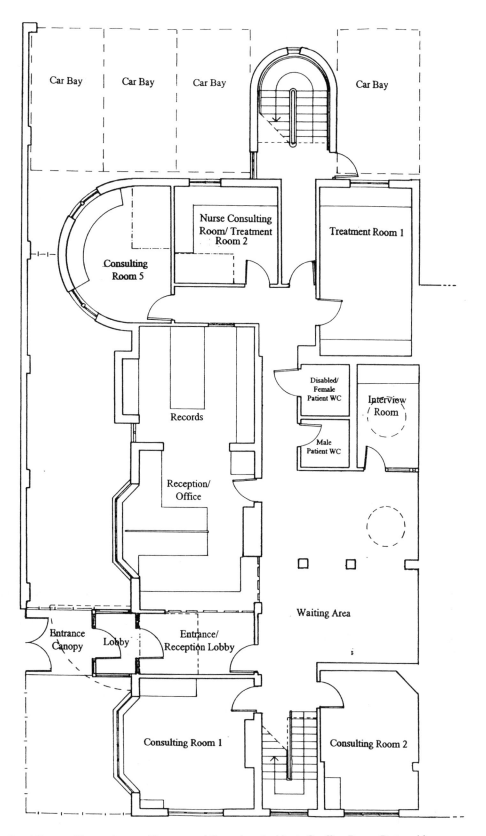

Figure 4.13 West Road Surgery, Newcastle upon Tyne: ground floor plan. Architect: Geoffrey Purves Partnership

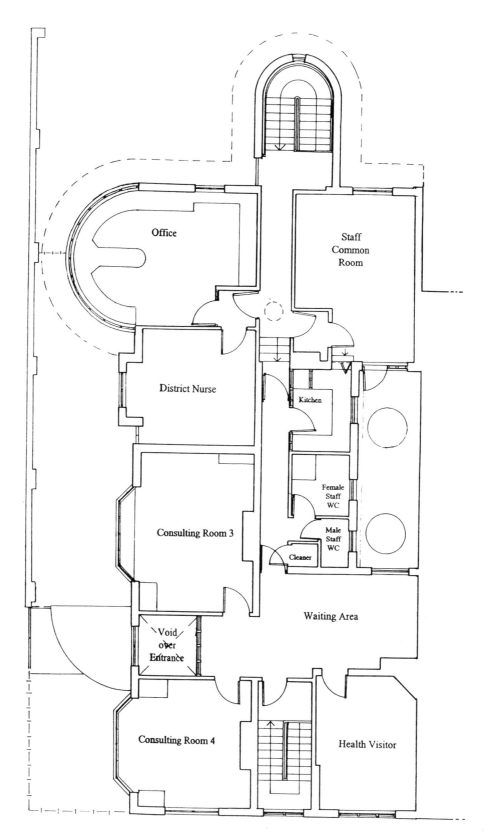

Figure 4.14 West Road Surgery, Newcastle upon Tyne: first floor plan. Architect: Geoffrey Purves Partnership

Conclusions

There are a number of obvious advantages now enjoyed by the refurbished building including:

- A huge improvement in the appearance of both the exterior and interior of the building. This has led to the building being shown greater respect by the patients.
- The building has now been completed and open for approximately 12 months and there are no signs of graffiti.
- Also, there has been no vandalism, except minor damage to the main staircase wall, and some petty thieving such as the stealing of the practice vacuum cleaner during a surgery session.

The building, therefore, has more 'dignity and presence' in the community. However, there are a number of remaining problems among which I would include the following points:

- The main waiting room displayed a slightly claustrophobic atmosphere.
- Dr Francis had previously conveyed to me the doctors' concerns about sound transmission in the first floor waiting area and it was very apparent in the main ground floor waiting area that the overhearing of conversations from reception staff by patients could give rise to breaches of confidentiality.
- Although the ambience of the ground floor waiting area was comfortable, well illuminated, pleasantly decorated and warm, the atmosphere did not seem to me to be especially friendly or relaxed. The very limited views to the outside, and lack of any other points of interest means that there is little visual stimulus. Would some internal planting, pictures on the walls, or a fish tank provide some visual interest? The hard wall surfaces do not help the absorption or muffling of conversations coming from the reception area. Also the hard plastic chairs do not help to improve sound absorption.
- These shortcomings result in the activities of the reception area easily catching the attention of patients waiting for their appointment. If they are not reading, or looking after a child, the reception area offers a focal point for patients to watch and listen, to which could lead to embarrassment for both patients and staff.
- The method of calling patients to the consulting rooms for their appointments seemed to vary between individual doctors and reception staff. Sometimes an intercom was used, sometimes a doctor came out to the waiting area to invite the next patient to enter for examination, and sometimes the reception staff called out a name and directed the patient to a particular consulting room. Is this variation a result of the doctor's personal preferences or is more discussion required to clarify the policy?

All of the above points, both positive and negative have aspects of management issues and design issues which merit further debate. I was left with the impression that although significant progress had been made in the overall quality of the building and the medical facilities now available to patients there is still room for refinement and improvement in the operation of the waiting rooms. I am sure this could be done for a very modest budget which would be cost effective and beneficial to patients, doctors and staff.

4.5.3 Approach: user questionnaires

A National survey of NHS patients was conducted in the final quarter of 1998. The Government is committed to carry out a similar survey annually to enable systematic comparisons to be made of the experience of patients. It will also allow comparisons to be made about the performance of primary care services in different parts of the country. The survey was administered as a self-completion questionnaire posted to 100,000 people and the results are based on over 60,000 completed questionnaires. The Department of Health said that the GP survey was designed to help assess the quality of general practice through the patients' eyes and covered a wide range of issues including access and waiting times, communications with patients, patients' views of GP's knowledge, out-of-hours care, courtesy, and the availability and helpfulness of other surgery staff and services including practice nurses and receptionists.

However, it appears that an opportunity has been missed to ask patients to comment on the quality of the buildings. There has been no attempt to connect the information potentially available from the self administered questionnaires sent to GP's (referred to in the last section) or to invite patients to address similar questions. It would be hugely beneficial if future annual surveys included a section about patient's perceptions of the quality of the built environment. Valuable data could be built up over a period of years about a range of qualitative issues. For example:

- did patients find the building convenient to use?
- did the building have a calming or relaxing atmosphere?
- was the building warm and comfortable?
- did it feel welcoming?
- was it accessible?
- did it function satisfactorily (e.g. toilets, soundproofing, privacy at the reception desk, was it clean)?
- were there views to the outside (to a garden or natural surroundings)?

Some of these points have been identified by the Picker Institute:

'The environment around us can set a mood, create a barrier, provide a distraction, give us pleasure or cause us harm. Yet, it is surprising to find that little systematic research has been done examining the impact of the health care environment on its consumers – patients, family members and clinicians. How these consumers are impacted by the physical or built environment is poorly understood. Hithertofore, we have not had answers to questions such as:

What do patients notice in the physical environment when they go to a doctor's office, a hospital, or a nursing home? What stands out in their minds? What gets in the way? What matters most to them? What impact does the built environment have on them? ... Throughout health care, patients and family members are increasingly recognised as the 'experts' about the subject of quality of their experience – what matters, what makes them feel better, and what they need to help them recover, heal, and adapt to significant changes in their lives. Because they are truly the only individuals who can tell us this information, as we work to create 'life enhancing' environments in health care, we must understand how patients and their families experience those environments and what it is about them that matters to them most.' (Picker Institute, 1998.)

The important point of this data would be to make the connection between the quality of the environment and the quality of the medical services. If design is to be taken seriously then it is essential that hard statistical evidence is used to examine the quality of health care. There is an acute shortage of this type of data to back-up statements that health outcomes are improved from well-designed buildings.

4.5.4 Consequences and outcomes: establish 'best practice' criteria and identify objectives

Limited research has been undertaken to establish 'best practice' criteria but a three-year project funded by £150,000 from NHS Estates is underway at Sheffield University under the direction of Professor Bryan Lawson. Preliminary results have been reported during 2000 by both the Chairman of the Consortium, John Wells-Thorpe and Professor Lawson of Sheffield University. The Consortium consists of NHS Estates, South Downs Health Trust, Poole Hospital Trust and the School of Architecture at Sheffield University.

Although the research is directed at hospital patients there would appear to be a number of common denominators that would also apply to the care of patients in the primary care sector. The research methodology involved patients being invited to answer a series of questions, focus groups with a range of staff and professionals specialising in the design of health care buildings. An early report (Lawson and Perry, 2000) noted 'How articulate patients can be about the architectural environment and how importantly they regard it. More than a century ago, Florence Nightingale had noticed the importance of their surroundings to her patients, and our work confirms this.'

Their report goes on to say that 'The idea that our environment can contribute to our well-being is not extraordinary, and yet it has received relatively little attention.' Importantly they remind us that 'The architectural environment should be considered as part of the service and not separate from it.' It is this connection between environmental benefits and health outcomes that has been missing in much of the research undertaken to date and the examples set by this piece of research needs to be followed up by more studies of a similar nature.

4.6.1 Criteria: there should be a high level of expectation with building design

Traditionally the assessment of the quality of care given by GP teams has concentrated on clinical factors. The role of the building has tended to have a low priority, despite the enthusiastic promotion of good design by Architects in NHS Estates. Quality indicators have been better at assessing technical competence and the use of functionality to satisfy compliance with government policy. The design process has lead to doctors talking to the NHS rather than to their patients, and key performance indicators have consequently been developed from the point of view of the service provider rather than the patient.

Different criteria need to be established so that user expectations can be measured and tested. It can be argued that the NHS is the last of the great nationalised industries and that the view of the patient as a consumer has not been given sufficient priority in assessing the needs for buildings in the primary health care sector. Recent research by the National Primary Care Research Development Centre examines these issues in its booklet *Quality Assessment for General Practice: Supporting Clinical Governance in Primary Care Groups* (Roland *et al.* 1998).

'What is quality?
In approaching the assessment of quality, it is helpful to have a mental framework of what quality actually is. In our view, quality of care for individual patients depends essentially on access and on effectiveness: can patients get health care, and is it any good when they get to it? Within effectiveness, we recognise the need for both technical and interpersonal skills. Both are key requirements for high quality general practice care.

Quality of care is determined by:

- timely access to care
- high quality clinical care (e.g. diagnosis and clinical management)
- high quality inter-personal care (e.g. listening, addressing patients' concerns)

Good management and effective continuing professional development are important requirements for delivering high quality care. These may be reflected in a PCG's approach to clinical governance and are, therefore, discussed in this paper.

At a population level, equity is important to ensure that some groups in the population are not specifically disadvantaged in the care they receive. Cost is also important in order to maximise available resources for the population as a whole. Both quality and cost will be of great importance to PCG's, however, we believe they should be kept conceptually separate.

There is no single measure of quality in general practice, nor do we anticipate there ever being one. The range of aspects of care which we detail in this paper cover a wide and diverse range of issues, and emphasise the complexity of assessing quality of general practice care. We believe that quality assessment will always require assessment of a range of aspects of care. To seek a single 'quality score' would misunderstand the nature of general practice.'

The need for patients to receive good health care can be fundamentally influenced by the quality of the buildings where this service is provided. We need to raise patients' expectations, and to view the quality of the health environment in the same way as they would assess the environment of their home, their holiday accommodation or the buildings where they shop.

4.6.2 Question: what is the level of design expectation (patients, doctors, staff)?

The level of design expectation will vary between patients, doctors and staff. Patients in the UK effectively have no influence over the quality of their health care environments.

They are provided with the facilities on a 'take it or leave it' basis unless they are subscribers to private medical insurance. Private facilities respond, to a limited extent, to ensure that environments are provided that offer patients satisfaction, but the pre-eminence of the clinician remains the dominant influence. At the primary care level choice and flexibility is extremely limited; the starting point almost without exception is the NHS GP.

Patient views need to be determined on a range of factors including:

- access and availability
- continuity of care and the opportunity to see the same person throughout their illness over a period time
- ability to make complaints about the care they are receiving
- choice about which doctor they see
- information about their doctor's organisation and management of the practice.

The performance of the building should be assessed against the patient evaluation of:

- availability and accessibility
- technical competence
- communication skills
- interpersonal attributes
- organisation of care.

The brief for a primary care building needs to review and incorporate the levels of service which a doctor seeks to achieve against the above factors. Only then, do the influences of a patient as a consumer begin to bear upon the design of the physical fabric. The best buildings, of course, solve some of these issues intuitively and it is difficult to establish the quantitative methodologies to provide accurate assessments of individual buildings.

4.6.3 Approach: questionnaire

The survey form shown in Table 4.6 was developed by the Geoffrey Purves Partnership. Based on the environmental quality checklist proposed by the NHS Executive in *Environments for Quality Care* publication, this expanded list of factors has been used to evaluate a health authority's building stock of doctors' surgeries.

The survey was conducted to determine the following:

- physical provision of accommodation and facilities.
- extent to which each practice currently meets the criteria for *Environments for Quality Care*
- condition of building fabric.
- potential for expansion.

The survey took, on average, a period of one hour at each site. Surveys were conducted at various times during the day between 8.30 am and 6.30 pm. Particular care was taken to avoid any disruption to surgery activities and the co-operation of doctors and staff was, in most cases, readily forthcoming. Surveyors were generally accompanied by the Practice Manager or Receptionist, when available. A number of doctors, predominantly those who were quite clearly in the better equipped premises, were keen to describe the services which they currently offered and would wish to offer.

4.6.4 Consequences and outcomes: assess results and make recommendations

The survey form set out in Table 4.6 was also used to appraise the expansion potential for each site to meet the provision of additional services for the full primary health care team and the shift of services from secondary and community health sectors. The empowerment of patients can, and should be taken further.

Professor John Howie has developed the questionnaire in Table 4.7, and it is interesting to see the emphasis placed on the quality of life. It asks patients to consider their sense of well-being. What Architects need to do is translate these social indicators into architectural responses when they designed new primary health care facilities.

Patients need to have greater confidence in ascertaining their aspirations and expectations regarding the quality of the environment of their primary health care facilities. The therapeutic benefits from giving patients personal control over their environment seems to be widely accepted, despite the limited amount of research to use as evidence for these views. Architects have the opportunity to bring greater invention, variety, and domesticity to the design of primary health care buildings in the future.

Table 4.6 Sample of survey form

Identity Number Exterior Photographs Name of Practice Address Time of Survey Date of Survey Existing Floor Area Number of Floors Estimated/Plan/Measured Dwelling			
Q	**The Site:**	**Yes/No**	**Additional Comments**
1	Good access to public transport?		
2	Adjoining property in good condition?		
3	Attractive planted external areas?		
4	Does building appear welcoming?		
		Number	
5	Existing car parking spaces?		
6	Potential car parking spaces?		
		Yes/No	
7	Adequate access for mini bus/ambulance?		
8	Is entrance easy to see?		
9	Can interior be seen from entrance?		
10	Is there level access?		
11	Easy access for prams/disabled?		
12	Porch or lobby with pram space?		
13	Can reception be seen from entrance?		
14	Is counter open & comfortable for patients?		
15	Is counter open & comfortable for staff?		
16	Security – is counter wide/high?		
17	Security – is there CCTV?		
18	Security – is there a fixed screen?		
19	Security – is there a sliding screen?		
20	Confidentiality – seating too close to recep		
21	Confidentiality – adequate dist. to seating?		
22	Confidentiality – sectioned off?		
23	Confidentiality – interview room?		
24	Low section for elderly/wheelchairs?		
25	Good sight, desk to entrance?		
26	Sight lines by direct view?		
27	Sight lines by mirrors?		
28	Sight lines by CCTV?		
29	The patient call system is by GP/reception		
30	The patient call system is by light/buzzer		
31	The patient call system is by tannoy		
32	Is there provision for moor mobility?		
33	Is there provision for poor sight?		
34	Is there provision for poor hearing?		
35	Is record storage separate from recept.?		
		Number	
36	Number of fixed seats?		
37	Number of loose seats?		

Table 4.6 *Continued*

		Yes/No
38	Are the seats comfortable?	
39	Are the colour schemes restful?	
40	Hap hazard storage?	
41	A view outside?	
42	Pictures to look at?	
43	Visible links with the community?	
44	Space for children to play?	
45	Feature play equipment?	
46	Are there just toys?	
47	Play area visible from entrance?	
48	Play area screened to mask sound?	

	The accommodation – room/space for:	Level/No
49	Waiting area	
50	Reception	
51	Records storage	
52	Records admin	
53	Consulting rooms, less than 11 sq m	
54	Consulting room, 11 sq m or more	
55	Exam room, less than 6.7 sq m	
56	Exam room, 6.7 sq m or more	
57	Treatment room, less than 17.5 sq m	
58	Treatment room, 17.5 sq m or more	
59	Nurses room, less than 11 sq m	
60	Nurses room, 11 sq m or more	
61	Practice manager	
62	General office	
63	Fundholding office	
64	Kitchen	
65	Staff room	
66	Doctors seminar	
67	Storage rooms	
68	Male patient toilets	
69	Female patients toilets	
70	Unisex toilets	
71	Disabled patients toilets	
72	Male staff toilets	
73	Female staff toilets	
74	Unisex staff toilets	
75	Disabled staff toilets	
76	Is there temporary waiting in corridors?	
77	Are patients routes as short as possible?	
78	Is staff circulation not in waiting room?	
79	Are signs legible?	
80	Are signs permanent?	
81	Are signs paper?	
82	Are there good pictorial signs?	
83	Are signs multi-lingual?	
84	Are signs in correct location?	
85	Are signs appropriate?	
86	Are there heating systems?	
87	Is there a ventilation system?	
88	Are there instant water heaters to sinks?	
89	Thermostatic valves to radiators?	
90	Is there flexible lighting for work?	
91	Is there a computer network?	
92	Are there telephone lines for appointments?	
93	Are there telephone lines for private use?	

Table 4.6 *Continued*

94	Is there a separate modem line?				
95	Is there a separate fax line?				
96	Is there an internet line?				
97	Is there an ISDN line?				
98	Is the telephone system adequate?				
99	Is there a pay phone for patients?				
100	Is there an alarm to insurer standards?				
101	Is there natural policing from reception?				
102	Is there a panic button?				
103	Is there an escape route for staff?				
		Year			
104	Age of construction? Pre 1850 1850–1899	1900–1918		1919–1944, 1945–1964, 1965–1980, 1980–	
105	Roof material	Slate		Tiles Felt Other	
106	Wall material	Brick		Render Conc.panel Other	
107	Window material	Wood		Steel Aluminium UPVC	
108	Door material	Wood		Steel Aluminium UPVC	
		SATIS%	**Min Rep.%**	**Major Rep.%**	**Renew%**
109	Roof structure?				
110	Roof finish?				
111	Gutters and rainwater pipes?				
112	External wall structure?				
113	Floor structure?				
114	Floor finishes?				
115	Internal wall structure?				
116	Internal wall finish?				
117	Ceiling finish?				
		Number			
118	Double glazed windows				
119	Single glazed windows				
120	Doors				
		SATIS%	**Min Rep.%**	**Major Rep.%**	**Renew%**
121	Electrical wiring?				
122	Space heating system?				
123	Water heating system?				
124	Mechanical vent system?				
125	External works?				
		Yes/No			
126	Are rooms, corridors at least 1.2m wide &				
127	One consulting room accessible to all?				
128	Any other uses on premises?				
129	Confidentiality by sight in clinical rooms?				
130	Confidentiality by sound in clinical rooms?				
131	Building maintenance economical?				
132	Is energy conservation addressed?				
133	Well-being building conveyed by sight?				
134	Flexibility in relation to future needs?				
135	Specialist rooms?				
136	Multi-purpose rooms?				
	Expansion Potential	**Yes/No**		**Area Available M Sq**	
137	Space for extension at ground				

138	Space for extension at first		
139	Space for extension at second		
140	Space for extension at roofspace		

	Provision Ranking	**Yes/No**
1	High quality, full pri. care, no invest 3 yrs	
2	Good cond. 50–80% check, potential Gr.1	
3	As 2, but limited potential expansion	
4	Ave. cond., 30–50% check, but has potential	
5	As 4 but limited potential expansion	
6	Minimum standard, but has potential	
7	Minimum standard without potential	
8	Very poor but potential	
9	Very poor, recommend closure	

ID number/locality						
Level						
Room type						
Floor area						
	Yes	No	Good	Fair	Poor	Comments
Natural light						
Double glazing						
Natural vent						
Mechanical vent						
Air conditioning						
Radiator						
Electric heating						
Gas fire						
Utility lighting						
Quality lighting						
Wall lamp						
Fitted shelves						
Fitted cupboards						
Fitted worktop						
Washbasin/sink						
Carpet						
Hard floor						
Wall finish						
Tiles						
Adequate storage						
Record storage						

Table 4.7

	Much better	Better	Same or less	Not applicable
As a result of your visit to the doctor today, do you feel you are:				
Able to cope with life	❏	❏	❏	❏
Able to understand your illness	❏	❏	❏	❏
Able to cope with your illness	❏	❏	❏	❏
Able to keep yourself healthy	❏	❏	❏	❏
Confident about your health	❏	❏	❏	❏
Able to help yourself	❏	❏	❏	❏

(Source: Howie *et al.*, 1997, 1998.)

4.7.1 Criteria: buildings should be enjoyed and include works of art

> That the arts can be therapeutic is not of course a new idea. But it is an idea whose time has come. (Sir Richard Attenborough, 1989.)
>
> The arts and humanities in health and medicine is an idea whose time has come. (Sir Kenneth Calman.)

Art in health buildings is usually thought of as a recent phenomena and it is certainly true there has been a surge of interest, and awareness of the benefits, in recent years. However, the Victorians decorated their public buildings, including hospitals, with paintings and sculpture celebrating great personal achievements. Proud of their financial and technical progress benefactors were recorded for posterity by these self-indulgent acts of artistic patronage. This legacy is still with us, often exercising the minds of today's administrators as to the best way to incorporate these works in new hospital buildings.

An interesting historical anecdote illustrates the introduction of the arts in health.

As early as 1912 it is suggested that Nijinsky was taken ill during a visit to London with Dyaghilev's Ballets Russes and was taken to St Stephen's Infirmary, a Victorian workhouse-turned-hospital on the site of the Chelsea and Westminster Hospital. On his recovery, three days later, legend records that he performed L'Apres-midi d'un faune and that Dyaghilev had 'distributed gold sovereigns to patients and staff' (Loppert, 1999).

Susan Loppert, in charge of the arts programme at the Chelsea and Westminster Hospital has developed an impressive track record of integrating public awareness of cultural issues into a healing environment. Music, opera and the visual arts all have an important part to play in raising the environmental quality of the building for those who visit it. Under Dr Rosalia Staricoff the hospital is now an important research centre for examining and quantifying therapeutic benefits and patient outcomes resulting from environmental factors.

Art is seen no longer as recording the 'great and the good' but as enhancing public enjoyment; indeed art should not be seen as an adornment to a building or a space but integral with the design of the environment as a whole.

Elsewhere in this book it is argued that quantifying the cost benefits of the intangible qualities of art presents today's designers with insuperable obstacles. Perhaps these difficulties can be put into perspective if the concept of quality is not divided into tangible and intangible benefits. Our perception of intangible benefits is categorised thus only because the factors involved are more difficult to quantify. With more research perhaps meaningful conclusions will be able to be drawn and the mysteries of concepts such as welcoming, relaxing and calm will be given quantifiable characteristics for the architect to manipulate. In this way the control of environmental qualities will emerge as the future path to improving patient outcomes by offering therapeutic

benefits. Today we are still groping for scientific evidence, using the defence of philosophical concepts, but this is changing. There is growing awareness of the need for more research and over the next few years our intuitive instincts will be tested and challenged by the results.

Florence Nightingale had this intuitive foresight of therapeutic benefits in health care nearly 150 years ago. Writing in her 'Notes on Nursing – what it is and what it is not' in 1859 she recorded:

> 'The effect in sickness of beautiful objects, of variety of objects, and especially of brilliancy of colour is hardly at all appreciated. Such cravings are usually called the 'fancies' of patients. And often doubtless patients have "fancies", as e.g. when they desire two contradictions. But much more often, their (so called) "fancies" are the most valuable indications of what is necessary for their recovery. And it would be well if nurses would watch these (so called) "fancies" closely ... I shall never forget the rapture of fever patients over a bunch of bright-coloured flowers. I remember (in my own case) a nosegay of wild flowers being sent me, and from that moment recovery becoming more rapid.'

Going on she expanded on her views of the connection between mind and body in the healing process:

> 'This is no fancy. People say the effect is only on the mind. It is no such thing. The effect is on the body, too. Little as we know about the way in which we are affected by form, by colour, and light, we do know this, that they have an actual physical effect. Variety of form and brilliancy of colour in the objects presented to patients are actual means of recovery. But it must be slow variety e.g. if you show a patient ten or twelve engravings successively, ten-to-one he does not become cold and faint, or feverish, or even sick; but hang one up opposite him, one on each successive day, or week, or month, and he will revel in the variety.'

And long before today's view that blue is a colour inducing coolness and depression and that red suggests warmth and invigoration she had recorded:

> 'No one who has watched the sick can doubt the fact, that some feel stimulus from looking at scarlet flowers, exhaustion from looking at deep blue, etc.'

About 10 years ago there emerged a strand of research looking more closely at art in health. Initially, it was predominantly centred around a discussion about the inclusion of works of art, meaning the display of visual images. However, the pioneering work by Professor Peter Senior and others through the Arts in Health Programme has stimulated a wider discussion. It has acted as a catalyst for a new enthusiasm to take onboard the concept of environmental quality assisting in patient recovery rates. This recurring theme has been identified by many including Ann Noble.

'The Hospice Movement is the response to the failure of main stream hospitals to meet the needs of terminally ill people and their families and there are many wider lessons that can be learnt from them. The fear, and for some, the likelihood, of dying are very real and ever present in all hospitals; yet requirements which are fundamental to the design of hospices – such as surroundings which are reassuring and inspiring, with views of sunshine – are either totally absent from modern hospitals or are regarded as no more than optional extras.'

However she goes on to explain the difficulties:

'The value of and the need to provide a therapeutic environment in hospitals are surely axiomatic but the best way of achieving them is less clear. One reason for this is the complexity of interactions between patients, staff and the building.' (Noble, 1999.)

The success of the Arts in Health Movement should not be underestimated. It has motivated the wider debate which is now rapidly accelerating to examine the therapeutic benefits from an improvement in the environmental and design qualities of the building fabric. Art, in the sense of pictures of a wall, has been the key to unlocking the bureaucratic attitudes in health administration. However, art is integral with good design and not an agent to dress up mediocrity.

In 1996 (Parker, 1996) it was still being debated whether or not NHS Estates should provide more central direction and encouragement for art, and foster research into its therapeutic benefits. There were certainly some who thought that it was best left to individual bodies, and there has been a reluctance by the NHS to become involved in design issues. Only recently, have these views begun to change, and it will be some time before the culture of the service provider switches to the awareness required to satisfy consumer demands.

The concept of art in health buildings is at the heart of 'value for money' evaluations. There is a case for saying that health care is itself an art with a scientific basis (Downie, 1994) and this is difficult to reconcile with the current NHS view that art in health needs to be justified by evidence to support funding. As Lord Robert Winston has noted, science only asks the questions; it is an enquiring process. Healing is a more all embracing concept; it involves our minds and our feelings and our spirits as well as our bodies. It is therefore perfectly natural to go along with Handel's view and accept that music can heal our sadness. As Downie points out 'The most obvious common ground between healing and the arts is morality.'

As these more rounded views begin to become widely accepted a number of research groups are beginning to examine how to demonstrate 'value for money' for good design. At the University of Sheffield under the Chairmanship of John Wells-Thorpe, Professor Bryan Lawson is engaged on a research project and at the University of Nottingham, Dr Phil Leather is developing research methodologies to examine those aspects of design that contribute towards the creation of a therapeutic environment. He states in his draft report, 'A Comparative Study of the Impact of Environmental Design upon Hospital Staff and Patients' (February 2000) that:

'Not surprisingly, then, the unfamiliarity and strangeness characteristic of the hospital environment has been found to generate strong negative emotions, including threat, vulnerability and fear, together with those associated with suffering and death (Brown, 1961). Ulrich (1991) argues that such emotions derive directly from a design ethos, which emphasises the functional delivery of health care at the expense of patient needs. The result, he concludes, are hospital designs which are 'psychologically hard' and 'unsupportive' and which work against the 'well-being of patients'.

'Psychologically hard facilities have this negative impact upon patient well-being either because they are experienced as stressful in themselves, or because the effort needed to cope with them adds to the total burden of illness. Psychologically supportive designs, on the other hand, facilitate patient coping with the stress known to accompany illness and are thereby complimentary to drugs and other forms of medical technology in fostering the process of recovery. An important goal for design, then, is the creation of hospital facilities that convey a positive image, e.g. fostering an environment that patients find pleasant and relating and which are thereby conducive to reduced stress and improved well-being.'

Creative arts can (Steel, 1999):

- alleviate stress
- reduce boredom
- provide reassurance
- give comfort
- increase motivation and mobility.

Art is to be enjoyed and it can take many forms: the visual arts, including sculpture, the dramatic arts, music, poetry and, of course, architecture.

The influence of this trend was identified and has been described as 'the best medicine'. Take, for example, extracts from an article published in 1998:

A high-level group of doctors, academics and healthcare practitioners met in Windsor recently to launch an 'arts on prescription' campaign. Their aim is to encourage the use of art – from poetry to pottery – to promote longevity and healthier living. Dr Robin Phillip, a senior clinical lecturer at the University of Bristol, drew attention to one of the potential benefits of the scheme: "We spend £81m a year in Britain on antidepressants, and the cost per patient can be as high as £300 a year. If we can wean just a few of these patients off such drugs through the use of arts in healthcare, then it will be worth it."

If the idea of expecting sculpture to alleviate dermatitis, or Debussy to cure depression, sound airy-fairy nonsense cooked up by new age idealists, think again. The Hopi and Navajo tribes in North America have for centuries created sane pictures to heal their sick, and as early as the 4th century BC, Theophrasus – Aristostle's favourite pupil – noted that "the sound of the flue will cure epilepsy and sciatic gout".

One of the most vivid manifestations of Nightingale's "variety of form and brilliancy of colour" is to be found at the Chelsea and Westminster Hospital in London, which must be the only hospital in the world to have a donations box cast in bronze by Sir Eduardo Paplozzi, let alone a magnificent Veronese resurrection in the chapel and a marble sculpture by Dame Barbara Hepworth in its dermatology unit.

For all the entertainment value of much of the art she has installed, Loppert (Susan Loppert, Director of the Hospital Arts Project) is deadly serious about her work's purpose. "We are not a frivolous optional extra here," she says. "And nothing we do is depriving you of a bed, or a hip replacement, or vital clinical research. We see the hospital arts project as an equally important part of the healthcare we offer. It's long been known that if you're in a colourful, healthful environment, you do get better more quickly."

Mens sana in corpore sano was how the Romans put it, and an awareness that health is a function of consciousness is taking hold in the West, despite the efforts of drug companies to persuade us that if we take more pills we shall be saved. As Freeman adds: "What we do is therapeutic, but it's not therapy. In creating a stimulating engaging environment, we are shaking off the shackles of hospitals being places where you come to die".' (Wright, 1998.)

4.7.2 Question: what are the benefits of 'artworks' in design?

As the therapeutic benefit of good environmental design takes hold a number of research groups are trying to scientifically analyse these intangible concepts. It seems that our society today cannot accept the philosophical arguments without scientific proof. What they really mean, is that accountants need to give politicians and other decision makers, simple arithmetically answers; in our market driven economy best value has come to represent the only way in which investment decisions can be taken. Ask Tony Blair why he goes to Tuscany for his holidays – probably not because it came out best from a value for money assessment of holiday locations! He more likely relied on his intuitive judgement that recognises quality, the same process which has led him to state that 'We know that good design provides a host of benefits' (DCMS, 2000).

Current research which is providing valuable evidence includes:

- The Exeter Evaluation (Peter Senior and Peter Scher).
- The Chelsea and Westminster Hospital Research Programme (led by Rosalia Staricoff).
- A research project at Nottingham University, funded by NHS Estates, initiated by John Wells-Thorpe and led by Dr Phil Leather.

There is also a group of architects working in the health field who are actively promoting the importance of environmental issues to achieve high quality architecture in their health projects. This includes work on a number of recent PFI hospital projects, although criticisms continue to emerge about the early examples of this genre.

In north-east England, there have been innovative projects undertaken within the Northern Arts area including:

- Arts in Health in Gateshead.
- The Ophthalmology Department, Royal Victoria Infirmary, Newcastle upon Tyne.
- Children's Oncology Department, Royal Victoria Infirmary, Newcastle upon Tyne.

In the primary care field, also in north-east England, there have also been interesting examples of the integration of art in small refurbishment projects.

Some of these projects are described in Chapter 11 including the use of stained glass in the Denton Turret Medical Centre and a range of visual arts projects co-ordinated by Dr Christina Cock at the Oxford Terrace Medical Centre in Gateshead.

It is interesting to note that the results of the academic investigations, for example the Exeter Evaluation and the Chelsea and Westminster work, are directed at the administrators. That is, the researchers feel that their efforts must be directed to the administrative decision makers. Would the focus be more beneficially directed to an analysis of patient requirements rather than patient awareness? Should we be asking patients what they think should be introduced, or form part of, future health buildings?

In the same way as a patient going into hospital may decide which books to take, or which music tapes to pack in their bag, which artwork would any of us choose to take into hospital with us? Perhaps this directs us to the work being undertaken at Nottingham University, by Dr Phil Leather and his team where they are attempting to assess a range of intangible senses such as warmth, comfort, friendliness, cleanliness, and a whole range of other human responses which make up a feeling of well-being. In short how to design a building that lifts your spirit.

4.7.3 Approach: a summary

As pointed out in the last section the pendulum is swinging towards general acceptance that there are real benefits to be gained from better environmental quality in our health buildings. Most of this work has been done in hospitals because primary care buildings are smaller in scale, cost less, and have a shorter design period. We have seen a wide range of innovative ideas, and high quality designs built during the last 10 years. These exciting buildings need to be encouraged and the many good examples brought to the attention of both doctors and clients. The danger is in not stifling the freshness of these ideas by imposing cumbersome procurement routes which drain all excitement from the buildings as they are put through the mangle of bureaucratic assessment, reassessment, and financial controls.

4.7.4 Consequences and outcomes: develop design guide recommendations

A review is underway to re-examine the NHS guidance notes for primary health care buildings. Existing guidance has focused on an analysis of accommodation. Advice in the future should include design requirements for the range of new facilities including health care centres, health kiosks, drop-in and walk-in facilities and local health care resource centres.

Historically, the major omission is that the issue of design quality has been omitted.

There is a rapidly growing awareness of the importance of design quality in the procurement of public buildings (see the recently published document *Better Public Buildings*, DCMS with a foreword by the prime minister – 'The best designed hospitals help patients recover their spirits and their health'). Many others in the procurement process now advocate this approach including Sir Stuart Lipton of CABE and Kate Priestley (Chief Executive, NHS Estates). However, the key factor is about emphasising the quality of the product rather than the quality of the construction process. Building Note 46 concentrates on functionality and although Building Note 36 touches on the issues of environment and design a new document should go much further to encourage the establishment of design objectives for any new primary health care project. This should be a fundamental requirement in the preparation of a brief and be flagged up at the beginning of the document.

The quality aspirations of all users should be established, particularly as seen from the view of the patient as a customer. The briefing process must be more than a product of functional design achieving prescribed schedules of space standards within certain cost limits.

Right at the beginning of the document there should be a section which encourages the design team to set out the quality aspirations expected from the building. It needs to encourage future users of the building to think about what the ethos of the building should be; to set out what the building users want out of the building; and what are the intangible values that the designers aim to achieve. For example, should the building be:

- friendly
- efficient
- welcoming
- relaxing
- comfortable
- warm
- pleasant
- accessible.

An example of recent research along these lines is the draft report by Dr Phil Leather at the University of Nottingham commissioned by NHS Estates – it includes the following statement 'The design goal was to provide a warm and friendly environment in support of the competent and professional medical services delivered.' There should be a fundamental skew to the Facilities for Primary Care document so that this philosophy pervades the main thrust of the text. It should seek to encourage the achievement of high design standards through the eyes of the patient – the tests of functionality and cost should be a secondary, albeit essential, requirement of the procurement process for any new primary health care building. It must not be written from the perspective of the service provider, but with the needs of the consumer (i.e. the patient) given top priority.

The aim should be to establish design standards from the point of view of the patient first. After setting down the aspirations and ethos of the building, the tests of functionality and cost can then be applied. The other way around the environmental quality and user satisfaction levels are likely to disappoint.

5

Financial issues

5.1.1 Criteria: NHS has historically used cost parameters as a benchmark for design evaluation

We are told by Kate Priestley, Chief Executive of NHS Estates that 'the NHS is the most complex organisation in Europe. Employing 1 in 20 of the working population in the UK, the NHS has an annual expenditure of £42.5 bn.' The estate includes 11,000 GP surgeries. It is not surprising, therefore, that enormous challenges arise when fundamental changes are planned, such as modernising the procurement process for health buildings.

Unfortunately NHS Estates is locked into the Government's plans to prohibit traditional forms of contract in all but the most exceptional circumstances. From 1 June 2000 all central Government clients have been asked to limit their procurement strategies for the delivery of new projects to PFI, Design & Build and Prime Contracting. Refurbishment and maintenance contracts will be included in these procurement routes from 1 June 2002. The Treasury has said 'this means that traditional, non-integrated strategies will only be used where it can be clearly shown that they offer the best value for money. This means in practice that they will seldom be used.'

As already mentioned, the guidance notes for GP surgeries is heavily biased towards achieving value for money. Projects are expected to

- improve the quality and range of services in proportion to the extra cost
- promote the right pattern of services
- provide practice accommodation reasonable for the needs of the patients in the area.

The process flowcharts do not include an interchange with the patients, the ultimate client, and for whom the facilities are being provided. The business case is established on the perceived aims and objectives of the health authority and the doctors. For example, the *Guide to the Provision of Leasehold*

Premises for GP Occupation includes a 17-stage checklist of activities. At stage 4, prepare outline proposal, a series of key issues that should be examined is listed:

- The problem(s) that the project is aiming to address.
- Analysis of key issues of service need.
- Objectives of the proposals – which should be specific, measurable and achievable.
- Key benefits of the project and how these are to be quantified.
- What other options could meet the objectives of the project?
- Costs and implications of doing nothing, or doing the minimum.
- Building and other costs are reasonable and provide VFM. Other costs will include additional staff, IT and business rates.
- A statement confirming the commitment of all parties associated with the project.
- An outline of the risks involved with the project (e.g. security of rental income, assumptions, financial risks to the practice/NHS Trust/HA and other users) and what management structure will be in place.
- Identification of opportunities for other primary care users, e.g. dentistry, pharmacy, community nurses and other professionals involved in primary care.
- Analysis of potential facilities management content.
- DV's initial assessment of CMR.
- Environmental Impact Study.

This stage concludes with the following phrase. 'The impact of the scheme within the immediate geographical locality and, most importantly, an assessment of the added benefit of meeting patient needs.'

In *A Guide to the Size, Design and Construction of GP Premises* the introduction 'explains the principles of the Schedule of GP premises which provides maxima both in terms of size of premises and building costs attached to them. Also provided are guidance notes for the development of the design brief and the assessment of individual schemes.'

5.1.2 Question: why has NHS concentrated on time and cost parameters for health building procurement?

Until the past few years, the Government's approach to financing health care facilities, in line with all Government spending, has been based largely on negotiating lowest cost tenders within annual spending budgets. This tended to downgrade the consideration of whole life costs, and it is only recently that the Treasury has begun to promote 'best value' as the basis for selecting successful bidders for Government contracts.

Inevitably, this led to an approach within the NHS bureaucracy to concentrate on setting targets for different sizes of GP surgeries and offering guidance on the space standards that would be acceptable. This approach created a cultural background to the provision of buildings encapsulated within the framework of the 'Red Book'. Standards were set for accommodation, maximum allowances were set down for professional fees, and cost limits were established. These principles were developed over many years resulting in a well-established set of procedures with which doctors needed to comply to improve or redevelop their premises. The environmental quality of these buildings was given scant attention. The philosophy regarding design was essentially that the administrators of NHS funds would establish a framework of requirements and set cost limits in the belief that this would leave designers free to interpret, in an imaginative way, the built form.

Fortunately, because of the relatively short timescale between inception and completion for primary health care buildings, and the personal rapport between doctors and architects, many successful small surgeries have been completed over the last decade. However, there are many more of these buildings which could have been even better. There could have been more encouragement from NHS Estates to the doctors under their contract to build facilities that were more flexible, more responsive to their patients' requirements, and more likely to offer better value to the community.

Functionality has been a key test of previous appraisal systems, a process devised by the administrators or service providers with negligible attempts to ask patients what they wanted.

The new NHS Plan recognises the importance of putting patients first, and an exciting period lies ahead as new approaches to satisfying consumer demands begin to be developed and implemented. This is very good news indeed for both patients, doctors, and architects.

The legacy of the previous approach to procuring health buildings does create some problems for the future. Those doctors who have invested in their premises, and may have substantial loans outstanding against their property, may find that there is little alternative use for their bricks and mortar should they be interested in moving on to more exciting flexible facilities under the umbrella of a co-ordinated housing, social services, and health programme. A question of equity values, the approach of District Valuers and rental calcu-lations, and alternative resale values will all need to be considered and it may be that the Government will need to devise some systems to ensure that the problems of negative equity do not stifle development of health care services. These problems are likely to be greatest in those areas most in need. It is in those areas where property values are likely to be lowest, and the need for alternative combined resources may be greatest.

5.1.3 Approach: review historical bureaucracy and procedures for building procurement

The NHS is one of the last great nationalised industries to come under the spotlight of privatisation. Steel, coal, the railways, electricity and gas have all been privatised and the NHS is now going through this painful process of change. Although the Government is committed to the retention of the NHS as a public service the funding of services will include an increasing percentage of private finance. This will be particularly evident in the provision and financing of new buildings, including those in the primary care sector.

There had been a philosophy of scrimping and saving in the post-war period, during the 1950s, which the general public had accepted. The benefits of nationalisation had significantly outweighed the shortcomings now coming under the spotlight. The new NHS Plan reflects some these changing attitudes, in particular the influence of information technology and the importance of consumerism or putting the patient first.

At present, the NHS is not customer focused. Historically the perception (even if legally incorrect) was that the customer (i.e. the patient) had few rights and the attitude was along the lines of aren't you lucky to have a 'free service'. Although the Government recognises the need to change, this will not happen over-night. A panic investment cannot take place instantly, and there will a decade of changes as the new initiatives begin to be implemented.

This does raise the question of striking a balance between political influence and power and the responsibility for the delivery of high quality medical services. It could be argued, for example, that the long list of team members from the medical profession who have signed up to the NHS Plan may find themselves being held to account in future, and being expected to accept responsibility for the delivery of the Government's Initiatives. Perhaps the Government has neatly manoeuvred the medical profession into the decision of 'you agreed this plan – why aren't you delivering it?'.

Other countries have made greater strides in the introduction of joint venture agreements between public and private finance for their health programme. Obviously, the US market has long been driven by a competitive market economy and is dominated by a two-tier health service largely financed by health insurance. There is a safety net for those without health insurance but it is regarded by most as a backstop position. The best doctors, and the best equipment, are found in the private sector.

More meaningful comparisons can be found on our doorstep, or rather on the other side of the channel, in France. Some in the medical profession regard the French system as superior to the British NHS. Certainly, there are increasing reports of excellent health services being available in France, such as a patient visiting a GP in the morning, having a consultant undertake tests and further examination in the afternoon, and results being delivered the same evening. This may lead to some interesting unexpected developments. Medical politics in the UK has evolved as a process of the British Medical Association (BMA) acting like a trade union in its negotiations with its employer (the Government). Perhaps inadvertently, doctors have not given sufficient attention to directing their discussions to the customer (their patients). Architects have gone through these same traumas 20 years ago when the Thatcher administration turned the spotlight on the perceived restrictive practices of the architectural profession at the beginning of the 1980s. Mandatory fee scales for architects were abolished, and architects were thrown into the cauldron of the competitive open market place. Today, doctors find themselves at the centre of public interest, receiving wide publicity for those doctors who have strayed outside their professional boundaries with a series of damaging court cases and public exposes which has left the political leaders of the medical professional institutions reeling, and put on their defensive back foot. The Government has stolen the initiative, and doctors are caught between the demands of a vociferous and articulate public and an employer adopting an uncompromising stance towards conditions of contract and expectations of the quality of service.

Medical services will also become increasingly international. Already, along the south coast of England, people are travelling to the continent to seek medical treatment, and it can be expected that this trend will increase in popularity. Obviously, many people also come to the UK for highly specialised treatment, but for initial consultations with a GP consumers are likely to become more demanding, more selective, and more likely to ask for second opinions. It can be argued that this may lead to a privatisation of GP services, similar to GP services before the introduction of the NHS. Already, there is evidence that in our more affluent suburbs, personal recommendations between patients is creating a network of preferred GPs who are perceived to have specialist knowledge in certain areas. Patients are saying 'Let's go and see Dr A – I've heard he is very good with knees'. Patients are increasingly able and willing to pay for a second opinion. However, the privatisation of GP services, should this trend develop, will be heavily influenced by the pharmaceutical industry. It is difficult to predict how the pharmaceutical industry will react, if, for example, the supply of drugs through the NHS was to begin to decline and an increasing percentage of medication was prescribed by doctors privately. At present, if doctors leave the contractual arrangements between themselves and the NHS, they are no longer able to give patients the benefit of subsidised medication.

Further speculation leaves one to ponder whether the privatisation of GP services will be taken over by large commercial organisations, rather than left as a network of individual private practitioners as in the pre-NHS situation. Not that long ago every high street had a privately run optician's shop. Now, the market is dominated by a handful of large commercial organisations that employ large numbers of opticians within national networks of shops. There are those in the retail trade who have already spotted the opportunity for providing pharmacy services and next step may be GP services, within their retailing empires. How convenient it would become, when doing the weekly shop, to pop in to see a GP at the local supermarket, particularly if this could be done at a time convenient to the patient. Already, many supermarkets are operating 24 hours a day.

Time, remains a crucial component of the cost effectiveness of GP services. The personal consultation period between a patient and their GP remains a vital interface for that initial consultation. There are examples of bad doctors (in medical terms) who are popular with patients because of their personal charisma. There are even examples of doctors hauled before the disciplinary committees of their professional organisations who bring their own patients as witnesses to support their defence. Time spent with a patient is crucial if a sympathetic, healing environment is to be engendered. For example, in the Mayo Clinic in the USA, consultants see on average four cases during a morning session, but in a typical NHS hospital a consultant's caseload for a morning session is more likely to be 20 patients. For GPs, the national average consultation period in the UK is 8 minutes – all too short if a meaningful rapport is to be developed between doctor and patient and those subtle tell-tale signs are to be identified from a patient's unhurried description of their concerns.

Intuitively, therefore, one is led to believe that buildings in the future for primary health care services need to be friendly, non-threatening, and full of old fashioned concepts of comfort, light, cleanliness, warmth, and friendliness. They should relaxing, accessible, community based facilities which patients are keen to make full use of – to pop in for a chat; to ask a nurse, or a pharmacist or a social worker for advice.

5.1.4 Consequences and outcomes: identify benchmark minimum criteria. seek to demonstrate inadequacy of this approach

Hospital design in the UK over the past 50 years has been disappointing. With few exceptions, design quality has been bleak, institutional, and not responsive to patients needs. The procurement process has been too extended, design quality has been largely ignored, and functionality has remained king in a process dominated by the service providers and the administrators far removed from the interface between patient and doctor within the confines of a clinical ward.

Similarly, primary health care buildings have been constrained by a set of procedures contained within the 'Red Book' which is now outdated. There have been enlightened solutions in recent years, by architects who have enjoyed a sustained period of work in this sector but imaginative solutions have been inhibited by the cost limits and tests of functionality.

If the inadequacy of these systems is acknowledged, what are the criteria that should be applied to the next wave of primary health care facilities? We must move away from an appraisal of bricks and mortar and must look at patient requirements. We must establish different criteria that are not just based on a function of the process. We must look at issues in a more rounded and philosophical way – to consider what ethos is being sought and what do patients expect. The recent work of the Construction Industry Council (CIC) is exciting. They are seeking to develop new performance indicators for design. Their aim is to raise the standards of design, to increase 'delight' as well as functionality and consideration of whole life costs. 'They seek to engender a really articulate architectural conversation between client and design team'. The initiative is intended to introduce a 'common language' for each stage of schemes says Michael Dickson, current Chairman of CIC.

Others working on this Initiative include Sunand Prasad, who says the tool is about making sure design is included along with the more process based work of the movement for innovation. 'The key thing to remember in spreading this measurement culture that we are now in is that you cannot measure all the building successes with a process measurement alone'. The measurement of the quality of the product remains a key criteria, and this remains an allusive objective for all those working in this field. Various analogies are offered as a comparison.

'Even wine gets marked out of 10'.

'Gymnastics and other sports are marked – all sorts of things that require imagination'.

By developing quality indicators the CIC Group hope to ensure that added value is given to the professional services to ensure the quality of the built environment is enhanced. The quality indicators will seek to address the cultural and social aspects of aesthetics, and the appropriateness to community, as well as the utility value and technical performance and economy and sustainability of the buildings.

The design process needs to be extended by looking more sensitively at the early stages of design, and analysing the post evaluation exercises more rigorously. The CIC believe that the term Design Quality Indicator is more appropriate than Key Performance Indicator. Another analogy used by CIC is the comparison of design quality to Olympic diving, when a competitor is given points for execution that are then multiplied by a factor relating to the difficulty of the dive – the aesthetics of a building will function as a multiplier rather than a number that will become compared directly with hard issues, sustainability or life cycle costs.

Ultimately, the evaluation of the success or otherwise of these initiatives will be measured as the benefit of design on patient recovery times and staff effectiveness.

5.2.1 Criteria: life cycle costs are not fully considered (only initial capital costs)

Until recently life cycle costs have been relatively unimportant in the Government process of procuring buildings, including those for the health service. The tradition has been to award contracts predominantly on a lowest cost basis. The Treasury has now changed direction and the welcome interest in design quality is also manifesting itself in a reassessment of whole life costs.

This approach is encapsulated under the umbrella of 'best value'. All Government departments and local authorities are taking a broader look at 'best value' issues and this is providing an opportunity to develop new thinking about a whole range of tangible and intangible aspects of a building during its overall life span. At the simplest level, building material manufacturers are able to demonstrate 'best value' for their products not only as the result of initial costs but also taking into account maintenance schedules and renewal timescales. With design issues the growing recognition of user reactions and user satisfaction levels is beginning to influence the decision making process.

GP surgeries are too small to justify the competitive pre-contract procedures that potential development partners face under PFI procedures. The emerging policies from NHS Estates for their Procure 21 method of procurement are yet to be tested in the market place and the bundling together of groups of primary health care facilities seems to be a risky strategy. However there is a growing group of specialist companies forming partnerships with GPs to finance new primary health care facilities. Their success rate in putting together viable procurement packages is being helped because of the changes in attitude by District Valuers. District Valuers are moving towards the creation of a special class of valuation for medical facilities, whereas previously they were seriously disadvantaged by being included with residential or local commercial values. These high valuations that are being rentalised as surgeries are enabling contracts to be written for minimum of 25 year lease periods guaranteed by local health authorities under the terms of existing procedures.

5.2.2 Question: how do you evaluate best value?

The Construction Industry Council (CIC) has carried out innovative work to examine new performance indicators for design. Not only does this reflect changing attitudes within the architectural profession about the measurability of design, but it reflects the growing influence achieved by the CIC and also CABE (Commission for Architecture in the Built Environment) in influencing Government departments to look more closely at the beneficial effects and cost advantages that can be achieved through the implementation of good design policies.

Jon Rouse, CABE's chief executive, talked to 10 major UK businesses during the summer of 2000. All of them had a reputation for commissioning high-quality architecture and he wanted to find out two things:

- Where is the impetus coming from?
- What valuation methods are being used to ensure that design benefits are factored into investment decisions?

Interestingly, he highlighted the shortcomings of traditional valuation methods used by the surveying profession. The traditional property valuation method, driven by reporting purposes to include in company accounts provided little reflection of their design value. Similarly, replacement cost calculations offer no mechanisms to value the intangible benefits that well designed buildings can provide. On closer examination there are two main factors that determine corporate policy on architectural investment. First most of the companies think that design is important in the process of corporate change. The second factor is having a senior design champion in the company. So far as architectural value can be translated into financial values – greater book value, additional capacity or running cost savings – it is accounted for within a cost benefit analyses. And most of the companies also incorporated others, less tangible design benefits as 'top up' qualitative factors. These included potential increase sales, improved working conditions and contribution to change in corporate culture.

British Airways, one of the companies visited by Rouse identified other intangible benefits such as improved moral due to the less hierarchical office set-up, more efficient use of space through more intelligent layout, and productivity gains through new ways of working aided by the building. He offers three alternative valuation methods (Rouse, 2000):

- **Contingent valuation.** The method has its roots in welfare economics. It involves asking individuals affected by a project, such as people who might use it, to reveal their personal valuation of design elements. It has been used in the USA to measure the social and environmental impact of industrial buildings, and is recognised by the Treasury.
- **Analytic hierarchy process.** Developed by Thomas Saaty from an engineering perspective, AHP makes a 'hierarchy' or list of every factor – whether of quantity or quality – that influences a decision, with the most general and least controllable factors at the top of the list. By giving weighting and ranking to these attributes, and making decisions at each level of the hierarchy, one if left with a comparable set of alternatives that reflect both intangible and tangible costs and benefits.
- **Fuzzy logic.** Already used to control many of our domestic appliances, 'fuzzy logic' helps us accept a lack of precision in decision-making. It allows us to express our judgements about design with a level of uncertainty that is then used to influence the calculation of overall financial cost or benefit. Research in North America has examined the application of the method to real-estate decisions, with positive results.

It can be argued that the architectural profession would gain respect and confidence from clients by engaging more

fully with these financial and business ratios, and if successfully exploited would result in a greater commitment by corporate clients in concern for the built environment (i.e. architecture). These arguments equally apply to the health sector, not least to primary health care buildings. Indeed, the intense personal relationships and complex briefs demanded by primary care buildings may well increase awareness of intangible qualities with enhanced benefits in terms of user satisfaction levels by patients, staff and doctors alike.

In Australia, work has developed along these lines to create a 'design dividend'. CABE is developing similar criteria for use in the UK.

5.2.3 Approach: comparison with the 'Red Book'

The 'Red Book' has represented the *modus operandii* of GP practice in the UK for many years. It represents the outcome from a long period of development, periodic reviews, and updating of data. It typifies the outcome of a bureaucratic approach of controlling a very large organisation. The rules, costs limits, and schedules of permitted accommodation are very prescriptive, and it is remarkable that so much high quality architectural work has resulted from such a stifling environment. The wide range of innovative GP surgeries built over the past decade has been achieved in spite of the dead hand of officialdom. Fortunately, this framework of controls is now rapidly breaking down as new forms of procurement expand and develop in the joint public private partnerships that the Government is encouraging, but there is a long way to go.

Controls on loose furniture, tight budgets, discounted fee scales for professional services and other prescriptive requirements for accommodation requirements and overall floor areas made life difficult for both doctors and architects. A completely different approach to building design is required for the next wave of primary care buildings. They must be buildings that are flexible and can incorporate the demands of a knowledge based economy, respond to the rapidly changing demands for information technology, and different working methods which will develop from faster communications between doctor, patient and specialist testing facilities (e.g. X-rays, consultant reports). Government procurement methods must enable future buildings to be flexible shells within which highly serviced workstations can be developed and changed over short periods of time. For example, a doctor's consulting room may have entirely different requirements in five years time than it does today – although it is likely to remain the fundamentally important space within which patient and doctor exchange information.

5.2.4 Consequences and outcomes: evaluate and compare with other building types

Primary care buildings are usually small buildings. They need to be looked at in a different light to the large-scale strategic infrastructure projects which have dominated NHS policy making for half a century. Obviously, the larger capital sums required to provide a major regional acute hospital facility is quite different to providing a modest community based facility.

It is difficult, therefore, to understand the logic of expecting these two widely different types of buildings to be procured using the same, or at least very similar, contractual methods. It seems reasonable to assume that the smaller health facilities should respond to local conditions, be they rural or urban, and in a way which is sympathetic to the characteristics of the population it serves. A rural GP practice based in a village classified as a conservation area is likely to be designed in a quite different way to a city centre GP practice in one of our major cities. It is difficult to envisage how the briefs for a group of surgeries can be developed to fall under the umbrella of a common outline business case necessary for a PFI contract. The sheer diversity of locational influences is likely to inhibit sufficient common ground to enable such groupings to satisfactorily proceed. It could be argued that there would be some merit in having instantly recognisable GP surgeries in different parts of the country, but brand name images, reminiscent of small scale Tescos or Sainsburys supermarkets are unlikely to provide the responsive therapeutic environments which we increasingly believe are beneficial to health care. It is no more logical than to suggest that all churches should look the same – instantly recognisable spiritual havens where anyone could drop-in.

The very diversity of site conditions, location, topography, and local architectural tradition must be allowed to influence design decisions to provide a responsive and innovative building which is flexible for future needs. There is wide spread agreement that time spent on the briefing process is a good investment for the future cost effectiveness of a building.

This is neatly illustrated by the 1:5:200 ratio which relates to buildings' capital investment to maintenance and staff costs. CABE is highlighting the importance of this ratio where 1 represents initial capital cost, 5 is a reflection of the maintenance and repair costs during the lifetime of a building, and 200 represents the total cost of a building, predominantly made up of staff costs. It is clear from this ratio that the initial capital cost of a building is relatively insignificant when compared to the overall cost of a building during its lifetime. Not only that, but greater investment at the initial design stage may well produce economic benefits further down the life span of a building and therefore narrowing the ratio between these figures to the benefit of all concerned.

The evaluation of this architectural benefit represents the tip of an iceberg largely unexplored. Massive research and investment is necessary to redress the balance. There is a poor tradition of research in architecture, and the intuitive approach to design is the traditional artistic licence which is believed to be a core concept of architectural education. Statistical evaluation of intangible concepts has remained elusive and, in fact, may well have provided some of the mystery in subjective artistic criticism. The scientific traditional of searching for evidence to justify decisions has not been instilled in the architectural profession.

It is encouraging, therefore, that the Government has launched a new organisation, NHS LIFT (Local Improvement Finance Trust) first previewed in the NHS Plan and included in the Government's proposals for new legislation in the Queen's speech given on 6 December 2000. The intention is to mirror the PFI programme for hospital developments with a scheme suitable for family doctors.

By 2004, the Department of Health envisages 3000 GP premises, mostly in inner cities and poor estates – more than a quarter of the total – will be transformed by a £1 billion fund combining public and private money. NHS LIFT will be set up as a limited company, working jointly with the private sector. The Government's first allocation will be £175 million (Hawkes, 2000).

Alan Milburn, health secretary, foresees a complementary programme of public private partnership invested in primary care facilities to improve accessibility particularly in the most needy areas.

It is envisaged that the new facilities will also combine other services such as retail outlets, an optician's shop, pharmacy, or other related services. Similarly, the intention is to bring primary care and social services together to improve communications, co-ordination of needs, thereby achieving a one stop service for health, social services and housing.

6

Briefing issues

Quotations

The source of the following quotations is from a lecture 'Designing for Intermediate Care' at the RIBA, by R. James Chapman at the Design Quality Forum, London on 19 March 1998.

> There is a central quality which is the root criterion of life and spirit in a man, a building, or a wilderness. This quality is objective and precise, but it cannot be named. (Christopher Alexander – *The Timeless Way of Building*.)

> Quality is never an accident, it is always the result of intelligent effort. There must be a will to produce a superior thing. (John Ruskin.)

> All excellence is equally difficult. (Thornton Wilder.)

> Quality above all, is about care, people, passion, consistency, eyeball contact and gut reaction. Quality is not a technique no matter how good. (Tom Peters – *A Passion for Excellence*.)

> To fight against the shoddy design of those goods by which our fellow men are surrounded becomes a moral duty. (Nikolaus Pevsner.)

> Mammoth hospitals, built like dreary office blocks on a devastatingly functional basis, depress the spirits, however good the healthcare. (Prince of Wales – *A Vision of Britain*.)

6.1.1 Criteria: quality standards should be higher

In an earlier chapter it has already been pointed out that architecture is more about the quality of the product rather than the quality of the process. However important it is to improve the construction process, achieve cost efficiency, and consistency of workmanship we all respond to the environment in which we find ourselves. This is particularly so when we are using buildings at times of emotional stress, or heightened awareness. Health and religious buildings are two obvious examples when our responses to our environmental surroundings are likely to be particularly important. It is all the more surprising, therefore, that the track record of the design of health buildings has, until very recently, given little importance to the quality of design.

The rapid increase in the awareness of the importance of good design in health buildings is to be welcomed, and it is particularly gratifying that the Government now recognises the essential part that good design can play in the healing process. It would be churlish to dwell on the political aspects of this new concern, if seen from the eyes of the patient. A more cynical view would be that the politicians are merely reflecting the power of consumerism, and that they have recognised the importance of putting the patient first in the delivery of the next generation of health care services. Part of that improvement of services lies in the quality of the building used for health care.

Therefore, architects need to take this opportunity to work with their fellow professionals in medicine and help devise the methodologies necessary for introducing higher design standards. But what are higher design standards? One is immediately brought back to the reality of the Treasury rules for procurement and the need for architects to demonstrate quantitatively their qualitative concepts. Leading practitioners are now developing a range of processes to encourage this approach, led by CABE (Commission for Architecture in the Built Environment) under the direction of Sir Stuart Lipton. On the larger hospital projects it is recognised that the early contracts have led to disappointing results from the design quality aspect and building in a design ethos to the early briefing documents is now recognised as an essential ingredient if the finished building is to have 'delight' or a 'wow' factor.

In the USA, the Plaintree philosophy recognises the importance of viewing health care from the patient's perspective and emphasises the importance of focusing on 'humanising, personalising and demystifying the health care experience'.

The story is told by Robin Orr based on the experiences of a patient called Angie who, on admission to a San Francisco hospital, had been left uninformed, frightened, and intimidated to speak up or ask questions about her treatment.

' "Robin, why does it have to be that way?" Angie asked. "Why is it that we have created the health care system that has some of the finest technology – we can save people's lives; we can substitute artificial organs for diseased ones; we can do all these wonderful things in the name of scientific medicine. But somewhere along the line, what we know about human beings, about health and healing (words you don't even hear in hospitals), the importance of families, diet, and nutrition, and the impact of the environment on our well-being have been lost?"

At that point, the Plaintree Organisation captured my intellectual curiosity, as well as my feelings and dedication. I decided that I wanted to work with this wonderful organisation in San Francisco. The Plain Tree blueprint is based on continuity, accountability and education. It concentrates on providing a beautiful healing environment where people touch each other "one of the most wonderful things we can do for people who are sick, or well, is to touch them".' (Orr, 1991.)

6.1.2 Question: how should an architect be briefed for primary health care buildings?

In an earlier chapter the conventional approaches to design have been described. These are usually sequential processes and sometimes have built in checks to prevent, or at least discourage, a return to earlier stages in the process in an attempt to prevent time delays or budget excesses. This has been the case with NHS procedures, requiring that the brief is 'signed off' at the beginning of each stage and the 'brief acceptance certificate' becomes a quasi-contractual document binding on all parties. We have seen that more recent academic research into the process of design has highlighted the shortcomings of a linear process and for high quality results to be achieved it is important to recirculate around the decision making paths. To constrain the design process by tight timescales, and locking in the financial criteria at too early a stage can have a detrimental effect on the final results. The cost of design is often seen as being over important in comparison to the total costs of a building over its whole life span. Perhaps because architects work with space rather than time the profession has been brow beaten into submission to accept unrealistic timescales for the design period. This has arisen from procrastination and delays from the administrators and controllers of the procurement process who are often financially led in their decision-making processes.

However, quality is fighting back and the following section was written by Gordon Kirtley, an architect with Sheppard Robson who has been responsible for trying to improve the design quality output in his work on health projects. There is certainly a need for a record of what has been agreed at each stage

of the design, but the process will constrain client and designer alike if it does not allow, and indeed encourage, interaction between the briefing and the design process.

Notes by Gordon Kirtley

An important duty of the design team is to advise the client and users as to what can change – in the brief and the design – at each stage of design development. Inexperienced users can be helped in decision making if they are confident that they are not being bound in every little detail of what they see in the brief and on the drawings. Conversely, it is essential that they understand that some changes may significantly disrupt the design, programme and budget for the project. User groups – who perhaps go through the design process only once in their career – are often surprisingly unaware of what is significant to the design at each stage of its development. For example, changing the size of a door on a 1:200 plan may be viewed with trepidation while the potential ramifications of a late introduction of storerooms or sanitary facilities may not be appreciated. (Of course, one might argue that architects who overlooked such an omission were not doing their jobs effectively.)

A useful approach is to set out explicitly what is fixed at each design stage. It is equally important that busy nurses, doctors and admin staff are asked to commit themselves to detailed briefing decisions long before the information is really need by the architect, engineers and other designers. Too often users are asked to complete complex room data sheets before the accommodation requirements and plans have settled to an agreed configuration. The timing of information gathering is crucial to the success of the project and again, it is worth explaining the process to the client and users to help them commit willingly to the timetable.

This has an added benefit of focusing the client, users and design team on the conceptual and strategic issues which need to be agreed and resolved in the early design stages and which are easily confused and compromised by too much information at the wrong time.

This leads to another important briefing issue. How does the design team gain an understanding of those intangible values which lie at the heart of the client's purpose in building a new facility. Quantitative information – an area schedule for example – is vital to the success of the scheme but, with bench marking data and published guidance, it is relatively easily to reach an agreed statement of need. By contrast it is often difficult to draw out qualitative ideas – issues of style, ambience, feel and image. But, if these issues are neglected or absent from the brief, the end product may be a disappointment to the client, even if functionality and technical performance requirements are well satisfied.

In some work that I did recently with the Wellcome Trust, updating and extending design guidance for biomedical research facilities, I found that we were able to define a set of 'quality parameters' which summarised the Trust's value system in so far as it applied to assessment of the applications for funding laboratory facilities. Some of the parameters could be defined quantitatively – for example space standards and physical environmental requirements – but the Trust was also able to set out its requirements for less tangible components of quality such as environmental quality, interaction and collaboration and flexibility in use.

To turn again to process, briefing can be viewed less a sequential process than a gradual revelation of needs from a fog of uncertainty and indecision. Users often have a very clear idea – sometimes too clear – of some of their needs and almost total uncertainty in respect of others. The trick is to find points of reference within the set of often incoherent and imperfect information which is the normal starting point in taking the brief. This framework can be seen as a first, very crude statement which will eventually develop into a coherent model of the client's requirements. In this sense, briefing is not unlike designing a building – once the client has seen the first attempt, warts and all, a dialogue can begin and effort can be focused on filling in gaps in the information.

Drawing this information from the client and user groups requires considerable skill and experience. Techniques involving detailed checklists and formal question and answer sessions may not ask the right questions. It is useful to set an agenda to structure interviews, but often it is better if the interviewee is barely aware of this. Users will use different techniques to express their needs. Some come armed with schedules or drawings, others will talk about the strengths and failings of their existing accommodation or refer to an example which they like or dislike. Especially in the first meetings, it is essential that the users feel that they are setting the agenda and that they are free to express their opinions – even if sometimes these stray from the strict scope of the project at hand.

As the brief develops, priorities begin to shift. The divergent phase, when all ideas are welcome, gives way to a process of co-ordinating and resolving conflicting needs, ensuring that the balance between consistency and diversity in the spaces provide is deliberate rather than a product of ad hoc and idiosyncratic demands.

Two factors are then especially important. The first is that the briefing team should itself have access to a database of information – statistics, model layouts, case studies – which will provide a reliable benchmark to gauge the expressed wishes of the users. Secondly, the client team must have a decisive leader who is assigned the authority to reach and enforce decisions.

6.1.3 Approach: analyse MARU primer

MARU carried out an investigation into designing primary health care premises for the North West Regional Health Authority in 1996 and a document they produced explores the briefing process. It concentrates on the practical necessities of working within the 'Red Book' and the *Capital Investment Manual* and it identifies that both systems are divided into discrete parts by a series of gates that every project must pass through, making clear which stage any project has reached.

Importantly, the document recognises the necessity to return to design decisions from time-to-time, to re-examine previous design decisions. Another important point is also made: after the long and often torturous process of satisfying the NHS administrative procedures for approval and 'signing off' of design stages, there is often little enthusiasm, or sufficient incentive, to embark on the evaluation process. On completion of a project this inevitably means that there is limited feedback provided for the benefit of other designers who may be embarking on a similar design process, sometimes for an almost identical brief. This emphasises a point already identified; that is there is a need to extend the design process at

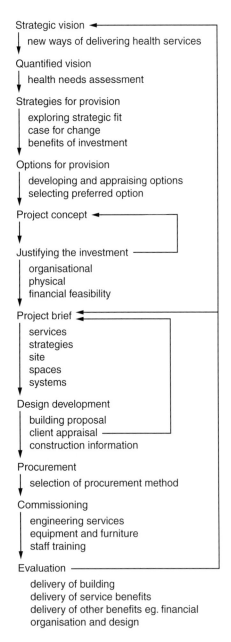

Figure 6.1 Source: *Designing Primary Healthcare Premises: A Resource*.

the beginning of a project as well as giving greater importance to the evaluation of projects on their completion.

The briefing tool set out by MARU is an excellent step-by-step analysis of how to navigate the practical realities of the NHS procedures that existed at the time of its publication. However, we now recognise the importance of giving greater priority to the needs of the patient and the philosophical stance of the brief needs to shift from the practical expectations of the service providers to the intellectual well-being of the real clients for the next generation of health buildings (see Figure 6.1).

6.1.4 Consequences and outcomes: develop design guide recommendations

The following notes are a typical specification for a brief for a health care building as proposed by Gordon Kirtley. A crucial component is the development of the ethos, aims and objectives of the project which should form part of the initial brief.

Typical specification for the brief of a health care building

The brief for the project should comprise a comprehensive, but concise, statement of the requirements of the client and the user groups, normally following the scope and format described in the *Capital Investment Manual*.

The brief comprises two parts: the initial brief and the full brief.

The initial brief should include the following:

- Introduction and overview:
  - ethos, aims and objectives of the project
  - key constraints
  - organisation
  - population.
- Operational policy statements for:
  - clinical functions
  - support functions
  - administration
  - reception, admissions, appointments
  - materials handling
  - waste management
  - security
  - domestic services
  - portering
  - car parking
  - sanitary facilities
  - staff amenities
  - visitor amenities.
- Design quality statement
- Schedule of accommodation; room-by-room schedule including:
  - unit area of each room type
  - number of rooms of each type
  - room occupancy.

- Functional relationships diagram:
  - network of adjacencies and links between scheduled spaces.
- Typical layouts (1:50) of key accommodation types showing:
  - key modular dimensions
  - generic equipment and furniture layouts.

The full brief should include for each room or space:

- Equipment list for groups 1–3 equipment.
- Requirements for:
  - key dimensions, including room height
  - wall, floor and ceiling finishes
  - daylight/blackout
  - acoustic requirements
  - doors and access (size, security, vision panels, etc.)
  - other special requirements.
- Room data sheets for engineering services requirements.

The client should appoint an equipment specialist who will liaise with the user group and collect detailed information on equipment items, including procurement proposals (e.g. existing equipment relocated, new equipment, etc.). The role of the briefing consultant will be to collate and co-ordinate this information.

Preparation of the brief

The initial brief and the full brief will be prepared in consultation with the client's nominated representatives.

A typical consultation process would include, for each user group, a series of three meetings:

- initial briefing meeting
- review of the first draft
- review of the final draft.

The briefing consultant will prepare an agenda and chair the user consultation meetings.

User groups

In addition to core user groups for clinical services, there should be special working groups for the preparation of the initial brief, including:

- interior design
- equipment co-ordination
- phasing and decanting
- health and safety
- fire safety (may be covered by health and safety)
- security
- facilities management and estates issues, including deliveries, waste, domestic services, catering and maintenance.

6.2.1 Criteria: there is no qualitative methodology to evaluate building design

Much of this book is about a comparison of subjective qualitative evaluation and evidence-based quantitative research. There have been several recent attempts to develop systems to give scientific credence to artistic concepts, and it seems that for the time being at least progress in this field is dependent on providing an economic justification for all design processes. We will look later at the appraisal processes to put applications for lottery funds into a priority list and the Higher Education Funding Council is also trying to design evaluation systems to judge the quality of design in our education buildings.

Pilot studies have been carried out by CABE to formulate design quality tools. The design quality indicators devised to evaluate quality have also been referred to in earlier chapters.

The key issue that emerges from an examination of these systems is that comparisons are being made between the expectations set out in the brief for a building and then compared with the results found in a post-evaluation study. However, the components of the brief are often very limited and it is therefore difficult to establish sufficiently worthwhile tests to measure the outputs from the finished building. This leads to the suggestion that the quality of the brief needs to be raised.

A number of approaches attempting to quantify the qualitative aspects of a design use an arithmetical approach. Essential, they are systems of point scoring against a series of scales judging performance. This leads to problems of assessment (MacNaughton, 1996) and the dangers and difficulties of assuming sliding scales of assessment which adopt a smooth or consistent gradient. More sophisticated models are required with more intensive research committed to this field.

There is undoubtedly very limited research either completed or underway, in this broad field and more sophisticated briefing techniques will not appear overnight. We should be less apprehensive about linking the philosophical concepts of complementary medicine with mainstream professional methods. Exploration of the holistic approaches to alternative medicine should be looked at in parallel with scientifically founded evidence produced from control experiments of environmental factors. The Glasgow Homoeopathic Hospital (see the case studies) is a good example of a recent building designed within the budgetary constraints of the NHS system and yet seeking out new ways to interpret a pleasing environment. It is often frustrating for designers who are constrained by a system that seems unable to see beyond the scientific parameters of progress based on experimental results.

Newspapers and magazines are full of articles about lifestyle: about how to remove stress from the workplace – about well-balanced diets – about 'making over' interior spaces. There is a new-found enthusiasm to control and influence our individual lives. The Prince of Wales, writing in *The Times* on 30 December 2000 says 'we should be mindful that clinically controlled trials alone are not the only prerequisites to apply a health care intervention. Consumer based surveys can explore why people choose complementary and alternative medicine and tease out the therapeutic powers of belief and trust.' With the medical profession under great pressure from society to become more responsive to consumer demands another article in *The Times* (19 January 2001) starts from the premise that health is more fundamental to happiness, well-being and prosperity than anything else. Surely this is the wrong way around? Good health is likely to result from happiness, well-being and prosperity and it is our failure to understand the historic values of a holistic lifestyle that has led us into the trap which assumes that a technical solution lies behind every medical disorder. Doctors have exploited the opportunity to let us believe they have the key to solve all medical problems and are the last of the professions to have their authority challenged: and they don't like finding that consumerism – patient power – is knocking on their door.

We should turn our attention to the quality of the environment; to the design of the places where we live and work and the therapeutic advantages that flow from the best examples. Doctors need to widen their horizons and understand the benefits that the humanities can add to our health. Science adds to our knowledge but philosophy and the arts make life worth living.

6.2.2 Question: what elements should be covered by a design brief – what is the process?

For primary care health facilities, the briefing process has been technically biased for the past 20 years or more. Working within financial constraints, and striving to achieve schedules of accommodation there has been an almost complete lack of qualitative descriptors.

Missing from these briefing documents has been a complete failure to adequately address environmental standards. We should be addressing many issues of quality, and describing the aspirations that we would like to see in our buildings. There should be a range of issues where standards and aspirations are explored and target performance levels established:

- lighting
- colours
- textures
- personal controls
- heating
- ventilation
- privacy
- dignity.

Similarly, we should be setting out the requirements of the building users:

- patients
- doctors (and other medical staff, e.g. pharmacists)
- nurses
- administrative staff
- technical staff.

We should also be exploring the requirements for external spaces. The space around the building, its entrance; issues of privacy, silence and dignity are all responses to our emotional needs which should be described in the building brief.

Buildings are not static. We should be offering flexibility and alternative uses over the lifetime of a building.

What related uses should be considered alongside the medical activities of a building? Will there be:

- a pharmacy
- social workers
- mental health staff
- a chiropodist
- dentistry
- other civic functions?

Where are the facilities to be located and what is the sites accessibility?

Transportation issues may well be as important or even more important than our traditional understanding of planning issues.

6.2.3 Approach: review standard architect job book with particular reference to GPP process

The following is a sample agenda used for an initial briefing meeting for a new surgery in the Midlands.

1. Introductions (include identification of named persons with delegated authority to speak for the surgery).

2. The existing surgery.
2.1 Perceived strengths/weaknesses of existing building.
2.2 Possible survey of existing patient/staff to assist in the identification of strengths and weaknesses.

3. The proposed design.
3.1 Discuss client's objectives, requirements and establish priorities and criteria for success.
3.2 Discuss detailed functional requirements of building users. Introduce two-phase room data sheets.
3.3 Discuss preferred spatial relationships and orientations.
3.4 Discuss any known historic planning and building considerations.
3.5 Signing off procedures.

4. Environmental considerations.
4.1 Likely car-parking requirements.
4.2 Likelihood of archaeological or antiquarian discoveries (from previous experience).
4.3 Known road widening or development plans.

4.4 Known problems with site, e.g. geographical conditions, hazardous substances.
4.5 Request for services information progressed by architects
5. Intended programme.
5.1 Discussion of key dates including progression of financial status with the district valuer.

Some of the issues that we are attempting to understand include:

- to define relationships
- to describe the ethos
- to understand and agree the programme
- to agree the line of responsibility and establish communications
- to discuss expectations
- to agree schedules of services and equipment to be provided
- to fix cost targets
- to review access, external spaces, desire lines, key site restraints, pedestrian and vehicular routes
- discuss working methods and administrative systems.

The financial constraints and schedule of room areas demanded by the local health authority form only a small part of the designer's brief. Many, indeed most of the issues in the above list are of no interest to the district valuer's assessment of rental levels which will be used to determine the rent allowance paid to GPs on occupation of their new building.

6.2.4 Consequences and outcomes: comment and expand on existing procedures

The 'Red Book' policy continues to focus on room areas and cost parameters but new procurement systems will emerge. The NHS Plan is moving in the right direction. The new financial proposals through LIFT will introduce private finance and increase the flexibility of procuring new primary health care facilities.

We can anticipate that there will be fewer partnerships, and that doctors will move towards being salaried employees of primary care trusts. Younger doctors, in common with many other professions, are increasingly reluctant to take on the financial responsibilities of a partnership in an economy that has seen sustained and steady growth with security of employment prospects. Financial success and security can often be achieved without taking on commercial risks. The historical advantages of partnership are increasingly being overtaken by new structures for professional services.

Therefore, we can see a major shift towards greater concern for design quality as more sophisticated measuring systems are introduced to evaluate 'value for money'. Much more research is required to develop accurate appraisals of whole life costs. From an environmental stance, all five senses of the human body should be considered.

Plate 1 The Centre for Life: aerial view. Photographed by Sean Gallagher

Plate 2 Wideopen Medical Centre, Newcastle upon Tyne: external view. Architect: Geoffrey Purves Partnership

Plate 3 Lintonville Medical Centre, Newcastle upon Tyne: internal corridor. Architect: Geoffrey Purves Partnership

Plate 4 Gosforth Memorial Centre, Newcastle upon Tyne: reception/ waiting area as built. Architect: Geoffrey Purves Partnership

Plate 5 West Road Surgery, Newcastle: external view. Architect: Geoffrey Purves Partnership

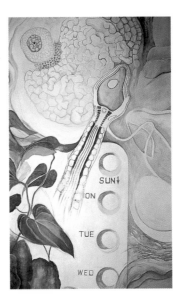

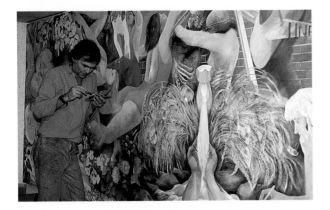

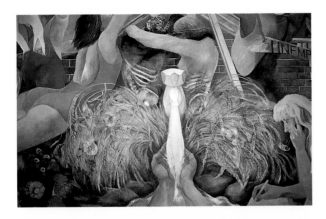

Plate 6 St Paul's Medical Centre, Carlisle: Cycle of Life mural by Barrie Ormsby

Plate 7 Forth Valley Bellsdyke Hospital: exterior view at dusk. Photographed by Morley von Sternberg

Plate 8 Glasgow Homoeopathic Hospital. Architect: MacLachlan Monaghan

Plate 9 The Haven Trust, London: exterior looking into reception. Architect: Devereux Architects (with Martin Hay), Partner Peter Hughes, Associate Darius Umrigar. Photographed by Nathan Willock

Plate 11 Martin House, Boston Spa, Leeds: external view. Architect: Wildblood MacDonald

Plate 10 Maggie Centre, Edinburgh: external view. Architect: Richard Murphy Architects. Photographed by Alan Forbes

Plate 12 Naomi House, Winchester: external view. Architects: Wildblood MacDonald

Plate 13 Greenwich Millennium Village: waiting area. Courtesy of English Partnerships/Henderson

Plate 14 Claypath Medical Centre: external view

Plate 16 The Lawson Practice, London: external view. Photographed by Andrew Putler

Plate 15 Hammersmith Bridge Road Surgery: corridor at dusk. Photographed by Paul Tyagi/View

Plate 17 Hove Polyclinic: reception. Architect: Nightingale Associates. Photographed by Charlotte Wood

Plate 18 Neptune Health Park, West Midlands: aerial view plan. Photographed by Penoyre and Prasad

Plate 19 Shrewsbury Intermediate Care Centre, London: entrance foyer

Plate 20 The Pulross Centre: front elevation. Photographed by Dennis Gilbert, VIEW.

Plate 21 Alexandra Health Centre and University Clinic, South Africa: external view. Photograph by Christopher Malan

Plate 22 Children's hospital: lobby. Architect: SBRA. Photographed by ESTO

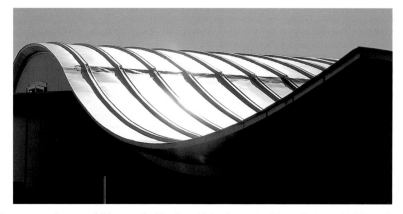

Plate 23 Ando Clinic, Japan: wave form roof. Photgraphed by Satoshi Asakawa. Architect: Tada Yoshiaki Architect & Associates.

- touch
- smell
- sight
- hearing
- taste.

Some research work is underway paying particular attention to these issues (John Wells-Thorpe, who is chairing a research group based at Sheffield University under the direction of Professor Bryan Lawson).

6.3.1 Criteria: building design should lift the spirit (there should be a 'feel good' factor)

An article published in *Hospital Design* (Rogerson, 1996) set out the case that hard facts are needed to convince hospital administrators that good design brings therapeutic benefits. Since that time, the awakening of interest in this subject has spread widely, and as we have seen the Government has now accepted the arguments and is looking for the evidence to underpin its ambitious spending plans in the NHS. Under a previous administration, the junior health minister in 1996, Tom Sackville, addressing a conference chaired by John Wells-Thorpe said that 'we have an enormous responsibility to get this right ... buildings with architecture and design that lift the spirits of patients need be no more costly than the depressing, austere buildings so familiar to many who use and work in the NHS.' Already, there were anxieties about the influence of the PFI procurement procedure with the minister going on to say 'I will not pretend PFI particularly helps [design quality] but it need not hinder it either.'

Therefore, we have seen the pendulum of opinion steadily shifting towards acceptance of the importance of good design in health buildings.

In the mid-1990s, conference speakers were still needing to remind their audiences that they were not doing the taxpayer a good turn by automatically opting for the cheapest option. What was needed was more serious research to form the basis on which therapeutic advantages could be measured.

Another influential architect at that time was Richard Burton of Ahrends Burton and Koralek, who understood the need to create calming environments and to look at design from the point of view of the patient. He pointed out 'designs which are calming when one is healthy can be depressing when is in a subdued state ... satisfaction measures are not enough – we need to measure behaviour and outcome.' This pioneering work has had an effect on policy within Government circles and prime minister Tony Blair now advocates high-quality design for civic buildings.

At the beginning of the twenty-first century, therefore, we are in a much more receptive culture to accept and understand the therapeutic benefits that can arise from well-designed primary care buildings. New design performance indicators are being developed to include a 'delight factor'. Research at Sussex University under the direction of David Gann is investigating:

- Functionality:
  - does the building perform its purpose
  - what is a building's productivity?
- Whole life costing:
  - sustainability
  - in use costs/adaptability
- Delightfulness:
  - is it a focal point in the community?
  - what do passers by think?
  - effect on the mind and the senses

These issues are not just about measuring the performance of buildings but about raising public awareness of the quality and delight that can be enjoyed from well-designed environments (Weaver, 2000).

6.3.2 Question: how important is therapeutic well-being?

The following interview outlines the case for good design in health buildings that can lead to faster patient recovery.

Notes on a meeting with Richard Mazuch, RTKL, 19 July 2000

Richard is an architect and has been with RTKL (a USA firm of architects) in London for about two years, having previously worked with Percy Thomas (a large commercial architectural practice with extensive hospital experience). For an American firm they have clearly excelled in the UK.

He has a number of research interests, and is working with MARU on a series of workshops held at the RIBA (this was referred to again by Michael Baum when I met him later in the day).

We had a wide-ranging discussion and he talked to me about his interest in the connection between Swedish and Japanese cultures. He drew parallels between the two countries having a culture and history of developing human-scale relationships into their built environment. He was fascinated by the grids and modules developed out of Japanese floor mat sizes, and the use of natural materials which is also very evident in Swedish traditional design. He also highlighted the importance in both countries of the relationship between external and internal spaces – very formal in Japanese design but also very important in Scandinavian architecture where views of the natural landscape are often framed by windows to give carefully considered views from inside a building. This has been exploited in more than one example of Scandinavian Church architecture where the view from the nave looks out over the altar through a large window onto a view of nature. I mentioned that there was a recently completed PhD thesis at Newcastle that explored the relationship between the work of Alvar Aalto and Sibelius.

He moved on to talk in more detail about the scientific evidence he was interested in collating to support these views and gave two examples:

(1) The brain reacted differently to a view of Lombardy poplars (i.e. a rhythm of vertical elements) compared to viewing an avenue of trees with a more rounded form (e.g. oak or horse chestnut trees) – a more pastoral scene. He talked about a different pattern of alfa and beta brainwaves being recorded.

(2) A combination of relaxing music and pleasant smells reduced recovery times.

In both cases he talked about the effect of these external influences on the human immune system. He also talked about the propensity to induce an epileptic fit by the use of certain colours (e.g. avoid yellow especially) and the pattern of light fittings in a ceiling when viewed from a patient lying horizontally in bed. He compared this with the brainwave activity when viewing tree-shaped patterns.

He said it was well known that a cool blue interior was likely to reduce blood pressure compared to vibrant reds that had the opposite effect.

Finally, he talked about the relationship between internal and external spaces again and the design of large Roman villas which would have a lounge for each season: spring, summer, autumn and winter. This was also brought down to the human scale and he reminded me that Romans also used different crockery at different times of the year – implements that were more appropriate to the food which was being eaten during a particular season.

I asked him if he was aware of the exhibition at Belsay Hall showing a collection of sitooteries. These fascinating pieces of design represent a range of expressions of how to create a relaxing place to seek refuge in the external environment. Somewhere to go and sit in peace and contemplate the world.

6.3.3 Approach/review: literature

From the first signs of research progress coming from the work of Roger Ulrich, the USA has been at the forefront of environmental design quality work in health buildings. Much of it has been centred around a group of people working at the Texas A&M University, together with a further group of specialists who have created the Center for Health Design, based at Martinez in California (www.healthdesign.org).

More recently, a series of research initiatives has developed in the UK, with considerable interaction between MARU (London), Manchester, Sheffield, Nottingham, and Durham Universities, all of whom are developing research outputs. Several international conferences have been held and the output of properly researched papers examining various aspects of environmental design, and the therapeutic benefits that can be achieved, is steadily increasing. Wayne Ruga is an architect, and was responsible for founding the Center for Health Design, and organising its first international symposium in 1986. Now working in the UK at Manchester University he is interested in the relationship between the environment and our culture. He asserts 'that in order to improve an

organisation's environment you must first improve its culture, giving the patient the empowering Plaintree model in the US as a successful example in health care' (Parker, 2001). The challenge to bring together robust evidence-based data and combine it with the philosophical theories of human nature continue to give difficulties to research groups around the world.

The Center for Health Design has produced a number of reports, including the following four studies particularly of interest for the design of primary health care facilities:

- Design evaluation of six primary care facilities for the purpose of informing future design decisions.
- Gardens in health care facilities: uses, therapeutic benefits, and design recommendations.
- Consumer perceptions of the health care environment an investigation to determine what matters.
- An investigation to determine whether the building environment effects patient's medical outcomes.

In the UK, MARU has been a leader of research into the design of health care environments and has produced a wide range of documents and publications, some of which are referred to in this book. The difficulty for academics remains the requirement by Government policy makers that research must be evidenced based before priorities are changed in the procurement process for new facilities. The requirement to demonstrate economic advantage continues to be a tough hurdle to clear for qualitative research. For example, work undertaken by the Department of Design and Architecture at the University of Luton, looking at the design implications of the Patient's Charter identifies the shortcomings in the questions asked of patients about their perceptions of the building environment:

'The design variables highlight the conflicting views of some patients when comparing information or data. The results showed that questions relating to the patient's perception of the built environment generated an average response on the aesthetics and functional aspects of the hospital. Whereas questions relating to their immediate well being and personal relationship with medical and professional staff generated a higher response from patients.' (Amoah-Nyako and Henderson, 2001.)

The spiritual approach to healing has been the subject of a comprehensive review by the Church of England (*A Time to Heal*, 2001). This report brings up-to-date the work of an earlier commission set up in 1953 which was the first time members of the British Medical Association and the Church of England had met officially to tackle this subject together.

The complexity of these relationships leads back to the wide conceptions of life and the world which Bertrand Russell in the introduction to his *History of Western Philosophy* describes as philosophical and the product of two factors 'one, inherited, religious and ethical conceptions; the other, the sort of investigation which may be called scientific, using this word in its broader sense'. He contends that all definite knowledge belongs to science and all dogma belongs to theology. 'But between theology and science there is no-mans land, exposed to attack from both sides; this no-mans land is philosophy.' The design of health care environments occupies this space.

6.3.4 Consequences and outcomes: develop design guide recommendations

During the research for this book the approach to design quality in health buildings has significantly changed. Positive support for good design is now being given by the Government and the effect of this change of policy is cascading down through a variety of commissioning bodies and agencies with responsibility for approving projects in the primary health care sector.

This is excellent news for all architects, and doctors can expect higher quality buildings than sometimes was the case 10 or 20 years ago. Architects should exploit the opportunity to develop a brief that reflects design quality as the primary benchmark of any new commission. There is ample evidence to support approval for putting patient priorities first. Seen from the perspective of the patient let us consider three key elements of an architectural brief:

- *quality* – to set the standard for well-being
- *functionality* – to check the technical performance
- *cost* – to ensure economic viability and value for money.

Taking these in order the following bullet points highlight a series of issues which should be discussed, and written into the brief before design work commences:

Quality

- 'Building a 2020 vision: future healthcare environments' by the Nuffield Trust (Francis and Glanville, 2001) summarises the changing attitudes towards designing health care buildings, including primary care facilities. It offers an excellent overview of likely future trends and is the product of a series of focus groups consisting of some of the most informed health care professionals working in the UK in the period 2000/01.
- Quality needs to be viewed from a wide perspective including the social and community values which new buildings should seek to meet.
- Aspirations and ambience are both words which invite a description of the cultural environment within which a building will sit, and which extends beyond any perception of its physical limitations.
- Patients and staff, as well as doctors should be asked for their views.
- The World Health Organisation's view that the single most important factor for health in a hospital is the atmosphere, captures the sense of well-being that flows from a well-

designed environment. The therapeutic benefits of this approach are accepted, as the increase in the literature of evidence-based research demonstrates.

Functionality

- The brief should list all technical standards that are required to be met. This will include both NHS space standards and statutory regulations.
- Performance specifications should be reviewed and discussed with all users so that expectations of colour, light, sound, and other environmental factors are understood. This will include the Disability Act to ensure compliance with all legislation for accessibility. Several recent documents provide guidance and checklists to simplify this task for architects.
- Security and external accessibility, e.g. transportation links, pedestrian routes and other practical aspects of the building fitting into its urban context need to be assessed.
- Flexibility of the building shell over its anticipated life span.
- Multipurpose community uses.
- Location.
- Sustainability – consider the choice of materials and the economic and environmental factors. An analysis of benefits arising from local services may show considerable improvement in lifestyle and well-being.
- Construction methods – the Government is encouraging a variety of techniques for larger projects (including large health buildings) to show economies of scale such as repetition and standardisation. This is to encourage construction to be seen as a manufacturing process. With smaller projects, usually the norm for primary health care buildings these perceived advantages are usually harder to achieve.

Cost

- Procurement routes are changing. PFI is advocated by the Government for large projects but has limitations for small projects.
- LIFT (Local Initiative Finance Trust) offers new challenges for primary health care facilities through the primary care trusts and primary care groups. Procurement methodology will evolve and new models will be tested over the next few years.
- Direct construction costs must be judged to give value for money.
- The cost to society brings to bear more complex economic analysis including lifecycle costs. Indirect costs, as well as the direct construction costs, need to be considered such as pride in the locality and lifestyle satisfaction issues. What value is placed on a sense of well-being?

Some of these issues have been discussed with regard to the design of school buildings. CABE, in parallel to their interest in health buildings, are working on education projects.

Richard Feilden, a CABE Commissioner with responsibilities for education has compiled a list of 10 key steps to ensure a high quality design results for educational projects and it is worth repeating the list for consideration within the health sector.

- Clear organisation, a legible plan and full accessibility.
- Spaces that are well proportioned, efficient and fit for their purpose.
- Well-organised circulation which is sufficiently generous.
- Appropriate levels of natural light and ventilation and use of environmentally friendly materials.
- Attractiveness in design, comparable to that found in other quality public buildings.
- Good use of the site, public presence as a civic building to engender local pride.
- Attractive external spaces offering appropriate security and a variety of settings.
- A layout that encourages broad community access and use out of hours.
- Robust, non-institutional materials that will weather and wear well.
- Scope for change in both the physical and information and communications technology environment, and the possibility of extension where appropriate.

6.4.1 Criteria: new briefing documentation is required

Very little has been written about design quality in the briefing process for primary health care buildings. The guidelines produced by NHS Estates concentrate on the technical and financial aspects of a brief, and these are discussed elsewhere in this book.

Many new initiatives are underway within the NHS system, and this includes the procurement of new buildings. The PFI process is well underway, and an intermediate form of procurement is under development by NHS Estates known as Procure21. Seeking to bridge the contract value range between £1 million up to £25 million the development and gestation period has been delayed by fierce criticism from both the construction industry and the design professionals. With a supply chain process focused on limiting the number of organisations involved in the procurement procedures there is a threat that many medium-sized consultants and contractors, with a wealth of experience in health projects, will be squeezed out of the system. As a response to the Egan philosophies of improving quality, scant attention has been given to raising the design standards of new health buildings.

At a time of great change in the NHS, driven by a Government which is the first in a long time to have a clear vision for the future of health in the UK, there is an opportunity to refocus on some of the briefing policies, and move towards a procedure which recognises design quality, rather than production quality as the key criteria for good health buildings in the future. Much encouraged by CABE, there is a surge

of interest in addressing these questions and new guidance notes are urgently required.

Enlightened NHS Trusts should be encouraged to take risks with design champions who can spearhead a drive for greater innovation, and provide a willingness to challenge traditional solutions. Consumers (i.e. patients) will soon realise that higher standards can be expected and the slow accumulation of research into therapeutic benefits of design may increasingly be an unacceptable reason for the Treasury to resist innovative design. Good ideas can too readily be shelved using the convenient excuse that further research is needed. Playing safe stifles innovation and existing bureaucratic procedures must not be allowed to stand in the way of progress. More research programmes are needed, that seek to bridge the gap between the quantitative research of the type undertaken by Roger Ulrich and the quicker, but more variable results from qualitative methodologies such as questionnaires. A pilot study undertaken by CAHHM (Centre for Arts and Humanities in Health and Medicine) the research group based at Durham University is looking at the evaluation of design aspirations during the construction of the new PFI contract. It will seek to compare and contrast the policy aspirations set out in the design brief to the consultants, with the results achieved at the end of construction.

Some success is being achieved in Northern Ireland, where John Cole is leading a number of exciting initiatives to dramatically improve the quality of hospital design. First, he has tackled the gross and excessive discounting of architect's fees which resulted in an impossibly poor level of service, and which was inadequate to provide proper design skills. By setting a competitive, but realistic fee he invited a small group of consultants to prepare designs on a prequalification basis and then invited the teams to attend design interviews. The client then selected an architect to work up exemplar design proposals over a six-month period 'This allows the architect to go through the full evolution of ideas and concepts until he can understand our needs. We turn that into an exemplar design and issue it as part of the briefing in the next stage tender. All the bids are then measured against that design quality threshold by independent assessors' (Baldock, 2001). The same principles could be equally applied to the smaller project size of primary health care facilities. John Cole says that ultimately clients must face up to paying the right fees for the right service. 'Input always equals output. Unless you put the resources into a project, you can't get the detail, design options, creativity that you are looking for.'

Fundamentally, there needs to be a seismic shift in the balance between stating design aspirations and scheduling technical performance standards. We must throw caution to the wind and be more adventurous with our design ideas; we must tear away from the dogged adherence to traditional briefing philosophies in the health system and put our quality aspirations first. It doesn't matter whether it is master planning, or urban planning on a large scale or the interior spaces of a private house, we must be clear about the quality of life which we want to enjoy when using the product of the building process.

6.4.2 Question: how do you identify (prioritise) the key decision processes?

The use of key performance indicators (KPIs) has evolved out of the KPI Working Group which has been looking at these issues on behalf of the Department of the Environment Transport and the Regions.

They identified seven major groups:

- time
- cost
- quality
- client satisfaction
- client changes
- business performance
- health and safety.

The key project stages

In order to define the KPIs throughout the lifetime of a project, five key stages have been identified (see Figure 6.2):

(A) *Commit to invest*: the point at which the client decides in principle to invest in a project, sets out the requirements in business terms and authorises the project team to proceed with the conceptual design.

(B) *Commit to construct*: the point at which the client authorises the project team to start the construction of the project.

(C) *Available for use*: the point at which the project is available for substantial occupancy or use. This may be in advance of the completion of the project.

(D) *End of defect liability period*: the point at which the period within the construction contract during which the contractor is obliged to rectify defects end (often 12 months from C).

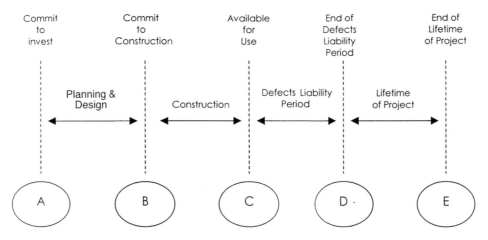

Figure 6.2 Key project stages.

Table 6.1

Procurement System	Typical Milestone at Key Point/Stage				
	A	B	C	D	E
Traditional (designer-led)	Appointment of led designer	Appointment of lead (main) contractor	Handover of built facility for use; payment of all non-retention monies	End of defects liability period (often 12 months); payment of any retention monies	End of useful life
Design & Build	Appointment (if any) of consultants prior to main contract	Appointment of lead D&B contractor	Ditto	Ditto	Ditto
Construction Management	Appointment of lead designer	Appointment of construction manager	Ditto	Ditto	Ditto
PFI	Appointment of 'Special Purpose Vehicle'	Appointment of lead contractor (if different), or sanction to proceed with construction phase	Handover of built facility for use	End of defects liability period if relevant	End of concession useful life; on-going payment to contractor

(E) *End of lifetime of project:* the point at which the period over which the project is employed in its original or near original purpose ends. As this is usually many years after the project's completion, this is a theoretical point over which concepts such as full life can be applied.

Interpretation of the key project stages

For the most common systems of procurement, experience of the first year's use of the construction industry KPIs suggests the following common interpretations of the five key stages. However, given the diversity of modern procurement systems and the many variations in practice, it may be appropriate or necessary to adopt different interpretations.

The KPIs

The KPI groups and their associated indicators are shown in Table 6.2.

The definitions for these indicators and guidance on their use is given in the section on KPI definitions.

It is self-evident that all of the above issues relate to the delivery process of a building to improve the quality of the product. I have argued throughout this book that an additional factor needs to be considered, which is the quality of the product, or 'delight' of the finished building. These intangible aspects of a building are much harder to identify, of course, and therefore tend to be overlooked by systems of assessment. How do you prove the cost effectiveness of an environmentally satisfying space? Inevitably, one returns time and time again to the challenge of balancing subjective qualitative issues against quantitative data used in an accountancy manner.

Extract taken from Department of Environment, Transport and the Regions (2000) UPI Report for The Minister for Construction.

Table 6.2

Group	Indicators	Level
Time	1. Time for Construction	Headline
	2. Time Predictability – Design	Headline
	3. Time Predictability – Construction	Headline
	4. Time Predictability – Design & Construction	Operational
	5. Time Predictability – Construction (Client Change Orders)	Diagnostic
	6. Time Predictability – Construction (Project Leader Change Orders)	Diagnostic
	7. Time to Rectify Defects	Operational
Cost	1. Cost for Construction	Headline
	2. Cost Predictability – Design	Headline
	3. Cost Predictability – Construction	Headline
	4. Cost Predictability – Design & Construction	Operational
	5. Cost Predictability – Construction (Client Change Orders)	Diagnostic
	6. Cost Predictability – Construction (Project Leader Change Orders)	Diagnostic
	7. Cost of Rectifying Defects	Operational
	8. Cost in Use	Operational
Quality	1. Defects	Headline
	2. Quality Issues at Available for Use	Operational
	3. Quality Issues at End of Defects Rectification Period	Operational
Client Satisfaction	1. Client s Satisfaction Product – Standard Criteria	Headline
	2. Client Satisfaction Service – Standard Criteria	Headline
	3. Client Satisfaction – Client Specified Criteria	Operational
Change Orders	1. Change Orders – Client	Diagnostic
	2. Change Orders – Project Manager	Diagnostic
Business Performance	1. Profitability (company)	Headline
	2. Productivity (company)	Headline
	3. Return of Capital employed (company)	Operational
	4. Return on Capital employed (company)	Operational
	5. Interest Cover (company)	Operational
	6. Return on Investment (client)	Operational
	7. Profit Predictability (project)	Operational
	8. Ratio of Value Added (company)	Diagnostic
	9. Repeat Business (company)	Diagnostic
	10. Outstanding Money (project)	Diagnostic
	11. Time taken to reach Final Account (project)	Diagnostic
Health and Safety	1. Reportable Accidents (inc fatalities)	Headline
	2. Reportable Accidents (non-fatal)	Operational
	3. Lost Time Accidents	Operational
	4. Fatalities	Operational

6.4.3 Approach: interviews

The following four interviews illustrate the range of views and priorities from a range of senior people working in this field.

Interview with Peter Senior

Notes on an interview with Peter Senior, Arts for Health, Metropolitan University of Manchester, Manchester. Interview held 10 August 1999.

Arts for Health is a research and consultancy department at the Metropolitan University of Manchester which is directed by Peter Senior, who is known as a leading advocate for the promotion of art in health buildings.

I was introduced to his assistant, Philip Pugh (who was originally a craftsman painter and decorator) and David Haley his research co-ordinator. Kath Beavan is their administrator.

Before the meeting I had sent Peter Senior a number of background papers about my research, including the matrix, and the two articles I had written in the *AJ* and *Hospital Development*. He began by referring me to Peter Scher's book about *Patient Focused Architecture* with whom he had collaborated. He also kindly provided me with a copy of a video (£10) that accompanies the book.

He outlined the background to his current work that had started in Manchester in 1973 by trying to bring arts and health together in the hospital environment. Peter Senior had been appointed as the first hospital 'artist in residence' at St Mary's Hospital, Manchester enhancing patient environments. He built up a team of six artists, eventually becoming 14 people, all working from an artistic point of view during the 1970s. He had co-authored the book *Helping to Heal – The Arts in Health Care*, which had been supported by the Gulbenkien Foundation.

Peter Senior had also been part of the Advisory Group set up by Tom Sackville, the then Minister for Health, and told me that NHS Estate's publication *Better by Design* had been written by Mike Nightingale. He referred to a number of other key people who were involved in the programme for introducing art into health buildings at that time including Geoff Mayers, chief architect at the Department of Health, Howard Goodman, also at the Department of Health together with Ross McTaggart and Ann Noble. He thought Ann Noble, currently Chairman of Architects in Health as being well worth talking to.

We then discussed the April 1999 conference which he had organised as a world symposium in Manchester and which had been attended by 500 people from 27 countries. By all accounts this was an important event, and I have arranged to receive the conference proceedings that are due to be published in October. Peter went on to tell me that he was advising the French government that had set up a scheme to co-ordinate the work done in both the health and culture ministries.

Referring back to the early work developed since 1973 and the formation of a research group, Peter said that the Nuffield Group had supported this work and that Sir Kenneth Calman had been involved in this work. Apparently he is interested in literature, the arts, and the humanities and believes that doctors as a group would benefit from being better educated in these fields.

The clinical approach to health care tends to eliminate humanity, and does not aid the process of healing. In the introduction to Peter Scher's book *Patient Focused Architecture for Health Care* he refers to Florence Nightingale's comment written in 1885 that 'the first requirement in a hospital is that it should do the sick no harm'. The clinical approach treats the symptoms but not the cause. The Nuffield Trust supports Arts in Health and encourages arts and humanities in medicine. Generally, the view is that doctors might look more broadly at human life. Peter Senior mentioned that Professor Calman had given a series of talks at the RSA on the relationship between the arts and medicine.

Regarding the World Symposium in April 1999, he mentioned that Roger Ulrich had written to him after the event saying that it had been a most important occasion for him – high praise indeed. Yet Arts in Health is flourishing as a group. The present procurement methods mean that architecture is being constrained. Architecture should catch the spirit. Art is not usually in the brief for new health buildings and the commissioning process is holding at bay art in the health estates process. With regard to GP surgeries, doctors are more directly involved as clients and therefore there is more opportunity to discuss and involve arts and artists in the building process. Peter Senior feels passionately that the arts in health programme cannot be avoided.

He had attended a meeting last week about the co-ordination of arts and sports programmes by the present government. This had been arranged by the Department of Culture, Media and Sport and the Department of Health will be asked to speak to the Arts Group Policy Action Team 10. The government is advocating social inclusion and encouraging opportunities for everyone to be involved. In France he referred to creative *animateurs*, who had been chosen because of their excellent communication skills and their ability to raise aspirations. Art and sports should not be seen in isolation and he referred to Barcelona as an excellent example of the benefits of co-operation in these fields. He thought that increasingly a wide range of initiatives were going on all over the world, and that there was big political capital to be gained through these ideas.

Turning back to his work at the Chelsea and Westminster Hospital he described how he had been closely involved in the introduction of the arts programme which had received very favourable publicity. His unit at the Metropolitan University was funded by a mixture of research funds and consultancy fee income and he believed that the Ministry of Health now recognised the importance of an Arts in Health programme which should be focused at community level.

This impacted on the design process in many ways, including the design for the disabled. He made the interesting observation that hospital patients are temporarily disabled people, and although no architect today would not design for the disabled there was still a large conceptual learning curve needed for designers in this field.

Briefly turning to America, he referred to Wayne Ruga, an American who organised an annual conference every November on environmental issues in health buildings. He noted that a number of American architects were setting up branch offices in the UK to take advantage of the increasing workload in this sector in the UK.

At the conclusion of the interview a number of issues were touched on briefly including the work by artists in Gateshead, led by an enthusiastic arts and recreation officer, Mike White, and the work done at the RVI by Waring and Netts. Germaine Stanger of Northern Arts had been involved in this process and had introduced Dick Ward an artist from Tynemouth who had done some exciting and interesting work. He suggested that I should contact Dr Kevin Windybank, at the Teenage Cancer Department of the RVI where some external murals of the Bigg Market had provided a simulating environment for some very ill teenagers. Time was running out and Peter Senior kindly agreed that it would be useful to keep in touch and exchange views from time to time.

Lecture: 'the arts and health'

The following is a report of a lecture by Professor Sir Kenneth Calman, Vice Chancellor for The University of Durham to the North East region of the RSA on 12 October 1999.

Sir Kenneth started his address by saying that the health record of the population in north-east England was not very good when compared to the rest of the UK. There were significant health problems and he identified five main influences:

- *Genetics*: so far we have been unable to change our genetic makeup but this may change in the future with new bio-medical technology.
- *Environment*: in a broad sense the physical environment influenced our health and in particular urban spaces have been important (e.g. plague of London, Victorian town houses, industrial pollution, etc.).
- *Lifestyle*: three areas are particularly important: smoking, physical fitness and drugs.
- *Social and economic factors*: employment patterns and social exclusion influence where we live and the manner in which we live.
- *Health service*: how is health care delivered and what level of service is provided. This is the least important factor in changing the standard of our health.

The quality and length of life are most influenced by the first four factors.

Sir Kenneth then moved on to discuss the influence of the arts on our health and well-being. He included all the arts, including literature, drama, music, and the visual arts. He said that when he was teaching medical students he had used literature, and in particular short stories, to illustrate ethical issues. In 1984 there was a combined literature and medicine course to discuss ethical and moral issues.

He encouraged his audience to think about what influences our health beyond scientific intervention. For example:

- with doctors does art help?
- with patients does art therapy work?
- does art in the community engender a better sense of well-being?

Calman referred to the work being undertaken by Mike White, Director of Art and Community Work in Gateshead MBC and also to Andrew Mawson who was working in the London's east-end. Community Art was a developing and evolving concept but he questioned how you measure the effectiveness of Community Art. The Nuffield Trust was co-ordinating work in the UK and had established a Centre for Arts and Health. He was interested to explore if the arts make a difference to the quality of life.

He was sure that the arts can play a great part in health care and thought that many hospitals can be depressing. The Marie Curie Centre in Newcastle was an example of a good-quality building which could make a difference to how we feel.

For art in health to become a significant influence in the architecture of health buildings he emphasised that architects would need to demonstrate the quantifiable benefits brought by this approach within business case proposals for new projects.

Moving on, he explored the balance of mind and body and the influence this had on our health. How receptive are we to artistic influences, and he especially referred to music and how it can effect our mood. It may not provide a cure to disease but it may allow you to cope with the problem more constructively and make you feel better.

Following his appointment as Vice Chancellor at Durham University he had secured funds for the appointment of a Director for a research group to study the influence of art and health and he expected this post to be established shortly.

Sir Kenneth ended his well-received address with a 'tongue in cheek' suggestion that perhaps we ought to have a government department of health and happiness.

Interview with Rosalia Staricoff

Notes on an interview with Dr Rosalia Lelchuk Staricoff, Director, Research Project, Chelsea and Westminster Hospital, London.

I met Rosalia at the Chelsea and Westminster Hospital, following my discussion with her at the Stockholm conference. The Chelsea and Westminster Hospital was opened by the Queen on 13 May 1993, and was designed by Sheppard Robson, architects. The development of an arts programme for the new hospital was led by three consultants: Mr James Scott, Dr Adam Lawrence and Dr Richard Staughton and works of art were commissioned at the drawing board stage. The Director of Chelsea and Westminster Hospital Arts is Susan Loppert, who is a winner of the Creative Britons Award sponsored by Prudential. The design of the building is in the form of a series of atria which are covered with translucent panels which allow patients and staff to be aware of the external weather conditions. For example, on a sunny day shafts of sunlight penetrate down into the lower floors of the building.

The arts programme concentrates on the provision of high-quality art which is open to public view and also provides an extensive programme of live performances of theatre, dance, music and opera. The whole programme is funded by private donations, and falls outside of the NHS budget. Certain walls in the hospital are, in effect, an art gallery with artists booking space many months in advance, some of them, I was advised, achieving good sales of their work. There are also a series of large three-dimensional works of art displayed in the atria, including mobiles, sculpture, and wall hangings (e.g. a series of paintings running through several floors representing a waterfall).

This has led to questions arising about patient benefits from this programme of artworks, and hence the appointment of Rosalia to carry out research work. This research is the first scientific 'Study of the Effects of the Visual and Performing Art in Healthcare'.

During my short visit she kindly gave me a whistle stop tour of the building and also explained her research programme. She had interviewed clinical staff to identify if there was a perceived clinical benefit and this has led to a series of evaluations being undertaken. Clinical staff have been enthusiastic in their support for her work.

- A consultant in chemotherapy was interested in assessing if arts can lower the level of anxiety amongst outpatients coming to the hospital to receive chemotherapy treatment. Using an internationally accepted scale of assessment a study was set up to record patients' responses in absence (control group) or presence of live music (trial group). Patients receiving their treatment were exposed to 40 minutes of music and she said the effects were immediately obvious. Some patients didn't want

the music to stop and others, who were withdrawn and nervous, became more communicative and responsive.
- Another experiment used a six-week rota of art exhibitions. The paintings were provided by 'Painting in Hospitals' and represented different types of art. The results for these studies are now being analysed in collaboration with a medical statistician.

Ms Lelchuk Staricoff also described how they were moving onto research with women and children, but she pointed out that the Ethics Committee had not approved any work with children. They were currently discussing the establishment of a programme in the maternity department looking at different stages of pregnancy – looking at post-natal, anti-natal and delivery rooms. All the protocols had to be agreed in advance with the ethics committee.

Note: a large donation box in the form of a sculpture designed by Sir Eduardo Paolozzi stands in the entrance area. For another example of Sir Eduardo Paolozzi's work see the sculpture recently erected outside the recently refurbished Central Square building adjacent to Newcastle Central Station.

Interview with Sir Donald Irvine

Notes on an interview with Sir Donald Irvine, President of the General Medical Council

I met Sir Donald Irvine shortly before he steps down as President of the General Medical Council, at the end of a term of office spanning six-and-a-half years and covering a period of considerable change in the medical profession. He has overseen a shift in emphasis towards consumer pressure for greater autonomy in the management of an individual's health care. However, he said that he is not conscious of a shift in government policy for the design quality of health buildings. His perception is that the government continues to give priority to functionality and cost when evaluating funding priorities and that the government has not shown interest in design quality.

Having worked for Sir Donald as a client, over 10 years ago, when he was senior partner of a GP practice in Ashington, Northumberland, he was advocating the importance of good design, and the benefits that could flow through to patient care if a building environment added to a sense of well-being. He went further, and said that he believes that it is a duty to promote a sense of well-being and that the working environment was very important for doctors and staff.

The health service does not have a good record in these matters and successive governments have neglected design, quality and the ethos of health buildings, including primary health care buildings. He is a great advocate and supporter of the pioneering work carried out by Avedis Donabedan in developing the structure, process and outcome of patient care and patient satisfaction levels. As a pioneer in quality measurement in medicine, he also foresaw the importance of quality of the environment and linked the goodness of care with the goodness of the environment.

He believes that architects and doctors should combine to create better buildings and referred to the wave of good primary care surgeries that have been built over the past two decades under the cost rent scheme. However, primary care was moving on, and society demanded that primary care should be community focused. There was a change in the social agenda as patients become increasingly demanding as consumers. With greater

wealth, the middle classes of the UK could afford to be more selective and this was driving the policies for future health buildings of which the government must take note. Well-designed buildings for primary care in the future must, therefore, reflect the needs of an individual community and provide the services required by the people living in the vicinity of the new building.

Primary health care: questions/issues for discussion

- List of advisors in national plan – no construction representatives.
- Doctors – moving away from owning property – salaried members of PCTs.
- Patient focused primary care – effects of telemedicine, new technology, e-mail appointments.
- Influence on new primary care buildings:
  - flexibility/change of use
  - additional facilities
  - a 'different' place.
- NHS direct/walk-in centres/mobile clinics.
- The patient as a consumer/consumerism.
- Comparison with opticians/commercial business employing the professionals – will this happen to GPs (e.g. what are Boots the Chemist's plans)?
- The arts and humanities: Sir Kenneth Calman's new research group (CAHHM) in Durham (Director: Dr Jane MacNaughton) Centre for Arts and Humanities in Health and Medicine.
- Future training of doctors – a holistic approach.
- Environmental factors for 'healthy living' – better patient outcomes shown by research in hospitals.
- NHS as property owners/PFI/Procure21.
- Importance of the building fabric in delivering medical services? – Government priorities.
- Evaluation of South Tees new hospital.

6.4.4 Consequences and outcomes: establish briefing process recommendations

Start with quality.

If design quality is to be of a high standard consultants need to be adequately remunerated and therefore deep discounting of professional fees is completely counterproductive to achieving buildings which will delight the user, and more significantly to the Treasury they will be poor value, almost certainly, when judged long term on a value for money basis. What appears to be a premium cost at the beginning of a project may seem a very small sum indeed to pay for a facility which will offer long-term efficiency, and as an added bonus provide an attractive pleasing and comfortable environment for all users of the building.

The briefing process should start with the aims and objectives being set out clearly and precisely. Time should not be skimped and there are many well-established methodologies which can be deployed to explore the needs of future building users through (e.g. face-to-face interviews, user groups), as well as identifying an individual project champion who is going to drive forward the whole concept.

In other sectors of construction, and the commercial office building sector is a good example, there has been considerable development in researching the procurement methodologies. As might be expected, they tend to be based on management philosophies, derived from a business school approach to efficiency, accountability, logic and analytical audit trails to demonstrate a rigorous examination of all the issues. But medical buildings are different: the emotional responses are highly charged by most patients when visiting a health facility and the spiritual dimension is brought more sharply into focus than when walking into your office for another day at work.

Putting it rather simply, design methodologies have evolved along a linear route from inception to final design, and this has been the case for most building types. More recently, design methodologies have become more sophisticated, with the benefit of additional research, and the circular nature of some design decisions have been built into some design approaches, and these were looked at in Chapter 3. The business school approach has been excellently developed for commercial buildings, particularly by Frank Duffy and his practice DEGW. A recent book by his colleagues *Managing the Brief for Better Design* sets out a thorough review of the briefing process (Blyth and Worthington, 2001). But I would argue that the book leaves largely unanswered the question of how to deal with an assessment of quality factors. We must build on the pioneering, and very important work of this group of researchers and take the briefing process for medical buildings into the realms of delightfulness. Indeed, Robin Nicholson who wrote the forward for this book is a leading advocate of the campaign within the architectural profession, supported, as we have seen, by CABE, and now taken on board by the Government itself to introduce the emotional responses that influence the design of buildings. If we are suc-

cessful in achieving this, then indeed we will be producing civic buildings of dignity again, an art which was lost throughout much of the last century.

How to achieve this, of course, is a much more demanding and complex issue – but this area of research will provide a fruitful source for the improvement of procuring health buildings in the future. So how do we go about it? Tentatively, I would suggest, by putting the emotional factors ahead of the technical requirements. Ultimately, the two sides of this equation will be balanced on the pivot of 'value for money'.

The quality issues which might be considered include:

- What overall impression does the client want the building to convey? The consulting room remains a fundamental interface between doctor and patient. What atmosphere does the doctor wish to create? Are there options? Is there a couch and a coffee table for a more relaxed atmosphere for sensitive conversations rather than the traditional answer of diagonally across the corner of a desk? Obviously, this begs a question of how long consultations should last, and the answer obviously is that they will vary from case to case. However, it is obvious that there is all the difference in the world between a short consultation to deal with a sore throat and the discussion which may be needed with a patient facing a serious operation.
- The design of a primary care centre will be heavily influenced by the system used by patients to call the next patient. It is a flashing light, an intercom, or even the doctor coming out to greet the patient individually.
- Consider environmental aspects: view of nature; five senses – touch, smell, taste, hearing, vision; atmosphere – homely relaxing, professional relaxing.
- Connections with the outside: urban context; entrance/ approach; communications/transport links.
- Spending time thinking and writing about the 'delight' factor which medical buildings should strive to achieve is the starting point to a successful briefing process.

7

Measurement of design quality

The measurement of design quality is an area of study that several large organisations have started to take an interest in over the past few years. It is likely that this is a reflection of consumerism,[1] and an awareness to respond ever more closely to the needs of an organisation's customers. It is also the result of greater affluence in our society leading to more time to enjoy those aspects of life which improve its quality. The start of the twenty-first century will see the flourishing of a second renaissance conceived in the last decade of the twentieth century when leisure time meant for many people that they could enjoy a longer life, good food, music, and show an interest in the design of their personal space beyond that ever experienced by any previous generation. The plethora of television programmes giving advice on gardening and decorating and redesigning houses illustrates the potential demand for high-quality environments and an awareness of well-being. What is much more difficult to achieve, is to attempt to measure these design qualities, and give them quantitative values. Most families now have access to a car and people seem to be able to make the value for money judgements necessary in choosing a particular model. Likewise, we all make value for money judgements when deciding on everyday purchases for clothes and food. However, the construction industry has for decades been wedded to the concept of lowest price as the best procurement route for new buildings. Slowly, and to some extent reluctantly, this outdated concept is being brought into line with other consumer products but there is a long way to go before wholelife costing is seen as a better way to judge the performance of a building. As architects well know, the problem often starts with exceptionally low fee bids reducing consultancy remuneration for design to meagre and pitiful levels – the result being an almost inevitable dilution of design quality.

Fortunately, these ideas are being superseded and the trickle of good design statements is rapidly turning into a torrent of support for better public buildings.

The measurement of design quality has frequently been understood to be an assessment, in numeric terms, of the relative values of various aspects of a building's performance (some quantitative examples are given in Chapter 3). This might vary from the subjective assessment of the emotional responses of an individual to a particular building, to the measurement of the efficiency or effectiveness of building services when tested against a performance specification. For example, the efficiency of a heating system can be compared to the design standards set in a performance specification; does the temperature in a particular room achieve the target temperature within the design tolerances? However, it is more difficult to provide meaningful data by asking a visitor to a GP surgery whether or not the entrance area was welcoming, by expecting that person to score their opinion on a scale of 1–10.

The crude mechanisms implicit in this type of analysis are easy to criticise. However, the shortage of serious research in this field has left designers vulnerable to criticism by those responsible for allocating capital expenditure where detailed business case studies are regarded as a pre-requisite before expenditure can be authorised.

The difficulties caused by this lack of information has been increasingly recognised over the last few years and the measurement of design quality is entering a period of greater scrutiny by those responsible for allocating funds for future building projects. Much work remains to be done, and the techniques need to be developed and refined so that more sophisticated models can be used for better evaluation of design quality.

NHS Estates – *Better by Design*

In 1994 NHS Estates produced an excellent booklet *Better by Design* (NHS Estates, 1994) which sets out a statement of good intentions. It recognised the need to focus attention on better-quality design in the health sector and it urged all those responsible for commissioning health buildings to be more vigilant in their pursuit of excellence. At that time, the control of design quality was seen to be largely the responsibility of architects commissioned to design buildings using the strict guidelines of data sheets and cost limits set out in the copious documentation provided by the business managers in NHS Estates. Although full of good intentions, was it more that a wish list of aspirations, seeking to cajole those responsible for commissioning health buildings to pay greater attention to design quality? With the benefit of hindsight, it is easy to see that the well-intentioned aims of this booklet lacked the teeth that its authors no doubt wished it should have. More importantly, it was a first step in the process of opening up greater interest in design quality in health buildings.

In the foreword to *Better by Design* the then junior minister of state for health, Tom Sackville, quoted Florence Nightingale 'The very first condition to be sought in planning a building is that it shall be fit for its purpose. And the first architectural law is that fitness is the foundation of beauty. The hospital architect may feel assured that, only when he has planned the building which will afford the best chance of speedy recovery to sick and maimed people, will his architecture and the economy he seeks be realised.' Mr Sackville went on to say that 'The new NHS structure will help the procurers of health buildings to meet the challenge. Decision making has been brought closer to the grass roots. Not only do Trusts have a greater responsibility to all the community served, but there is also greater freedom than ever before to influence the quality of their estate.'

The document ahead of its time when published went on to set out a number of statements setting targets or aspirations for those responsible for commissioning health buildings. It also contained appendices giving a checklist of design pointers and offering guidance on selecting design teams with a view to raising the expectations and standards of quality and cost. It also recognises the inherent potential that patients may recover more quickly in a well-designed building.

However, the document offered no mechanisms to quantify, or evaluate these statements of good intentions, or aspirations. It is not until more recently that more work has been done on developing analytical methodologies for measurement techniques.

It recognises the need to make statements about aspirations and design expectations but does not offer any mechanisms to actually measure design quality. It exhorts clients within the health sector to aim for high standards, but at the time, there was no alternative process other than to build within the technical framework of cost limits and space standards defined by the NHS.

English Partnership – *Time for Design*

Several other major commissioning bodies have made attempts to define design standards, and explore mechanisms for evaluating design quality in projects for which they commissioned. English Partnership set up regional design panels. The intention was to subject projects that were being commissioned to an independent panel of experts for an informal check on design quality. This attempt at self-appraisal by a client was in response to their recognition that design quality matters. English Partnership (1998) also produced a booklet *Time for Design* which offered advice on good practice in building, landscape and urban design. In comparison to the NHS Estates document, the booklet produced by English Partnership offered guidance and advice mainly about the context of buildings in the urban scene. Prefaced by Lord Rogers it anticipated that some of the concerns explored by the urban white paper, 'Towards an Urban Renaissance'. It set out to encourage good practice and listed design principles which were mainly about environmental good manners and respect for the neighbourhood in which the building was to be built. It linked good design with commercial sense and placed a high value on the sense of place. It reminded designers to consider site assessment, environmental impact, energy efficiency, transportation linkages, and the impact that buildings have on the community in which they are situated. It states 'English Partnership seeks to involve the community in the design process.' By consultation with community groups a dialogue will be established to provide information about their aspirations and expectations. It is people who regenerate places, and not places that regenerate people (see Chapter 9).

It does include a section about the changing workplace and the need for flexibility in buildings but no formulas are offered to measure design performance. The limitations of these guides shows, on the one hand, how they were at the forefront of thinking, and yet the construction industry remains constrained and locked in a time warp of design and build procurement systems where wholelife costs were discussed but invariably dismissed on the basis of minimum capital expenditure on completion. This may say as much about the funding of construction in the UK, both in the private sector, and also in Government expenditure.

Royal Fine Art Commission

In the education sector, the design quality in higher education buildings was explored at a Royal Fine Art Commission seminar held on 21 November 1995 with a keynote address by Lord Palumbo (Royal Fine Art Commission, 1996). In the same way that therapeutic benefits are now being recognised in health care design it foresaw the potential benefit that 'Buildings should be of such quality that they impress their users and those to see them, so aiding in the most subtle way the learning process.' This is a crucial connection linking economic benefit to good design but no evidence base was offered to back up this theory. Increasingly, the linkages were being made by informed thinkers that good design offered real cost benefits. 'Universities depend for their funding upon perception of value, for it is value which attracts the students who ensure the flow of funds. Architecture is an expression of value and the reputation of universities will depend, at least in part, upon the extent to which their building programmes fulfil that concept of value and project visions of excellence'. Richard MacCormac expressed these sentiments in his paper to the conference, which was entitled 'Filling the Purpose of Architecture in Higher Education'. This trend towards greater interest in the measurability of design quality has led a number of groups to undertake studies and prepare reports on this subject. NHS Estates produced an advisory document looking at the improvement of quality and design of health care buildings. The Treasury assembled a high powered group of contributors who contributed towards the preparation of Technical Note No. 7 – How to Achieve Design Quality in PFI Projects. More recently the Construction Industry Council (CIC) prepared a report 'Can we measure the Quality of Design in Buildings?' These themes are picked up by CABE who are providing a pivotal and overarching role in focusing attention on the importance of design quality in the future building stock of England

Design quality benchmarking

The NHS Estates' approach (NHS Estates, 1999) has been to look at the development of a design quality benchmarking method. It is based on a scoring technique, which can be used to evaluate both design proposals and completed buildings. The work of NHS Estates acknowledges that health buildings create a number of special demands on designers including:

- *Complex functions*: a huge range of surgical and medical sciences, transport, logistics, support and social functions, including high-tech equipment and IT systems, as well as restaurant and leisure areas. Not only the preserve of hospitals, increasingly these activities will need to be considered as part of primary health care buildings.
- *Range of types of health care*: design must deliver buildings that reflect service needs, ranging through local primary care facilities, mental health care day facilities and major acute hospitals.
- *Therapeutic environments*: improving the quality of design for health buildings involves no only the consideration of its civic and social contribution, as well as providing the best environment to heal and reassure patients, and provide staff and visitors with high quality surroundings. Research illustrates the links between good design and recovery, security and efficiency. Sadly limited in extent, this area of work needs to be expanded and developed.

The promotion of high-quality design is a combination of meeting functional requirements, and providing an enhancing environment for the healing of patients. 'It is this convergence of architectural aspiration, with functional requirements in an appropriate healing environment, which makes health buildings unique ...'. Figure 7.1 illustrates NHS Estates ideas.

The development of a quality benchmarking method by NHS Estates has been described in Chapter 3.

They have devised a framework of the main characteristics of design quality. As the model and benchmarking methodology are developed the complete list of criteria will be identified.

Similar themes have been explored up by the Construction Industry Council (CIC) who have extended the work of NHS

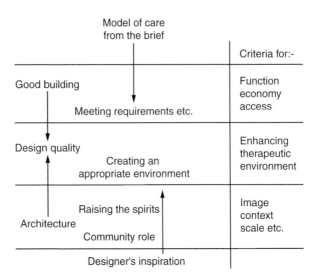

Figure 7.1 Architecture for health care. Source: NHS Estates, 1999

Estates, the Housing Forum (Housing Performance Indicators), MARU (Medical Architecture Research Unit), M4I (Movement for Innovation) and others. Clearly, the interest in this field is broadening rapidly and over the next few years it can be anticipated that a large body of research work will emerge and extend our understanding of the measurement of design quality. Until such time, we will continue to debate the challenge between scientific and social responses, discussing the tangible and intangible components of evaluation techniques. Of course, the intangible concepts may become tangible if measuring techniques become sophisticated enough to quantify the human responses and emotional reactions which we normally associate with subjective (or intangible) reactions.

Construction Industry Council

The CIC report opens with Corbusier's view of design quality 'In assessing design quality, it has to be remembered that each individual has a different proportion of artistic and spiritual or scientific and social response to the design at hand.' He argued that there is a creative tension between spiritual man and economic man where knowledge of man and of physical laws are the drivers of creative imagination, beauty, freedom of choice, etc. Indeed the actual response to a building or construction for each individual comes from the balance of their individual response to the range of stimuli – social, spatial, acoustical, visual, thermal to the environment at hand. (See also Figure 7.2.)

Commission for Architecture and the Built Environment

In searching for the next steps in measuring design quality a number of research groups are engaged on explorations of

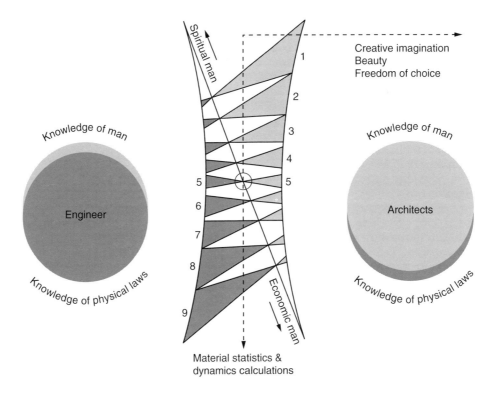

Figure 7.2   Source: CIC, www.cic.org.uk

this task. The CIC, working on behalf of CABE 'Has set up a multi-disciplinary group to make proposals for performance indicators to measure the effect of design on the satisfaction gained from building development. This initiative response to the prime minister's focus on design and value and the Government's view that quality of design is the essential feature in success of development and customer satisfaction.' Interestingly, it accepts the premise that design can be considered within two broad categories: product and process.

Product and the assessment of the construction process is represented by M4I issues and product looks at the concept stages of design and procurement methodologies. The report goes on to state 'Measurement of customer satisfaction is a partly abstract process which couples "tangible" performance indicators to "intangible" assessments. The CIC study is to focus on the added value which professional services bring to delight, functionality and added value of developments in the built environment.'

Susan Francis of MARU is attributed with the formulation of a framework for the evaluation of design quality encompassing the overlapping features of therapy (delight), function (purpose) and sustainability (resources). They are defined as follows:

• Therapy related to user perception, the psychology and to the appeal performance base.
• Function to use for health care, of the site and satisfactory operation.

• Sustainability to social purpose, economics and environmental performance.

Manning (1991) is quoted as distinguishing between the subjective environmental qualities and physical environmental qualities:

Environmental quality (subjective)	Environmental qualities (physical)
character	temperature
atmosphere	illuminance
ambiences	sound levels
images, etc.	ventilation rates, etc.

All of the above approaches accept a differentiation between subjective and quantifiable factors. In other words, there is an acceptance that there are tangible and intangible qualities that need to be considered in the assessment of the design of a building. However, let us suppose that intangible concepts are merely aspects of design for which only limited techniques have been developed so far – at least so far as their involvement in the interpretation of architectural factors is concerned. The measurement of 'architectural meaning' is central to the work being undertaken at Nottingham University. Perhaps, at some time in the future we will be as adept at measuring whether or not a building is comfortable, relaxing, or friendly, as easily as we are able to measure temperature and energy consumption today.

Another example of an attempt to stretch measuring techniques to value design is the urban research carried out by CABE (2001). This work found that good urban design:

- Adds economic, social and environmental value and does not necessarily cost more or take longer to deliver.
- Delivers high investment returns for developers and investors by meeting a clear occupy demand. It also helps to attract investors.
- Enhances workforce performance and satisfaction and it increases occupier prestige.
- Delivers economic benefits by opening up new investment opportunities and delivering more successful regeneration.
- Helps to deliver places accessible to and enjoyed by all.
- Benefits all stakeholders – investors, developers, designers, occupiers, public authorities and everyday users of developments.

Table 7.1 Making architecture accessible (source: NHS Estates, 1999)

	General concerns:
Economy and sustainability	
Example criteria:	
• economic building	Life cycle costing
• energy usage	
• low maintenance	Flexibility for change
Efficiency	
Example criteria:	Design for reduced operating costs
• logistics	
• workflow	
• durability	Well organised building
Functionality	
Example criteria:	Space standards and relationships
• convenience	
• comfort	
• privacy and dignity	Therapeutic environment

Note: architectural quality is subjective. The following part of the framework aims at making architecture accessible.

- How can we describe our architectural aspirations?
- How can we recognise a good architectural composition?
- What are the means of expression and how can we read them in our visual environment?

Good architecture
- civic/social
- life-enhancing   *What it's about*
- aesthetic

Concept
- context
- scale   *Creating a composition*
- harmony

Expression
- form and space
- light and shade   *The raw materials*
- colour and texture

Table 7.2 Example checklist (source: NHS Estates, 1999)

Good hospital design should:

Be good architecture
- contribute positively to its community and civic context ❏
- provide a pleasing composition ❏
- be aesthetically uplifting both externally and internally ❏

Fit into its surroundings
- be a good neighbour to adjoining buildings ❏
- fit well on the site and meet Town Planning requirements ❏

Create a user friendly, healing environment
- a pleasant, external appearance, with a human scale ❏
- an obvious main entrance and easy-to-find special entrances ❏
- a welcoming entrance and reception area ❏
- a simple, clear plan for easy wayfinding ❏
- a reassuring internal appearance with views to the outside ❏
- natural daylight and ventilation to occupied areas ❏
- comfort and privacy where needed ❏
- space, colour, light, views, and art to enhance healing process ❏
- pleasantly landscaped surrounding areas and internal courtyards ❏

Provide a safe and secure environment
- design for health and safety ❏
- clear fire planning principles ❏
- design for security control ❏

Provide easy access for
- ambulances, public transport, service vehicles and fire appliances ❏
- cars for visitors and staff with adequate car parking ❏
- pedestrian access to the building ❏
- easy access for disabled people ❏
- separate access for goods deliveries and waste disposal ❏

Reflect appropriate health building standards
- be based on appropriate space standards ❏
- reflect Health Building Notes guidance ❏
- reflect Health Technical Memoranda standards ❏

Be efficient
- in relationship of functions ❏
- in movement of people and distribution of supplies ❏
- in utilisation or space ❏

Be economic and sustainable
- in staffing and operation ❏
- in energy utilisation ❏
- in building maintenance ❏

Be flexible
- adaptable to respond to change of use ❏
- expandable to meet changing demand ❏
- phaseable for planning, construction stages or future development ❏

Specify appropriate constructional standards
- Building materials and finishes should be appropriate to use ❏
- finishes should be easy and economic to maintain ❏
- Engineering systems should be organised for ease of use and future adaptation ❏

This research, undertaken by the Bartlett School of Planning at the University of London on behalf of CABE, was based on commercial examples of property development. However, the same techniques could be transferred to the health sector, including primary health facilities.

The market economy, driven by public companies reporting to their shareholders bi-annually through Stock Exchange reports inevitably means that capital employed is measured against short-term performance returns and it seems that it has all been almost impossible to extend these arguments to take note of the longer term benefits of good design when applied to wholelife costing within the building industry.

The launch of the urban and rural white papers, by the Government at the end of 2000 marked another step in the move towards greater understanding of the complex relationship between quality of life, wholelife costs, and the short terms of building procurement systems in the UK. At long last a series of recommendations begin to address the issues we need to consider to ensure the future provision of high quality urban spaces. Inextricably tied up with both planning and transportation policies the scale of these issues falls far outside the scope of this book. However, there may well be a cascade effect from the macro-economic issues discussed in these two white papers to the micro-economics of the health sector, and in particular primary health care buildings.

It is precisely the balance between these issues attempting to define the quality of life and the pragmatic requirements of a market economy that has led to a pilot study being initiated at the new PFI hospital for South Tees Hospital Trust. A £120 million project commenced on site early in 2000 and is due for completion in the spring of 2003 has an ambitious and forward-looking brief. It sets out parameters for patient care, and a high quality healing environment. The PFI contract has transferred accountability of the design team from the client (South Tees Hospital Trust) to the contractor (Mowlem/Crown House Engineering).

Urgent studies are needed to allow the measurement of these conflicting issues so that value judgements can be made about the success of the procurement route.

Note

1. Consumerism is the rise of customer influence over the suppliers of goods and services. Underpinned by the Human Rights Act, consumers now exert considerable strength in negotiating contracts and the law generally leans towards the individual rather than an organisation (e.g. employer, manufacturer, or service provider) if a dispute arises.

8

Procurement routes

The condition of the existing estate

Procurement routes are changing. Primary health care facilities are becoming larger multi-functional 'healthy living centres' offering integrated health and care services. A variety of agencies and professional skills will work in buildings serving the local community. Private finance will be provided by specialist developers and local initiatives will ensure greater control of matching requirements will services.

This will have the benefit of allowing the new community facilities to include a wider range of services such as pharmacies, dentists, physiotherapists, and alternative or complimentary medical practitioners to all work under one roof.

As health and care services become more integrated the new community buildings, or healthy living centres, will grow in size and become multi-functional with a target of 500 new healthy living centres by 2004 opportunities for small and medium practices are set to expand. Building costs can be expected to range between £500,000 and £5 million.

The health minister, Alan Milburn, has said when he announced the publication of a report on the progress as necessary to improve the NHS Estate (February 2001):

> 'One-third of our hospitals were built before the NHS was created, and one-tenth date back to Victorian times. You cannot deliver twenty-first century care in nineteenth century buildings.
>
> For too long investment in NHS infrastructure has been a low priority when it should have been a high priority. Capital investment in the NHS was lower at the end of the last Parliament than it was at the beginning. The consequences are plain for all to see. Buildings that are shoddy, equipment that is unreliable, hospitals that are out of date.'

Kate Priestly, Chief Executive of NHS Estates when speaking at the CABE conference in London on 6 February 2001 restated that the NHS has the largest property portfolio in Europe. However, 30% of the estate was built before 1940.

As part of NHS Estates' plan to raise the importance of design quality to meet the aspirations set out in the NHS Plan 2000 the biggest ever hospital building programme in the history of the NHS has been launched with a £7 billion capital investment planned by 2010. By then, 40% of the NHS Estate is planned to be less than 15 years old. Part of this plan is to achieve a £1 billion investment in primary care facilities.

Construction targets

Primary care buildings have faired better during the last 20 years, with some excellent projects having been constructed, showing innovation in design and procurement. Potentially better is to come following the announcements in the NHS Plan:

- refurbish or replace 3000 GPs premises
- build 500 'non-stop' primary care centres by 2004

The formation of primary care trusts is an important policy change creating separate legal entities that can own property and act as clients. Previously GPs were the main client body, often raising their own commercial loans to finance surgery buildings. Problems of negative equity have arisen and this has discouraged younger doctors to take on the responsibilities of debt to finance their partnership aspirations. The attractions of salaried employment has encouraged specialist developers to offer long term leases for new premises.

How are these ambitious investment plans going to be achieved? The construction industry as a whole is witnessing an upheaval in its procedures, and procurement routes, which are more radical than at any time in the past 50 years. In the mid-1980s over 70% of construction was procured using 'traditional' contractual arrangements but this had reduced to less than 40% by 1998. The past 20 years has seen an unprecedented upsurge in new contractual arrangements between client and builders which has all had an impact on the way in which design teams have been employed and briefed. There has been a decline in the traditional role of quantity surveyors, the emergence of project managers as a separate professional discipline, design and build contracts have offered maximum price building costs but all too often there was disappointment about the finished building. The translation of design aspirations often led to disappointment in the realisation of the finished product. Buildings were often over budget, delivered late, and had too many defects. The Latham Report (1994), *Constructing the Team*, was the first major investigation which set out to examine how buildings were commissioned and built in the UK. This was followed in 1998 by the Egan Report, *Rethinking Construction*, and this document concentrated on improving the construction industry by viewing it as a manufacturing process. It identified targets to reduce defects, reduce costs, encourage standardisation of components, and offer continuity of work by encouraging the major clients to enter into framework agreements with selected contractors and design teams.

Many architects were concerned about the implications of these reports on their profession believing that their influence would be diminished and that they would be marginalised by big guns in the major contractors and client bodies – and for a while these concerns were probably well founded.

More recently, stimulated by a refocusing of effort in looking at the quality of the product, as well as the quality of the process there has been a resurgence of concern for high standards of design. These arguments are covered elsewhere in this book. Society has become more aware of the importance of a sustainable, environmentally friendly environment and is developing an understanding for designs which embrace the quality of life factors – the joy and delight that architecture can add to the fabric of society. This highlights the need to fundamentally shift priorities in the current briefing process. The ethos of the organisation must be the springboard for the development of the brief.

Procurement routes are therefore changing, and developing to reflect these requirements:

- Criticism of the PFI route: architects have felt their influence constrained by often being expected to work speculatively, or at peppercorn rates, during the competitive bidding stages of appointment often taking many months (if not years) to reach a conclusion and to feeling subservient to the main contractor after their novation in a winning team and sometimes loosing authority over their own designs.
- Procure21: the NHS Estates proposals for meeting Government expectations for repeat business to a selected list of approved large contractors but subject to much criticism by medium sized architects and contractors.
- The newly proposed LIFT scheme promises to meet many of the difficulties inherent in the other procurement routes particularly for primary health care facilities.

The potential damaged caused by the marginalisation of small- and medium-sized enterprises in the procurement route is considerable with a loss of skills, resources, and local knowledge. There should be a rejection of policies that polarise organisations as either small or very large. The damage done to medium-sized contractors, architects, and many others in the design process is likely to be enormous.

Local Improvement Finance Trust

The imminent launch of the Local Improvement Finance Trust (LIFT), is a new initiative to stimulate the funding and operation of future primary health care facilities. This proposal has superceded the earlier concept of batching primary care facilities together to form the 'critical mass' necessary to carry out improvement work under PFI rules. Newcastle had been a pilot study area for the batching of 32 primary health care buildings to create such a single contract opportunity under PFI rules. The outline business case (OBC) had been prepared, but for a variety of reasons the number of sites was reduced to 22. Extensive and helpful comments were received on the OBC from the regional office. However, the launch of the NHS Plan included proposals for LIFT which is designed to introduce private finance in a structure which devolves responsibility down to smaller building blocks at a regional and local level. Figure 8.1 illustrates how initial funding provided by the Treasury and the Department of Health passes to an independent company that would seek additional funding from institutions in the private sector. This company would have a Board of Advisers and oversee the allocation of funds to regionally organise LIFT companies. These in turn will attract further finance from local authorities, housing associations and primary care trusts and would operate with local boards.

The regional LIFT companies would then seek to enter into joint venture agreements with local developers to provide new local primary care facilities. Hence, the initial Government funding is designed to lever in a substantial proportion of private finance. A concern is whether the local companies would be of sufficient size (i.e. big enough) to provide competencies in the key areas of:

- strategy
- construction
- facilities management and health services.

It might be anticipated that all these skills may be difficult to find within one company which would be of a size commensurate with the scale of project envisaged at a local level (see postscript at end of Chapter 12).

Local responsiveness and flexibility

To provide high quality local primary care facilities requires flexibility, and a local responsiveness to the needs and requirements that are particular to a community. It can be argued that the provision of the physical building should be separated from the provision of health services and the attendant facilities management needs during the life of a lease. Other sectors of the building industry and property market make clearer distinctions between the provision of the buildings and the operation of the services within them. As discussed elsewhere the office market has clearer structures which govern the way buildings are commissioned and occupied. Although some building owners occupy their own building, a much more sophisticated briefing process has evolved in recent years to enable a greater understanding of flexibility, efficiency and satisfaction by the people who use the spaces. The development of similarly comprehensive briefing documents should be a pre-requisite for all new primary health buildings.

Within the structure of NHS Estates regional responsibilities are also limited to an expenditure level of £25 million. This will also limit the size of packages which can be put together at a local level if responsibility and accountability is to be kept within the communities requiring the services. Site acquisition is likely to be a critical factor, and location is a crucial component in the success of a primary health care building.

It seems essential, therefore, to ensure that this imaginative initiative is fully explored at a local level, to ensure that the mechanisms are in place to provide the flexibility and responsiveness which will be required to its success. Medium sized developers, consultants and construction firms will need to work together so that collectively the competencies required are provided. This fundamentally different approach to PFI will encourage a 'bottom up' rather than a 'top down' approach to new solutions.

There are those who argue for repetition, and standardisation in the provision of primary health care facilities leading to ideas of the same building being reproduced on many sites. An analogy might be drawn to the standardisation of fast food outlets such as McDonalds, or even the larger supermarket operators such as Tesco or Sainsbury where there is a standardisation of building design. However, the health service is not dispensing commodities; people do not go to their GP to buy off-the-shelf products and the diversity of services suggests that primary care demands a more flexible solution which will respond to local needs, and the peculiarities of a particular community. Perhaps there will be components of a building which could be standardised but health care needs to accommodate the social values that can flow from flexible and humane spaces.

Government aspirations for good design

With better design being seen as part of New Labour's 'Cool Britannia' architects find themselves in the position of political encouragement from the highest level. How is this manifesting itself on the ground? The public sector programme being led by Sir Steve Robson at the Treasury may have some validity for the handful of big hospitals which NHS Estates has to deliver over the next few years. But how will it be able to implement this policy for the multitude of small community based health projects that are going to form the backbone to the primary care health sector in the future and that will need to mesh with local conditions. Their success will depend on the ability to be flexible and responsive to compliment existing patterns of housing, education, shopping, and transport systems.

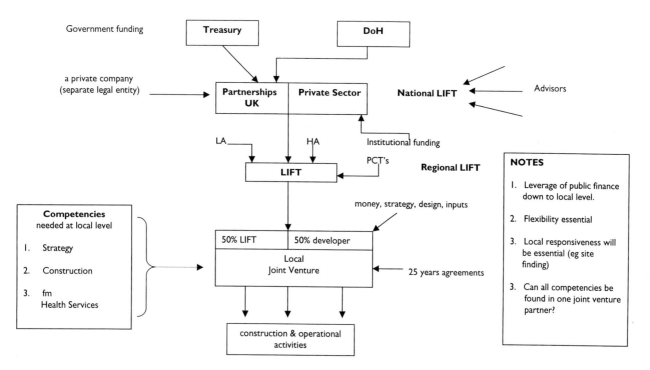

Figure 8.1 Diagram of possible structure for LIFT (Local Improvement Finance Trust)

The emphasis coming out of PPG3 which the private house building companies are being asked to follow places the emphasis on good design very much at the level of the local planning authority. Although PPG3 recognises that there may be building technologies to be examined by the house builders the emphasis is on 'small is beautiful'.

Therefore, is good design sitting in the middle of procurement methodologies that are diametrically opposed? The Government is encouraging partnering which is perhaps a response to dealing with decades of frustration in delivering big projects behind programme and above budget. The Egan philosophy of productivity benefits and economies of scale have yet to be proven in the construction industry where each project is a unique product. It is very different to the production line technologies of twentieth century economic theory of supply and demand. A knowledge based sustainable environment has more to do with recognising the uniqueness and individuality of each site.

The challenge for NHS Estates is to find procurement methodologies that meet Treasury objectives, that don't stifle high quality design, and offer flexibility, not standardisation. The Government has set out its aspirations for good design and is looking to the private house building industry to rise to this challenge. However, will it be able to achieve the same high standards of design for the big public sector projects via partnering? Perhaps the private sector might just have an opportunity to demonstrate its flexibility and responsiveness by producing better quality designs, that are also better value, be it for housing, or privately funded community health projects.

Local competencies

Partnering at small and medium levels of contract size also offers potential for productive working relationships. If the LIFT programme is to be successful co-operation at a local level to allow specialist skills to flourish would seem to argue against all the necessary competencies being provided by one organisation. One possible split is:

- strategic
- construction
- facilities management and health services.

By allowing competencies to evolve at local level suggests the willingness to consider separately function and ownership of primary health care facilities. The provision of health services and their management and maintenance are quite different to the skills required to build a high quality flexible building, that is sustainable, environmentally friendly, and efficient to run. The LIFT programme by encouraging the leverage into the system of private finance provides every opportunity to develop the more sophisticated marketplace for the provision of primary health care buildings.

9

International trends

We have seen how the development of Western medical practice is returning, once again, to being patient centred, although the reasons today are very different to those of previous centuries. This trend is bringing the most advanced medical techniques and practices back onto a path that is converging with the aspirations of the poorest countries in the world. Western civilisations, with advanced scientific technologies in the medical field have once again begun to understand the importance of alternative therapies and a more holistic approach to healing environments. Poorer countries, struggling to finance sophisticated medical policies continue to provide a community based primary health care service often involving traditional remedies.

World Health Organisation: health for all

The most important achievement for international public health over the past 50 years is that today people are living longer. The average life expectancy at birth has increased dramatically from 46 years in the 1950s to 65 years in 1995. The gap in life expectancy between rich and poor countries has narrowed from 25 years in 1955 to 13.3 years in 1995. Today, common standards can be applied throughout the world as global expectations move towards an environmentally friendly, sustainable, and socially just framework for all mankind. The founders of the World Health Organisation (WHO) defined health as 'A state of complete physical, mental and social well-being and not merely the absence of disease of infirmity'. The declaration of Alma Ata adopted in 1978 at the international conference of primary health care jointly sponsored and organised by WHO and UNICEF, stated that primary health care (PHC) was the key to attaining health for all as part of overall development. The conference defined PHC as 'Essential health care made universally accessible to individuals, families and the community by means acceptable to them, through their full participation and at a cost that the community and the country can afford'. The conceptual framework for health for all was defined in 1977, when the Thirtieth World Health Assembly decided

that the main social target of governments and WHO in the coming decades should be the attainment by all citizens of the world by the year 2000 of a level of health that would permit them to lead socially and economically productive lives.

Clearly, the year 2000 has come and gone and as the new millennium began 1.3 billion people continue to live in absolute poverty although health for all remains the cornerstone of WHO's institutional vision. It has become increasingly clear that this conceptual framework has to be revised and updated to answer the new socio-economic, technological and epidemiological realities brought about by profound changes in global magnitude. That is why the WHO is developing a new holistic health policy based on the concepts of equity and solidarity, emphasising the individuals, the families and the communities responsibility for health, and placing health within the overall development framework.

The UK: a rich country

The UK, the fourth richest economy in the world in 2001, has placed the individual patient at the centre of its health care policy for the future as set out in the NHS Plan 2000. Very poor countries in sub-Sahara Africa, and elsewhere in the world, might equally well have similar health policy objectives. This converging path is encouraging news, and will allow greater transfer of skills and resources between rich and poor countries than was ever possible when resources were concentrated in large technologically based hospitals.

The advent of the information age will now allow specialist skills to be taken to patients in their home environment. Common sense suggests that this approach is preferable to transporting individuals vast distances across the world sometimes to a different cultural environment.

Environmental and quality of life factors can be allowed to flourish. Home and community based primary care services will be able to communicate with each other between countries as well as between urban and rural locations within their own domain.

These policies would seem to encourage the development of the humanities in medical training. For example, the courses being developed by CAHHM at the University of Durham will encourage doctors to take a broader view of life, and encourage trainee doctors to broaden their education by undertaking modules in a variety of humanity subjects such as philosophy, the arts, and architecture.

These issues will pose large questions for WHO and there has been criticism that it is concentrating increasingly not on communicable diseases that threaten whole populations and strike the young hard, but on 'lifestyle' diseases such as high blood pressure, cancer, heart disease and depression.

'This shift is wrong for many reasons. None infectious diseases pose individual, but not public, health risks and do not require the same degree of international co-ordination as the fight against contagious epidemics. Second, because they mostly strike after the age when poor people in poor nations expect to die they are by definition rich country illnesses ...'

WHO's first duty of care is to the millions who die young in poor countries of treatable diseases.' (Anon, 2000c.)

Primary health care buildings provide a vital link to achieving these aspirations no matter where in the world they are built.

India: a policy for both rich and poor

In poor countries traditional healers as the resource of primary health care are a vital component of health care. In India to encourage motivated and bright young professionals to join primary health care services it is proposed to introduce new services so that health care management of the country is provided with competent people who would also be assured of an attractive career in medical services. In recent years the rich Indian health culture has gone through serious neglect. However every effort is being made to revitalise local health traditions by supporting the effects of exist-ing local and traditional health practitioners. This will provide about 500,000 traditional health care practitioners to contribute towards ensuring that people's health costs are low in their own community settings.

The strategy for revamping the primary health care system in India in the future includes a range of objectives which would be valid for any population group in the world. Present policy makers in the UK would feel comfortable with the same criteria. The list includes:

- Active participation of the people in managing their own health and that of the communities where they live.
- Optimum utilisation of existing primary health care infrastructure to remove the current inertia and to gear them up to meet the present and future challenges of health care.
- Active participation of voluntary organisations in the planning, monitoring and implementation of health programmes, particularly in the vulnerable areas.
- Ensuring a disciplined and responsible growth of the private sector both in curative as well as preventative and promotive care.
- Revitalisation of local health traditions and strengthening of local practitioners so that they can play important roles in health promotion, throughout the country.
- Decentralised district level planning with flexibility to cater to the local needs and constraints.

These points draw heavily from the report for the sub-group on Rural Health and Indian Systems of Medicine and Homeopathy, constituted by the Planning Commission, Government of India and chaired by Mr Alok Mukhopadhyay.

It is exciting to see these global perspectives and the new opportunities opening up for an equality of health policy for everyone. Undoubtedly it will be sometime before it is possible to achieve full internationalisation of specialist services. Technology will be used for the benefit of patients in parallel with the advancement of science. The use of IT to distribute information after the age of technology opens up exciting opportunities to provide equity.

Table 9.1 Comparison of key indicators of health expenditure and life expectancy for a selection of developed countries

	Total health expenditure per capita (£cash) 1997	Total health care expenditure as percent of GDP	Infant death rate per 1000 live births (1997)	Male life expectancy at birth (1997)
Australia	1140	8.4	5.3	76
Denmark	1582	8.3	5.2	73
France	1397	9.6	4.8	75
Germany	1666	10.7	4.8	74
Ireland	837	7.1	6.2	73
Japan	1458	7.1	3.7	77
Netherlands	1210	8.6	5.2	75
New Zealand	827	7.5	6.9	74
Sweden	1355	8.6	4.0	77
United Kingdom	907	6.8	5.9	75
United States	2455	14.0	7.8	73

Source: Office of Health Economics, *Compendium of Health Statistics*, 12th Edition 2000

The cross-fertilisation of cultures, the exchange of healing and traditional alternative therapies and the introduction of humanities hint at a civilised and culturally based health policy. As cultural barriers come down between nations it will be easier to accept and understand that for example traditional remedies derived from the natural environment in the Amazon jungle may have applications in the UK. Scientific explanations can be investigated but we must encourage the exchange of resources and knowledge even if at first some aspects may seem alien to recent health policy in the rich countries of the world.

The design of primary health care buildings will reflect this shifting paradigm and will also have similar characteristics of accessibility, flexibility, and sustainability, designed in an environmentally friendly manner compatible with local conditions. The checklist of requirements for a good primary health care facility will be much the same anywhere in the world although, of course, the physical results when built may differ widely. The important starting point is to consider the same lists of technical and emotional characteristics and allow the environmental conditions of the locality influence the design solution.

India has examples of both high technology centres of medical excellence to areas of rural poverty with primitive health facilities. It straddles the international range of health care provision and demonstrates the validity of the WHO policy for 'Health for All'.

Cambodia: a poor country

In Cambodia there is an excellent example of a primary health care project funded by the Australian government through the Australian Agency for International Development. Its aim is to achieve a sustained technology transfer in recipient countries through an integrated team effort. Here we see the introduction of a national policy on primary health care based on the WHO declaration of Alma Ata which was passed by Royal Decree in 1995.

'[Primary Health Care is] essential health care based on practical, scientifically sound and socially acceptable methods and technologies made universally accessible to individuals and families in the community through their full participation and at a cost that the community and country can afford. It forms an integral part both of the country's health system, of which it is the central function and main focus, and of the overall social and economic development of the community.'

Cambodia has significant areas of need that have determined national priorities. The current infant mortality rate is approximately 89 per 1000 live births. Overall per capita health expenditure in Cambodia is approximately $26.5 per year. Donor agencies spend approximately $5 per capita. The government's contribution to health costs was $1 per capita in 1998. This amount is scheduled to increase to $6 per capita by the area 2002. Households frequently have to go into debt to pay for inpatient medical costs. The National Health Development Plan provides for the development of a system of health centres and referral hospitals that will respond to the basic health needs of the population. As part of the Australian Aid Programme a programme to build health centres has been implemented and some examples are shown in the case studies.

Cambodia's primary health care policy is based on internationally recognised principles. These are regarded as core characteristics essential for all primary health care activities in Cambodia. In implementing activities all agencies and activity participants should adhere to the following six principles of the Royal Government of Cambodia Policy.

Principle one: universal accessibility and coverage in relation to need

The Royal Government of Cambodia affirms the right and opportunity of all people to access and utilise basic health and related services. As national resources are limited, it is vital that available resources are managed effectively. Planning and co-ordination of Primary Health Care activities should respond to community needs while avoiding unfair distribution of resources or duplication of activities.

Principle two: community participation in health and development

The Royal Government of Cambodia seeks to improve health and promote national development through community participation in health and development activities.

Principle three: intersectoral action in health

The Royal Government of Cambodia recognises that effective planning and implementation of primary health care activities requires close co-operation by many different government, non-government, community and private organisations, as well as the participation of international agencies and organisations.

Principle four: appropriate technology and cost effectiveness

The Royal Government of Cambodia affirms the right of all people to effective, reliable, low cost health and related services which are provided in a way which is affordable and acceptable to the community. Health service providers should be properly trained and skilled for their roles. All treatment should be provided through the use of safe procedures and properly functioning equipment. Cost effectiveness should be considered intersectorally and nationally, as well as within individual projects and activities.

Principle five: sustainability

The Royal Government of Cambodia priorities the development of sustainability characteristics in health and community development activities. This should occur through; promoting accessibility and coverage of services; actively supporting community participation in activities; fostering intersectoral co-operation and action by government, private and non-government agencies; and using appropriate technology and cost effective management and technical systems. The government is committed to increasing the national health budget to support sustainability of existing and planned health related initiatives.

Principle six: monitoring and evaluation

The Royal Government of Cambodia recognises that appropriate monitoring and evaluating systems must be established for health and community development activities. National monitoring and evaluation systems will be further developed and improved. The goal of these systems will be to ensure resources and used appropriately; to document process, impact and outcome characteristics of activities; and to create opportunities to evaluate activities and compare different strategies.

These principles embody universally accepted objectives that transcend cultural, heritage, race, religion or wealth and provide a common thread for progress to be followed in the future. They are consistent with the more narrowly focused subject of briefing explored in this book. The understanding and measurement of the therapeutic benefits arising from good environmental design is equally important whether designing a health centre in rural Cambodia or an affluent urban area in Western Europe.

Priorities may change in different countries of the world but the unity of a 'Health for All' policy underpins the need to design primary care buildings which provide a holistic healing environment.

10

A strategy for the future

Policy guidelines

In a global context the objective for primary health care must be to build on the current international trends: to identify the common strands in the policies of both rich and poor countries to create an international framework for health care. The previous chapters set out the aspirations of the World Health Organisation (WHO) setting down criteria that high standards of primary health care should be the expectation of all the peoples of the world. Race, colour and creed will become subservient to the need for patient-centred policies to flourish regardless of whether it is in a poor country torn apart by the strife of heavy debts or the obsessively materialistic culture of a rich society. The people of both rich and poor economies should be striving to create a lifestyle that concentrates on the well-being of the individual as a major contributory factor to the health of everyone. The globalisation of expertise, already recognised in management structures of large multinational companies, will develop in the health sector. There will be universal acceptance of the need for high-quality primary health care services in every country of the world, and the challenge is to recognise that the social and economic dynamics of the diverse cultures in the world can become complimentary to each other to achieve this goal.

Large multinational companies (such as Kodak and Coca-Cola) already have a pan-continental management approach to their business strategy, and the economic significance of these major corporations is larger, and therefore more powerful, than many smaller developing countries. At the beginning of the twenty-first century we are already familiar with the marketing of products in both rich and poor countries. We need to adjust our thinking to enable health policies to flourish in the same business style which has been successful for the marketing of consumer goods. Expert medical skills can be parachuted into impoverished regions of the world in the same way that you can buy a Kodak film in Cambodia as well as the USA.

With regard to primary health care buildings let us consider the architectural and medical challenge set by this approach to put patient care first, wherever that person happens to live in the world.

The architectural challenge can be summarised as follows:

* to formulate a brief
* to develop a design process
* to set out the ethos of the building
* to create a healing environment
* to understand better the medial constraints of the specific location.

The medical challenge might be summarised as follows:

* a policy for patient focused primary care that can fulfil the medical needs within the economic, cultural, and environmental constraints of the area
* the development of the transfer of skills and expertise (on a global scale)
* to acknowledge the therapeutic and environmental benefits that can be brought into play as part of a health programme.

These two sets of challenges set out to combine art and science to offer a holistic philosophy for health care.

Focusing on patient concerns and cares, these can be grouped into what the Picker Institute calls the eight dimensions of patient-centred care (MacRae, 2000):

* respecting a patient's values, preferences and expressed needs
* access to care
* emotional support
* information and education
* co-ordination of care
* physical comfort
* involvement of family and friends
* continuity and transition.

The president of Picker, Susan Edgman-Levitan, PA often says that if you want to have a cost-effective strategy, let your patients re-design it. If you want an expensive, complicated one let the clinicians or administrators address it. We will come up with all these programmes, and all the patient says is, 'All I want you to do is to leave a card at my bedside so I can remember to write down questions for my doctor, or, "Let me eat when I feel like it".'

In essence, it is the health care providers who need to be imbued with this radical approach to the provision of health care facilities. The real point of leverage, as stated by Dave O'Neil, President and Chief Executive Officer of the Center for Health Design are the health care providers – the chief executive officers, boards, physician leaders, nursing executives, and other who make the decisions about the organisation (O'Neill, 2000). This approach seems to remain true whether you are talking about the management of the NHS in the UK or the establishment of primary health care policies in countries such as Cambodia, or South Africa.

Building briefs

Previous chapters have explored several key components of a brief:

- procurement methods
- funding arrangements
- ownership
- performance criteria.

The future development of procurement methods will involve a number of criteria including:

- the cost of design
- the management of design
- the measurement of emotional responses.

The interaction of these factors will influence the chosen procurement route. For instance, the increasing preference for private finance will almost inevitably sharpen the assessment of funding institutions when they look at the cost of not only the design process, but also the proposed building solution. The management of design will diversify across a broad cross section of approaches as the criteria for the finished building begins to be more precisely defined.

There seems to be an inevitability in the UK that funding arrangements will shift towards money being sourced from private funds. As we have seen, doctors are increasingly less interested in owning the freehold of their premises, and the traditional NHS policies will become more fluid and less concerned about setting out strict models for ownership and management.

Ownership

The trend rapidly emerging of private finance being introduced to fund new facilities will have a significant effect on the employment of GPs by the service provider. A variety of other commercial uses will mean greater independence and individuality as new facilities are commissioned. On the one hand, local initiatives will create a rich diversity of specific design solutions, but there is also likely to be a trend of major corporations creating chains of GP surgeries. We already know that Boots and Tesco are examining the introduction of primary care services within their retail outlets. Therefore, we can expect that two competing policies may emerge. High quality solutions stimulated by specialist developers responding to local requirements and standardised 'shops within a shop' as the major retailers identify brand images for marketing primary health care services. These changes have already happened with the provision of optical services, and can be expected to be integrated with primary health care services. A wide range of other services may also be introduced so that a cocktail of inter-related health services will form the basis for a lifestyle marketing opportunity for the major retailing groups.

What are the performance criteria? The brief must first of all address the ethos of the proposed new facility. What is the quality of the environment going to be, and how is this to be achieved? Is it to be performance related, and therefore cost driven, or will it be accessed on quality? The case studies illustrate the consequences of those solutions which have been centred on cost criteria against those where clients have been more attuned to achieving higher standards of quality, and a sense of well-being in the place being created. In the longer term, how will society judge these divergent criteria?

- *The cost of design.* Start the briefing process with an unshakeable aspiration not to compromise on quality. This inevitably means a commitment to spending time on the process and consequently implies an acceptance that design fees should not be treated parsimoniously. Too often low fee bidding cripples the design team's ability to allocate sufficient time to establish and evolve the brief. Taken over the total life-span of a building, design costs are a very small percentage of the total expenditure which will include building costs, future maintenance and repair costs and staff costs (see Section 5.2.4).
- *The management of design.* There are many other guides to the management of design briefing which are logical, analytical and scientific in their approach to the problem but how do you build in the 'delight' factor. Time must be allocated to thinking about emotions, and discussing ideas, which must be encapsulated in a written document.
- *The measurement of intangible or emotional responses.* We must develop methods which allow the measurement of emotional responses to environmental conditions. Much more work is required to build on the emerging body of research to demonstrate the validity of subjective decisions often assumed to be justified only by the personal experience of architects. Equally doctors need to be encouraged to think more laterally and to become sympathetic to the role of the humanities in health care.

Design guides: checklist to establish briefing process recommendations

Aims and objectives

A healing environment can be judged as a balance between the interface of technical standards and emotional responses. The success of the building in contributing to the quality of life will be the result of the designer's ability to meet this challenge.

Will the building provide good architecture and good medicine?

- *Mission statement*:
  - what is the practice philosophy? – its ethos?
  - what are the implications for a patient focused service?
  - how will customer (patient) satisfaction be measured?
  - will there be a 'delight' factor?
- *Procurement route*:
  - who will own the premises?
  - how will it be financed? (what is the ratio of public and private finance?)
- *Quality issues*:
  - key relationships/operating systems for consulting room/examination, reception area and doctor/patient interface (e.g. call system).
- *Flexibility*:
  - will other functions be accommodated (e.g. pharmacy, dentist, social services, etc.)
  - what is the anticipated lifecycle for the building?
  - operating criteria (e.g. 24 hour opening).
- *Design expectations*:
  - list criteria required or sought under emotional and technical standards of design (see Table 10.1)
  - assessment of value for money or value engineering.

Table 10.1

Technical standards	Emotional responses
Schedule of rooms	Environmental aspects
Functional requirements	• view of nature
Room sizes	• the five senses
Area of building	– touch
Room data sheets	– smell
Performance specification	– taste
• heating/ventilation	– hearing
• lighting	– sight
• acoustic	Atmosphere
• electrical	– homely
• thermal (building shell)	– relaxing
• cleanliness	– welcoming
Cost limits	– professional
Value for money	– caring
Life cycle costings	– accessible
	– friendly

Privacy
Patient control over environment
Post-occupancy evaluation – user satisfaction

- *External relationships*:
  - site location/urban context
  - transport links/communication systems
  - 'green' characteristics
  - entrance/approach
  - accessibility.

Assessment tools

In summary, a selection of assessment tools is available to the medical and architectural professions to evaluate the performance of future health care facilities. These include:

- key performance indicators
- simple checklists of objectives and criteria
- spider diagrams to create visual comparitors
- patient satisfaction interviews
- post-occupancy evaluations
- architectural quality assessments (both qualitative and quantitative)
- cost-benefit analyses.

Obviously, many different tools may be used to evaluate a particular project. In some parts of the world, the standards of expectation may vary widely and it is important to recognise these distinctions, for example, if using patient satisfaction interviews.

Academic research programmes

The fear of hospitals (and primary health care facilities) often arises out of environmental images rather than physical or medical traumas. Dr Phil Leather explores some of these issues.

'Many traditional hospital designs, however, create a very different image, one which is strange and alien to many. Carver (1990), for example, compares being admitted to a modern hospital to "entering an alien spacecraft", where the atmosphere can be "intimidating and unfamiliar". Veith and Arkkelin (1995) suggest that the mere mention of the word "hospital" is enough to conjure up "thoughts of long sterile hallways, stainless steel utensils, banks of life-monitoring equipment, people in white uniforms rushing to and fro, specialised rooms for specialised functions, wheelchairs lined up at elevators, and the smell of rubbing alcohol and disinfectant."

Not surprisingly, then, the unfamiliarity and strangeness characteristic of the hospital environment has been found to generate strong negative emotions, including threat, vulnerability and fear, together with those associated with suffering and death (Brown, 1961). Ulrich (1991) argues that such emotions derive directly from a design ethos which emphasises the functional delivery of health-care at the expense of patient needs. The result, he concludes, are hospital designs which are "psychologically hard" and "unsupportive" and which "work against the well-being of patients".' (Leather, 2000.)

Leather's work is one of the few research programmes in the UK which looks at validating the relationship between design, image and well-being.

'The clear obvious conclusion which follows is that positively appraised environments are beneficial to patient satisfaction and well-being. At the very least, they are conductive to the generation of positive moods. Beyond that, however, there is also evidence that they are associated with increased mental capacity, lower drug use and a shorter post-operative stay.

It remains the case, however, that the way in which we see and experience the environment is a largely holistic affair. It is difficult, for example, to see the Eiffel Tower without reference to its specific cultural context. Blackpool Tower must undoubtedly have many structural features in common with its French counterpart, but its meaning and image are very different. In part at least, these differences derive from the fact that Blackpool provides a very different cultural context from Paris. It is this context-related meaning which influences our behavioural responses to them as much as, if not more than, their individual physical characteristics. So, too, with the hospital environment, where the identification of the role of discrete design elements will never replace the need to understand and be able to delineate the overall image and meaning deriving from a particular configuration of physical elements. This research has sought to take some tentative but important steps along this road.'

Some of these issues are also explored by Professor Patsy Healey, an urban planner, who is interested in the factors which influence 'place quality'.

'A central hypothesis of in my own recent work has been that, despite all our consciousness of mobility and global interconnectedness of our contemporary world, the qualities of "places" matters to us. Place quality matters with respect to where we live, the places of our daily-life routines. It matters with respect to the places we like to visit. Some places also have symbolic important for us, as cultural assets, symbolic referents. The places of our daily life and of the cultural referents important in the society in which we live are also important for our identity. Some people are fortunate in that the places where they live, and the cultural referents of the society they live in, re-inforce their sense of belonging and identity. Others experience the opposite, alienation and exclusion.

There are also impacts on health, well-being and environmental qualities. There is much evidence that the social ambience of a place affects the people who live there.

The location of such distressed places within city regions is not neutral as regards environmental qualities.

The government response to the emergence of neighbourhoods of concentrated poverty and ill-health was often in the past to seek to redevelop them, with new physical structures. Yet many people who experienced this treatment found it disruptive, undermining the delicate balances which enabled them to survive. They often wanted to hold on to their own "places", the only place many of them might know well and know how to get by in. These days in Europe, there is much more effort to work with residents to identify locally-helpful programmes. Another typical government response has been to treat the various problems people experience "sectorally" – as an "education issue", or a "housing issue"; a "health problem", an "unemployment problem" or a "crime problem". But this "splits up" people's lives into a set of compartmentalised needs. In the UK, it is now widely recognised that a multi-sector or "holistic" approach is needed. But this implies a different kind of governance to well-established cultures and practices in many government department and agencies. What kinds of transformation in the way government is done are needed? How do such transformations take place?' (Healey, 2001.)

These academic studies highlight the challenge in identifying the problems and offering solutions to provide a healthy environment. A major investment in research programmes is needed if the results of existing studies are to be consolidated and translated into policy directives.

This view is endorsed by the British Academy which advocates an extension of the quality of life programme. The Academy suggests a major EU-wide analysis of issues such as income and financial deprivation, work and labour markets, health and ageing and the dynamics of well-being. The quality of life as a research theme would include many strands including health and ageing, cities and the local environment, and arts and heritage (British Academy, 2001).

11

Case studies

Introduction

We have seen how there is a coming together of policy objectives throughout the world regarding the needs of primary health care services – a convergence of ideas that focus the provision of services on the patient and the delivery of health care at a local level. The success of the World Health Organisation's (WHO) Health for All Policy forms the bedrock for the strategic direction of national health policies in many parts of the world. It bridges both rich and poor economies, and, for example, in South Africa the complex political problems are challenging the health authorities to provide an efficient health care service to people with widely differing economic backgrounds. Within a short period of time the South African policy has changed from focusing on acute hospital provision to a rapid response programme of providing primary care clinics. Similar attitudes are now prevailing in other countries around the world.

The following projects from different parts of the world show the range of responses to the provision of primary health care facilities. It is remarkable how global trends are becoming unified – a common agreement that patients should come first and that the medical care and that the buildings provided for these services should be focused on the patient. The briefing process for architects is no more than recognising the juxtaposition of these skills to provide an environment which cares about people and listens to their needs. It should not be driven by an over zealous concern to satisfy accountants – costs and floor space calculations only form a part of delivering health care buildings that work. The range of architectural responses illustrated acknowledges the importance of good design. There is a rich vein of work being developed and we should be full of optimism for the future of small health buildings serving the needs of primary medicine around the world.

The illustrations and case studies look at a range of primary care buildings. They include projects that have been funded by both private and public money using a range of procurement methods. The largest number of examples come from the UK. However, a selection of international examples

has been chosen to illustrate the diversity of architectural design, and the high standards that can be achieved from very different starting points. They all have in common the aim to put patients first, and to provide a humane caring environment for their well-being.

United Kingdom

Some of the best examples of successful small-scale caring environments in the UK have been created outside of the NHS procurement route. There are many examples of good design where clients have been looking for a more sensitive approach to provide facilities for special health needs and in the hospice movement.

Art in Health Care

We have seen (Section 4.7) that the background to the current wave of enthusiasm for better design in health care environments included the introduction of art in a wide range of buildings. There are many innovative examples of NHS projects that have been improved by the introduction of art works. Typical of this approach is the work done by Northern Arts (much of it under the guidance of Germaine Stanger and Mike White). This also has resulted in the establishment of artists' residences after the completion of original commissions in four local hospitals. They have been instrumental in encouraging and helping to see through to completion a range of projects including those listed below.

A GP's waiting room, St Paul's Medical Centre Mural, Carlisle

Dr John Anderson was well acquainted with the work of artist Barry Ormsby. On moving to a newly built surgery, he envisaged a mural by Barry as a feature in the waiting room.

Dr Anderson needed to convince his partners it was a good idea before contacting Carlisle City Councils Arts Development Manager, Mick North, to help put together a funding package.

123

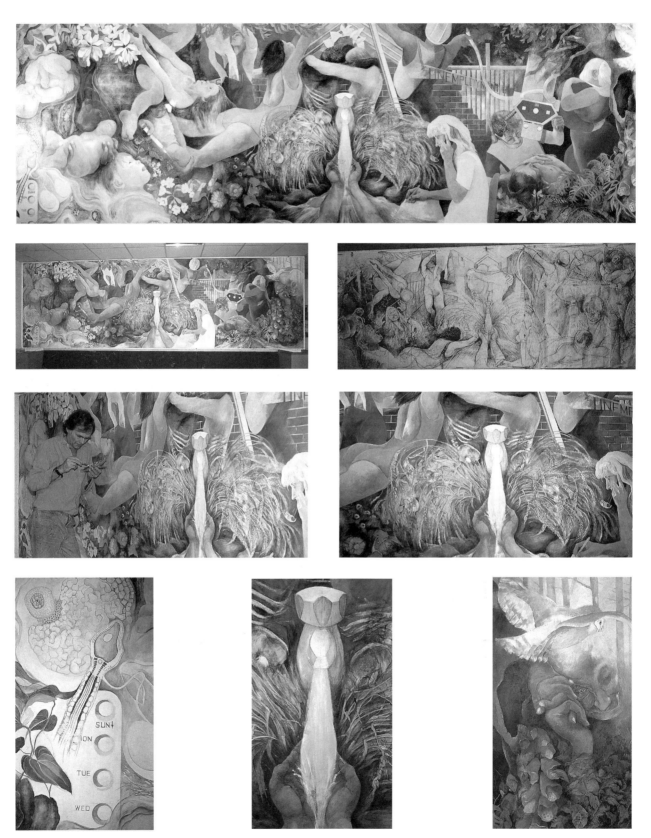

Figure 11.1 St Paul's Medical Centre, Carlisle: Cycle of Life mural by Barrie Ormsby (also in colour section)

This was achieved through the Art in Healthcare Initiative (Northern Regional Health Authority/Northern Arts Funding), the Cumbria Family Health Service Authority and sponsorship.

The work took eight months to complete. It was painted while people waited to consult their GPs.

The theme of the work is the life cycle and the medical use of plants. The mural pays reference to the major factors in establishing sound mental and physical health.

Oxford Terrace Medical Centre, Gateshead

This medical practice at Bensham in central Gateshead extended and refurbished to designs by the Geoffrey Purves Partnership is the base of an Arts in Primary Health Care Development Programme. In 1999/2000 an arts residency with sculpture Michelle Newman was established in the practice, following on from taster art sessions in the surgery waiting room. A number of the art works are on display at Oxford Terrace, some created in previous Arts in Health Projects.

The principles which have informed the Arts in Primary Care and Community Health Projects can be summarised as follows:

- The role of Arts in Health in the Community is different from the role of Arts in Health in Hospitals (which is still,

Figure 11.3 Blue Nude by Lisa deLarny. Exhibited at Oxford Terrace Medical Centre (1995)

Figure 11.2 Oxford Terrace Medical Centre, Gateshead: sculpted relief titled: 'Helping Hands' by Lisa deLarny. Architect: Geoffrey Purves Partnership

Figure 11.4 Detail from silk painted curtain. Made during Nicola Balfour's artist's residency at Oxford Terrace Medical Group in 2001. Photographed by David Daniells

in the main, concerned with commissioning artworks and art therapy).

- Surgeries and the localities they serve should be places where we learn to be healthy.
- The arts – and friendly artists – can shape contexts in the community to provide mediating images for health education so that people are touched rather than indoctrinated.
- The re-integration of art into health checks the dehumanisation of medical science and it is essential for both mental and physical health promotion.
- There is a relationship between creativity and wellbeing, and to encourage people's laden creativity the Arts in Primary Health Care can be domestic, communal and celebratory.

Dr Christina Cock is responsible for overseeing the programme of art in this practice which involves literature as well as the visual arts. 'Poetry helps to take people's mind off the reason why they are coming to see the doctor – it relieves anxiety'. Queuing to see a GP can be a lonely and anxious experience and a human touch can prove to be very helpful. Poetry sometimes does that work better than anything, touching without imposing. It can make the waiting experience less lonely. The practice also encourages artist's residencies. Nicola Balfour who specialises in textiles worked with staff patients, community groups and refugees who live locally and use the surgery during 2001. During the residency her work has involved a huge number of people from discussing ideas in the waiting room to practical workshops in silk painting.

Children's Cancer Ward (Ward 16) Royal Victoria Infirmary, Newcastle upon Tyne (Architect: Waring & Netts)

The philosophy of the design approach adopted by the architects (Waring and Netts) in redeveloping this ward, part of a large Victorian hospital, was to create an environment specific to the needs and aspirations of teenagers. They sought to achieve informality and to incorporate artwork relevant to teenagers which would assist recovery. Their design solution included:

- Bedrooms for two or three patients with plenty of room for access, drip trolleys, wheelchairs, etc.
- Soft, warm colours and interiors, very modern in feel, with dado and picture rails and decorative wallpapers.
- Use of materials and detailing such as wood strip vinyl flooring, hardwood and coloured ceramic tile dado rails and different bedding, soft furnishings and light fittings.
- Individual notice boards at each bed for personalising, and timber veneered vanity units.
- Separate modern kitchen with dining area for teenagers use, linked to upper levels lounge area with comfortable chairs, television, built-in book shelves and display, focal fireplace.
- Built-in workbenches with hidden lighting and computer outlets to allow school and academic workspace.

- A redundant corridor was widened and fitted out as a 'hanging out' and social space. This included seating, pool table, telephone booth, vending machines and views over the adjacent flat roof courtyard and mural.
- An ensuite bathroom links each bedroom, and this was finished in blue and yellow glazed ceramic tiling and feature 'dressing room' lighting to the vanity unit. A specifically commissioned ceramic tile mural depicting a seaside scene with waves and dolphins was centred on the main wall.
- Artwork, funded by the GlaxoWellcome Trust and the Hospital Trust, was used extensively in the scheme. The centrepiece was a large external mural painted on ply sheets on a steel frame mounted on an adjacent flat roof, visible from the main internal corridor. After extensive consultation with the teenage patients, their unanimous choice was a view of the social scene based on the famous 'Bigg Market' area of Newcastle. This is extremely humorous and very popular with patients. The same artist used many of the caricatures from the Bigg Market mural to imitate finger painting on condensation by acid etching on glass. This was used extensively in existing windows and bathrooms to achieve privacy.
- A high-quality main entrance was provided from the main corridor and included veneered panelling with the names of major sponsors. A further large piece of commissioned art depicted many of the best known Tyneside features including the bridges and St James' Park, home of Newcastle United football team.
- A highly decorative, complex pattern was commissioned and designed for a suspended ceiling tile, and laid as a central feature in treatment room. This was to provide some interest/distraction for patients undergoing unpleasant treatments.
- In addition to the building and interior design features, the air of informality was extended to staff not wearing uniform.

Figure 11.5 Children's Cancer Ward, (Ward 16) Royal Victoria Infirmary, Newcastle upon Tyne: lounge for teenagers. Architect: Waring & Netts

Figure 11.6 Childrens' Cancer Ward, (Ward 16) Royal Victoria Infirmary, Newcastle upon Tyne: bathroom with etched glass

Ophthalmology Department, Royal Victoria Infirmary, Newcastle upon Tyne

Another initiative at this hospital (known to everyone on Tyneside as the RVI) was a project to visualise, fund and install art in the newly completed ophthalmology department, one of an increasing number of new buildings within the site. An excellent booklet describes the process. Quoting from Germaine Stanger (in 1998):

'In January 1996 I toured the nearly completed Ophthalmology building with the then chairman of the RVI, Anne Galbraith, whose idea it was that the building should contain a variety of artwork if the bulk of its cost could be met by the National Lottery. To our delight the project was granted a National Lottery award of £82,263.00 in April 1997.'

Aware of the fundamental need for artwork to be integrated into the design process the report tactfully says:

'To marry artwork with architecture and to simplify the funding process, works of art should ideally be considered from the outset of any new building.

The Ophthalmology building echoed the more familiar path of clients recognising the need for artwork when a building nears its completion. An arts programme interwoven in and around the building process is part of the architect's vision. It is much more difficult to hold onto that "vision" when the building is in use and visual ownership has, theoretically, passed from architect to staff and the general public.'

Funded by an Arts Council Lottery Grant nearly £100,000 with additional funding of £10,000 being provided by several local sponsors.

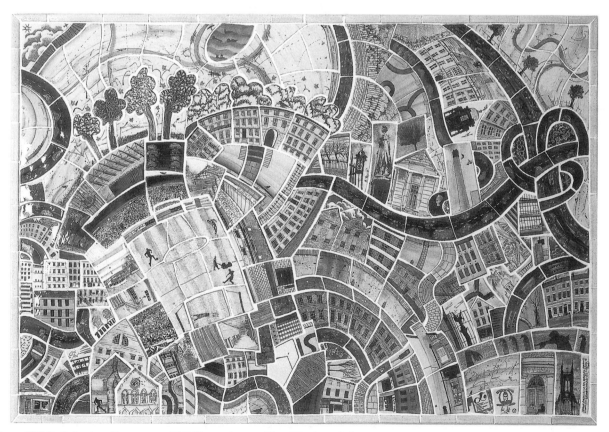

Figure 11.7 Opthalmology Department, RVI, Newcastle upon Tyne. The Scott Collection, commission for the Royal Victoria Infirmary, Leazes Panel. Underglaze and inglaze painting and prints on porcelain tiles.

Denton Turret Medical Centre, Newcastle upon Tyne

The design by the Geoffrey Purves Partnership incorporates a central top-lit waiting area which has views out to the adjoining Dene and includes a 20 m² area which can be separated, if required, for a variety of community welfare and health-related activities. The top lighting helps to create an attractive and welcoming environment which has been exploited by the enthusiasm of the GPs who ran a competition for local art students to win the commission for a stained glass screen. The winning design depicts a chronological history of the local area. The surgery is near Hadrian's Wall and the design includes screens from the fall of the Roman Empire. The artist, Carol Bryce drew on the region's rich history. The screen is divided into seven sections, each 1 m², and it chronicles the history of Denton to the present day. Scenes mark the collapse of the Roman Empire – depicting by a broken column, the closer of the area's 28 pits, and the opening of the new surgery on Kenley Road with the Tyne Bridge in the background.

Although not primary care facilities, the next two examples from the Royal Victoria Hospital, Newcastle upon Tyne illustrate creative environmental enhancement within the smaller scale of departmental areas in a large hospital.

Special needs and cancer care buildings

The provision of facilities for the care and treatment of cancer patients has seen the development of many sensitive and caring environments. The selection of projects illustrated brings together descriptions of the buildings that encompass the key arguments outlined in this book. Although many of them have been built within the constraints of financial limits that are either the same or, at least, very similar to NHS standards the briefing process has formed the central pivot around which the client, patients, and architect have developed with the medical teams, buildings which put the healing environment at the top of the list of priorities. There is an overriding concern that the patients who will be using these buildings need to be able to enjoy their surroundings, often because there are no conventional medical remedies to their illness. Where conventional medical remedies have reached the end of the line, this seems to stimulate the desire to search for a more humane architecture. This lesson, quite simply, should be taken on board for all primary health buildings.

Fortunately, this approach has rapidly gained wider acceptance and a series of GP facilities are now being designed that reflect this philosophy. There is a wish to provide services at a community level, in buildings that are friendly and accessible. There is more humility in the design approach where technology is important but subservient to the needs of people.

The five schemes illustrated in this section all provide outstanding high-quality environments. The architect's accounts describe a concern to use natural materials and to create spaces that have been conceived as a response to human emotions. The functional and technical requirements have not been allowed to over-ride the emotional criteria in

Figure 11.8 Denton Turret Medical Centre, Newcastle upon Tyne. Architect: Geoffrey Purves Partnership. Stained glass window depicting chronological history of the local area. Artist: Carol Bryce

the design process. We should learn from these examples and transfer the design philosophies to general practice buildings. It is also interesting to note that both the Forth Valley and Naomi House projects are based on a curved plan and both architects talk about the intimacy and spatial qualities that these shapes provide.

General practitioner surgeries

If the special needs and cancer care buildings illustrate an outstanding concern for designing sensitive environments then the GP buildings demonstrate the rapidly changing procurement routes that are revolving in primary health care. We have seen that the special needs and cancer care buildings have had more opportunity to explore the development of a design brief outside of the constraints normally imposed by the NHS procedures. With GP buildings the pressures for development have focused on the procurement route and a variety of models have begun to emerge. Primary sector finance is being introduced, both by the Government through its LIFT initiatives as well as by developers offering comprehensive building services to health providers. PFI contracts have explored batching GP premises together to form larger contract values. The projects which are illustrated include a variety of procurement routes, as well as several examples from the last generation of cost rent generated projects based on the principles laid out in the 'Red Book'.

The best of the new examples succeed in not only embracing new procurement and financing routes but also rise to the challenge of producing high-quality architecture with stimulating environments and an understanding of the therapeutic benefits that good design can provide. Over the next few years the opportunity to explore these trends should be grasped. The design and theory of a patient-focused architecture needs to be shared internationally. We can expect to see a new wave of buildings offering spatial flexibility, patient accessibility, and a caring environment. Pushing at the boundaries of this work is a group of professionals who have recognised the need to mix disciplines, and design buildings that are humane and contribute to the built environment.

During the past decade there are very many excellent examples of primary care buildings. The RIBA Clients Advisory Service (CAS) lists over 600 practices with experience of designing primary health care buildings and their database provides a substantial track record of competent buildings. Many are excellent, and will continue to provide a good service to patients for many years. Some of these good examples can be found on the NHS CD-ROM 'Design Quality', and, of course, the NHS booklet *Environments for Quality Care* published as long ago as 1994 provides a selection of exemplar projects from around the UK.

More recently, the results of innovative architects working with sympathetic medical practitioners have explored a number of approaches to improve environmental quality and these have been discussed elsewhere in this book. Issues such as the introduction of artworks, stained glass, improved disability access (including mobility, audio, and visual impairments) have all added to the knowledge base for buildings used for primary health care purposes.

Community facilities

As we have seen, a variety of solutions have been designed to meet the multifarious requirements of local circumstances both in the UK and around the world. These buildings are invariably complex and lay down a challenge for the clarity of the design to be preserved during the procurement route. Hence, the buildings encapsulate the often conflicting objectives of 'product versus process' discussed more fully in earlier chapters.

They are a test of the British Government's policies to achieve high standards of design while seeking to introduce private funding including the use of PFI contracts. This has led to differences of opinion within the architectural profession. On the one-hand academics such as Susan Francis, at the Medical Architecture Research Unit says 'Over the past 10 years some of the most successful designs have come through primary and community settings.' However she is concerned that NHS LIFT will mean the batching of smaller buildings within a given area to form larger contracts that will be procured through framework agreements. This, she believes, will lead to a lack of site-specific work and will attract consortia which might not otherwise be interested in jobs of this scale. Mike Nightingale of Nightingale Associates does not share such a pessimistic view. He says, 'We do both building and interior design in the health sector so are well set up. It is a good time to be specialising because there is a wealth of work and a feeling that days of utilitarian hospital architecture are over: first the Egan Report suggested good design was good patients and now CABE is working with the Government through the NHS Design Forum on the importance of good design. Starting small with clinics will give small firms a chance to get in, but they will have to show competence and an ability to cope with complex work. There is evidence that PCT's will be quite entrepreneurial about procuring buildings' (Richardson, 2001).

Of course, the other major factor in the shape of primary health care buildings of the future will be the working practices of GPs themselves. Doctors are under increasing pressure in the UK to modify their working practices, look again at job descriptions and the work that may be undertaken by nurses, and their involvement, if at all, in the financial structure of the ownership of medical buildings. The examples illustrated in the UK and in other countries illustrate the range of work and approaches adopted for primary health care community facilities in response to these changing needs of both the medical and architectural professions.

The next generation

The testing ground for primary health care buildings of the future, or to use a generic term, healthy living centres, is most likely to be in the community sector. Rich opportunities for innovative design, imaginative briefing, and new methods of funding and procurement will shape the next generation of small health buildings. There are, therefore, many exciting challenges ahead for both doctors and architects to work out new arrangements of co-operating professionally so that these two honourable professions can forge a closer relationship and a common objective of building a healthier lifestyle for everybody who will use these buildings.

No doubt, different solutions will emerge as private finance influences the public funding of the NHS. The briefs for community buildings will have to balance the need for flexibility with multipurpose rooms and the need to offer more specialised facilities closer to a patient's home. In the USA, a range of specialised facilities has tended to emerge where there has been sufficient wealth to support the demand for those services. Therefore, there are many medium-sized buildings in the USA providing specialised community services in, for example, cancer care, ambulatory clinics, care of the elderly, cardiac centres, clinics for children and other medically discrete treatment centres. Other parts of the world continue to focus on patient centred therapies. The Western civilisations, predominantly English speaking, should look more closely at alternative health philosophies. Chinese traditional medicine, including herbal, acupuncture, and mental therapies will become better understood in future years and more research should be undertaken to look at the whole body approach to well-being which has been adopted by the Chinese.[1] The dilemma of affluent societies is highlighted by these two different approaches. Where wealth alone doesn't solve lifestyle health problems there is a greater willingness to look more closely at human attitudes towards health. There was, perhaps, a closer correlation between the philosophy of health, and therefore the facilities which society provided for the ill, in the Chinese and Roman civilisations of 2000 years ago than there is today in our Western civilisations. These arguments return us to the importance of the brief to reflect the ethos of the client. Architecture and medicine need to work together to build healthy living centres for the future.

Case study 1: Forth Valley Bellsdyke Hospital

Architect: Foster and Partners – a project for the mentally ill commissioned by the Central Scotland Health Care NHS Trust.

The following is by Ken Shuttleworth part of the team of architects from Foster and Partners that worked on this project.

Forth Valley phase I

Working on the Forth Valley Bellsdyke Hospital projects has been a labour of love. Its the sort of project we are rarely approached to do. I'm not sure why as it presents a fascinating problem to solve. The project captured our imagination and interest and we worked relentlessly to fulfil our aim to simply produce a scheme that would match the worthiness of the cause.

The projects are for people who are mentally ill. In our view they deserve a better environment than they are, so often, given. The patients have special needs yet their 'architecture' resemble, or in fact in many cases actually are barracks. The patients are the unfortunate victims of events beyond their control, and our hearts went out to them. We felt we had to do something to improve their environment their living standards and hopefully therefore the life of people who are far worse off than ourselves.

Yet despite these good intentions it was a real challenge to meet the budget and the timescale the project demanded as we had from a standing start in October, to spend £750,000 by March in order to achieve the spend rate demanded by the client who, if he didn't spend the money, would lose it.

We started with very intense meetings with the administration, medical and nursing staff to fully immerse ourselves in the needs of both patients and staff. The meetings were very positive and the client body a joy to work with. Out of this process we evolved a series of buildings.

The first phase we designed as a crescent of seven identical six-bedroom houses which focus onto a south-facing landscaped garden. The second phase is a tri-spoked form, housing more segregated patients and a third, separate amenity building is shared by the whole Bellsdyke hospital.

The overall challenge was to meet a really tight government controlled budget and satisfy the desires of both the client and ourselves, to provide a substantial improvement in living standards.

The most direct comparison was with the latest existing buildings affectionately know as 'the bungalows' which had low ceilings, minimal window area, dark narrow corridors, wasted space, blank white walls, ill conceived tiny bedrooms with segregated living, dining and kitchen area. To us, although new, they were miserable and didn't offer a pleasant atmosphere to live in, whether one was mentally ill or not.

Our main concern was to try to ensure the buildings were sympathetic to the patients needs. Many suffer from manic depression and schizophrenia. Often they feel persecuted and that voices are talking to them. Spot lights could be seen as menacing 'eyes' so needed to be avoided, sharp angles antagonised, dark corners could be perceived as dangerous, overhangs as oppressive. Also they may be prone to violent outbursts and attempts at suicide. However, their condition varies and sometimes they would be sociable and other times, they wished to be alone. They need comfort, constant attention, supervision by understanding nurses to ensure their own and others safety. Also, they all smoke continuously.

Our response in phase I was to provide buildings that offer a wide variety of spaces. Firstly, the south-facing garden, like a village green with an intense landscape contained on its north side by a crescent of houses. This is the heart of the community and the focus for all the houses.

Inside the houses we designed a large open plan 'family' living, dining and kitchen area. The social focus of the house with discreet sitting and dining areas within the space. The space has a high vaulted ceiling, with top light, to allow the use daylighting throughout and natural ventilation to relieve the smoke. By contrast, the bedrooms are highly personalised spaces with focused external views of trees for patients to have their own completely private space.

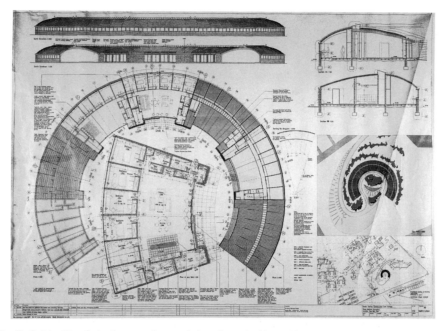

Figure 11.9 Forth Valley Bellsdyke Hospital: plans, sections and elevations. Architect: Sir Norman Foster and Partners

The more public spaces face south and the private spaces face north onto a tree belt, none of the bedrooms are over looked and each one has its own uninterrupted view of the landscape.

Within the living space there is an 'inglenook' where two people can sit and feel secure and play cards in front of a cosy 'fire'. The nurse's space also doubles up as a meeting and discussion area.

These different types of space offer a range of use possibilities and attempts to be sympathetic to the different moods and needs of the patients.

Figure 11.10 Forth Valley Bellsdyke Hospital: exterior view. Photographed by Morley von Sternberg

Throughout the scheme we used natural materials as a key design decision. Such as stone and wood around a garden to ensure a continuous link back to nature, natural things and reality.

The whole seven houses form crescent as a cluster – a hamlet of 56 people – a little community. The curved form in both plan and section is a comforting gentle response to the brief and avoids unnecessary aggressive sharp forms.

We also used standard products but to create a unique form. For instance, we used windows directly out of a catalogue but we put them together in ways not previously envisaged by the manufacturers. By putting standard windows together we created a continuous ribbon of windows on the north side and used standard patio doors again butted together on the South side to give a continuous view of the garden.

We also were keen that each house has a different name reflecting the type of wall climber on the entrance wall to each the houses, which include roses, wisteria, virginia creeper, etc. Why not rose cottage?

The final touch was the colour of the rooms – they are all different and each house is different to give a range of moods and breakdown the usual clinical white.

Phase I has been a joy to work on and has given the team a very real sense of purpose and satisfaction.

Forth Valley phase II

In 1995 Foster and Partners were appointed as architects to design additional accommodation to complement and extend the facilities for psychiatric patients within the grounds of Bellsdyke Hospital. As part of the redevelopment and masterplan a new informal campus is being created that is residential in scale rather than utilitarian. The phase II brief asked for res-

Figure 11.11 Forth Valley Bellsdyke Hospital: exterior view at dusk. Photographed by Morley von Sternberg (also in colour section)

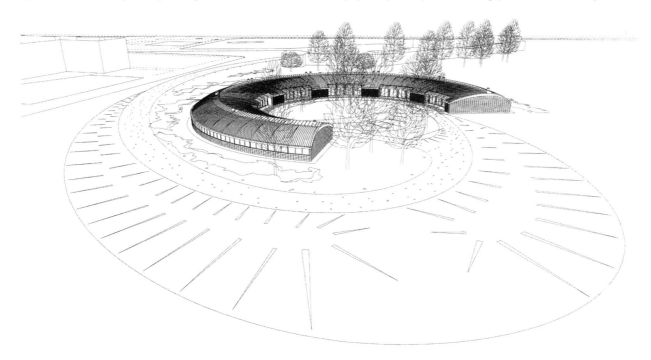

Figure 11.12 Forth Valley Bellsdyke Hospital: computer-aided design perspective

idential accommodation for 24 long-term psychiatric patients and recreational facilities to also serve the existing phase one accommodation, completed by Foster and Partners in 1995. While the phase I residential unit was designed to create a sense a community with bedrooms leading off shared sitting rooms, the phase II residential wing is designed for patients who require a higher degree of care and the building is flexible enough to create secure units if required.

Working within a tight budget, the aim was to create a warm humane environment to lift the spirits of the patients and avoid a cold, clinical institutional atmosphere. The buildings use timber, blockwork, render and state to create a domestic environment which integrates sensitively with the wooded site and surrounding buildings. The new buildings respond to phase I in their orientation, form and materials and sit within the existing tree clusters, creating a unified and harmonious development.

The new 800 m^2 tri-spoke residential building has three accommodation wings linked to the central nursing support by a series of sitting and dining rooms. The building is designed to be flexible, allowing the wings to function either in isolation or to be interlinked. Each wing has its own separate colour scheme, which helps the residents to orientate themselves. Bedrooms are located along the perimeter of the building taking advantage of daylight and views. Internal spaces and corridors use rooflights to admit daylight and ensure privacy. Due to the serious nature of the patients' illness special design features have been incorporated.

Within the square recreation building, a series of spaces lead off the large main central hall which is top lit by roof lights. This 400 m^2 building will be used by patients from phases I and II.

Construction of phase II began in January 1996 and was completed in March 1997. The total cost of phase II was approximately £1.5 million.

Case study 2: Glasgow Homoeopathic Hospital

Architect: MacLachlan Monaghan.

Dr David Reilly, the 'champion' who had the vision to create the Glasgow Homoeopathic Hospital describes the project as follows:

'We aim to help people self-heal – if possible from their disease, but always from their suffering. We wish to create a space, a place, an atmosphere, an approach and an experience that helps this healing happen. We strive to treat each patient as a unique individual and whole person, recognising that their inner and outer life can have a significant impact on the processes of disease and healing.

We seek to discover what is of value within traditional and complementary care, and integrate this with the best of orthodox care, blending the arts and sciences of healing. We recognise that our work as carers requires us to address out own understanding, health and wellbeing. We aim to share this knowledge and experience with our individual patients, and with the community.'

An architectural competition was held and extracts from the brief are reproduced below. The success of the idea is described in an article written by Sandra Hempel, 'Healing Space', published in *Health and Homoeopathy* Spring 1999.

The brief to the architects of the new Glasgow Homoeopathic Hospital is summed up with deceptive simplicity. They were asked to create a place of beauty and healing. When the hospital welcomed its first patients, it was clear that the building did indeed fulfil that considerable expectation.

The driving force behind the £2.2 million project, the hospital's lead consultant physician, David Reilly, admits to being nervous as the doors opened, however. He had lived with the vision for a long time and, although the staff were consulted the whole way through the design process, he waited anxiously for the first reactions of staff and patients to the completed building.

He need not have worried. 'It has all been overwhelmingly positive,' he said. 'People have been almost shocked by the beauty of the place.' Glasgow's planning department has just announced that it sees the new building as setting a standard to which other hospitals should aspire.

The key themes are lights, space and harmony. The building makes the most of natural daylight and all of the patient rooms face outwards, with windows and doors on to what will soon be landscaped gardens. The aim is that people in the building should always be aware of the world outside.

The materials are as natural and environmentally friendly as possible. The floors and blinds are wooden; the roof is zinc – chosen because it is recyclable; real lino is used for floor covering; and chairs and sofas are made from cane or leather. The colours are restful, with walls of pale apricot and sofas in soft mulberry.

The final cost per square metre of the building is no more than that of a conventional NHS hospital, although this money was raised entirely from charity.

Great attention has been paid to small details, such as door handles, light fittings and the shape of the chairs. Stained glass is used for the patient bathroom windows and tiny red mosaic tiles for the basin splash-backs. An artist, Jane Kelly, was commissioned to lead the collaboration to define environmental design. Her response has been to create a colour and materials palette inspired by the sources of homoeopathic remedies.

The building is intended to meet both the physical and the psychological needs of the patients and staff who use it, rather than forcing them to adapt to or suffer from its demands. It is all part of the holistic healing process.

Dr Reilly says that his strong views on what was needed come from his past experiences of working in hospitals that made people feel uncomfortable. 'We wanted to avoid the subconscious triggers in the environment that induce anxiety. Most patients in a hospital feel intimidated.'

The second, which will have to await the results of more fund-raising, will include a water therapy area, an academic area for conferences, research and teaching, a multi-use space for therapeutic arts such as dance and music, and possibly a café-bistro and retail pharmacy. 'We have a dream that I call a wellness centre,' said Dr Reilly. 'People could come here in the evening and have water therapy, massage or aromatherapy, and enjoy good food in the café-bistro.'

The care that the hospital offers is unique, Dr Reilly believes, and it is now delivered in a setting that reflects and is indeed part of the approach.

'There are two main activities. The first is the integration of orthodox and complementary therapy and this is not just words, it really happens. The full range of orthodox investigations and treatments is available through the NHS Trust.

Second, we are about whole-person medicine, which embraces and harmonises many types of medicine.'

Dr Reilly believes that the big challenge now is to transcend the artificial divisions within medicine.

'This is really in its infancy. If you come to accept the merits of homoeopathy, Chinese medicine, herbalism and other complementary medicines, you then have to look at how you treat a given patient. When do you use a particular therapy? And what do you do when homoeopathy doesn't work? When orthodox medicine doesn't work? When acupuncture doesn't work? How do you help people to adjust?

The question of the effective therapeutic relationship is very important in all this. If there is a healing, constructive relationship between doctor and patient, then together we can go forward and look for answers.'

Figure 11.13 Glasgow Homoeopathic Hospital: entrance. Architect: MacLachlan Monaghan

Figure 11.14 Glasgow Homoeopathic Hospital: external view. Architect: MacLachlan Monaghan

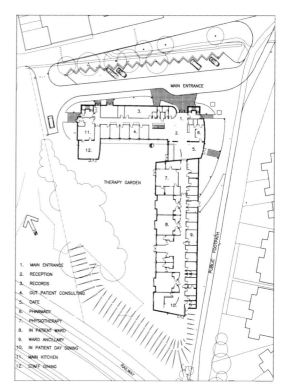

1. MAIN ENTRANCE
2. RECEPTION
3. RECORDS
4. OUT-PATIENT CONSULTING
5. CAFE
6. PHARMACY
7. PHYSIOTHERAPY
8. IN-PATIENT WARD
9. WARD ANCILLARY
10. IN-PATIENT DAY DINING
11. MAIN KITCHEN
12. STAFF DINING

Figure 11.15 Glasgow Homoeopathic Hospital: site plan – phase I. Architect: MacLachlan Monaghan

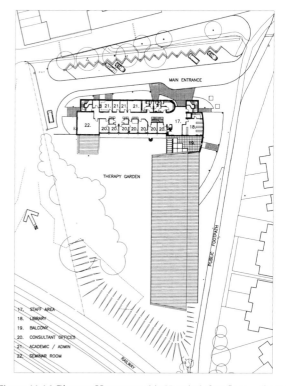

17. STAFF AREA
18. LIBRARY
19. BALCONY
20. CONSULTANT OFFICES
21. ACADEMIC / ADMIN
22. SEMINAR ROOM

Figure 11.16 Glasgow Homoeopathic Hospital: first floor – phase I. Architect: MacLachlan Monaghan

Acupuncture, autogenic training, massage and relaxation training are already well integrated into the care at Glasgow, but Dr Reilly and his staff intend to explore the boundaries with other therapists.

Dr Reilly stresses, however, the need for careful evaluation of the effectiveness of care: 'Some healing disciplines have a lot of common ground with compassion and therapeutic engagement. We try to understand that any result is attributed to. It calls for rigour and discernment.'

Dr Reilly is now looking for a new sub-title for the Glasgow Homoeopathic Hospital that will accurately reflect the work being done there, including the fact that homoeopathy is one part of a wider approach to care: 'We are now moving into a new century and this is a new hospital to tackle the vision.'

The Brief (extracts)

'Healing is a natural process. The task of the healer is to facilitate this process.'

Glasgow's new homoeopathic hospital will serve as a focus of care that will draw on modern and traditional approaches to create good medicine. This will be an important building. This new hospital will signal its healing purpose to viewers from the outside. It will also create a harmonious interior environment which will help in the process of healing.

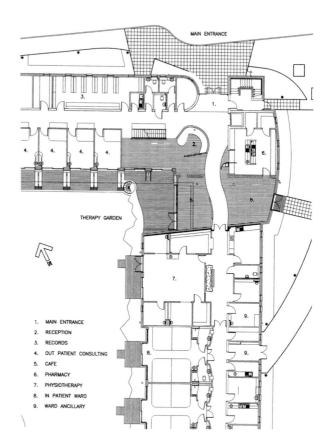

Figure 11.18 Glasgow Homoeopathic Hospital: site and part ground floor plan. Architect: MacLachlan Monaghan

1. MAIN ENTRANCE
2. RECEPTION
3. RECORDS
4. OUT PATIENT CONSULTING
5. CAFE
6. PHARMACY
7. PHYSIOTHERAPY
8. IN PATIENT WARD
9. WARD ANCILLARY

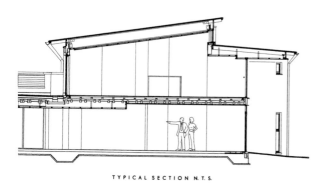

TYPICAL SECTION N.T.S.

ELEVATION TO SOUTH N.T.S.

Figure 11.17 Glasgow Homoeopathic Hospital: part section and elevation. Architect: MacLachlan Monaghan

Healing and this building both:

- take the materials of the natural world and draw them together in a form which is greater than the sum of their parts
- have ancient roots but look to the future
- are positive agents of change.

The people of Glasgow, in common with many communities, are increasingly demanding whole person forms of care. For over one and a half centuries the Glasgow Homoeopathic Hospital has pioneered an approach to healing separate to mainstream medicine as that has developed and changed.

In its relationship to Gartnavel Hospital this new building will signal the current, mutually supportive relationship between complementary and orthodox forms of care. As a separate building of distinctive character the new homoeopathic hospital will also emphasise its role in helping people to self-heal and in disseminating information on that process.

Glasgow's new homoeopathic hospital will be among the first significant buildings to be created in the period leading to Glasgow's celebration of its role as UK City of Architecture & Design 1999. This is an important project for the city.

Figure 11.19 Glasgow Homoeopathic Hospital. Architect: MacLachlan Monaghan (also in colour section)

Background

The practice of homoeopathic medicine in Glasgow goes back to the 1840s. Glasgow Homoeopathic Hospital has been based at its present location since the early part of this twentieth century. In common with the rest of Britain, demand for complementary medicine in west-central Scotland has steadily increased over recent years. The demand for outpatient services has increased by 30% since 1987 with referrals exceeding available appointments by 30% each month.

The need for improved homoeopathic facilities in Glasgow is exacerbated by a substantial demand for teaching and research in the field. The homoeopathic hospital's academic departments organise multidisciplinary modular courses which are the most popular of any postgraduate medical course offered in the UK. Over 100 students a year undertake the 1-year introductory course and around 50 go on to the second and third years. A total of 20% of Scottish GPs have completed the introductory course.

Location and site information

The site is situated within the grounds of Gartnavel General Hospital and extends to approximately to half an acre.

Visual and urban design objectives/materials

The new homoeopathic hospital will meet unique and special demands. It should be a building of the highest quality which signals its special function. As a significant new building designed at the outset of Glasgow's reign as Britain's City of Architecture and Design 1999, the new homoeopathic hospital will be a focus of considerable attention and should serve as a model to which similar facilities should aspire.

New accommodation: phase I

In addition to conventional medical practice Glasgow Homoeopathic Hospital offers a range of therapies including homoeopathy, acupuncture, neurotherapy, relaxation therapy and hypnosis. The bulk of this treatment is conducted in outpatient clinics but the hospital also has occupational therapy and physiotherapy departments on site. The new facility should be designed for future functional flexibility as clinical practice may change.

The Glasgow Homoeopathic Hospital cares for over 600 inpatients and day-cases a year. These patients require a range of services from 24-hour assessment to palliative care in the atmosphere of a therapeutic community. The new Hospital will have 15 beds which will be able to be used flexibly by in-patients, day cases or by patients only requiring overnight accommodation prior to their treatment.

It is intended that other patient accommodation will be used flexibly by different members of the multidisciplinary team working with individual, or groups of, patients. Staff and patients should be able to move easily between different parts of the Hospital. 15,000 out-patients attend each year, are seen by medical and nursing staff and their prescriptions are dispensed on site. Although every area of the hospital is busy, it is important that the general environment preserves patients' privacy and generates a peaceful and healing atmosphere.

Careful attention should be paid to providing barrier free access to people with mobility problems. Although only a few people with disabilities have to use a wheelchair all the time, they should be able to use the new hospital or visit friends and relatives with the minimum of inconvenience. The need for hospital visits for people with temporary mobility constraints (through illness, accident or even just being accompanied by a small child) should also be accommodated. Both phases of the new hospital should be designed with these considerations in mind.

New accommodation: phase II

As, in effect, the national centre for the development of complementary medicine and its holistic integration with orthodox care and a centre for scientific research, the second phase of the new facility must also integrate a library, academic research and teaching facilities. Enhancement of treatment and rehabilitation facilities will include a hydrotherapy pool, amongst other features.

Landscape/trees/planting

Homoeopathic medicine draws extensively on natural resources. It is, therefore, appropriate that the new building sits comfortably within its 'natural' setting. The possible importance of plants and trees to patients' feelings of comfort and security should be acknowledged and the planting of the areas associated with the new hospital might acknowledge the special properties of medical plants. The new building should integrate with its immediate environment.

Building and engineering services

The new building will be largely self-sufficient. While it will draw on the specialist medical resources of Gartnavel General Hospital and share laundry facilities, inpatient catering will be on site. Delivery and waste disposal should be planned to be as discreet as possible and away from inpatient accommodation.

Both building and engineering services should be designed to take account of best codes of practice with consideration of experience gained from successful contemporary hospital buildings. Suggestions of innovative means of reducing energy consumption would be welcomed by the client.

The quality of lighting to both the exterior and interior of the building is a further consideration in ensuring patient comfort. While the necessity of adequate lighting for elderly patients and those with poor sight is acknowledged, care should be taken to avoid glare and the sterility of fluorescent 'wash' lighting. Ease of control of lighting and energy saving measures should be considered. Lighting should, in general, be designed for low energy consumption. Office lighting should take account of the widespread use of computer terminals and the relevant European regulations.

Figure 11.20 The Haven Trust, London: exterior looking into reception. Architect: Devereux Architects (with Martin Hay), Partner Peter Hughes, Associate Darius Umrigar. Photographed by Nathan Willock (also in colour section)

Case study 3: The Haven Trust (Cancer Support Unit)

Architects: Devereaux Architects (with Martin Hay). Partner: Peter Hughes, Associate: Darius Umrigar

The following account is from a letter from Peter Hughes, Director, Devereux (23 April 2001 to the author).

'We first became involved in this project in February 1998. The project was introduced to this office by Martin Hay, a project architect working with us at that time. Martin had developed the scheme as a private job to Stage D before joining us. Devereux were then appointed by The Haven Trust to take the project through to completion with Martin acting as project architect. Martin has since left this office.

The funding for this project was raised through a series of charity events, and an on-going fundraising campaign. This process also continued during the construction stage, with many components and building materials pledged as donations to the Trust. These materials included plasterboard, light fittings, kitchen fittings, floor finishes, furniture, etc.

As there was no NHS precedent for this building type, the actual briefing process did not follow normal NHS procedures. The brief was formulated by Martin Hay in collaboration with members of the Trust, based on certain assumptions for room sizes. A degree of flexibility was built into the layout in anticipation of future change. However, this had to be achieved within the constraints of the existing building.

During this process close collaboration was maintained with leading breast cancer consultants from the Charing Cross Hospital. The centre also has links with the nearby Royal Marsden Hospital.

The site in Fulham, London, was also chosen for is close proximity to Charing Cross Hospital. The Haven is located approximately 3 minutes walk from Fulham Broadway underground station'.

The centre has received wide publicity and further reading can be found in Fairley (1997) and Scher (2000). The following extracts are from Peter Scher's article in *Hospital Development*:

'The Haven Trust was set up by art dealer Sarah Davenport. She realised the need for humane support to women at all stages of breast cancer (estimated at one in 11 women in the UK) when her children's nanny was diagnosed with

Figure 11.21 The Haven Trust, London: ground floor reception. Photographed by Nathan Willock

Figure 11.22 The Haven Trust, London: 'Tree of Life'. Photographed by Nathan Willock

it and was offered no information or support beyond a cup of tea. Sarah Davenport auctioned her own collection of paintings and with powerful backing (e.g. from Prince Charles, Sophie Rhys Jones, several important financial players in the city, national newspapers and magazines, as well as leading oncology specialists) raised the funds needed to develop and operate the centre. "No one", she said, "should ever have to face breast cancer alone".

An abandoned Welsh Presbyterian Chapel in Fulham that had been converted into a drama school was purchased. Martin Hay of Devereux Architects then worked with the client to develop and formulate the brief and to design the conversion of the building.

The ambience of this interior is enriched by gentle curves, for example in the suspended ceilings, the lift and stair enclosures, and the reception desk. There are high quality materials and finishes, e.g. timber flooring and rich carpets, and a number of commissioned art works by the Prince of Wales' Institute. These include a small fountain, a ceramic "Tree of Life" mural and the stained glass window. The colour scheme and lighting are also very successful and the architects have been able to incorporate numerous recesses and niches where flowers or other decorative elements may be placed. The design and furnishing is all of-a-piece, and an environment of very high quality has been achieved.

It seems certain that this centre, now named "The London Haven", will flourish, and there are plans to raise funds for establishing other centres elsewhere. It offers, free of charge, a drop-in facility, appointments with spe-

Figure 11.23 The Haven Trust, London: Detail stained glass and chairs. Photographed by Nathan Willock

cialist nurses, complementary therapies, counselling and support as well as professional advice, information and support on the telephone. The centre also has links with local oncology services at the Charing Cross and Royal Marsden Hospitals. The questions raised in my mind on seeing such a facility need serious consideration though the answers may not be easy to find.

Is this a better approach than that provided by the NHS or are these charities filling an unacceptable gap in NHS provision? Is there a unique benefit to patients in obtaining these very precisely targeted services from completely independent providers? Is the informal relationship with the NHS more appropriate and, if so, why? Can we envisage a future in which most serious conditions will be treated in specialist centres located wherever the sponsors choose? Specialists "isolated" at these centres may not readily be able to consult colleagues in other specialities about separate symptoms that their patients may develop.

The contrast between the support patients can obtain at the London Haven and what is offered in most parts of the NHS is scandalous. Indeed that is what led to the very existence of the Haven Trust. If we truly want a health service of excellence we would not rest until our government made sure that the NHS matched the standard set by such as this centre. It can be done in the NHS as I saw at the Glasgow Homoeopathic Hospital and when the design of the building matches the quality of the service the results are outstanding. Out of a disused Victorian chapel, the Haven Trust

Figure 11.24 The Haven Trust, London: sectional perspective. A drawing by Peter Hughes

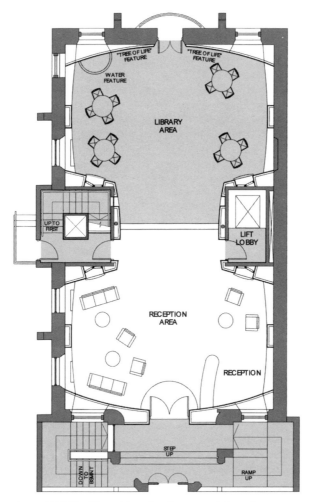

Figure 11.25 The Haven Trust, London: ground floor plan

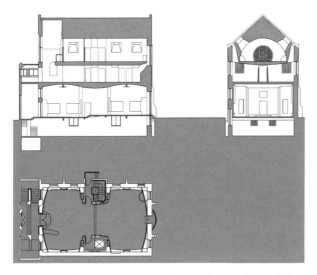

Figure 11.26 The Haven Trust, London: sections and ground floor plan

and Devereux Architects have made a new healthcare facility of the highest quality and I believe it will have a truly positive effect on the health outcomes of its users.'

Case study 4: Maggie Centre, Edinburgh (cancer support centre)

Architect: Richard Murphy Architects.
The following is Richard Murphy's account (18 June 2001).

Maggie Keswick Jenks founded the cancer care centre after her own diagnosis with cancer and her experience of how the National Health Service dealt with that period in her life. She became very interested in the idea of a place which was not run by the hospital, but had patients on the board and could get information on lifestyle issues such as diet, yoga, beautician, massage, and many other non-mainstream responses to the disease. She persuaded the Western General Hospital in Edinburgh to donate a disused stable and eventually we were appointed as the architects. The briefing of the building was complex as Maggie had many ideas as to what might happen there although the building itself was extremely small to accommodate everything. Essentially though shining through the whole experience was the idea that it should be as non-institutional as possible (no corridors) and the domestic model of a house was quickly arrived at. It should also be as open and as flexible as possible and hence our idea of single space with rooms that can be added or subtracted by the device of folding sliding doors. On entering the building, there is a big space which contains information, staircase/library, and lots of light and then views into smaller spaces of the familiar domestic nature of a kitchen and a living room and upstairs are two counselling rooms.

The building opened in 1996 and became an immediate success and quite quickly it was realized that an extension to double its size was needed. The cancer care centre movement has now grown with Edinburgh remaining as its central administrative base so there was need for more offices, a second counselling room, and a large activities room which is capable of subdivison. The extension completed this year has seen the building grow in two opposite directions, a two-storey development to the west and a new single-storey activity room to the northeast. In this way, the central space remains central to the building and although doubled in size, we hope the final complex remains non-institutional.

Architecturally, from the outside, extending one of our own buildings has been relatively easy as the original conversion envisaged the stable building as a shell into which an inner building was placed and this can be read clearly by the non-alignment of walls and glass block panels, etc. with the original openings. This inner building has then been extracted to the exterior in both directions so that the extensions are, we hope, relatively seamless affairs in both directions.

Figure 11.27 Maggie Centre, Edinburgh: external view. Architect: Richard Murphy Architects. Photographed by Alan Forbes (also in colour section)

The following article about the Maggie Centre, written by Catherine Croft appeared in *Building Health* a supplement of *Building Design* February 2001.

'Somewhere to come home to.

As a result of Maggie Jenck's experiences of cancer care, she set up the first Maggie's Centre cancer caring centre – using domestic scale and open layout to give patients "a home they wouldn't have quite dared build themselves". Now, with new schemes from, among others, Frank Gehry and Daniel Libeskind in the pipeline, there are plans for six centres.

For June Langstaff, a patient at Edinburgh's Western General Hospital undergoing five weeks of radiotherapy for breast cancer, the first Maggie's Centre was a real refuge. She describes the hospital's oncology department as being like "an enormous castle fortress", but says that walking through the door of Richard Murphy's nearby tiny table conversion made her "feel cuddled": cared-for from the very start. Given their objectives, this has to be the best tribute both architect and client could have ever hoped to receive.

The Maggie's Centres – and there are soon to be six of them, in Edinburgh, Glasgow, Dundee, Sheffield, Cambridge and London – have a very special brief. When Maggie Keswick Jencks was told that her own cancer had recurred and she had only three to four months to live her overworked consultant had no time to talk to her and her husband (critic Charles Jencks). Minutes after breaking the news to them, he was saying: "And I'm so sorry, dear, but could we move you to the corridor, we have so many patients waiting ...".

Maggie was determined that she would do all she could to ensure that the same didn't happen to anyone else, and that there was somewhere both cancer patient and their friends and relatives could go for information, support and to have time to adjust and think.

The Maggie's Centre cancer caring centres (the first of which she was able to be closely involved in as a new treatment gave her 18 months' remission), are not hospices, but places providing information for those faced with a bewildering range of complementary therapies and advice about diet, exercise, and relaxation, as well as complex decisions to make about conventional treatment. As programme director Andrew Anderson summarises, the Maggie's Centres "are both a bolt hole, somewhere it's okay to cry, and they are about making patients better, more demanding 'clients', who don't just feel pushed around by a system they can't control".

The brief for the new projects combines what has been learnt from Edinburgh with Maggie's original ideas. Each centre will be built in the grounds of a hospital with a specialist oncology department, but it is the anonymous, frighteningly institutional atmosphere of a large hospital that is to be avoided at all costs.

Corridors are eliminated, and it is important that on entering each building there are no dark corners and it is easy to see and understand the whole layout. As well as a small seating area with a fire, there is a prominent kitchen table, and plenty of spaces where it is possible to sit on the periphery but not feel excluded, so that patients can take their time deciding what activities or conversations they wish to participate in.

The relationship with the exterior is also important, and views of trees and nature are especially valued by both staff and patients. The site for the Dundee centre has to be the

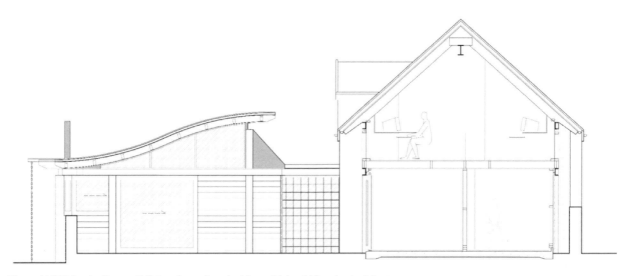

Figure 11.28 Maggie Centre, Edinburgh: section. Architect: Richard Murphy Architects

best yet in this respect: it looks down onto the river Dee and a separate fundraising project is seeking money to construct a lake in front of it, with a island for contemplation reached by a narrow bridge.

The brief states: "we need to think of all the aspects of hospital layouts which reinforce 'institution' – and then unpick them", and concludes by hoping that patients will experience each centre as feeling 'like a home they wouldn't have quite dared build themselves, and which makes them feel that there is at least one positive

aspect about their visit to the hospital which they may look forward to".

In Edinburgh, Murphy's original 1996 project has been extended, adding a larger multi-purpose meeting room, another consulting room and more offices from which to oversee all the new centres. It is still very small, and the domestic scale that is the key to its success is skilfully maintained.

A second centre is underway, with a £360,000 lottery grant as part of the funding package. Like Edinburgh it is

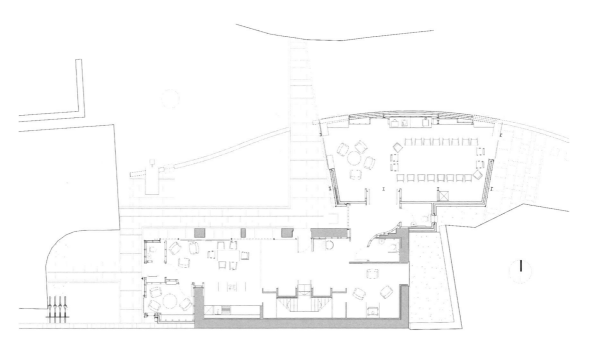

Figure 11.29 Maggie Centre, Edinburgh: ground floor plan. Architect: Richard Murphy Architects

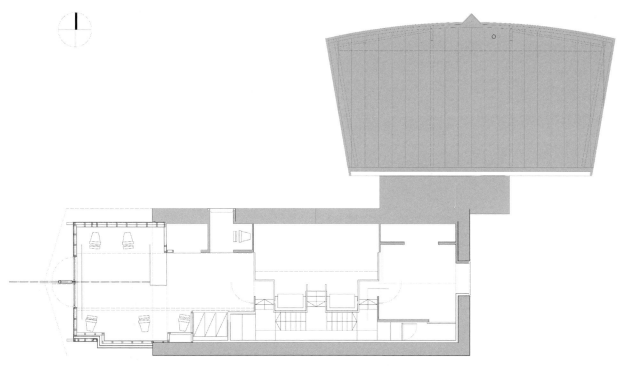

Figure 11.30 Maggie Centre, Edinburgh: first floor plan. Architect: Richard Murphy Architects

a conversion, this time of a small Victorian gatehouse at Glasgow's Western Infirmary Hospital. It too is designed by a local Scottish architect (Page & Park, best known for the Glasgow Lighthouse building). Again the kitchen is at the heart of the building. The library is at the base of the castellated turret and will be lit from above, and there will be a relaxation room in a lead-clad extension raised a half level to increase privacy.

The next two centres, however, are causing much more excitement: Frank Gehry is designing the Dundee Maggie's Centre, while Daniel Libeskind is working on a scheme for Cambridge. both Gehry and Libeskind were friends of Maggie's and have donated their time for free. Centres for Sheffield and the Charing Cross Hospital in London are also planned, but as yet no architects have been selected.

Rather than resorting to a committee, this very personal approach to developing each project will be enormously aided by having Marsha Blakenham acting as client. Blakenham, whose own home epitomises the relaxed open-pan ethos sought for the cancer care centres, was a close friend of Maggie's and will liaise closely with oncology nurse Laura Lee who treated her and now heads the Edinburgh Centre. "We are absolutely not rolling out a franchise", she says. "We want every Maggie's Centre to have its own distinctive identity".

The importance of good design and aesthetics is as important to her as to all the other key players (she is a painter and potter when not fundraising and inspiring others). She is aware that using "star architects" will generate extra interest and facilitate fundraising, but she is adamant that neither she nor Charles Jencks is putting an intellectualised architectural agenda at the top of their list of priorities.

Indeed, although Jencks sees the way in which Murphy weaves together the old and the new as post-modern, he also emphasises that the centres are "not pushing a most-modernist line". He sees Gehry's experience of the vernacular as particularly relevant and hopes that each project will combine modesty with "great inspirational architecture".

Frank Gehry remembers Maggie as "a very special lady: close to sainthood". His office has been working full time on the Dundee Centre as "a labour of love" for four months and has designed everything including the furniture and the light fittings. Stirling-based James Stephens Architects is now producing working drawings and will supervise the project on site. The initial models were rejected for being "too Ronchamp-like". Gehry admits that they were "excessive: a tour de force – nice sculpture but irrelevant". He is very aware that some people have seen the anonymity and low-key exterior of the Edinburgh centre as key to its success and that the last thing the organisation wants is to be accused of commissioning fancy architecture for the sake of it. He has sleepless nights over this very point and says that Maggie finally came to him in a dream and told him to "calm it down".

The latest version is more modest: in his words "more subtle and laid-back". His initial image of a tower as a "beacon of hope" is retained, but a flamboyant mini-Bilbao roofspace has been replaced by a folded stainless steel sheet (titanium would have been too expensive), across

143

which he hopes that soft cloud shadows will ripple. This corrugated roof form was inspired by the folds in the sleeve of a blouse worn by a woman in a Vermeer painting in the Metropolitan, a postcard of which is pinned over Gehry's desk and reminds him of Maggie.

Daniel Libeskind has yet to commit himself on paper. Blakenham describes his scheme as "just a twinkle in his eye", but he has been talking about producing a "tree house" for the very tight site at Addenbrookes Hospital in Cambridge.

He is extremely excited by the ethical content of the project and is aiming to produce "not just a shallow image, but a place that is interesting to be in and dignified". In many ways the project is the exact opposite of his Jewish Museum, which overawes and disorientates the visitor. Libeskind is also highly unusual in that he has gone straight to building large, public buildings, rather than starting with small domestic projects – although he is now also working on a villa in Majorca which is about the same size as the Maggie Centre. He will be presenting initial concepts at the Soane Museum at the end of February.

As for the future, there is no doubt that the Maggie's Centres are fulfilling a very real need and the concept could spread further. New advances in genetic testing for cancer-causing genes will create additional demand for counselling, information and support.

However, as yet the organisation feels that six centres is enough, and that they will want time to learn from the first generation of buildings, and consider how the charity's structure could grow before commissioning any more. Although cancer affects men and women more or less equally, 70% of the visitors to the Maggie's Centre are women. Staff are convinced that this is just symptomatic of the British male's reluctance to discuss feelings, but it might be worth considering whether the kitchen-table domestic ethos is less appealing to men. There has also been some criticism of the *House & Garden*, comfortable middle-classness of the atmosphere.

Gehry believes that "we underestimate what architecture can do: we don't play enough", and the Maggie's Centres have certainly encouraged inventive play focused on very serious ethical issues. But for architects, perhaps the most heartening aspect of this very worthwhile project is the recognition by both client and building users that buildings can empower people and make them feel good about themselves, and that this is worth paying a bit extra for.'

The final test will be the post-occupancy evaluation of this series of buildings. Will they achieve the objective of providing an environment for the caring interaction of human emotions or will the aspirations of architect 'prima donnas' submerge the objectives of the brief with an over concern for form? This approach stands at the opposite end of the spectrum to design by management, cost planning and space planning allocations.

Phase II

Since it opened in November 1997 Maggie's Centre has attracted a large number of visitor and friends and the range of activities that takes place there has widened considerably. During that time the need has become apparent for a series of meeting rooms for larger groups or more strenuous activities.

The additional accommodation required two large meeting rooms, a consulting room for visiting therapists and a permanent office. While the new extension doubles the floor area of the centre, it is designed to preserve a domestic scale. All the activities of the new are visible from the original centre space, which still functions as the front door to the centre.

The extension is in two independent directions to the west and to the north east. The western extension is two-storey with administration on the top floor and additional consulting room on the lower floor.

The extension to the north-east is conceived as an independent but linked building to the original. This is a single volume which can be divided unequally and extends with a rendered retaining wall along its northern boundary to form a terrace on the eastern side and a boundary to the garden on the western side. Again the materials are the same as the other extension with a lead roof, steel framing and Douglas Fir framed windows. the monopitch roof is designed to admit south light into north facing rooms while its sinusoidal form deliberately avoids any conversation with the roof pitch of the existing building.

Case study 5: Martin House and Naomi House (two children's hospice projects)

Architect: Michael Wildblood, Wildblood Macdonald.
The following is the architect's account.

Martin House

Selection of architect

In the late Autumn of 1984 we were telephoned to ask if we were prepared to enter a 'limited competition' for the design of Martin House, a new children's hospice, to be constructed at Boston Spa near Leeds.

We would not normally participate in an unofficial competition of this nature but as the proposal was:

1. for what seemed to be an immensely worthwhile charity
2. on our doorstep (3 miles from our office)
3. likely to offer possibilities for future work on this new building type.

We threw ourselves wholeheartedly into the project, making a model of our sketch proposals over the Christmas holiday.

In early 1985 we were appointed as architects for Martin House.

Briefing process

- The first move in the briefing process was a visit to Helen House in Oxford (the only children's hospice in Western Europe at the time). I spent a full day there washing up, playing with the children and talking to parents and staff, a day worth more than a week of reading in the briefing process. (The Reverend Richard Seed, the Chairman of the Martin House movement, had been a Curate in Oxford and knew Helen House well.)
- Helen House could not be 'copied'. It had been built in the grounds of a convent with many of its administrative functions undertaken elsewhere. Martin House had to be 'stand alone' and totally 'self-contained'.
- The client briefing team comprised the administrator, a paediatrician, an oncologist, two parents of subject children and a representative of the board of governors. The head nurse was appointed during the detail design, and joined the client group at that stage.
- The essential elements of the brief which soon emerged were:
  - A children's hospice had to be very different from an adult hospice. It was not a place to die in, but a place where children with life-threatening illnesses could come with their families for respite care.
  - It therefore had to be school, holiday camp, but mainly home, all rolled into one.
  - It had to be as little like an institution as possible.
  - A careful balance had to be struck between it being like a normal school or home and it having the nursing aids and equipment (which can be unsightly) needed to assist the work.
- The milestone decisions (town planning strategy, approval of budget, acceptance of tenders, etc.) were taken by the board of governors.

Fundraising and procurement

In parallel with the development of the brief and the design,
the board of governors undertook a major fundraising exercise to cover the construction and fitting out costs (circa £2 million) and an endowment fund to finance the anticipated £0.75 million running costs (1987 prices).

The majority of the funds were raised by the general public and bodies such as The Lions and Rotary Club. A number of grants were obtained but virtually no funding was obtained from the public purse.

(Approximately 4% of the running cost is obtained from the public sector, the balance being raised by the general public and interest generated by the endowment fund.)

When a sum equal to the construction costs had been raised a decision to appoint the main contractor was taken. Traditional procurement routes were used.

The wish of certain individuals and bodies to donate in 'kind' rather than 'cash' posed additional problems relating to the need to adhere to the agreed specification and cost control of the project.

User group discussion

Apart from the involvement of subject children parents in the client group there was no user group discussion. This should be seen in sharp contrast with the design of a new teenage unit which is currently being designed. For this building there has been a very lively meeting of 40 young people who have exceeded their prognosis and outgrown the child-centred ambience of Martin House.

Flexibility and sustainability

The site in Boston Spa was chosen because:

- It was close to the A1 (2 miles) for ease of access from a large part of northern England.
- It was on a bus route from Leeds and Wetherby.
- It was on the edge of a large village/small town with pubs, shops and other facilities within walking distance.

Figure 11.31 Martin House, Boston Spa, Leeds: external view. Architect: Wildblood MacDonald (also in colour section)

- It was within the catchment area of a GP practice that could offer support.

It was resolved at an early stage that the building need not be capable of expansion. It was agreed that expansion should take the form of the construction of new hospices elsewhere rather than jeopardise the planned 'homely size of eight children's bedrooms (+2 contingency rooms and support accommodation).

Extensions have taken place over subsequent years but these have been in answer to required improvements for support facilities rather than to the overall capacity of the building.

Naomi House

Selection of architect

Our selection as architects for Naomi House followed a visit of Trustees from Winchester to Martin House, who were undertaking research prior to the setting up of a similar facility in Wessex.

They were told by Martin House Administration 'you should use our architects!'

Briefing process

- The selection of the site (which had ramifications on the design of the building) was much more critical for Naomi House than had been the case for its predecessor. A

planning refusal for a site near Romsey led to an extensive site search and caused the acceptance of the offer of land within the grounds of a nursing home to be readily accepted. The offer was for a smaller parcel of land (2 acres rather than 4) and came with an insistence upon a traditional building vocabulary.

- The client briefing process was much less involved than Martin House. It was led by a trustee who was the works bursar of a local higher educational establishment, the administrator (a retired army officer) and the local general practitioner. But a great deal of reliance was placed upon us as architects for the delivery of similar facilities to those provided at Martin House.
- We became so concerned that we were assuming responsibility for both design and brief that we insisted upon a full day presentation to the full board of trustees. It covered all aspects of the design and systems to enable them to 'share the ownership' of the building.
- The design has many similarities with Martin House in terms of size, linear structure and protective overall plan shape. Improvements undertaken in Yorkshire: the provision of en-suite facilities for parents and enlarged care team offices, were incorporated. But differences such as a less overt 'Christian' foundation, a better hydrotherapy facility and a more 'additive design' distinguish it from its predecessor.

Figure 11.32 Naomi House, Winchester: external view. Architects: Wildblood MacDonald (also in colour section)

Fundraising and procurement

Fundraising and procurement took a similar route to Martin House. In terms of fund raising there was a more developed organisation with town groups committing themselves to achieving target sums. The full endowment sum target of £5 million was reached prior to the start of construction.

User group discussions

There was virtually no user group discussion. Being a new facility in a new area, this was difficult to arrange. Much reliance was placed upon the Martin House experience.

Flexibility and sustainability

As with Martin House, it was agreed that the building need not be capable of expansion. However the simple cross wall construction and abundance of roof voids will allow some modification in the future.

The siting of the building has similar locational qualities too. It is adjacent to a main trunk road, within 10 miles of a major city, but at a local level is within walking distance of village pubs and shops.

Naomi House, was described in an article published by *Building* (24 October 1997) and the following extract by Martin Spring describes the design approach.

In 1990, Peter Lee, a rural Hampshire GP, found himself faced with a distressing problem. A local couple were unable to attend a school concert in which their child was performing because their other child was so severely handicapped that he could not be left, even for one evening and with nursing care. In the event, Dr Lee went beyond the normal call of GP duty and baby-sat for the evening.

Seven years later, Lee has helped solve such problems in a permanent and spectacular fashion. A children's hospice,

Hospice ground-floor plan encourages togetherness

The 10-bedroom children's hospice is shaped like a horseshoe encircling the children.

① The 10 children's bedrooms are given pride of place on the ground floor, facing southwards to a walled garden.

② Each child has a small external patio reached by a french window.

③ A central corridor forms the main circulation spine.

④ The dining and living rooms are clustered at the east (a) end of the spine; specialist areas are at the west (b).

⑤ Ancillary accommodation forms four spurs to the north of the horseshoe. The four wings contain: (a) entrance and offices, (b) plant rooms, (c) nurses' and parents' rooms, and (d) a non-denominational chapel.

Cross-section illustrates child's scale

The 55-room building has been reduced in apparent scale and made homely so as not to intimidate vulnerable children.

① The entire complex appears to be an extended single-storey house, with double pitched roofs that sweep down to low overhanging eaves.

② An upstairs floor of staff rooms, parents' bedrooms, store rooms and an escape corridor has been partly hidden within the roof space.

③ Principal ground-floor rooms benefit from the extra headroom.

④ Children's bedrooms and ground-floor corridors borrow daylight from rear rooflights through concealed light shafts.

⑤ Service ducts have been neatly concealed alongside a central spine wall. No ducts, flues or external pipework mar the rustic brick and tiled exterior.

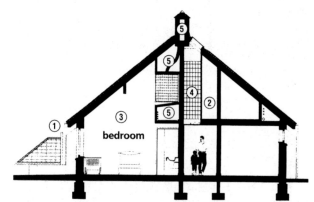

Figure 11.33 Naomi House, Winchester: plan and section. Architect: Wildblood MacDonald

purpose-built just outside the village of Sutton Scotney, now offers luxury hotel accommodation where children with incurable diseases and their families can take short breaks from their otherwise constant stress. Named Naomi House, the hospice was entirely funded and developed by a trust set up by Lee and many others, who raised a total of £5m in private donations in southern England.

The form of the building, completed in June at a cost of £2.25m, is as extraordinary as its purpose. The first thing to strike the visitor is its arts-and-crafts revival style. The building exudes Lutyens from every handmade brick, rustic roof tile and gable end chimneypiece. The second prominent feature of the building is its rounded, horseshoe layout that partly encloses a large south-facing garden.

Naomi House was designed by architect Michael Wildblood, the UK's only expert in children's hospice design. Wildblood's Yorkshire-based practice, Wildblood Macdonald, also has first-hand experience of restoring Lutyens architecture, notably Goddards in Surrey.

Even so, the idea of borrowing a traditional style did not originate from Wildblood. It came from Mrs Cornelius-Reid, who donated the site on her estate in return for a dozen red roses presented each Midsummer's Day and after whose daughter the hospice is named.

Non-institutional design: more relevant than the arts-and-crafts styling is the building's horseshoe format. Taking pride of place on the concave side of the horseshoe are 10 children's bedrooms, each with its own french windows opening out on to shared south-facing patios that merge into the communal walled garden beyond.

"The gentle curve embraces the children and gives a feeling of being equal and together", explains Wildblood. It also gives a non-institutional twist to a basic building layout around a central corridor.

All the other 45 rooms of the hospice are wrapped behind, above and at either end of the sequence of ground floor bedrooms. Plugging into the back, or northern side, of the horseshoe are four wings containing main entrance and offices, services plant, parents' bedrooms and a non-denominational chapel.

Wildblood describes the hospice as "a holiday camp, school, but mainly a home – all rolled into one", and has designed it to be as welcoming and non-institutional as possible. At the same time, he has tried to give the building a strong identity, partly to have an immediate impact on visitors, who only stay for a few days and partly to soak up the garish modern plastic toys and children's paintings that will accumulate.

In this sense, the traditional styling of the building has not been a hindrance. "I didn't weep buckets when we were stuck with a traditional style," admits Wildblood. "It has helped create a feeling of home and domesticity, though balanced with the need for proper equipment."

The building is brought down to a child's scale, with low eaves, even though much of it is two-storey. Natural tactile materials are used throughout – local handmade bricks and tiles on the outside, and natural timber on the inside.'

Case study 6: The Cornerstone Centre (primary care resource centre)

Architect: Fairhurst Design Group, Manchester.
This account of the project was provided by Tropus Project Solutions, The Cornerstone Centre, Manchester.

Introduction

The Cornerstone Centre is one of the first primary care resource centres to be developed in the country. The building is located on a prime site, in an area of Manchester currently the subject of major redevelopment. The building was developed as a PFI contract by McBains for the Mancunian Community Health NHS Trust. The building contract was basically developed on a design and build basis. The main contractor being John Turner & Sons of Preston. The appointed architect was the Fairhurst Design Group of Manchester.

The building is not only used by the Mancunian Community Health NHS Trust but also by the North Manchester Health NHS Trust who have relocated their consultancy and physiotherapy services from the old Ancoats Hospital which is in the process of being demolished.

Briefing process

The briefing process was lead by the Manchurian NHS Trust Director of Facilities, Mr Mike Dean, who was responsible for determining the operational requirements of the various services including those of the other user groups. The output specification and room data sheets were developed by the architect, Mike Dean, and the service providers along with McBains over a period of 3 years.

Due to the nature of the building the briefing process required precise details especially regarding the specialist equipment for example in the dental area which required the assistance of a contractor who specialises in the design and installation of dental equipment. The ethos of the building is to provide health care for the local community and to make the building available to the community to use in the evening when parts of the building can be made available. This resulted in the need to agree a design which was flexible, secure and practical for both out of hours use and operational use for NHS staff during normal working hours.

The requirements of the North Manchester NHS Trust also required detailed scrutiny in order to establish a design suitable for use by the various consultants and nursing staff. In the design of consulting rooms, particular attention was paid to the clinical areas where specialist equipment is used, such as X-ray viewers, autoclaves and the storage of medical equipment.

Mancunian Community Health Trust requirements

The Trust have developed facilities for the following services:

- Dental – there are four surgeries, an X-ray room, X-ray development area and a preparation room. Two of the surgeries have a gas scavenging system which allows general anaesthetic to be used together with a recovery room. However, current legislation does not allow general anaesthetics to be carried out. These facilities are supported by a dedicated reception area and office area.

- Orthoptics – an area was designed to allow for eye tests and general examinations to take place. Particular attention was paid to the size of the room to provide the required distances for examinations. The provision of equipment in this area determined the general layout and special requirements.
- Audiology and speech and language therapy – these are two separate services, however the outcome of the discussions with these departments regarding the user requirements has resulted in common areas being provided. Within the brief for audiology unit is a requirement for the treatment of the walls to remove any reverberation. Particular attention has been paid to wall treatment and soundproofing. Consideration had to be given to noise disturbance from services such as ducting in the ceiling void and pipework.
- Podiatry – two surgeries have been provided for these services together with a writing area and IT base. During the discussions with the user group it became apparent that the location of electrical sockets was critical. It is important to have as much flexibility to allow for the podiatrist to operate either right handed or left handed. It is also important to provide a writing area in each surgery. This allows the podiatrist to complete patient notes at the point of treatment.
- Mid-wife services/baby clinic – although these services are not provided each day, the building has been designed to be flexible in offering facilities. An area known as the group activity room has been provided. This room off the main reception area has its own storage area, kitchen, store room, toilet and baby change area. This room is suitable for many varying uses such as a meeting room, training area and counselling facility. It was important to provide the toilet, change area, kitchen and store. This allowed for the self-contained facilities suitable to suit the various uses of the room and to avoid disturbance and provide a degree of confidentiality.
- Seminar and training facilities – like other organisation facilities for meeting and training sessions are sometimes limited. At the Centre two dedicated areas are available. These rooms are as a result of the briefing process located remote from the main clinical areas. Consideration had to be given to provide separate access and security to other parts of the building when the rooms are used out of normal hours by community groups, etc. Within the design the areas had to be made as flexible as possible and in close proximity to toilet areas. Each room has TV video facilities and projection equipment for training purposes. The design layout had to cater for the projected maximum population of the areas. Therefore in the training room a sliding dividing screen is provided to allow maximum use or to divide the room for smaller groups.
- Reception area – as mentioned earlier the centre not only serves the Mancunian Community Health NHS Trust but also other users such as the North Manchester NHS Trust who have the consulting room and nursing facilities. In consultation between both trusts the design of the reception and waiting area has been designed to accommodate three reception staff. Two staff employed by the Community Trust and one member of staff employed by North Manchester Trust. In the preparation of the design brief, particular attention was given to providing a pleasant friendly area with the capability of being secure, flexible and to provide seating for patients visiting all the services within the centre. Although all clinical services are located on the ground floor it was not by agreement considered a requirements to have designated areas. It was also, again by agreement with the users, considered necessary to provide a small play area with toys for young children to use whilst waiting to be attended to.
- The enquiry counter was the subject of much debate. Taking into consideration the need to provide a friendly environment the major point of debate was the need to provide some form of screen between the public and staff. It was agreed by all parties that no screen would be provided at the time the building opened. It was agreed that for a period of three months the question of a screen would be monitored. After this period it was found that there were no security issues and that the screen was not necessary. This resulted in a contract saving in the order of £5000.
- Security – the Manchurian Community Trust have some 32 health centres and clinics in the Manchester area. The policy is not to have any form of high level security such as CCTV systems or security guards. This was not always agreeable to all parties. Security has been only provided in the form of shutters to all ground floor windows and to two first floor windows which provide roof access.
- General office accommodation – accommodation is provided at first-floor level in a large open plan area. This accommodation was agreed to be flexible to house Trust staff such as health workers, district nurses and outside agencies such as home start and having a voice. The brief called for flexibility of services including power points and IT sockets to cater for the immediate and future needs. The briefing process with senior staff agreed that as the main office is open plan, an area should be provided for confidential one-to-one sessions. Two small areas have been provided in the form of small enclosed rooms with glazed wall.
- Facilities management – the property is owned by Tropus Project Solutions as such a dedicated facilities manager is based at the centre. The role of the facilities manager is to ensure that the building is always available for its use and maintained in a clean and tidy manner by contractors employed by the company.

North Manchester Health NHS Trust requirements

North Manchester Health NHS Trust appointed their own project manager to provide a design brief for their requirements which included consulting rooms, clinical area and

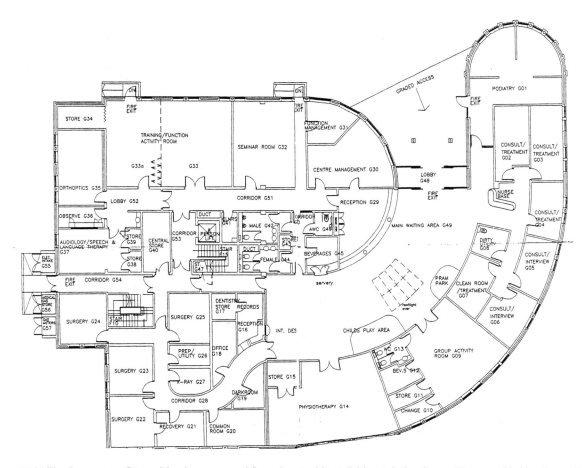

Figure 11.34 The Cornerstone Centre, Manchester: ground floor plan. Architect: Fairhurst design Group. Notes provided by: Tropus Project Solutions

facilities for physiotherapy. The project manager consulted direct with the Trust's users. During the end period of the construction period there were minor problems with the general layout of some areas which resulted in some minor changes to room layout. This was due to a change of mind in terms of desk positions, etc. It is important that such changes are avoided. There was an agreed 'cut-off' point but changes in staff can be problematic on any project. With the reception counter there was a lesson to be learnt. Sometimes it is worth monitoring a situation for an agreed period before making costly changes.

Conclusion

It is vital that in the briefing process consultation takes place with the end users. The management does not always have the hands on knowledge of the day-to-day operations of services. Hindsight is always a wonderful thing but can be extremely expensive. The minor details are as important as the major details. Additional sockets, for example, are costly and unless the project manager has an understanding of the user requirements items such as sockets can be missed. It is imperative to agree furniture and equipment require-

ments room by room, especially clinical equipment which may require specific services.

The briefing process should consider every option available. In the design of a new building there is always the opportunity to change work practices which can be more effective and less costly to manage.

The following extracts are from the Cornerstone Centre, Operational Policy and Principles of Operation.

Introduction

The Cornerstone Centre is an East Manchester locality base for services provided by health and partner organisations. Services provided should be locally sensitive and responsive to need. It is also a community facility and the public will be encouraged to book rooms and use it as a centre for advice and support.

Philosophy

The Cornerstone Centre is a resource that is available to the local community, the non-statutory sector, NHS and other appropriate agencies. Rooms within the centre will not have the names of services on them in keeping with the principle of multi-purpose rooms. The centre will be an example of successful collaborative working and patient-focused care.

All users and potential users of the centre will be entitled to representation on the centre management committee, which will be empowered to make decisions about services provided within the building.

Aims and objectives
- Staff will follow good customer service practices.
- Professional staff will work in a truly multidisciplinary way and ensure that the services provided to patients are seamless.
- Community use of the centre will be actively encouraged, such that they feel ownership of the building.
- It will not be possible to block-book multipurpose rooms.
- Office space will also be, on the whole, multipurpose.
- Non-statutory organisations and the local community may receive preferential treatment when booking rooms.
- All users of the building will be entitled to attend regular site meetings, where are aspects of the running of the building will be discussed.
- Patients will be encouraged to make comments, suggestions or complaints about the centre.

Objectives of the centre's staff
- To work in partnership with the local community.
- To try and meet unmet needs which have been identified.
- To work in a truly multidisciplinary way, with good communication and regular clinical meetings and aiming to share one set of case notes per patient (MCHT only).
- To learn from other professionals within the multidisciplinary team.
- To follow best practice and evidence-based treatments.
- To seek out members of the public who would benefit from the services offered.
- To provide expertise, information, advice and support to meet all needs.
- To work in a welcoming and flexible way which suits the needs of the public.
- To focus on prevention.
- To promote equal opportunities and be sensitive to cultural and religious beliefs.

Principles of operation

1. The overall running of the centre will be overseen by the centre management committee, which will consist of representatives from all users and potential users of the facilities.
2. All room bookings will be made through the reception and the receptionists will aim to work in an integrated way such that they can cover for each other during lunchtimes, absences, etc.
3. The aim is that most rooms can be used by anyone. Rooms will not be dedicated to a particular service or agency.

4. Office space will also be, on the whole, multipurpose, with few dedicated desks or dedicated office areas. The single rooms upstairs will not be allocated as they are to be used for confidential discussions. Staff should not leave belongings on desks or in drawers, but there will be lockers provided.
5. Generally, the multipurpose rooms cannot be block-booked and there will be a limit as to how far in advance they can be booked, but there will be some discretion if the room is only booked for one or two sessions per week, or for external training, etc. People or services should not leave equipment or possessions in rooms after use and must clear them up at the end of their session.
6. Community use of the facilities is to be actively encouraged, such that a target for this will be set. One-third of all bookings for the multipurpose rooms should be from the community. To meet this target community bookings will get priority on some occasions.
7. Non-statutory organisations will be encouraged to use the centre and their requests may receive preferential treatment.
8. To encourage communication between different disciplines it is hoped to pilot a system where only one set of notes is held for each patient (MCHT only).
9. Multidisciplinary clinical meetings will be held on a regular (monthly) basis to discuss improvements in ways of working, sharing clinical expertise and to improve understanding of each other's roles. Clinical outcomes and quality of services provided will also be discussed.
10. Regular site meetings will be held where all aspects of the building will be discussed, i.e. the way it operates, any faults, repairs or improvements needed, etc.
11. The centre will operate within the policies and procedures of MCHT.
12. A suggestion box will be introduced and comments received will be discussed by the centre management committee.
13. All agencies and members of the public who use the building will agree to abide by the above principles.

Please note the Mancunian Community NHS Trust has been re-organised. The main occupiers are now 'North Manchester, NHS Trust'.

Case study 7: Greenwich Millennium Village (primary school and health centre)

Architect: Edward Cullinan Architects.
The Millennium primary school, hall and health centre, within the pioneering Greenwich Millennium Village, is a practical demonstration of the Government's vision of sustainable urban communities. In a new kind of facility for this new community, education and health care are linked on one, relatively small, site and provide fully integrated services.

The three interconnected buildings reuse a typical brownfield site and are placed by the north-west entrance to the new village, beside the pedestrian route to the Millennium Dome.

Right by the village entrance stands the school hall, which is also a public hall, whose circular form creates a symbolic gatepost or lighthouse for visitors and villagers alike.

In the spirit of the Millennium Village the buildings are built right up to the pedestrian piazza, and all the entrances open directly off it; the space of the piazza is framed by rippling walls of English larch.

The more private rooms of the buildings, classrooms, consulting rooms, waiting and treatment rooms face due south onto their own gardens and playgrounds. By facing all the main rooms due south and by the use of protective awnings, the buildings will benefit from useful passive solar gain in winter, whilst still cutting out the heat and glare of the higher summer sun.

The sustainable character of the buildings include this passive solar design, very high levels of natural day-lighting and insulation and low rates of air infiltration. Furthermore it uses the Termodeck system of passing the fresh air through the holes in the pre-cast concrete slabs to provide passive cooling in summer and 100% fresh air all the year round; thereby the school meets the most demanding Department for Education guidelines.

The landscape to the south of the school and health centre is designed for the benefit of both school and village. Close to the school are small playgrounds for infants, while further away is a more vigorous playground for juniors; beyond lies a floodlit all-weather pitch. This landscape is contained within a densely planted ring of hills created from recycled material.

Innovation in the school and health centre: key distinguishing features

Lifecycle costing:
- sustainable materials with low embodied energy

Figure 11.35 Greenwich Millennium Village: waiting area. Courtesy of English Partnerships/Henderson (also in colour section)

- specification of natural and/or recyclable materials with avoidance of pvc
- durable materials self-finished where possible.

Energy:
- high levels of insulation to reduce running costs
- high degree of air tightness to reduce heat loses.
- double-glazed, low e glazing with an overall low u value to the external envelope
- south facing to maximise solar gain
- Termodeck – energy efficient heating, cooling and ventilation system
- automatic sensors for lighting.

Meeting new educational standards:
- meeting fully the standards of bb 87 and bb 90
- ventilation – continuous fresh air to proscribed rate of air changes in excess of new legislation for health in educational buildings
- daylighting – achieving 4% natural daylighting (lightwells) – reduces energy use
- acoustics – designed to achieve a reverb time of 0.8–1.0 seconds to teaching spaces. Also partitions to achieve 51Db reduction, doors and screens 37db.

Extended school facilities:
- food tech – an area for sitting, eating and socialising before and after school
- enlarged practical area for hobbies, arts and crafts
- library and shared ICT area for study support
- new guidelines for teaching spaces – larger class areas sufficient for whole-class literacy, numeracy and other class-work
- greater amount of soft external play in proportion to hard,
- large designated areas for storage.
- early years centre – has capacity to offer an extended day for 48 weeks a year.

Special educational needs (SEN) :
- anticipated 25% of pupils will have SEN (physically disabled, visually impaired, behavioural difficulties, hearing difficulties)
- designated spaces – personal care suite, large and small group room, assessment room, changing/shower room, disabled toilets
- links to the health centre – physiotherapy, nurse support, etc.

Information technology:
- following new curriculum guidelines with designated areas for IT teaching
- electronic whiteboards, video conferencing and cable connections to most rooms
- extensive trunking for maximum flexibility in use

Community use:
- after hours school club, creche and early years nursery
- one-stop-shop – to inform the villagers of local events and opportunities

- all-weather pitch and badminton court available for hire – revenue for school
- drama/music studio available for after hour classes
- open learning centre and community rooms available all day for adult learning.
- school hall available for theatre, community events and ecumenical use.

Health centre/school:
- baby clinic
- medical checks, school nurse, SEN support, etc.

Transport:
- limited parking to discourage car use to the facilities
- integrated bus links
- tube and river bus link nearby
- encouragement of cycling and walking through cycle lanes, 150 m cycle hitching rails to the buildings, buildings set within a pedestrian street and a village extolling pedestrian movement.

Landscape:
- indigenous species planted
- diversity of planting – woods, shrubs, aquatic landscape, wild flowers and grasses, scented and tactile plants around play areas
- area for childrens' planting
- re-use of a brownfield site.

The primary school

The primary school is for 420 4–11 year olds, initially one form of entry rising to two in 2003 or when required. Its basic accommodation is in line with DfEE Building Bulletin BB82, and its floor area is that recommended for these numbers (1568 m^2). The school is one of the first to comply with the new demanding requirements of BB87 and BB90 with regard to low energy usage, guaranteed ventilation provision and exemplary natural lighting. The gross floor area of the primary, early years and adult facilities is around 2800 m^2.

Figure 11.36 Greenwich Millennium Village, façade. Courtesy of English Partnerships/Henderson

Figure 11.37 Greenwich Millennium Village: detail – corner seat. Photographed by Morley von Sternberg

The school will have its own early years centre (EYC) with, when fully open, full-time equivalent places for 50 3–4 year olds, 14 2–3s, 10 1–2s, and a crèche for the use of parents attending the health centre or other activities in the school. The nursery playrooms will benefit from close working with the adjoining pair of reception classes. The EYC will have the capacity to offer an extended day to under-5s for 48 weeks of the year, with integrated provision of education, care, health and family services along early excellence and sure start principles.

A small turning and parking area is provided for disabled access and deliveries, but most people will arrive on foot or cycle. To cope with the visitors expected, the reception area is bigger than usual and designed for separate access by – and security of – the different user groups.

The school and EYC will be fully inclusive of children with special educational needs (SEN) with disabled access to all parts of the complex, and rooms for SEN assessment, support and hygiene. The internal acoustics of the teaching spaces have been designed to meet the needs of SEN pupils and to make concentrating on lessons easier for all users. Physiotherapy and other services will be available in the health centre, and specialists can easily reach the school to work with pupils where appropriate.

To allow for SEN assistants, aids and two computer trolleys in each classroom, the classrooms are 57 m^2 in area – sufficient for whole-class literacy, numeracy and other classwork. Supplementing them are 12 m^2 group rooms shared between pairs of classes to enhance SEN and ICT work.

The school will be equipped with state-of-the-art educational technology, including electronic whiteboards, video-conferencing and cable connections to nearly every room. It

will be a national test-bed for new equipment and methods as well as being at the heart of the Greenwich Grid for Learning, linked to local networks, schools in the nearby education action zone and the Internet. The library is large enough to act as a media resources centre for pupils, and for adults there is a small open learning centre.

In line with the national childcare strategy, the school has been designed to offer wraparound care and holiday play schemes. The school's food technology space will have a sitting and eating area for breakfast, afternoon snacks and socialising, before and after school. The specialist practical area will be larger than normal, for hobbies and arts and crafts. The hall and studio will be available for after-school games, dance and drama. The library and shared ICT area, and sometimes the community room, can be used for study support. There will be a store for the local education authority (LEA) play service, and the play workers will share a multi-agency office. All these spaces are located near each other for security and ease of management while the rest of the school is closed. The school playground and pitch will also be easily accessible out-of-hours.

The hall

Local events can take place in the community room, the large studio and the hall. They will also have changing rooms and use of the school's all-weather pitch. The hall is big enough for recreational badminton or other indoor games; it is equipped for theatrical events and suitable for religious use. The entrance to these facilities will be separate from the school and EYC, and can be supervised from the premises manager's office out of school hours.

Family support will be provided by a multi-agency office, a parents' room and a kitchenette. Other shared rooms will be available for counselling and meetings. There will be a wide range of adult education and training opportunities during the school day in the open learning centre, community room and health centre. Out of hours, the hall, studio and some other schoolrooms will also be available.

The health centre

The health centre has been designed for a full range of primary care as well as promoting healthy living and preventative approaches to medicine. Its reception area will include a one-stop shop for information and advice. The centre will supply some specialist services to pupils with SEN, and in turn will share use of the crèche, SEN and community spaces for meetings, exercise classes or courses. Its garden will be a soothing visual focus for the patients' waiting area, and offer opportunities for therapeutic and sensory experiences.

Building services

The building services strategy combines guaranteed continuous fresh air supply in excess of new legislation for health in educational buildings with exceptionally low energy costs and passive cooling in hot weather. The design is the culmination of extensive consultation with DfEE regarding the optimum means of compliance with BB87.

The heating and ventilation of the school and health centre is achieved by passing tempered air through the hollow cores of the pre-cast concrete floor slabs using the Termodeck system. This method exploits the thermal storage capacity of the building fabric itself, enabling the building to moderate its own internal climate. The net result is that occupied areas receive 100% fresh air, with free night-time cooling available in summer using the cooler night time air to flush heat from the thermal mass of the roof and the floor, which store this cooling for use the following day. The boiler plant is a fraction of its normal size due to super insulation and efficient heat reclamation of both casual heat from bodies and from electrical equipment and solar heat gains; energy savings of 56% of that used in a comparable naturally ventilated school, designed to meet the current building regulations, are anticipated.

Advanced modelling techniques were employed to optimise the use of day-lighting levels in the classrooms on both floors through the use of light (and ventilation) wells at the rear of the classrooms.

Energy efficient artificial lighting has been used throughout, using tubular or compact fluorescent lamps with high frequency control gear, with presence detection in the classrooms to minimise wasteful lighting usage.

This is designed to produce:

1. 56% energy savings when compared with a similar naturally ventilated school designed to meet the current building regulations
2. free cooling in summer to 23°C
3. carbon dioxide generation of 10 kg/m^2/year
4. daylight factor of between 3.5 and 4%.

The structure

The upper levels of the ground include bands of weak clay and peat so all the new structures sit on concrete piles which extend down into the terrace gravels. Cast *in situ* driven piles were used as this produces a sealed bore which stops potentially contaminated perched ground water seeping down into the gravels. There is also no spoil from this method of piling which is important where ground contamination may be present. The piles are connected by grids of reinforced concrete ground beams which also support the concrete ground floor. The ground beams were designed to allow the positions of piles to be varied on site if, for instance, a pile hit a buried obstruction and had to be abandoned. This was expected to be a distinct possibility as the new buildings straddle two groups of old piles which originally supported large storage tanks. The ground floor was cast over an impermeable gas membrane and granular fill layer which allows any gas to migrate harmlessly to the perimeter of the building.

The superstructures of the classroom block and health centre are simple two-storey steel frames with the floors formed from pre-cast hollow core concrete planks to provide for the Termodeck system with a reinforced *in situ* concrete topping. The school hall has different servicing needs and has *in situ* concrete floors. The steelwork is exposed and intumescent painted in many areas which necessitated close working with the steelwork fabricator and the architect on the detailing of connections. The design uses a mixture of fixed and pinned connections between the beams and columns which provide the necessary lateral stability but also limit the transfer of forces where this would be problematic.

Landscape

The landscape of the site has been treated as an integral part of the overall design and complements the buildings and their sustainable design.

The play area is surrounded by landscaped mounds, which are planted with a mixture of vegetation ranging from grass and ground cover through to shrubs and trees. The species have been selected to provide a variety of forms, colours, textures and seasonal variations and are predominantly indigenous species. A series of routes through the planting have been created to form an 'ecological trail' along which specific areas have been planted to form differing habitats such as meadow areas, pioneer scrub and climax woodland. A small pond and wetland area has been created to provide examples of wetland habitats.

The school play area is finished in macadam with coloured patterns and games painted on the surface. Timber shade structures provide protection from excessive exposure to sunshine. To the south lies a floodlit all weather pitch for football and other games for people of all ages.

The bulk earthworks and remediation of the site included the removal and treatment of contaminated material. Steep reinforced earth banks formed part of the landscape works.

Construction

The contract was let in two stages, enabling the contractor to commence initial works at an early stage and to influence the buildability of the designs.

The work has been progressed proactively between the client, design, construction, cost consultant, and site and project management teams within a partnering charter. Subcontractors were brought on board early to obtain their input and to iron out any co-ordination issues.

The site has been run in a business-like manner with health and safety given the highest priority. Planning and looking ahead has been key to ensuring progress and efficient construction. The high specification and innovation has presented challenges, which have been met with the teamwork and planning described above.

Project management, cost control and health and safety

Project management for such an innovative facility within a tight programme, a standard Department of Education budget, an innovative brief and a multiplicity of users has been a challenge. Early two-way briefing meetings were held to ensure full understanding by the team of the requirements, and by the users of what was being provided. Risk management and value engineering was carried out to facilitate maintaining the budget and programme, established by the cost consultant, the client and project managers. The client played a proactive part throughout, reducing decision time and providing early feedback.

Case Study 8: Claypath Medical Centre, Durham

Architect: Michael Litchfield, Howarth Litchfield Partnership.

The following notes were provided by the architect on 14 February 2002.

Initial selection process for the architect

Howarth Litchfield Partnership were approached by the Claypath Medical Centre following their enquiries with other medical practices within the area and visits to some of our projects. We were appointed following interview.

Briefing process/consultations with doctors

A very extensive briefing process included the assessment of the working arrangements of the existing practice and the opportunities that a new development would provide to improve service delivery and efficiency. Detailed studies considered record and administration systems, reception arrangements, the introduction of patient waiting over two different levels and the development of both consulting and nursing suites.

Funding/procurement route

The practice had the support of the County Durham Health Commission and pursued a cost rent scheme.

The project was fully designed and detailed including furniture, fittings and decoration. Competitive tenders were obtained from builders and the project completed under a fixed price tender.

User group discussion – patient participation

There were extensive discussions within the practice, drawing upon the expertise of the partners, administrative and nursing staff. Design approaches were reviewed and finalised prior to the tender process.

Patients, many of whom were also local residents, were invited to give their opinion of the proposed site and the final design prior to submission for planning approval.

Design qualities/environmental issues

During the briefing and participation exercises, several sites were identified and assessed.

The selected location was in several ownerships following the demolition of buildings when a new dual carriageway and roundabout had been created leading into the centre of the historic part of Durham. The site was the leftover gap, between the historic Georgian houses leading steeply to the town centre and terrace Victorian housing sloping away from the site to the north.

The design was, therefore, developed to link the scale of the two housing areas and draw on the materials, proportions and gable design typical of the historic heart of Durham city. The proportions of the Claypath Medical Centre carry a vertical emphasis and utilise render, brickwork and slate for the contemporary form.

The design received the enthusiastic support of the planning authority as a significant townscape design within the conservation area. The building wrapped around the inner courtyard containing the car parking while the main façade provides a new entranceway to Durham city from the east.

Flexibility/sustainability issues

The internal layout introduced services for patients on both floors by providing consulting, nursing and patient areas. The

Figure 11.38 Claypath Medical Centre, Durham: external view. Architect: Michael Litchfield, Howarth Litchfield Partnership

Figure 11.39 Claypath Medical Centre, Durham: external view

practice has found that this flexibility has been extremely successful and has enabled them to respond to on-going developments in the delivery of primary health care.

All heating, lighting and access control systems incorporate low-energy building management. The construction materials are all from renewable resources.

Costs – lifecycle costs

The costs of the scheme were in accordance with Schedule 51 of the Statement of Fees and Allowances. This allowed for additional costs related to the use of natural slate, the curved form of the building and cast iron gutters as planning requirements of the conservation area.

Life cycle costs were considered in the selection of high-performance boilers, zoned control to heating and the sustainability of materials.

Urban context/site location

The Claypath Medical Centre previously occupied a four-storey Victorian property on a steeply sloping site leading into the centre of Durham. The practice and patients were very

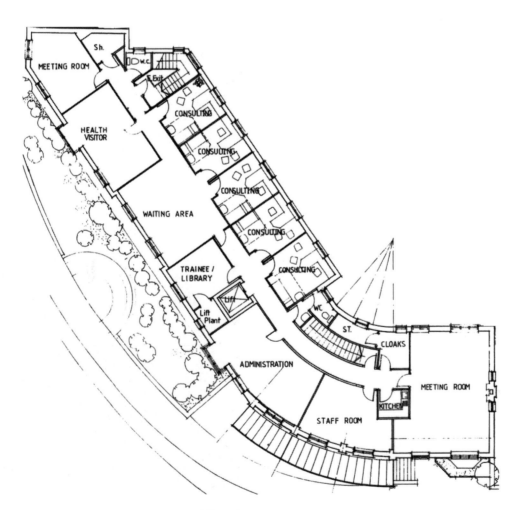

Figure 11.40 Claypath Medical Centre, Durham: ground floor plan

keen to identify sites which provided improved access by public transport and was on a relatively flat site. With Durham being extremely hilly, the number of appropriate sites available was very limited.

The site as identified was in several ownerships and, in part, was used for a playground. It was necessary to identify a new site for the repositioning of the playground and assemble the site. In addition to ownership, one of the adjacent properties claims of way which, after extensive legal enquiries, provided not to be established. The purchase and valuation of the site was achieved with the support of the district valuer.

Transport linkages

As noted above, it was extremely important to identify a site with space for doctors and staff parking but, most particularly, public transport.

Case study 9: Hammersmith Bridge Road Surgery

Architect: Guy Greenfield.
The following notes were provided by the architect (23 May 2001).

We were appointed in 1996 after a selection procedure and a limited ideas submission to the doctors by short-listed firms. Our clients were the Hammersmith, Ealing and Hounslow Health Authority, the Bridge Avenue Group Practice (end users) combined with the Riverside Health Care Trust who occupy part of the first floor (co-end users).

We were briefed by the doctors and presented separately to the doctors and the health authority. The doctors' brief consisted of little more than a schedule of accommodation. The doctors appointed a partner as intermediary between ourselves and the practice members though group meets were also held. We consulted separately with the Riverside Health Care Trust.

The building was funded as a development directly by the health authority with purchase agreements in place with the group practice. The district valuer valued the building at completion and the purchase by the GP partners is now ongoing.

The building was built under a JCT contract and traditionally tendered.

There was no patient participation other than patients' views voiced through the GPs.

Physically, the building is a conventional load-bearing blockwork structure. There is therefore little flexibility in the internal arrangement for future re planning. The arrangement of single corridor with rooms off would suit a large variety of uses outside health care. From an environmental viewpoint, the building is mostly naturally ventilated, many of the materials are natural (slate and timber floors), the copper cladding is recyclable.

The construction cost was £1.25m.

Figure 11.41 Hammersmith Bridge Road Surgery: exterior detail with steeple. Photographed by Paul Tyagi/View

Figure 11.42 Hammersmith Bridge Road Surgery: corridor at dusk. Photographed by Paul Tyagi/View (also in colour section)

Figure 11.43 Hammersmith Bridge Road Surgery: stair detail. Photographed by Paul Tyagi/View

Figure 11.44 North Croydon Medical Centre: triple height reception area. Photographed by Timothy Soar

The building is located just off the end of the M4/A4, adjacent to the Hammersmith and City, District, and Piccadilly tube lines and is well served by many bus routes.

Case study 10: North Croydon Medical Centre

Architect: Allford Hall Monaghan Morris Architects.
This project was widely acclaimed when completed and has been published in the *RIBA Journal* (May 1999). It is also included on the NHS CD-ROM 'Design Quality Portfolio' where it is described as an elegantly designed surgery for a small general practice in an urban environment. The building has an air of competent efficiency with a welcoming atmosphere. A survey of users and building technical managers have approval ratings of 81% and 85%, respectively. These are very high. The scheme has also received a 1999 RIBA Award for Architecture.

The practice was established in 1910 and is now located in a socially deprived area. The requirement is for a place of calm where patients can wait in peace, move about without complication and feel confident during an examination. It should be characterised by skilful manipulation of space and light.

Figure 11.45 North Croydon Medical Centre: stair detail upper. Photographed by Timothy Soar

John Welsh, writing in the *RIBA Journal* (May 1999) said:

'The problem, as AHMM [Allford Hall Monaghan Morris Architects] and the client put it, was one of space and light. Why, if you are ill or, God forbid, dying, would you want to enter some dingy waiting room? And would you feel comfortable being treated in a cupboard? Surely, patients want to enter a place of calm, a building planned to allow them to wait in peace, to approach the consult-

ing room without complications and to feel confident during an examination – and all this on a corner site 8.5 m wide and 21 m long.

The architectural qualities add up not to some fancy place more appropriate as a shop, but rather the suggestion of medical efficiency way beyond that of a small surgery.

It is this balance, between what should be in a surgery and what it could be through architecture, that marks out this building.'

Second floor plan

First floor plan

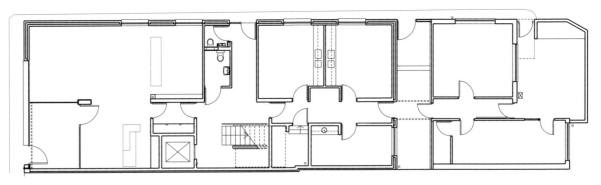

Ground floor plan

Figure 11.46 North Croydon Medical Centre: plans

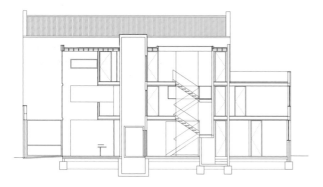

Figure 11.47 North Croydon Medical Centre: section

Case study 11: The Lawson Practice

Architect: Ahrends Burton and Koralek.
The following is the architect's account.

The primary care centre at St Leonard's Community Hospital in Hackney, north London, has been designed for the Lawson Practice and City and East London FHSA.

The project, which was initiated in response to the Tomlinson Report, involved writing the brief, assisting in establishing and securing funds for the scheme, which included GP premises, training unit and community facilities, a minor injury treatment centre and a 10 bed inpatient unit. The two latter functions have been held over until funding is available from the purchasers.

The majority of the space in the current proposal is taken up by the six-doctor GP practice, a community nurse base, the training unit and minor surgery; but the scheme is capable of expansion. This led us to consider how the design of this type of building could achieve a planning system capable of ordering space, structure and services – the purpose of the exercise being to reduce the design time and achieve an early start on site.

Figure 11.49 The Lawson Practice, London: reception area. Photographed by Andrew Putler

The building is designed to allow expansion in the future. Surveys of users and managers of the building fabric by NHS Estates show satisfaction ratings of 86% and 84%, respectively. These are high. The building has received an industry award for energy-conscious design.

The Lawson Practice comprises a team of six GPs, supported by two practice nurses and various administrative and training staff. It is also the base for the Turkish Advocacy which was developed to promote a good health policy within the local Turkish community. The centre will also be the base for various topical seminars and presentations and other lectures.

Figure 11.50 The Lawson Practice, London: external view. Photographed by Andrew Putler

Figure 11.48 The Lawson Practice, London: external view. Photographed by Andrew Putler (also in colour section)

Initial selection process for architect

The local health authority appointed Anne Noble as the architect/health facility planner, who drew up the shortlist.

Briefing process/consultations with doctors

Initial brief prepared by the above architect, design brief recorded in database prepared by ABK with client.

The client was Lawson Practice and East London and the City Health Authority.

Funding/procurement route

Funding was from the NE Thames Regional Health Authority, Dalston City Partnership and a loan to the Lawson Practice.

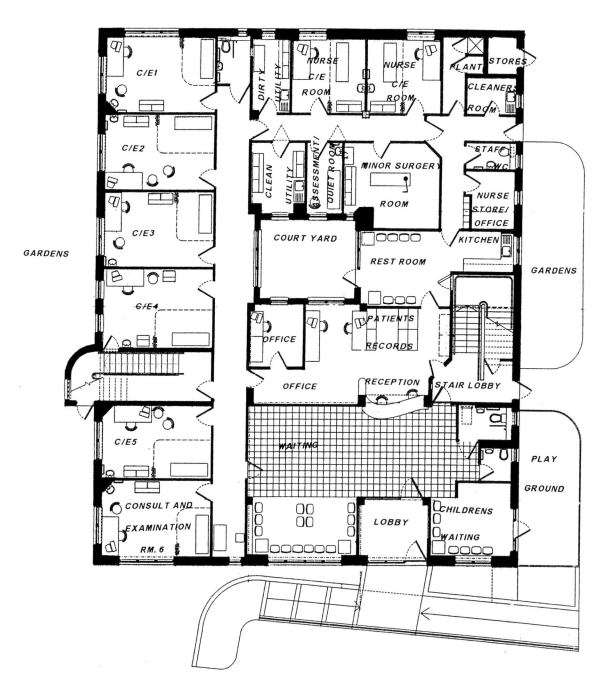

Figure 11.51 The Lawson Practice, London: ground floor

User group discussions – patient participation

There were user group discussions but no patient participation.

Flexibility/sustainability issues

An additional consultancy room and a minor surgery room were included.
Allowance made for flexible space for offices, research, teaching, library. Expansion is foreseen on the site.

Drylining systems used for partitions to allow for re-planning of space.

Energy conservation by good insulation and natural ventilation

Costs – lifecycle/site location

No choice of site. Expensive foundations due to deep excavations through land which had been built on for 600 or so years.

Transport linkages

There are two bus routes. The practice serves the local community – most people walk, the doctors tend to use bikes

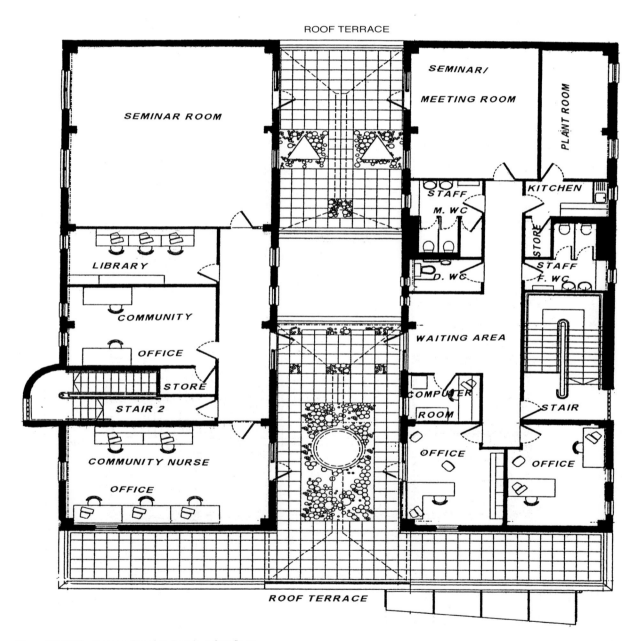

Figure 11.52 The Lawson Practice, London: first floor

Case study 12: Rushton Medical Centre

Architect: Penoyre and Prasad.

While the building is designed to house four existing local GP practices, it is also capable of accommodating a number of future options in line with new thinking about primary health care: grouping of small practices to provide better resources; an autonomous major procedures/diagnostic suite; space for group activities and a range of ancillary and complementary services; perhaps GP managed beds.

The ground floor has a central top-lit mall running the length of the building which acts as circulation as well as waiting space. On one side are the consulting and treatment rooms and on the other the administration and services spaces. This, combined with the provision of four separate entrances from the street, allows the creation of various sizes of practice premises or the uniting of the whole to make a single large health resource centre. The upper floors project out successively creating sheltered parking and entrance space.

Abundant natural light and measures such as high insulation standards and a warm air system with heat recovery conserve energy and reduce fuel bills. The surgery on the first floor has its entrance, stair and waiting areas glazed for visibility from the street, to make access easy and legible.

Scheme description

Client's brief

The Family Health Services Authority worked with a group of local and unsuitably housed GPs in South Hoxton to find a site and develop the brief for a large enough building to house all the local practices as well as some community health services. It was felt that the building should also be flexible enough to accommodate future changing patterns of use.

The need for a substantial improvement of the predominantly one- and two-hander practice premises, and the advantages of large scale, better resourced practices had been in discussion in the City and East London FHSA since the late

Figure 11.53 Rushton Medical Centre: external view. Photographed by Dennis Gilbert/View

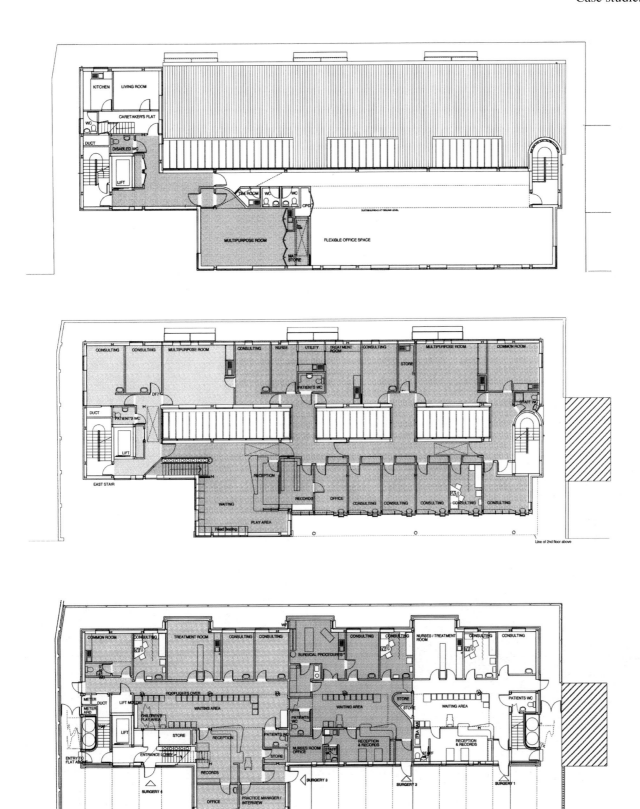

Figure 11.54 Rushton Medical Centre: plans

1980s. A complete audit of primary care premises in its area in 1991 confirmed this need but also the practices' wish to remain separate, at least initially. Initially this building will separately house four existing local GP practices. However, it had to be designed to be capable of accommodating a number of future options in line with new thinking about primary health care such as grouping of small practices to provide better group activities and a range of ancillary and complementary services. The project was executed using private finance, with the developer retaining the design team originally commissioned by the health authority.

The design

The building was designed to have a strong civic presence and to be perceived by its users as a building of health. These aspects are emphasised by the bright Mediterranean colour of the rendered walls visible from across Shoreditch Park.

The ground floor has a central top-lit mall running the length of the building which acts as circulation as well as waiting space. On one side are the consulting and treatment rooms and on the other the administration and service spaces. This, combined with the provision of four separate entrances from the street, allows the creation of various sizes of practice premises or the uniting of the whole to make a single large health resource centre. The upper floors project out successively creating sheltered parking and entrance space.

Abundant natural light and measures such as high insulation standards and a warm air system with heat recovery conserve energy and reduce fuel bills. The surgery on the first floor has its entrance, stair and waiting areas glazed for visibility from the street, to make access easy and legible.

Planning history

The site had been earmarked for a health development in consultation with the local planning authority.

Construction

The foundation system of vibro improvement with stone columns and shallow reinforced concrete pad footings was used on this site (a former garage). The use of a steel frame, pre-cast floors and concrete stair flights enabled the superstructure to be erected quickly allowing easy access for the following trades. By supporting floors and roof decking on the lower flanges of 203 mm deep UC sections the soffits were kept virtually flat allowing great flexibility for services distribution. High thermal mass is achieved by both the floors and the perimeter walls of dense blocks which even out the day and night time temperature variation. The walls are protected by a skin of render on insulation. Galvanised cantilever eaves and verge brackets allow the top deck sheeting of aluminium to project well beyond the perimeter walls.

Funding arrangements

The FHSA funded the project to tender stage, at which point it was taken over by a third party to be developed and leased back for health use. The FHSA was able to make a capital grant to the project from its London Implementation Zone allocation of funds.

Case study 13: Stanhope Health Centre

Architect: Panter Hudspith.

Background

This project highlights the challenges open to talented architects who can influence the quality of health care provision of primary and community care for the whole of Weardale an area which covers approximately 250 square miles and a population of 7300. The local hospitals are Bishop Auckland General (15 miles) and Shotley Bridge (20 miles), but the area is remote and is seriously affected by harsh winter weather for about 5 months of every year, when main roads are often impassable and access to the hospitals thus made very difficult.

The following notes are based on the architect's notes which formed part of the business plan dated June 1994.

Stanhope Health Centre is the base for a five-doctor partnership, which became a fundholding practice in 1993. The practice had developed its services in the space available: a number of clinics were held and the practice contracted to provide community psychiatric services, physiotherapy and ENT clinics on site.

Stanhope is generally seen as the centre of the Dales and consequently a focal point for patient care. The areas remoteness means that the doctors have traditionally had a major role in the provision of accident and emergency services in the community. In addition, the Dales are a popular centre for activity holidays and holidaymakers who attend the surgery for their emergency treatment instead of using the accident and emergency services.

Built in the 1970s it had suffered from the normal wear and tear of 20 years' constant use, gradually becoming too small and inappropriate for the way a contemporary practice should operate. Some of the rooms were being used for different purposes than they were originally designed for, often with inadequate sound proofing, and patient confidentiality was sometimes compromised.

Options and requirements

Stanhope Health Centre needed to be a flexible and high standard building in order to provide the wide range of services which need to be accessed by the population of the Dales.
- Minor surgery was undertaken and there was a need to have two treatment rooms; a dedicated clean room as well as a general purpose room.
- Clinics needed to be held such as diabetic and vascular clinics as well as ante-natal and baby clinics.
- Services should enable the practice to offer facilities according to patient need. The service needed to improve patient access and confidentiality.

- Community services had been inadequate. There had been no rooms which could be used for group sessions, e.g. mothercraft.
- Patient care – the health centre had not been patient orientated. The waiting room was regarded as inadequate, too hot in summer and too cold in winter. The reception desk was considered unwelcoming and there was no disabled access or toilet facilities.

Solution

Having identified that there were a number of serious problems in the way the health centre was operating and that it did not meet future needs, a decision was made to explore options for improving the services offered. Refurbishment of the existing building was determined to be the best option for a number of very sound reasons.

There was good onsite parking and lay-by space for community service vehicles and disabled patients. There was available land at both the front and the rear of the site for expansion.

The existing layout of the building enabled many of the rooms to be reorganised in a rational and efficient manner with minimal movement of partitions.

Figure 11.55 Stanhope Health Centre: waiting area. Architect: Panter Hudspith. Photograph by Simon Hudspith

Existing services in the building were mainly positioned in large ceiling and floor voids that facilitated easy removal and extension. The local planning department gave a very favourable response to the proposed extension.

The site building and car parking were currently owned by the Department of Health, thus eliminating site capital costs, and realising a health service asset.

Refurbishment of the existing building proved to be the most pragmatic, appropriate and cost-effective route available to the health centre and the decision was made to proceed with that option. The doctors were fortunate to have creative architects who rose to the challenge of developing an effective brief. They prepared a document to identify, in detail, the functional and qualitative requirements for both the building as a whole, and each individual room. An initial questionnaire was issued for consultation to each member of the health care team which was then processed by the architect into a briefing document that became the basis for the design development. Their skill in analysing and interpreting the data collected before starting to provide physical solutions is a powerful demonstration of the importance of quality issues in the design process and particularly highlights the significance of a well-developed brief.

Case study 14: Hove Polyclinic

Architect: Nightingale Associates.

Description of the building

The polyclinic is a relatively new building type. Certainly, South Downs NHS Trust and Brighton Healthcare, who rent space in the building, had few such building types to refer to as precedents; those already designed being either much smaller or in converted accommodation.

The services which are provided include medical and surgical outpatient clinics, X-Ray and ultrasound, physiotherapy, pain management, speech and language therapy, chiropody, podiatry, hearing tests, child health clinics and development checks, parentcraft and postnatal sessions, ECT treatments, psychological therapies, including psychology, psychotherapy and behaviour therapy.

Whilst the schedule of accommodation was a relatively easy matter to establish, the manner in which it was to come together was something to which the Trust gave considerable thought. They produced a design ethos statement (reproduced below) to assist the designers in their response.

Land for the polyclinic was identified in the development control plan to the north-east of this large site, offering distant views of the sea to the south. The land falls north-east to south-west across the site, offering the opportunity of creating a lower ground floor for administrative areas, storage and plant space. This permitted a larger upper ground floor footprint, ideal for the main patient areas, with easy level access from plentiful adjacent car parking and public transport bus services. The facilities on this upper ground floor

Figure 11.56 Hove Polyclinic: reception. Architect: Nightingale Associates. Photographed by Charlotte Wood (also in colour section)

are configured around the main reception area, which includes a small café and waiting areas, designed in such a way that patients can easily be directed to their treatment area. The consulting and minor surgery wing to the east has a 'V'-shaped roof, permitting the use of high level glazing to achieve privacy. Speech therapy and audiology are situated at the quieter south-west corner of the site, away from traffic noise. The X-ray suite has a central space lit by a large roof light, again ensuring privacy for gowned patients. Physiotherapy is provided under a curved, floating roof with high level glazing on all four sides, creating a light, airy space for patients and staff.

The psychological therapy suite is a self-contained space and, being at first floor level, provides a degree of privacy for the patients attending it. They have a separate reception waiting area, adjacent to a central open courtyard around which the individual consulting rooms and group therapy rooms are arranged.

Internal finishes are limited to a very small palette. Only three wall colours are used with white predominating in the waiting and circulation areas. Only light colours are used internally, giving maximum benefit from direct or indirect natural lighting. The Trust have commissioned three separate works of art which will soon be installed in the building. External finishes are similarly very limited: red brickwork (to match the bricks selected from the adjacent Mental Health Resource Centre) together with some small areas of white rendered panels. Aluminium windows and glass block walling are used in the fenestration, with a mill finished standing seam aluminium roof, which lends itself to the simple geometric shapes of the roof, defining the separate functions within the building.

The design team was under considerable pressure to deliver a building within a fixed budget and a timetable related to other hospital closures. The consequent result was achieved to programme for £1000/m^2 and fully satisfying the client's expectations.

Client's ethos statement

The following aspirations were included:

- The clinic should be light and airy to give the impression of health and well-being.
- The building should provide a safe, comfortable and welcoming environment.
- Natural indirect lighting is essential to allow maximum privacy and best working conditions.
- The main reception area is to be the hub of the building.
- The environment in the main areas must demonstrate a child-centred approach.
- Older people will be a main user group and their needs must be paramount in the design of the building.
- The polyclinic could become a focal point in the local community, which should encourage people to come to receive health care.
- There is a need to resolve the tension between safety and security issues for public buildings.
- The colours and textures chosen should be an integral part of the design.
- Because the polytechnic will be in use for many years, timeless features, such as natural finishes, a feeling of lightness and space, and smooth rounded edges would be welcomed.

Figure 11.57 Hove Polyclinic: external view at dusk. Photographed by Charlotte Wood

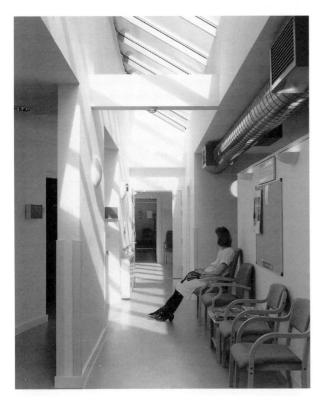

Figure 11.58 Hove Polyclinic: waiting area. Photographed by Charlotte Wood

Case study 15: Neptune Health Park

Architect: Penoyre and Prasad.

The building forms part of an ambitious urban regeneration initiative within a City Challenge programme, in which the health park provides a combination of public services on a central site in Tipton.

Intended as a community building, the health park contains a GP surgery, primary health care unit, cafeteria, meeting rooms and a Citizens Advice Bureau. Different activities are organised within discrete areas, but focus collectively on a concourse space containing the cafeteria and health information bureau. The building is designed to be as open and welcoming as possible with access to the various facilities for up to 18 hours a day. A café terrace overlooks the canal, making a place for various waterside activities.

The building is constructed in loadbearing masonry, rendered and insulated externally to provide an energy efficient enclosure of high thermal mass. Roofs are either metal or flat with a roof terrace for staff incorporated at second floor level.

Background

Sandwell is a borough located in the industrial heart of the West Midlands and is bordered by Birmingham, Wolverhampton, Dudley and Walsall. Tipton is one of the six 'towns' of Sandwell and lies to the north-west of the borough. It is one of the most deprived areas in Sandwell with low income levels and high dependency on benefits.

Neptune is a flagship community and health care facility, which provides local access to a number of services in one place. The realisation of the building itself signifies a partnership between a number of different users who have worked together for the past 6 years to make Neptune a reality. The key members of the partnership are Sandwell Healthcare, the Black Country Family Practice, Murray Hall Community Trust, Sandwell Health Authority and Tipton Challenge. These agencies are in turn supported by the local people. The partnership aims to develop more integrated working practices between health care agencies and other businesses in Tipton, and to increase local ownership and involvement in health.

The notion of integrated working between partners, staff and community is an underlying philosophy of Neptune – not just within the building, but throughout its links with agencies in Sandwell. The services developed are highly flexible, multipurpose, multidisciplinary and multi-agency with shared resources, policies and training. This is called the 'spirit' of Neptune – not just a collection of services in one building but a real partnership with each agency signing up to a new type of organisational culture to meet the needs of patients and users.

Neptune could be described as a 'one-stop shop' for health. As well as seeing a doctor or a physiotherapist, people are able to enjoy a cup of tea, browse in the information centre, walk by the canal or sit in the gardens – a new type of health building where people can use many of the facilities without needing an appointment to enter the building.

The design

The building project was launched with a design competition in 1995 and won by a multidisciplinary team lead by Penoyre

and Prasad Architects. The team were appointed in 1996 and the detailed brief and design developed in close collaboration with the project team. The design is based around the following principles:

1. the facilities are grouped around a central space, the concourse
2. the facilities are self contained but disposed such that they may benefit from one another
3. the visiting public can feel comfortable and welcome whether they have appointments or not. By the way the building and its entrances are positioned the design enables people to drop by or even pass through
4. more private and intimate spaces are located away from the public eye to respect the dignity of people needing to use the health care services provided
5. the design symbolises an open and inclusive approach to health care and health information
6. the building is flexible and anticipates provision of services not yet available
7. interiors are designed to avoid any 'institutional' atmosphere. Colour and maximum use of daylight make light and bright spaces. Wherever possible corridors are naturally lit and vary in size and shape along their length.

Site planning

Situated on a bend in the Wolverhampton Canal at the Southern end of the High Street this is a prominent site n the centre of Tipton.

The site is accessible from the canal bridge at the southern end of the High Street and from Sedgeley Road West to the south. The building is positioned alongside the canal with a landscaped parking area to the south. Principally one and two

Figure 11.59a Neptune Health Park, West Midlands: aerial view plan. Photographed by Penoyre and Prasad (also in colour section)

storeys the building rises to three storeys at the High Street, end forming a drum like landmark at the bend in the canal.

The two principal entrances lead into a concourse at the heart of the building where visitors arrive in a double height space that accommodates a café and information area. This is the social hub of the building from where all other areas of the building can be reached. On one side are the commercial pharmacy and optician and the community workshop spaces, on the other the GP surgery, the Black Country Family Practice, and the Sandwell Healthcare facilities. A stair and lift lead up across a bridge to the Citizens' Advice Bureau.

Construction

The building is constructed in loadbearing masonry in the main part with a steel frame supporting the Concourse roof. A large brick wall faces the car park, other walls are faced in a combination of brick and render. The render is laid directly over a thick layer of insulation on blockwork walls, providing an exceptionally high degree of thermal insulation, whilst allowing the internal environment to benefit from the thermal mass of the building structure. The roofs are in aluminium where pitched, and asphalt where flat providing a long lasting low maintenance external envelope to the building. The building services have been designed for simplicity and maximum energy efficiency to suit the varying levels of occupancy in the building.

Special awards

As this building creates a brand new focus for a deprived local community, and because it contributes as much to the social well-being of Tipton as it does to the built environment, we believe it should be considered for the Centre Vision and Urban Design Special Awards.

Figure 11.59b Neptune Health Park, West Midlands: view from canal. Photographed by Penoyre and Prasad

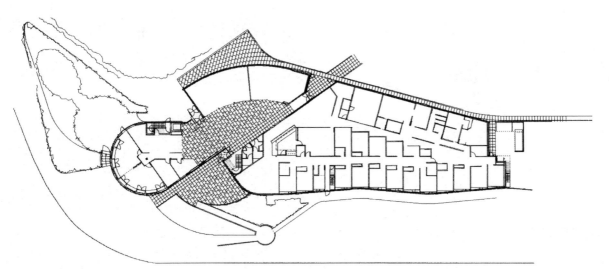

Figure 11.60 Neptune Health Park: perspective of entrance area

Case study 16: Newhaven Downs Polyclinic

Architect: Penoyre and Prasad.

The polyclinic serves the community of Newhaven and the residents of the recently completed elderly care home on the same site. The building contains physiotherapy and chiropody departments alongside mental health interview facilities and consulting rooms for visiting GPs. There are specially designed rooms for consulting with children and for speech and language therapy. The polyclinic is a public facility intended to be both welcoming and easily accessible for all. To this end all areas are located on one floor, around a generous and well lit waiting hall. The building has been designed as a multi-use flexible facility to a specific current brief, but pays reference to changing service needs in the future. Consulting and interview rooms are designed to allow this future potential for change.

The clinic is constructed using orange–red-facing brickwork with painted timber windows. The roof is covered with a standing seam aluminium sheet with generous overhangs. The main waiting hall is lined with timber panels above door height with a north-facing clerestory and glazed wall to the south-eastern aspect.

Client's brief

South Downs Health NHS Trust required a new building on an adjacent site to the recently completed Elderly Care building (also by Penoyre and Prasad) to provide outpatient and clinical facilities for the local community of Newhaven. The services provided by the polyclinic would give additional support to those provided in the elderly care building and the wider needs of the community.

The building provides local facilities for physiotherapy, chiropody, speech therapy and a base for the community mental health team, as well as having a range of bookable consulting and interview rooms for visiting GPs and consultants to hold local clinics. There are specially designed rooms for consultations with children and for speech and language therapy.

The establishment of the brief was part of a consultation process, which brought together all of the intended users and providers of this new service together with the design team.

Figure 11.62 Newhaven Downs Polyclinic: waiting area. Photographed by Andrew Siddall, Penoyre and Prasad

The design

The polyclinic is a public facility intended to be both welcoming and easily accessible for all. All of the facilities are located on one floor level and are arranged around a generous and well-lit waiting hall. This allows the building to be easily understood by new visitors and for it to be easy to manage. The building has been designed to cater for the diversity of uses that are currently demanded but is capable of flexibility to allow for future changes with minimal disruption.

The design of the building meets the client's requirement for an efficient and flexible building which is easy to maintain and is constructed from low maintenance materials.

Figure 11.61 Newhaven Downs Polyclinic: external view. Photographed by Andrew Siddall, Penoyre and Prasad

Figure 11.63 Newhaven Downs Polyclinic: waiting area. Photographed by Andrew Siddall, Penoyre and Prasad

Construction

The building is located on the side of the chalk downland overlooking Newhaven and Lewes to the north and is built on insitu concrete ground beams that span the variable strata. The external walls are traditional cavity construction with warm orange–red-facing bricks to match the elderly care building. The walls of the meeting room project out as a bay in blue self-coloured render to give the building its own identity on the site. The low-pitched roofs are clad in mill finish aluminium standing seam 'Ziplock' sheets. The generous overhang at eaves and ridge are formed in specially made aluminium bullnose profiles that incorporate the gutters and roof ventilation details. The roof verges also express the roof profile in aluminium forming a series of silver planes that create low and high eaves and the opportunity for clerestorey lighting to the central waiting areas. The windows are high quality pre-finished timber and are used to form a large glazed screen at the end of the waiting space. The building has been designed to allow for future expansion at the end of the waiting space if additional services are demanded.

Case study 17: Shrewsbury Intermediate Care Centre

Architects and interior designers: Tangram Architects and Designers. Design partner: Douglas Jackson.

With hospitals increasingly becoming centres of specialisation, the new Shrewsbury Centre at Forest Gate in London provides a model for intermediate care to the local community.

The development, with Tower Hamlets NHS Trust Newham Healthcare and Newham Community Services NHS Trust as the client, brings together group practice and community accommodation with consultant, treatment and

Figure 11.64 Shrewsbury Intermediate Care Centre, London: entrance foyer (also in colour section)

diagnostic facilities including X-ray, venepuncture, clinical measurement and a diabetology unit.

Initially the client's intention was to locate specific accommodation within two separate converted buildings. When Tangram were appointed as architects the potential was explored to link the buildings and provide an opportunity for staff to meet and collaborate in developing health care needs. As well as enabling the accommodation to be perceived as one building, the linking structure also provides a focus for the local community and includes a multipurpose room for meetings and health education projects.

The task of linking the buildings was complicated by the change in level between the floors of the two buildings and the resultant 'cascading' roof geometry imaginatively resolves the problem.

The work was undertaken in phases in order to enable the group practice to function throughout the period of building works. After phase 1 the group practice moved into the refurbishment area in order to allow phase 2 to be completed

Figure 11.65 Shrewsbury Intermediate Care Centre: external view of entrance

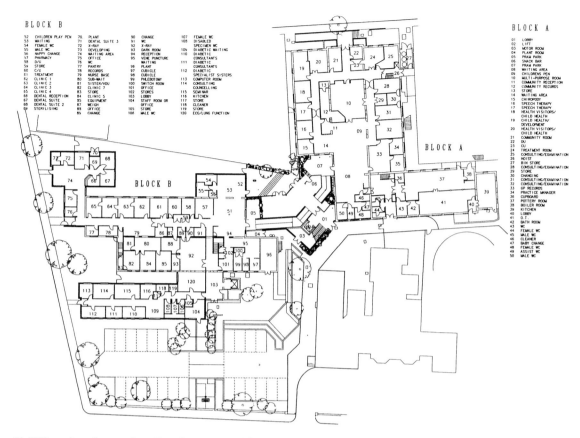

Figure 11.66 Shrewsbury Intermediate Care Centre: ground floor plan

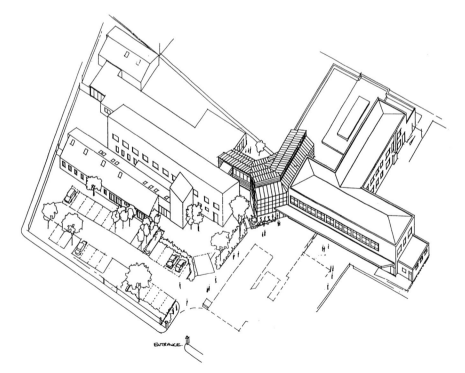

Figure 11.67 Shrewsbury Intermediate Care Centre: axonometric

Case study 18: Farnham Local Care Centre (community hospital)

Architect: HLM Design International Limited.

The following is based on notes provided by HLM Architects.

Background

The new local care centre replaces the existing hospital buildings, and incorporates a health centre for four GP practices, in-patient accommodation for 84 beds, and primary health care services with associated parking, landscaping and vehicular access facilities. It brings together a comprehensive range of services for the local community, in close partnership with GPs, social services and other agencies. The client (Surrey, Hampshire Borders NHS Trust) aims to provide local, high-quality services responsive to individual need, which promote health and independence in people's own homes, in GP surgeries, in hospitals and in specialist mental health facilities.

The site for the project, Farnham Hospital, began as a local workhouse infirmary at the turn of the century and evolved into a District General Hospital. This role has now been

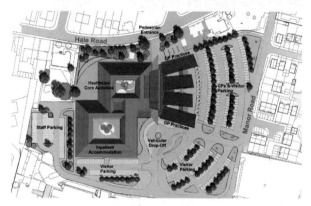

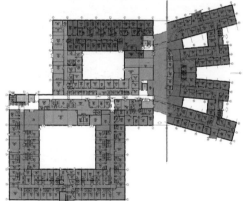

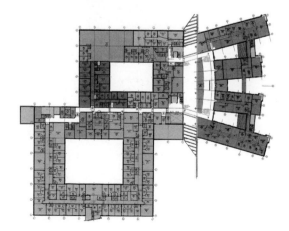

Figure 11.68 Farnham Local Care Centre: various views

superseded and the site was under-utilised. The new building will change Farnham Hospital into a more integrated health care complex. The challenge is to provide as many services as possible within very tight resource constraints and ensure that the health needs of local patients are met today, and provide flexible accommodation to meet the health needs of patients well into the twenty-first century. The architects believe that the local care centre complex will offer patients more accessible, streamlined and effective inpatient and outpatient service, better linked to diagnostic and therapy services as well as to locally based out reach services and GP practices. Patients will enjoy a better environment with more facilities and amenities and a more co-ordinated and personalised service. GPs will benefit from efficiencies achieved through development of speedy, direct access, more clinical protocols, diagnostic packages and access and feedback services.

Planning/design

The building is focused around a central reception atrium, which acts as a collection point for the visitors using the pedestrian access. This reception and general waiting space is in the form of a double height 'street' which separates the diagnostic care facilities (health centre) from the core treatment services and in-patient accommodation. The main feature of this space is the continuous spine wall that cuts through the entire width of the building, defining the entrances to the facility and 'collecting' visitors into the information heart of the centre. The spine wall is solid and free standing, and is punctured at various points to allow access to the health centre and natural daylight to filter through to the waiting areas.

The health centre element of the building consists of four separate GP practices and each one is contained in its own linear wing which radiates out from the central waiting area. Shared facilities link these wings and create small private courtyards providing natural daylight and amenity to the ground floor consulting suites. Each practice contains its own small sub-waiting area, flooded with light from the large glazed elements in the external walls.

From the outside, the elevations to the health centre are finished with a mix of brick and render and incorporate large glazed areas to the end of each wing to define the staff and meeting areas behind; each roof is a single, mono pitch design which further accentuates the GP practices within.

The central core facilities and in-patient accommodation are based around a simple courtyard design, providing natural daylight to the majority of habitable/patient rooms and easy access from one department to another. The central reception area is served by a pharmacy and café to the ground floor and provides direct access into the outpatients department. The large assessment facility on the ground floor allows access onto a private garden amenity space.

The project is financed through the PFI process.

Case study 19: Center for Clinical Research, Stanford University, California

Architect: Foster and Partners.

This project in the USA is not a health facility used by patients, but a research centre. However, it is included as a case study because it illustrates some of the design concepts which have been developed more fully in the commercial environment, but are applicable to health environments (see Chapter 4 especially Sections 4.2.2 and 4.2.3). The central courtyard, flanked by a range of spaces where research teams can work in greater privacy provides a flexible framework, and a high-quality environment. The architecture is providing a sophisticated envelope to enable human intellectual endeavour to flourish. The same objectives could be said to be true for any health centre.

The following notes have been provided by the architect.

Stanford University has long been recognised as a centre for clinical excellence. The new Center for Clinical Sciences Research provides the school of medicine with state-of-the-art laboratory and office space for its ongoing programmes of research into cancer and other diseases. Its design responds to emerging trends for interdisciplinary biomedical research and provides flexible, light-filled working spaces in which research teams can expand and contract with ease.

The brief called for close proximity between laboratories, core support areas and offices. Another important stipulation was natural lighting in the laboratory and office spaces. These requirements led to the development of a modular design, which allows close proximity between functional areas and research groups.

The 21,000 m^2 building consists of two symmetrical wings centred around a central courtyard. The wings are connected at roof level by a screen of louvres. By shading the courtyard from direct sunlight, the louvres create a comfortable environment for social interaction, and this space has become the social hub of the building. Offices overlook the courtyard through curved bay windows. A screen of bamboo

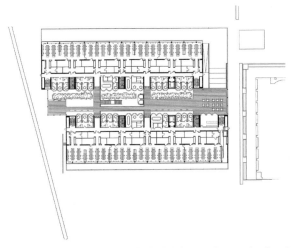

Figure 11.69 Center for Clinical Sciences Research, Stanford University, California: ground floor plan

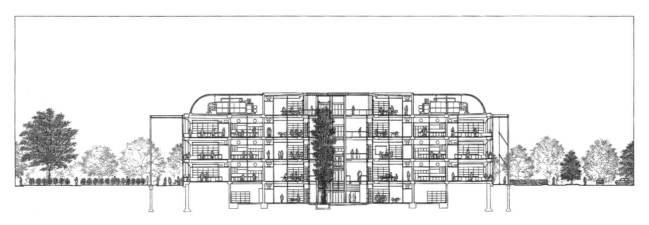

Figure 11.70 Center for Clinical Sciences Research, Stanford University, California: cross-section looking east

Figure 11.71 Center for Clinical Sciences Research, Stanford University, California: exterior view under louvres. Photographed by Robert Canfield

Figure 11.73 Center for Clinical Sciences Research, Stanford University, California: interior view of plaza. Photographed by Robert Canfield

Figure 11.72 Center for Clinical Sciences Research, Stanford University, California: interior view of classroom. Photographed by Robert Canfield

Figure 11.74 Center for Clinical Sciences Research, Stanford University, California: exterior view. Photographed by John Edward Linden

177

at ground level offsets the crisp lines of this space and affords greater privacy for office occupants.

Environmental systems take advantage of Palo Alto's climate, which is among the best in the United States. The offices are naturally ventilated for most of the year, with mechanical assistance on extremely hot days. Horizontal louvres over the outward-facing facades provide shade and correspond with a third-storey cornice line established on the campus by the neighbouring Hospital and School of Medicine Complex, designed by Edward Durrell Stone.

Seismic performance was another key concern: the campus lies close to the San Andreas fault and the laboratories contain highly sensitive equipment. In response, the building employs a concrete shear-wall structural system. Elements spanning beneath the courtyard rely on friction pendulum bearings to allow up to 0.5 m of seismic movement between the wings. Extensive computer simulations were conducted, including real-time animations based on previous earthquakes. The resulting system has become a major element in the building palette, and because of its high thermal mass contributes to the building's low energy demand.

Case study 20: The Pulross Centre

Architect: Penoyre and Prasad.
The following notes have been provided by the architect.

Intermediate care means medical, nursing, rehabilitative and respite care that can be offered to clients near their home without recourse to hospitalisation within acute facilities. The centre is one of a new generation of health buildings embodying the shift away from the hospital to a primary care-led NHS.

The centre is located in an area with a high index of deprivation and with health problems associated with such indicators. Its declared and positive philosophy is to regard health as 'a state of mental and social wellbeing, not merely the absence of infirmity'. As part of the delivery of this vision the new building has strong roots in the local community as well as sophisticated modern therapeutic facilities.

The design of the building responds to both the civic and therapeutic intentions of the centre's philosophy. With its curved glazed façade it presents a welcoming face to the surrounding neighbourhood. Within, great importance has been attached to the creation of a variety of accessible public places on the ground floor, including a café, also serving the range of clinics, therapy and treatment rooms. On the first floor are short-stay inpatient wards and individual rooms overlooking the garden. The landscaping, using the rubble of the hospital buildings that were once on site, creates a raised garden with level access from the first floor. The complex requirements of privacy and efficient operation are met whilst providing a calm yet stimulating sensory environment.

The building was reviewed by Katherine Shonfield in the *Architects' Journal* (22 March 2001) and her article highlights many of the recurring themes which are emerging in the architecture of a healing environment.

'The plan brings together two contrasting worlds. The first is the orthogonal, best-practice planning of treatment rooms, recorded in NHS design manuals and painstakingly evolved since the health service's inception. The second carries the building's message, expressed in the relaxed curvaceous flow of its social, circulation and administrative spaces. There is hierarchy but, appropriately for a building with democratic aspirations, no servant space.

Distinction rather than difference also characterises a rare sureness about colour. Attention to colour is echoed in the treatment of other less tangible and often overlooked aspects of architecture: acoustics and touch. Within the hall space, the combination of timber elements, carpeting and the asymmetric overhang of the nurse's point, gives the place a pleasing sound of inhabitation of the recognisably institutional cacophony of reflected noise or a depressing hush.

The Scandinavian impression is underlined by a distinctly unEnglish and luxurious sense of physical comfort. The intention is that the building blurs artificial boundaries between medicine and the rest of life.'

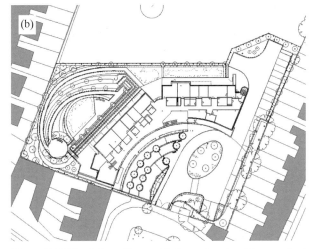

Figure 11.75 The Pulross Centre: (a) Front elevation. Photographed by Dennis Gilbert, VIEW (also in colour section). (b) Site plan.

South Africa

South Africa provides an excellent opportunity to examine the development of a health policy based on improving primary health care resources. At the crossroads of political and economic direction the country has had to deal with the sharp contrast between an affluent community with demands for world class hospital services set against poor quality rural services, sometimes with primitive facilities. Although the world's first heart transplant operation was carried out in South Africa by Dr Christian Barnard there was an underprovision of rural health care clinics with particular emphasis on the requirements for young women and children. SV Architects were the architects responsible for the documentation of the most significant primary health building programme in South Africa following the change in government in 1994. This work was presented to the Fifteenth Congress of International Hospital Engineering, a conference held in Edinburgh in 1998 by John Mehl of SV Architects. The following extracts explain the policy:

'The social and political background.

With the change in government in South Africa in 1994 the policy regarding the provision of health care facilities also changed. The States intention was to move the emphasis away from the first world hospitals and expensive specialised facilities and equipment to community-based primary health care.

To understand the reasons for the change in Health Policy one must take cognisance of the following recent statistics: In South Africa the ratio of urban to rural population distribution is 48.8%/51.2%. By comparison Britain has a ratio of 89.3%/10.7%. The birth rate per 1000 population is 34 compared to a world average of 25. Britain's birth rate is 13.3/1000 population. South Africa's population density is 33.9 persons per square km with Britain at 240 persons per square km. In Britain the passenger of km ratio is 34 times greater than in South Africa.

From the statistics it is evident that there is great demand for the provision of rural health care with particular emphasis on the requirements of young women and children. For economic reasons with the low population density the facilities can only be fairly basic and the State can afford nursing staff rather than qualified doctors.

Two of the most important aspects of the new 1994 Health Policy were therefore:
- universal access to primary health care
- free health care to pregnant women and children under the age of 6 years.

The nature of a primary health care clinic and infrastructure.

The model that has existed for several decades in South Africa is the rural primary health care clinic. Such a clinic serves a population of 5000 to 10,000 people and is generally staffed by qualified local nurses. The intention is that people requiring medical assistance should live not further than reasonable walking distance of such a clinic. (WHO standard: 5km or 1 hour walking time.) Where the ailment is so serious that it cannot be dealt with at local level the patient is stabilised if possible and thereafter transported by vehicle to the nearest hospital.

Prior to 1994 some 3000 such clinics had been built and there existed a shortfall of at least 1000 clinics. Taking population growth into consideration and the inadequacy of some of the facilities a further 1000 clinics were required. Therefore the real shortfall in1994 was probably closer to 2000 clinics.

Typically a primary health care clinic varying in size between 130 and 500 m^2 comprises several consulting rooms, a waiting area for patients, a small administrative component, staff facilities and toilets. Sleeping over accommodation for patients is not generally provided. Staff accommodation for nurses is generally desirable: it doubles up as a caretaker's facility; the provision of quality accommodation encourages nurses to stay or be attracted to rural communities; 24 hour nursing care is present. Depending on the birth rate surrounding each clinic a midwife obstetric unit is also frequently provided.

The crisis that developed in the provision of primary health care clinics.

The new 1994 ANC government in South Africa tackled the problem by allocating an unprecedented sum of £11 million for the construction of new clinics. The amount was budgeted for the remainder of 1994/5 and 1995/6 financial year and should have meant that at an average cost of £150,000 per clinic a boost would have been given to state funded Primary Health Care facilities by the provision of a further 83 clinics in that period of nearly 2 years.

At the same time the government wanted to achieve greater community participation in the development of the clinic designs than had been common practice in the past. Therefore the government embarked on a consultative process between local communities and consultants as they strove to augment the rural clinic infrastructure. While this approach was intended to engender good will the policy was in danger of floundering because the consultative process was lengthy and after 16 months of the 2 year period only £0.09 million of the £11 million had been spent and the ideas had not progressed beyond paper.

Central government advised health that these funds would be reallocated to other departments unless they could come up with a convincing business plan whereby they could use the funds before the end of the 1995/96 financial year ending March 1996.

The adoption of the fast track clinic building strategy in dealing with the crisis.

The newly appointed Director of Health Facilities Planning in the National Department of Health from August 1995 was an architect, Malcolm Jones. The day following his appointment the Minister of Health, Dr Zuma, "placed the problem in his lap" and asked whether a solution was possible. Mr Jones had been involved in Building Research for several years previously and had been particularly interested in exploring methods whereby the process of providing health care could be speeded up without prejudice to the quality or the cost thereof. Against this background Mr Jones developed a business plan in which the use of a fast track programme would enable construction to commence 17 weeks earlier than a conventional programme.

National appropriateness.
Pitching the appearance of the buildings and their consequent cost at the correct level was not easy. On the one hand the buildings had to be sufficiently pleasant so that health workers coming from finely constructed training institutions and asked to work in the clinics would not consider the working environment a deprivation. The buildings needed also to reflect the "new South Africa" where care for people on the fringes of rural society was expressed. Memories of the burning of schools because they were viewed by communities as inferior "hand-me-down" solutions from central government occupied the thoughts of the Task Team as they developed the documentation. Conversely the clinics are built with taxpayers money and criticism either from Treasury or the press for being over lavish had to be avoided. In a few instances local consultants felt it incumbent on them to "jazz up" the appearance of the buildings that they were responsible for, adding functionally superfluous "post-modern" gables. The press pounced on these cases. By and large the impression

gained by speaking informally to members of the communities and health workers is that the clinics are well received. Physical evidence thereof was apparent in one clinic where a nurse had rigged out a consulting room as her bedroom.

The design of these primary health care facilities raises interesting architectural questions about national appropriateness. The same conference paper describes the problem as follows:

'In January 1998 the South African government launched the equity in primary health care project. The focus will be on problems of the historically disadvantaged sectors of society, the rural African women and children in the former homelands. The project will seek to address long-standing health problems of malnutrition, infectious diseases, maternal and prenatal mortality and the new increasing problems of HIV/AIDS – problems resulting from basic human beings such as the lack of water, sanitation, housing, employment and rapid urbanisation. The success of the project will be seen through its contribution to improved life expectancy and reduced infant and child mortality rates, stabilisation of HIV/AIDS prevalence rates and a decrease in TB cases in South Africa.

As a case study the Alexander Health Centre and University Clinic in Johannesburg provides an outstanding case study of the high quality work which is being achieved in South Africa.

Figure 11.76 Philani Clinic in Kwa-Sulu Natal, South Africa. Architect: SV Architects

Alexander Health Centre and University Clinic, Johannesburg

Profile of the clinic

The Alexander Health Centre and University Clinic occupies a unique position not only in the community of Alexander, but in the social history of South Africa itself. Since its humble beginnings as a missionary mother-and-child clinic for the 20,000 strong Alexander community some 70 years ago, the clinic has grown from the original two-roomed corrugated iron building to a model community-based primary health care facility. Today it serves an impoverished community of around 400,000 people which is crammed into an area of just one square mile in extent on the edge of Sandton, the wealthy centre of South Africa's financial life. Few places illustrate as glaringly as these neighbouring suburbs the country's social dichotomy, born out of a long history of segregationist development. It is against this history that the ongoing evolution of Alex Clinic, as it is affectionately known, must be understood.

When the founding charity, the American Board Mission, decided to withdraw from Alexander to focus on other needy areas in 1939, the newly independent clinic was registered as a welfare organisation, and private benefactors permitted the construction 4 years later of new premises on 4-acres of land on the edge of the township. At this time the University of the Witwatersrand forged a symbolic link with the clinic, which became a training facility for medical students under a full-time medical director.

Over the following decades the clinic became a centre not only of health care, but of passive resistance in an increasingly adverse political climate. Increasing pressure from the government to see the residents of Alexander forcibly relocated under apartheid legislation, led from protest and boycott actions of the 1950s to ever worsening social despair and political tension. Major unrest in Alexander accompanied the 1976 Soweto riots, and kept escalating until, in 1986, it peaked with a mini-war in the streets. Alexander Clinic was specifically targeted by government for its unfaltering spirit through these years, first by imposition of a full financial

Figure 11.77 Alexandra Health Centre and University Clinic, South Africa: external view. Architect: Meyer Pienaar. Photograph by Christopher Malan

Figure 11.78 Alexandra Health Centre and University Clinic, South Africa: additional external view. Photograph by Christopher Malan (also in colour section)

Figure 11.79 Alexandra Health Centre and University Clinic, South Africa: another external view. Photograph by Christopher Malan

stranglehold and, in 1986 a series of firebomb attacks which were later found to have been perpetrated by the police's secret special branch under government orders.

At the height of this turmoil the clinic again emerged as a pioneering establishment, in using the climate of adversity as a driving force to explore community-based alternatives to health care delivery, and implementing its vision to the effect that it is today regularly held up as a model for community-based primary health care in South Africa. Its strong ties with the community were forged not only through the role it played in times of political hardship, but by implementation of a variety of new concepts. Literally each adult resident in Alexander was given voting rights at the AGM, to ensure the board of directors was truly representative of the community. In some respects, the clinic premises became a broader community centre, and the clinic itself launched satellite facilities, outreach programmes, educational drives and homecare initiatives in the township.

This very close integration of the clinic into the community it serves keeps guiding its ongoing forward planning. Following political transformation in South Africa the clinic has had to respond to ever new challenges – political faction fighting in the years of transformation, a wave of violent crime as the new democracy takes hold, ongoing social despair with severe problems of criminal violence, domestic and sexual abuse, regular scares for epidemic diseases, such as cholera, and an AIDS problem is disastrous proportions, with 70% of people volunteering for AIDS tests at the clinic in the year 2000 having test HIV positive. Today the clinic is re-assessing its role within the community in a strategic forward planning exercise, to address this new wave of challenges by exploring options for increased counselling services, preventative health care and focusing on the medical as well as social aspects of the HIV/AIDS pandemic.

At the same time the clinic is engaged in talks with the new government, to work out a mutually acceptable model for public/private sector co-operation. Currently the government, which follows a policy for free primary health care delivery, subsidises the clinic's operational expenses to an amount of 80%. With appeals for private donations increasingly difficult to motivate in a free democratic environment, the challenge lies in trying to secure full operational subsidies from government, without sacrificing the independence which has afforded the clinic its adventurous spirit in the past, and has permitted it to be a pioneer in exploring sustainable, community-based alternatives to health care delivery.

The architect's role in the clinic

The history of the Alexander Health Care and University Clinic shows a clear evolution in its operations, to adapt to ever-changing circumstances. The architect has to understand these underlying dynamics in order to contribute meaningfully to the clinic's ultimate aim of health care.

In 1989 Meyer Pienaar Architects were invited via the University of the Witwatersrand to formulate a plan for long-term involvement in the clinic. At that time the clinic was looked on with disfavour by the government of the day, but private donor funds had been secured for renovations and expansions. Projects at the time involved a full analysis of the clinic's premises and operations, renovation and rationalisation of existing facilities for improved efficiency, and addition of a new 24-hour casualty unit. Given the dynamic, evolutionary nature of Alex Clinic, the architects have over the 12-year period since these initial projects, become in a sense a partner in a long-term collaborative relationship.

Briefing process and community involvement

The Alexander Clinic is a truly community-based institution, and the residents of Alexander are proud and hugely protective of the clinic and its history. The board of directors is elected from within the community, with each adult resident in Alexander entitled to a vote at the AGM.

Since Alex Clinic is very much a dynamic institution, which has to adjust constantly to ever-changing priorities in its service delivery, the architects to some extent become part of strategic planning exercises. At masterplanning level the architects engage in talks with the working committees which review the clinic's services on a regular basis, and they pro-

actively contribute schematic design proposals to serve as a basis for the working groups' ongoing discussions. This is very much a process of parallel work by internal planning committees and architects focusing respectively on operational and infrastructural evolution of the clinic.

Out of the masterplanning reviews individual projects are identified and prioritised. These can range from small interventions (for instance altering of a few partitions) to larger capital projects, such as the new administration wing (1997) or the new antenatal clinic (2000),

For these projects the brief is compiled by the architects on the basis of extensive discussions with the client's steering committee as well as doctors and all the nursing staff of the particular department. Input from staff is crucial to ensure tried and tested working procedures are optimally accommodated and social or cultural aspects the architect may not be aware of are considered. Through a long history of very close involvement with the community and daily contact with hundreds of patients, the nursing staff is also the best conduit to channel patient-input back to the architects. The design brief is refined on the basis of sketches, followed by later more detailed scale drawings, with each design stage being submitted for input to the steering committee and staff. Where private sponsors are funding a project, they are also consulted to ensure that they are satisfied with the scope and quality of the product.

External design parameters, for instance given architectural context, recycling of existing structures for new uses, statutory regulations and recommended hospital design standards are incorporated by the architects during early design development stages.

Funding procurement route

Presently Alex Clinic receives 70–80% of its operational budget from government. The remaining operational expenses, as well as all funding for capital projects has to be raised in the form of private sponsorship. In the year 2001 the operational budget amounts to R20 million of which R14 million is paid by government, leaving a shortfall of R6 million before capital projects can be considered.

Figure 11.80 Alexandra Health Centre and University Clinic, South Africa: a further external view. Photograph by Christopher Malan

Figure 11.81 Alexandra Health Centre and University Clinic, South Africa: an internal view. Photograph by Christopher Malan

Fundraising for capital projects is normally separated from the ongoing fundraising work in the operational side. Once a new building project has been identified, the architects prepare design and presentation drawings, which are priced as accurately as possible by the quantity surveyors to provide accurate sponsorship targets.

In collaboration with the clinic's fundraising manager the architects compile brochures aimed at securing donor-funds. Such initial works is done at no fee, with professional fees only payable once full project finance has been raised. If circumstances permit, some of the professional fees may be waived and services offered as donations in kind.

Costs and sustainability

Naturally, it is of paramount importance that buildings are as cost-effective as possible, and care is taken that each new structure erected on the premises adds value beyond its immediate function. The initial buildings of the clinic were an assembly of loose structures with little unifying context. In many of the architectural projects this building fabric is reconfigured and re-used, to squeeze optimum benefit from existing assets. With each new addition to the clinic, the architects aspire to tighter aesthetic and functional integration of all buildings into an efficient whole. The main mechanisms which have been consistently applied for the last 12 years to achieve integration and environmental quality on the premises are carefully considered placement of new structures to optimise spatial coherence, the use of vibrant colours on the buildings and the use of landscaping to blend internal and external spaces into a pleasing whole. Beyond functional efficiency, the aim is to strengthen the clinic's qualities as a total healing environment.

Although frequently quality has to be somewhat compromised in favour of quantity, the buildings are of a robust nature, to give sponsors and users alike the peace of mind of a lasting investment. Individual buildings are domestic in scale, with a number of double-storey structures exploiting the sloping site which is developed on three different terraced levels.

The integration of buildings with gardens and incorporation of courtyards permits optimum use of natural environmental controls. All rooms receive daylight and are

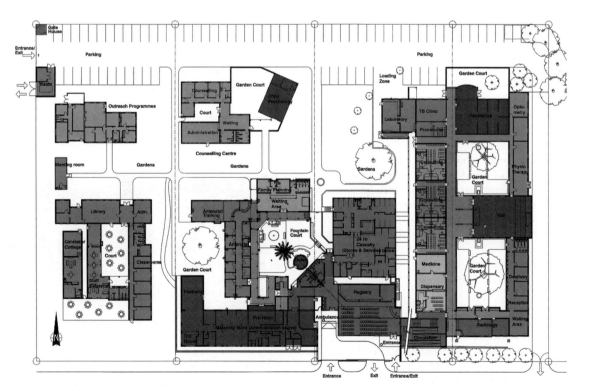

Figure 11.82 Alexandra Health Centre and University Clinic, South Africa: master plan. Drawings by Meyer Pienaar Architects

Figure 11.83 Alexandra Health Centre and University Clinic: proposed new entrance and registry. Drawings by Meyer Pienaar Architects

naturally ventilated through windows, with clerestoreys aiding convection flows through crowded spaces. Verandahs provide shaded and sheltered walkways and waiting areas, and all new additions are orientated and detailed to minimise reliance on mechanical systems.

Transport linkages

The clinic is located on one of the main access roads into Alexander, on the edge of the township. Few residents have private transport, and patients have to reach the clinic either on foot, or through the services of the active private minibus/taxi service. Realising that access to the clinic may be problematic a certain sector of the community, the Alexander Health Centre has established two small satellite facilities at strategic locations in the township for elementary consultations and procedures, immunisation campaigns and other services not dependent on the infrastructure of the main clinic. These satellite stations are supplemented by a mobile clinic, housed in a caravan.

In addition the clinic runs a variety of community health outreach programmes, in which nursing staff takes nursing care, preventative medicine and health education to the homes, schools and workplaces of the people.

Conclusion

During the briefing process for upgrade work 13 years ago, the director at that time, Dr Tim Wilson, insisted that a place of contemplation, a 'quiet room', should form part of the new buildings. This space was designed as a simple and modest circular room with a brick-corbelled ceiling and rooflight. This little space expresses the role of Alex Clinic throughout its turbulent history as a place not only of physical, but also emotional healing. An anecdote related by Dr Wilson illustrates how, as a community-based institution built on a long history of caring, Alex Clinic has become a true haven in a harsh and hostile urban setting: On seeing an old woman wander aimlessly through the premises, he inquired whether she was lost. Oh no, she replied, not at all. She only came there to hear the birds sing.

United States of America

For many years the USA has been a technology-driven affluent society. At the forefront of scientific enquiry its health facilities are as advanced as it is possible to provide in this world from the point of view of access to medical knowledge.

However, attitudes are changing and the assumption that technical expertise coupled with wealth leads inexorably to better health care is being questioned. New ways are being explored to provide health care services, not least because of financial constraints which are beginning to limit the funds available to invest in the health sector. Some of the large architectural practices who have produced the best work in America for large hospital programmes are beginning to look again at the way these major facilities are master planned and conceived. There is new interest in providing small-scale specialist facilities and a concern for environmental qualities that provide humane, comforting characteristics more in tune with the familiarity of home, rather than the relatively unknown atmosphere of a hospital. No doubt it is over simplistic to say that 'small is beautiful' but by providing smaller buildings close to the communities they serve, doctors and architects have a better chance of meeting the needs of patients.

There is discussion of hospital villages, using different architectural firms on one site. The quality of design and the therapeutic benefits from giving patients personal control over their environments seems to be widely accepted, despite the limited amount of research to use as evidence for these views. This change of scale illustrates a narrowing of policy differences around the world for primary care facilities. Specialist centres nearer the communities requiring the health services are bringing greater invention, variety and domesticity to the work of some American architectural practices. There are common threads in the philosophy of health care which are valid regardless of whether the health facilities are designed and built in California or Cambodia, New York or Namibia, which brings refreshing clarity to the importance of the relationship between doctor and patient. Architects need to refocus their attention on designing a caring environment for this fundamental process and resist the temptation of the ambitious large scale and usually impersonal architecture of big buildings.

Examples from three American practices are included, all of whom subscribe to the importance of high standards of environmental design and the therapeutic benefits which can flow from this approach. Although these are not examples of primary health care buildings they demonstrate the narrowing gap in setting design standards and establishing a high quality brief to achieve patient satisfaction in health buildings of all types. They also illustrate the development of specialist care centres.

SBRA (Shepley Bullfinch Richardson and Abbott) has been established for 125 years and health care is one of the

Figure 11.84 Bronson Methodist Hospital: corridor of light. Architect: SBRA. Photographed by ESTO

Figure 11.86 Children's hospital: lobby. Architect: SBRA. Photographed by ESTO (also in colour section)

three primary practice areas in which they specialise. Two of their projects for specialist health services illustrate their concern for high standards of environmental design including a new centre for women and children at the Bronson Methodist Hospital, Kalamazoo, Michigan and the new clinical building at the Children's Hospital in Boston, Massachusetts. Another health specialist is TK&A (TSOI/Kobus & Associates), founded in 1983 and a winner of many design awards. Their work for the Magee-Women's Hospital in Pittsburgh, Pennsylvania and the Brigman Women's Hospital at

Figure 11.87 Centre for women and newborns. Corridor and reception. Architect: TK&A (Tsoi/Kobus & Associates). Photographed by Steve Rosenthal

Figure 11.85 Bronson Methodist Hospital: child and pond. Photographed by ESTO

Figure 11.88 Centre for women and newborns. Reception. Photographed by Steve Rosenthal

Figure 11.89 Magee-Women's Hospital. Internal view. Photographed by Hendrich-Blessing. Architect: TK&A (Tsoi/Kobus & Associates)

Boston, Massachusetts illustrate the focusing of care and attention on specialist units within the American health care system. Although both of these buildings are large they represent a refocusing of attitudes to health care policy. Lastly, examples of Earl Swensson Architects work, including the Baptist Memorial Hospital, Collierville, Tennessee and the Samaritan North Health Centre at Dayton, Ohio show an interest in human scale domesticity in buildings which are otherwise large institutional projects.

Obviously, there are many other examples that could be gleaned from the large range of health care architecture being commissioned in the USA. Small jewel-like examples of work, to compare with the Maggie Centre in Edinburgh have not readily come to the surface in my search for buildings where the patient/doctor interface is the core value in the briefing process. As an eminent architect in one of the leading American firms of architects said to me: 'There seems to be a fundamental split in this industry between practices that focus on small, primary care projects and those that focus on large health centres, so I am afraid I can't offer much help.' My reply pointed out that the UK procurement route for small-scale health buildings such as doctors surgeries and community clinics was clouded in uncertainty. Concern has been expressed (by CABE and others) that NHS Estates attempt to solve this problem by the introduction of Procure21, and the batching of smaller projects into larger contract packages will give rise to difficulties. The LIFT programme is more promising but, obviously is still at an early stage in development. British Government policies are not consistent. For example:

Figure 11.90 Baptist Memorial Hospital. Lobby dining area. Photographed by Jonathan Hillyer Photography, Inc. Architect: Earl Swensson

Figure 11.91 Samaritan North Health Centre. Entrance. Photographed by Jonathan Hillyer Photography, Inc. Architect: Earl Swensson

- The Government is advocating better design standards in civic buildings.
- The NHS Plan has a very ambitious programme for investment in small-scale buildings (i.e. GP surgeries).
- The Government seems intent on pursuing building procurement through the PFI process (which is not suitable for small projects and is attracting a great deal of adverse criticism on the design standards achieved in recent health projects).

Funding for American health projects is also subject to extensive review and the balanced budget Act of 1997 has had the effect of reining in health care costs. Hilary Clinton's initiatives have spawned many mergers and both the medical and architectural professions as well as the entrepreneurial health care businesses are looking afresh at smaller community facilities. Importantly, this is also bringing therapeutic benefits as designs become more sensitive to the quality of human scale spaces and are patient focused.

Sweden

The affinity of Sweden with other northern European countries is evident in the approach being taken by a number of recent health care projects. There are similarities of scale, and

the use of natural materials in the majestic but demanding landscapes of northern latitudes. There is a frugal attention to detailing and a clarity of thought imposed by the economic restrictions generated by a sophisticated, affluent country but more tightly constrained in comparison to the resources of the USA.

This creates interesting models to compare between smaller or poorer nations where the design process becomes more focused on the human qualities and the personal interaction between patient and doctor. These principles have a validity regardless of the affluence of the country where health facilities are required.

The Norrtälje Hospital illustrates some of these principles and are described in the following extracts from the Architect's account provided by Ahmed Radwan.

'The 1980s were characterised by what was referred to in Sweden as ROT (renovation, rebuilding and extension). The idea was to exploit the qualities of the existing buildings, with a growing appreciation of the value of old panelled doors, stucco, stripped pine floorboards and tiled stoves, etc. In the health services, however, it is not so straightforward, as hygienic considerations and new technology often make it impossible to retain such environmentally valuable details. Whether to tear down or to preserve becomes here more a question of function and economy.

Today, the diminishing resources available to hospitals and the streamlining of both services and the use of premises, mean extensive changes to the existing buildings. Digital technology and new surgical methods have been transforming hospital routines in an ever increasing rate over the past few years. a great deal of hospital work that had previously required many days' hospitalisation can today be dealt with on an outpatient basis. More and more

Figure 11.92 Norrtalje Hospital: plan. Architect: Ahmed Radwan, ETV arkitekter ab

Figure 11.93 Norrtalje Hospital: entrance area

Figure 11.95 Norrtalje Hospital: reception

wards are being shut down. The old system of separate clinics is changing to one aimed at greater co-operation within the different areas of hospital activity.

The views, apart from creating a very pleasant atmosphere, also make orientation easier. This is equally important for a small-scale hospital.

We have made every effort to avoid long, dark corridors with ward rooms situated beyond the ante-rooms and bathrooms. Instead, the wards are gathered in groups, with the bathrooms so placed that the ward rooms have direct contact with the corridor.

There are never more than three paces separating the different rooms in any one group. Most of the lavatories and shower-rooms have windows.

The planning motto was "the green hospital focused on the patient".

Our aim was to let the hospital express its individuality. Norrtälje is a small town with relatively small-scale buildings. The existing hospital is of a modest scale and is largely three-storey. The building has been modernised, rebuilt

and extended in several phases. The new building has also been given a small-scale expression through a distribution of the volumes into smaller, generally two-story units.'

Cambodia

The Government of the Kingdom of Cambodia recognises that improving community health is essential for national development. Their national policy on primary health care states that it has been prepared as part of the Government's commitment to strengthening a primary health care approach to health and community development issues. Starting from this sound base, consistent with the objectives of the World Health Organisation (WHO) it is apparent that there is no difference in the philosophy and aspirations for a high quality of life between rich and poor countries.

An example of how this work is being promoted can be illustrated by the Aid Programme supported by Australia and managed by ACIL Australia PTY Ltd. ACIL Australia PTY Ltd is a privately owned Australian company formed in 1967, with its head office situated in Melbourne, Australia. It implements projects enhancing the living conditions of communities in developing countries and strengthens their local agencies. ACIL's mission is to maximise the benefits and values of the Aid projects it manages. Its expertise lies in its capacity to strengthen the capabilities of developing nations, government agencies at national, provincial and district levels, facilitating the involvement of local communities, ensuring project goals and objectives are achieved.

The Cambodia Health Promotion and Primary Health Care Project (CHPPHC) is funded by the Australian Government through the Australian Agency for international development and is managed by ACIL Australia PTY Ltd. ACIL is committed to achieving sustained technology transfer in recipient countries through an integrated team effort of clients, target beneficiaries and project staff, ensuring quality outcomes through providing the best available consultants and support teams.

Figure 11.94 Norrtalje Hospital: kitchen area for patients and staff

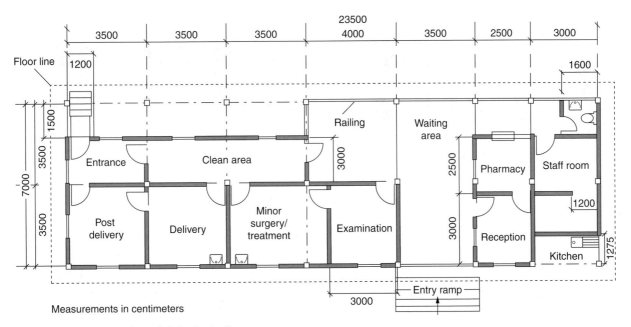

Figure 11.96 Standard plan for a clinic in Cambodia

The goal of the Health Promotion and Primary Health Care Project is to improve the health, knowledge and practice of both community and health workers in Phnom Penh and Kampong Cham Province. This is being achieved through training, provision of equipment, infrastructure development, health promotion, management support and community development.

The project is comprised of four inter-related components:

- national health promotion and primary health care
- Kampong Cham Province health service delivery
- community development and participation in health services
- project management monitoring.

The project has achieved much in the 3 years it has been operating. It has built the National Centre for Health Promotion, the Regional Training Centre in Kampong Cham and 15 commune health centres. All of these were made operational through the training of staff at all levels of the health care system.

Other important achievements include the development of national curricula for training of health care workers, as well as the national primary health care policy, obtained endorsement from all relevant local and international agencies. The project has also established and operationalised three district, 15 commune and 75 village development committees, funding and conducting health-related activities in 60 villages so far. Training of health care workers has been in both clinical and management areas. The project has produced over 30 health promotion materials which are currently being combined into health promotion campaigns.

The main project challenges have been working in a very resource scarce environment, landmines, and *coup d'état*.

These issues combined with limited human resource capacity have made a very challenging project.

Within this programme a standard plan has been approved which has been the basis for constructing 15 health centres. Although there may appear to be little direct connection between an aid programme in a developing country for primary health care facilities compared to the sophisticated research objectives of therapeutic benefits in high quality environmental design work it is, nevertheless, important to stress the fundamental patient/doctor relationships.

What this programme is seeking to achieve in Cambodia is a caring environment for the humane and sensitive treatment of patients by dedicated doctors in the best buildings available to them given the economic circumstances of their environment. These principles remain the same, as is said elsewhere in this book, whether the building is in Cambodia or California. The building provides the flux or catalyst for that essential interchange between the patient and their doctor. These buildings could trigger, with equal success, a sense of well-being, and stimulate the spirituality of healing which seems to be inherent in all mankind.

Further information is available in the Internet (www.bigpond.com.kh/users/chpphc).

New Zealand

Parallels can be drawn between New Zealand and Scotland with regard to the delivery of health care services. It can be argued that the two countries share some of the same issues of a widely scattered population, and a rugged landscape, certainly as far as the South Island is concerned. New Zealand is also grappling with rising expectations in the delivery of

Chow:Hill
ARCHITECTS
DEVELOPMENT CONSULTANTS

STRATEGIES NZ's First *SuperClinic*™

A PROJECT REPORT BY CHOW:HILL ARCHITECTS

DEC/JAN98

•*Manukau SuperClinic*™

•*Botany Downs SuperClinic*™, Howick

A *SuperClinic*™ in NZ

Manukau *SuperClinic*™, which was opened on 8 October 1997 by then Prime Minister Jim Bolger for South Auckland Health, is a new type of healthcare facility for New Zealand.

The *SuperClinic*™ is an ambulatory care facility accommodating seven clinical modules, offering specialist secondary care including orthopedics, ENT, audiology, paediatrics, ophthalmology, womens health, diabetic and geriatric services as well as 6 Operating theatres for day stay surgery in a range of disciplines including gastroscopy.

The *SuperClinic*™ also features the first digital radiology suite in New Zealand, allowing radiology and ultrasound images to be viewed at any location within the Middlemore network.

Ambulatory Care

Ambulatory Care has been one of the megatrend issues for healthcare throughout the world in the last ten years. As technology advances and healthcare service delivery becomes more patient-focused, more procedures and treatment episodes occur on an outpatient basis rather than involving overnight hospital care.

Well-designed ambulatory care centres can deliver healthcare more effectively, allowing patients to return to their homes the same day, contributing to their recovery and overall well-being.

The Concept

The 6500m² *SuperClinic*™ building at Manukau City, is believed to be the largest ambulatory care centre in the Southern Hemisphere.

The project had its genesis in 1994, when South Auckland Health recognised it was not able to continue to effectively meet future challenges of healthcare delivery to New Zealand's fastest growing and most diverse community from its current site and aging facilities at Middlemore Hospital.

The Crown Health Enterprise embarked on a $120m facilities modernisation programme over several years intended to achieve a variety of goals consistent with international trends in healthcare, including:

- redistribution of healthcare services into the community;
- decongestion of the Middlemore site;
- co-ordinated redevelopment of key Middlemore Hospital facilities;

The *SuperClinic*™ programme, which includes a sister clinic in Botany Road, Howick, is a key part of that facilities modernisation programme.

The *SuperClinic*™ concept is simply a secondary care facility located in the community with a full range of specialist public healthcare services under a single roof.

one

Figure 11.97 SuperClinics project report: Chow Hill Architects

Design Process

In determining the best model for the *SuperClinic*™ project, facility and operation, South Auckland Health canvassed best international practice and formed ongoing links with individuals and organisations throughout the world.

While funding and delivery are very different, ambulatory care and day surgery facilities in the United States were found to be the most useful models for the *SuperClinic*™ team.

A series of visits by clinical, management and design members of the team to ambulatory care centres and day surgery centres was an opportunity to learn first hand which features could be successfully transplanted to New Zealand.

Simmonds Healthcare from the US were engaged as healthcare consultants and assisted on clinical interface, briefing and outline design issues.

Chow:Hill Architects were engaged as Principal Consultants and assembled a team of specialist consultants to develop the outline concepts into detailed designs and contract documents under the guidance and co-ordination of project managers, Carson Group.

The detailed design and documentation process for the *SuperClinic*™ projects was very demanding in terms of time, quality and involvement at every level.

•*Typical waiting area*

We were required to:

- issue full sets of documents for audit review at 30%, 60% and 90% completion prior to final issue;
- participate in audit review/value management workshops;
- present computer animations of the facility to clinical workshops;
- assist in preparation of models, full-size mock-ups, and a test examination room to refine the design;
- participate fully in briefing discussions on service delivery and respond to major changes, in some instances while under construction;
- demonstrate calculations and estimates of building services aspects, such as energy performance, usually from first principles;
- liaise with a range of medical equipment suppliers to ensure detailed spatial, structural and services requirements were met;
- continue to maintain control on programme and budget.

This level of involvement is expected of consultants who are providing quality service to healthcare projects on a daily basis - they require a strong commitment from all participants.

•*Manukau SuperClinic*™
main entry & porte cochere

Change in Healthcare

Many of us regard change as an opportunity, but just as many of us regard change with suspicion, especially in public healthcare.

The *SuperClinic*™ projects were designed and documented in a climate of overwhelming change - change to service delivery, change to staffing levels, change to management and operation, and simply a change of environment - many of those involved needed to make the service and operation fit the facility just as much as the facility had to fit the service.

In a very real sense, the *SuperClinic*™ projects were also *leading* change at South Auckland Health, rather than *responding* to it as most projects tend to do.

For the design and construction team, including South Auckland Health's Estates & Engineering managers, it often meant no specific client or brief were available - no-one had built or operated a *SuperClinic*™ here before.

Judgements were made by the team based on research, experience and liaisons with clinicians and healthcare providers both here and overseas.

Success of this proactive approach to design in a changing healthcare delivery environment will continue to be measured by the ease with which current and future clinical services are integrated into the building.

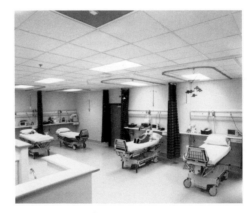

•*Day surgery recovery*

two

Figure 11.97 continued

Design Concepts

Change is a reality to healthcare delivery, as much as healthcare projects.

The *SuperClinic*™ is designed to facilitate both operational flexibility and future adaptability in response to service changes in a number of ways which may not be apparent on first sight.

The floor plan is based on a 1800mm dimensional module, allowing two rooms of 3.6m (measured centre to centre of partitions) and a corridor of 1.8m for each 9m structural bay, and is organised into "clinical modules".

Each typical clinical module has two patient corridors leading off the Waiting room, with examination rooms to the exterior, procedure and more specialist rooms to the interior, and staff corridors, Nurse Station and Reception between.

A clinical module breaks down issues of space ownership and territoriality, allowing more efficient scheduled use of facilities - a diabetic clinic one day, a pediatric clinic the next.

The module layout envisages the clinician moving between 3 or 4 examination rooms, consulting with patients prepared by a healthcare assistant, rather than the clinician waiting in the room for the next patient to be brought in - significant operational efficiencies are possible though this approach without compromise to service quality.

•*Typical module plan*

Each typical examination room and procedure room was designed and documented with a high degree of client input and control.

Every aspect was discussed, different configurations trialed, feedback processed from staff, every single stud and nog and each electrical, mechanical, data and medical gas outlet was located and drawn, all to satisfy the requirements of a wide range of clinical services within a typical room with little more than a change in bed position or an extra piece of equipment.

Other rooms, such as shared work offices, which fit the examination room modular size are constructed and fitted with services blanked off to allow easy conversion to examination rooms - in fact, late in the construction period, 2 rooms were converted, demonstrating the built-in adaptability of the design.

The team also assisted South Auckland Health to develop a standard in-house catalogue of modular knock-down joinery components - cupboards, drawers, shelves, benches - to allow easy, economical repair and replacement of elements and to facilitate control in a variety of future projects by allowing staff to order custom configurations from a range of catalogue components.

While none of these features are of themselves particularly exciting or glamorous, they are essential for any healthcare project seeking to meet the challenges of change in healthcare delivery now and in years to come.

•*Atrium and greeter station*

Design Treatment

Public buildings, particularly healthcare buildings, should not be ostentatious or overdone - they must be of an appropriate scale and quality and, especially in Manukau, be capable of expressing a wide range of culture and opinion.

To this end, the building is intended to be as inviting, welcoming and comfortable as a 6500m² building can be through use of a range of familiar forms and details:

- gable roof projecting at the entry - a form well known around the Pacific rim;

- concrete tile hipped roof, exposed rafters, eaves gutters - all familiar domestic details in New Zealand, albeit on a larger scale;

- coloured concrete block veneer cladding (used for the first time in New Zealand) with "punched" windows and articulated texture - rather than larger scale, commercial detailing like curtain wall glass.

The main internal feature of the building is the central atrium space, running full length, providing public entry to the front, staff entry to the rear, access and egress to all clinical modules and housing lifts, motor and hub rooms, public toilet and phone facilities.

All visitors immediately encounter a prow-shaped greeter station fashioned from laminated matai and staffed by friendly people to greet you in your own language and direct you to the appropriate module.

The atrium is intended to be as full of light and welcoming as possible with careful sizing and placement of double height spaces and skylights glazed with high performance solar control glass.

•*Upper level atrium*

three

Figure 11.97 continued

Construction Features

Structurally, the building is a 2-way moment resisting reinforced concrete frame, avoiding shear walls and braces which limit the adaptability of the spaces, with structural steelwork and timber trusses to the roofs.

Seismic movement is accommodated in 20mm joints to block veneer corners and at framing and concrete junctions.

The design of the building contributes to energy efficiency of the mechanical plant by balancing the amount of glazing with space volume, building mass and insulation, rather than an emphasis on curtain wall glazing,

All access and egress is through the atrium which also functions as a smoke reservoir and extraction zone in the event of a fire.

Acoustic treatment is an important feature of the *SuperClinic* - plywood lining is installed below roofing throughout to mitigate the effects of nearby aircraft noise on consulting areas.

Room-to-room crosstalk is minimised between treatment spaces by a combination of selected framed, lined & insulated partition systems, careful location of services outlets, solid core doors in steel frames with acoustic seals, heavy duty mineral fibre suspended ceiling tiles and, within the ceiling spaces, spun polyester acoustic baffles suspended from the roof or floor above for the perimeter of each room, closing the ceiling space into a series of baffled cells.

Tight control was asserted on the layout and position of all services, especially main runs, throughout the building to provide the client with the same degree of certainty and logic on services locations as other modular elements and to allow for future adaptability as much as possible.

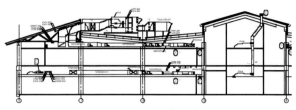

•*Cross section showing Mechanical services*

An 850mm minimum depth ceiling space is provided and all main services are kept in specific zones within the corridor ceiling spaces with branches into rooms as required - there was a policy of needing approval to leave the service zone assigned to a particular cable, pipe or duct.

Within walls, all services run vertically, unless specifically allowed otherwise in exceptional circumstances, allowing easy location of services for future adaptability and fixing medical equipment.

While this may seem heavy handed, South Auckland Health now has a building with a consistent and clear framework and a high degree of modularity - all of which have clear operational, maintenance and adaptability advantages.

Many of the architectural and building services features of the *SuperClinic* are subtle and hidden, but contribute enormously to the effectiveness and success of the facility.

The *SuperClinic™* Team

Client	South Auckland Health
Principal Consultants	Chow:Hill Architects
Project Architect	Darryl Carey
Healthcare Consultants	Simmonds Healthcare/ Miguel Burbano
Project Manager	Carson Group
Cost Consultants	Maltby & Co
Structural Consultants	Holmes Consulting Group
Civil Engineers	Harrison Grierson Consultants
Services Consultants	Rayner Cameron
Landscape Consultants	Priest Mansergh
Contractor	Hawkins Construction

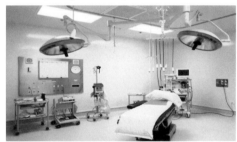

•*Day surgery operating theatre*

Chow:Hill ARCHITECTS DEVELOPMENT CONSULTANTS STRATEGIES

Chow:Hill Architects have developed expertise on a wide range of recent healthcare projects including:

* Extended Care Mental Health Unit, Otara, Auckland

* Development Planning for Middlemore Hospital, Auckland

* Taumurunui, Tokoroa, Te Kuiti Hospitals reconfigurations

* Emergency Suite & Trauma Centre, Waiora Waikato

* Laboratory Redevelopment, Waiora Waikato

* A variety of general practice and specialist clinics for public and private providers

For information and assistance on all types of projects, contact :

Darryl Carey

Chow:Hill Architects
PO Box 23593
Papatoetoe
AUCKLAND

Phone 09-2778260
Fax 09-2778261
darryl@chowhill.co.nz

Richard Hill

Chow:Hill Architects
PO Box 19208
HAMILTON

Phone 07-8340348
Fax 07-8342156
richard@chowhill.co.nz

design to deliver value

Figure 11.97 continued

health care services to world standards of excellence. This is leading to a shift in policy, away from large hospital complexes to the provision of more specialised local clinics.

Darryl Carey, an architect working the health care sector in New Zealand writes:

'As far as trends in primary healthcare facilities go, I believe NZ is no different from anywhere else in terms of mega trends. We are seeking fewer acute hospitals, separation of inpatient and ambulatory services, sometimes separation of elective and acute surgical services, a wider spread of ambulatory/primary care services throughout the community and an increase in the range of services offered in the primary/ambulatory environment, especially day surgery.

My sense is that, as in so many other areas, NZ is fairly quick to pick up on global trends and act on them, especially those from the US. As our funding/provider arrangements have more in common with the UK public health models (on which they used to be more closely based), some adjustments in US approach and standards are required.

We have recently seen our government restructure our health system to establish District Health Boards which, for the first time, are both funders of primary healthcare providers (including GPs) and healthcare providers themselves (as hospital operators). In theory, this should allow an opportunity for a comprehensive integrated approach to healthcare services in each district. The reality so far is that DHB funding is still centralised from the Ministry of Health and has not met DHB expectations. Many of our DHBs are well managed and financially strong, while others are less so. Many of them suffer from run-down facilities due to deferred maintenance and reduced capital investment in recent years (although this means that nearly every hospital in NZ has a fairly substantial project underway). Opportunities for cooperation and complementary services between DHB's have not really been realised.

The context this creates for all facilities is one of limited budgets and intense scrutiny by clients and Ministry/Treasury reviewers. We are always benchmarking our designs against comparable facilities from around the world. This may have something to do with a lack of a set of nationally agreed design guidelines and standards (like the NHS ones).'

New Zealand has developed the concept of super clinics, a secondary care facility located in the community with a full range of specialist public health care services under a single roof.

Scotland

Although Scotland is part of the UK, Scottish architecture, in parallel with the political changes which have led to devolution and the establishment of the Scottish Parliament, is

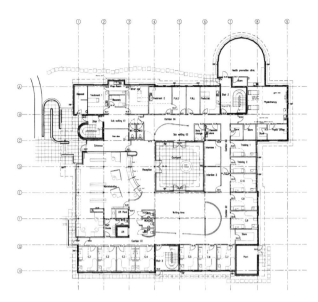

Figure 11.98 Dunbar Medical Centre: ground floor plan. Architect: Campbell & Arnott Ltd

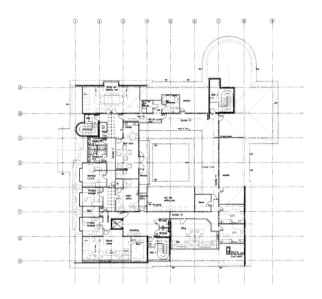

Figure 11.99 Dunbar Medical Centre: first floor plan. Architect: Campbell & Arnott Ltd

searching for a new identity. It is seeking recognition that its buildings should be assessed independently. The architectural profession in Scotland is flexing its muscles to raise the status of its cultural heritage and demanding a separate national appraisal of its work.

This nationalistic fervour is encouraging the development of links with other northern European countries (for example, Scandinavian countries such as Denmark, Sweden and Norway) where there are similarities of climate, culture and

Figure 11.100 Musselburgh Primary Care Centre: ground and first floor plan. Architect: Campbell & Arnott Ltd.

population density. The Nordic and Celtic traditions are encouraging a robust architectural response to the climatic conditions in Scotland, and the independence of its people. An affinity with nature, and the use of natural materials perhaps is one reason why they are already embracing the more inclusive or holistic approach of the next generation of health buildings. The world class examples of the benefits of therapeutic care for patients which have been achieved at both the Glasgow Homoeopathic Hospital and the Maggie Centre in Edinburgh demonstrate the benefits that result from small scale buildings using natural materials that are in tune with the environment. People engage with these buildings in a way which is impressive to see.

These ideas are also being pursued by other architects in Scotland, and the work of Campbell and Arnott is an example of what is being achieved.

They describe their approach as follows:

'Our approach to medical centre design is based on the recognition of the need for careful analysis for each practice's unique working methods and an understanding of the changes that inevitably occur. Our aim is to produce an effective and stimulating working environment benefiting both staff and patients.

In line with government policy, centres are now including an ever increasing range of community facilities. The practice is currently involved in a number of centres which are at the forefront of this trend.

The recently completed Craigmillar Medical Centre brings together Craigmillar Medical Group and the Durham Road Branch Surgery along with extensive community facilities including chiropody, dental, health, education and several multipurpose community consulting rooms. The building also provides office space for health visitors, community midwives and community nurses as well as serving as a base for the local health care co-operative. Recently opened by the Secretary of State for Health Mr Sam Galbraith the centre is set to transform the provision of health care in the Craigmillar area.

Other developments such as Tollcross will continue this trend with a centre which will include an extensive physiotherapy suite within the community facilities, whilst for a development in Dunbar the challenge was to reconcile the requirements of three individual practices operating under one roof along with its use as an out of hours base.

The Practice has also recently designed a new centre for Heriot-Watt University at their Riccarton campus. Currently under construction, the building includes dental and occupational health suites in addition to the medical practice's facilities.'

Figure 11.101 Monifieth Medical Centre: artist's impression. Architect: Campbell & Arnott Ltd.

Japan

Health care architecture in Japan towards to the end of the twentieth century focused on large hospital developments. A highly populated country, where individual houses are often very small, there is often little privacy or suitable facilities to care for the ill at home. The average stay in hospital is longer than in the West, although patients are expected to have made a full recovery before being discharged.

Eastern cultures have relied much more heavily on healing techniques which explore the relationship between mind and body and are conditional on an individual's spirituality. Faith and trust are integral components of medical protocols. It is somewhat surprising, therefore, to find that the Japanese government is encouraging the medical and architectural professions to explore the PFI process being promoted within the UK as a health building procurement route, when there is criticism of its design quality standards.

Figure 11.104 Ando Clinic, Japan: aerial view. Photographed by Satoshi Asakawa.

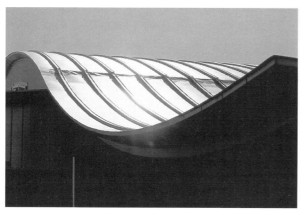

Figure 11.102 Ando Clinic, Japan: wave form roof. Photographed by Satoshi Asakawa. Architect: Tada Yoshiaki Architect & Associates

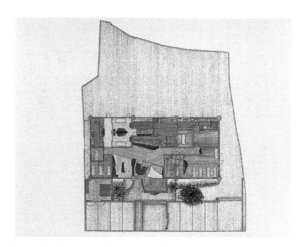

Figure 11.105 Ando Clinic, Japan: first floor plan. Photographed by Satoshi Asakawa.

Figure 11.103 Ando Clinic, Japan: internal view showing curving staircase. Photographed by Satoshi Asakawa.

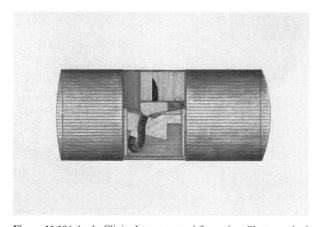

Figure 11.106 Ando Clinic, Japan: second floor plan. Photographed by Satoshi Asakawa.

Attitudes in Japan, as in other parts of the world, are moving towards a greater concern for patient focused care. To create an appropriate environment for patients is now regarded as being of paramount importance and the return to a caring environment as an aid to healing seems to be more compatible to older culture values of Japanese society before they embarked on their large hospital building programme. What is apparent from this very brief overview of health care attitudes in Japan is the trend towards greater priority being given to a high quality environment centred on the therapeutic benefits for patients. Here is another example where health policies are bringing medicine and architecture closer together. Examples of small clinics where the quality of the environment is uppermost in the minds of the designer provide yet another example of the importance between the patient and doctor interface. The Ando Clinic situated in a local temple town has a distinctive curved line to its roof. It has been designed with the image of a dragon in mind, and blends well with the surroundings according to the architect, Yoshiaki Tada Architect & Associates.

Note

1. The following note was provided by Jian-Guo Wu, a Chinese doctor who trained in traditional Chinese medicine at the University of Traditional Chinese Medicine, Guangzhou, a city in south China. He is researching project management techniques in the UK to see how they can be applied to the development of health clinics in China. He summarises the approach of traditional Chinese medicine (TCM) – one of the four quintessences of Chinese culture – in this description:

What is Chinese medicine?

To many Western readers, Chinese medicine may seem strange and unreliable. It is hard for them to understand why the needle and herb can cure the disease. It is the case, even in China, that some Chinese look on TCM as a mysterious thing. But it is a truth: as you know, China is a country that has a long long history and magnificent national culture. And TCM emerged at least 3000 years ago (in Chinese history, that is Shang Dynasty – 1000 BC), and has serviced the Chinese people for about 3000 years. Generally, TCM is a unique system of diagnosis and health care approaches. It is based on a profound philosophy and the concept of the universe outlined in the spiritual insights of Daoism (one of the Chinese religions), and it has produced a highly sophisticated set of practices to cure illness and to maintain health and well-being. These practices include acupuncture, herbal remedies, massage, diet, meditation, and both static and moving exercises. Although they appear very different in approaches, they all share the same underlying sets of assumptions about the nature of the human body and its place in the universe.

The basic theory of TCM

TCM can be traced to 1000 BC, but the first and most important classic of TCM had been completed during the Qin Dynasty (200 BC). The classic Huang-di Nei-jing (Inner Classic of The Yellow Emperor) – firstly build up TCM theory completely. Many basic concepts of TCM were expatiated in this work such as the fundamental substances in TCM, the meridian theory and the basic approach to diagnosis and treatment and so on. The basic substances include: Qi, Jing, Xue, Jin-Ye and Shen. Qi means 'energy', 'vital energy'. Jing can be translated as 'essence', governing growth, reproduction and development. Xue means 'blood', but not merely the physical substance that is recognised as blood in Western Medicine. It nourishes the body and Shen. Jin-Ye, which means 'body fluids', is considered to be the other organic liquids that moisten and lubricate the body. Shen can be translated as the mind or the spirit of the individual. The Meridian system consists of twelve main channels, each links together one by one into a cycle of circulation. And the basic substances (Qi, Blood, etc.) flow in the channels. Each channel has many specific, recognised acupuncture points. Actually it is hard to understand and it is impossible to explain the above concepts fully in one English word or phrase.

Medicine: East and West

Perhaps someone still argues whether TCM is science or not. But TCM has been developed in China for several thousand years before Western Medicine was introduced into China in the Qing Dynasty (about 100 years ago). In fact, Medicine East and West are two quite different ways of seeing, and thinking about the body and disease. Western Medicine is concerned mainly with isolatable disease categories or agents of disease and tries to change, control or destroy them. The Chinese Medicine, in contrast, directs the attention to the complete physiological and psychological individual. Illness is a pattern of disharmony of the whole body (entity). Treatment aims to restore harmony and to rebalance the interconnections between all aspects of the organism.

Anyway, TCM is an old science but with good prospects. I am sure that the Chinese medicine will be widely accepted throughout the world in the next 50 years as:

- there are no side-effects
- no laboratory reports are required
- no stethoscope is necessary
- no aspirin is needed
- no antibiotics/penicillin need to be prescribed.

12

Way forward

'Architecture is also about the spiritual needs of people as well as their material needs. It has much to do with optimism, joy and reassurance; of order in a disordered world; of 'privacy' in the midst of many; of space in a crowded site; of light on a dull day. It is about quality. Increasingly, there has rightly been a focus on the commissioning of hospitals and other health care buildings of quality, durability and style.

Of course it will continue to be important to control costs, but aesthetic and architectural considerations must also be given proper recognition.'
Lord Foster (Quoted by Mr Chris Smith, as Secretary of State for Culture, Media and Sport at the Opening Plenary Session of the Arts in Hospitals and Healthcare Conference, held in Strasbourg, France, 4–6 February 2001)

'Increasingly doctors and other healthcare professionals will need to work more closely with their patients to explore which treatment the patient feels best meets their need. I believe the potentially powerful role of complementary therapies will need to be increasingly recognised and incorporated into an individual's healthcare.'
Prince of Wales (11 November 2000 at the Millennium Festival of Medicine Conference)

'You can have the most efficient procurement process in the world but if you don't have a decent design you will still end up with a second-rate building.'

Quality and quantity must be evaluated together, with quality receiving a far higher weighting. The client's design advisers should be just as important as the Quantity Surveyors.'
Sir Stuart Lipton (Chairman of the Commission for Architecture and the Building Environment)

'In public health, we've got to address the rising expectations of consumerism. People demand better buildings.'
Peter Wearmouth (NHS Estates acting Chief Executive)

This book has explored the relationship between buildings and health and touched on the intractable issues that confront architecture and medicine. Philosophers will continue to debate the meaning of art and science. However, one important and central aspect thrown up by these debates is the role that good briefing plays in the creation of primary health care facilities. This chapter is not a conclusion or a summary of the topics explored in the preceding pages because we are looking at a development process. Rather, it examines a number of ideas which may provide a fruitful path to follow in future, and identifies some of the challenges which need to be confronted for progress to continue.

The problem

We have seen that historically, when medical knowledge was limited, health care focused on the sense of well-being. Through the ages, scientific knowledge advanced and medical skills developed a pace. In the UK, the NHS has transformed medical expectations, but we now find that there is a return to the holistic approach to the care of our bodies. Technology and wealth have been found not to be the elixir of life. There is a plethora of intangible concepts with which to grapple and these questions will continue to be examined and debated in the search for a high quality of life. Good environmental conditions in the place where we live are the bedrock for good health.

The opportunity

The information age has given us the ability to share knowledge globally. There has been a new awakening of moral attitudes and responsibilities arising out of the Human Rights Act which is giving a greater sense of respect for the individual person. This is reflected in health care which is once again becoming focused on the patient as an individual. The case studies illustrate this trend in attitudes and approach to health care and we should be encouraged by the opportunities now being presented to capture the ethos coming out of thoughtful building briefs.

The target audience for the book is primarily architects and doctors but everyone involved in the provision of primary health care is increasingly aware that the individual must be the centre of their own health care, or well-being. There seems to be a universal acceptance that this policy can apply in both rich and poor economies. Health for All really is a policy for primary medical care which has no opponents, and crosses political boundaries.

The training of doctors is becoming more broadly based. Many University departments are now recognising that a scientific and technology based approach for medical education does not give a sufficiently well rounded training for the doctors of the next generation. Humanities are being introduced to the curriculum of medical schools which reflect the recognition that doctors need to treat patients in a more holistic manner. In the same way that Architects have moved on from the principal of 'a house is a machine for living in', so doctors are recognising that well-being is more complex than scientific enquiry alone.

The Government is also moving its position on health care policy with a new understanding of the importance of patients' needs. The requirements for health care are being assessed from the perspective of patients and there is recognition that the social agenda for health care needs to become more inclusive. Inevitably, this will lead to greater complexity in the organisation of services, and the crossing of boundaries between traditional concepts of health care, social services such as housing and the treatment of mental health issues. One is lead down the path of recognising the importance of the built environment to provide a humane place in which to live a healthy life. The opening few pages of this book described the historical importance of the home, and there is a growing weight of opinion which is returning to the home as the focal point and centre for health treatment in the future.

Trends

The case studies bring together a range of solutions from which it is possible to distil a series of common strands in the design approach.

- Policies around the world are concentrating on improving health care services at a primary level.
- There is universal attention to patient centred care irrespective of the size of the building, or wealth of the country, in which it is located.
- Architecture and medicine are talking to each other. The quality of the humane healing environment is seen as a positive benefit. The technocrats are acknowledging the contribution to health care from urban design. The quality of the place we live in is important to our well-being.
- Our well-being is reflected in the environmental quality of our new health buildings: smaller, community based flexible spaces, easily accessible and welcoming. They are designed for the benefit of the patient rather than the provider of medical services.
- There is a high incidence of curved shapes in the design of small health buildings. The building form envelopes the user, provides comfort and is reassuring. It is nonthreatening, and not confrontational. By a combination of form, light and colour buildings around the world straddle cultural differences with an architectural language which individuals can recognise whatever their mother tongue.

Future objectives

Doctors and architects need to work more closely together. Through the development of briefing documents, we should be optimistic about the opportunities that will arise for primary health care buildings in the future. They will provide the physical framework within which the complex social interaction of the community can engage with the medical profession. There is agreement that many of the better examples of good design for health buildings have been built in the primary care sector.

1. The brief should be the central and fundamental cornerstone for the provision of future health care buildings. It should set down the ethos and culture for the health care environment. Many of these over-arching objectives will be common to the design of a doctor's surgery anywhere in the world.
2. There are both strategic and practical levels of planning. It is at the practical level where there may be more substantial differences in the briefing document between one country and another.
3. The brief should set down the design aspirations. It will set out the 'wish list' and establish the sense of wonder which excites the spirit when good architecture is encountered.
4. The brief must bring together current ideas and anticipate future trends.
5. It must also capture the sense of change which is sweeping through the primary health care design field not just in the UK, and the USA, but in many parts of the world.
6. In another decade we are likely to find much broader acceptance of alternative therapies. In the West, we have only recently begun to understand and accept the contribution that alternative health remedies can bring. How much more there must be to learn about traditional Chinese medicine, for example, and environments such as the Glasgow Homoeopathic Hospital may well be the forerunner of many other buildings in the future seeking to combine traditional medicine, alternative therapies, and a high quality of environmental design.
7. More sophisticated linkages are likely to emerge. Key words and phrases to consider when writing a brief are:
   - government policy
   - community facilities
   - education (training)
   - sustainability

- knowledge (transfer of skills)
- value for money
- finance and funding
- flexibility
- communications
- location (accessibility)
- transport policy
- patient needs.

An examination of these issues will assist in establishing the strategic framework for the design of a new primary health facility. It may be helpful to prepare checklists on these points as an *aide-mémoire* during discussions with key members of the client and design team. This will give focus and direction to the establishment of both the strategic and practical aspects of the brief.

Design quality (or buzz factor)

Our modern understanding of a primary health centre was set out in the Dawson Report (1920) as 'An institution equipped for services of curative and preventive medicine to be conducted by general practitioners of that district, in conjunction with an efficient nursing service and with the aid of visiting consultants and specialists'. It remains a valid definition today, but during the intervening 80 years the earlier professional arrogance of architects and doctors has shifted markedly towards a more humane, understanding, and listening attitude. This approach is explored in the editorial of *Medical Humanities* (Evans, 2001).

'Medical humanities as an aspiration looks both forward and backward, seeking in part the *rediscovery* of a certain attitude towards medicine, its natural objects/subjects (patients) and its place in the cultural, artistic and scientific order. That attitude is embodied in the idea of a Renaissance Man or Woman embracing an interdisciplinary (even omni-disciplinary) view of the world, a universal gaze which is, on the face of it, no longer available to us in a world of runaway specialisation in knowledge. Consider how one might both celebrate "The beauty of the human form and the nobility of the human spirit" and peruse "An insatiable curiosity for the materiality of the here and now, a Faustian itch to explore ... ." – a universal gaze which, fused within an individual mind, may seem paradoxical, rather than merely daunting.

Be that as daunting – or as paradoxical – as it may, we suggest that one source of both moral and intellectual renaissance for the contemporary physician lies in recapturing a sense of *wonder* at the human body, its place in the natural realm and its miraculous functioning as the fount, and the medium, of embodied human experience.'

This view is echoed by the Government, by CABE (Commission for Architecture in the Built Environment) and many others in the architectural profession in recognising the importance of design quality and the need for a 'wow' factor. The excitement and vision that architecture can give to the

human spirit can be more readily seen as the basis of a health policy built around personal wellbeing. In short a holistic approach. Perhaps all this was foreseen by Antoine Checkhoff who said in a letter to a fellow writer:

'I thought then that the sensitivity of the artist may equal the knowledge of the scientist. Both have the same object, nature, and perhaps in time it will be possible for them to link together in a great and marvellous force which is at present hard to imagine'.

By closer co-operation the medical and architectural professions will be better equipped to answer in a more rounded and complete way our individual health needs.

The large commercial architectural practices in America are beginning to question the philosophy of creating very large hospital complexes, partly as a result of pressure on cost-fitting policies in the USA. The problems being experienced in the UK with the quality of the new wave of hospitals procured through the PFI process highlights the historical priorities given to functionality and cost standards in the UK building programme. The sheer size of some of the largest hospital projects invites comparisons with the grim environments of some large airport complexes, or even the new town developments of the 1960's. The government, fortunately, is now recognising the importance of good design and the limitations of a precocious project management profession which has mushroomed in recent decades. Perhaps the ambitions of grandeur on a larger scale would be better served by a more humble approach to meeting the smaller scale of human requirements of social interchange at a person to person scale. It is at this scale that the all-important relationship between patient and doctor takes place.

The gap between large practice, working on the big hospital projects, and those who are working on the smaller primary health care projects is a difficult one to bridge.

My own view is that NHS Estates' attempt to solve this problem by the introduction to Procure 21, and the batching of smaller projects into larger contract packages is unlikely to succeed. The LIFT programme is more promising but, is still at an early stage in development. Government policies are not consistent. For example:

- The Government is advocating better design standards in civic buildings.
- The NHS Plan has a very ambitious programme for investment in small-scale buildings (i.e. GP surgeries).
- The Government seems intent on pursuing building procurement through the PFI process (which is not suitable for small projects and is attracting a great deal of adverse criticism on the design standards achieved in recent health projects).

Recurring themes

The following list sets out a number of key ideas which have kept re-emerging throughout my research for this book, and many of them can be identified in the buildings illustrated in the preceding chapter.

- Emphasis on quality of architectural design:
  - importance of high quality environmental factors.
- Emphasis on the patient as an individual:
  - patient focused care as a local level of primary care being the hub of patient treatment rather than the start of a linear process of passing through various levels of specialisation.
- Building flexibility – design for change, openness, accessibility.
- Buildings have not played a key role in health policy, but need to in future.
- There has been insufficient recognition of the importance of environmental quality, and the effect that this can have on health care.
- Architects need to take up the opportunity to build on the new interest by doctors to embrace health and humanities.
- It is people that regenerate places, not places that regenerate people. Over reliance on economic, social and physical modelling techniques and statistical analysis at the expense of visual stimulus, under-values the importance of architecture.
- Visual stimulus is a key ingredient of the built environment. The delight of architecture should not be squeezed out of the built environment by analytical methodologies.
- The theoretical framework set out in Chapters 3–5 discusses the factors which will shape future primary health care buildings in four main groups:
  - policy
  - design
  - finance
  - briefing.
- Give status to the product as well as the process (think of design as well as construction).
- Put architecture back into health.
- The patient must come first.

A framework for the brief: the ethos

The key words and phrases listed earlier in this chapter will shape the brief and establish the starting point for defining the ethos of the building which is being commissioned.

Right at the beginning of the document there should be a section which encourages the design team to set out the quality aspirations expected from the building. It needs to encourage future users of the building to think about what the ethos of the building should be; to set out what the building users want out of the building; and what are the intangible values that the designers aim to achieve. For example, should the building be:

- friendly
- efficient
- welcoming
- relaxing
- comfortable
- warm
- pleasant
- accessible.

There should be a fundamental skew to the way briefing documents are written compared to the priority given to the tests for functionality and finance which have been the benchmark for commissioning primary care health buildings until recently. The brief should seek to encourage the achievement of high design standards through the eyes of the patient – the tests of functionality and cost should be a secondary, albeit essential, requirement of the procurement process for any new primary health care building.

Huge potential benefits are coming out of these changing philosophies in primary health care buildings which will influence the quality and procurement methodology for our health buildings at the specialised end of health care. Opinions are being voiced about larger hospital sites being broken down into villages, with different architects being appointed for specialist departments, or even viewing a hospital in terms of adjacent development within the urban planning of adjacent blocks in our existing city centres. Medical schools are responding to these challenges by the introduction of humanity courses. Architectural departments in our universities should similarly respond by giving greater attention to the training of future generation of architects in the health sector. There is little attention being given to the design of health buildings at either an under graduate level, or research programmes for post-graduate study.

Jessica Corner articulates some of the shortcomings from the eyes of the nurse when she says:

'the clinical setting adopts, through its architectural presence, both the interior design and building structure, a message of progress, cleanliness and efficiency. This takes precedence over comfort, reassurance, information or participation. The architecture supports the quite literal transportation of people into the world of treatment and its time dimensions ... . There is a process of separating people from normal life in the manner from which they are conducted from the hospital door towards all departments inside. ... Clinic, ward and consultation room structures reinforce the separation between patient and professional. ... These are the architectures of treatment and not of personal care.'

She goes on to argue that:

'Policy makers for healthcare need to determine the form of future buildings. Buildings, whether they are large hospitals or local surgeries, need to be different. They need to embody different meanings. In particular buildings need to convey recognition of people's sense of self, of "me", rather than promote, as they do now, the collective need for healthcare to get 'the job done' by controlling and processing patients.' (Corner 2001.)

Strategic components of a brief

Having established a framework of ideas or ethos, and understanding the context and networking requirements for a particular building in a specific location, the strategic components of a brief can be more precisely laid down. These will include:

- The vision:
  - how will the experience of visitors, patients and staff be enhanced by the building?
  - how will the design quality add to the expectation of excellent?
  - will be high quality environment be achieved?
  - will it be patient focused?
- The process:
  - select an appropriate procurement method to ensure that design quality isn't stifled.
- Urban design
  - will the building contribute to the sense of place?
  - will transport linkages work?
- Benchmarking:
  - is the building going to add to the level of competencies prevailing in the vicinity?
- Value for money:
  - will it represent 'best value'?
- Patient centred:
  - will the brief encourage good environmental design and achieve therapeutic benefits for patients and all other users of the building?
  - is it patient centred?

Practical components of a brief

After the ethos of the project has been defined, and the strategic objectives have been agreed, the practical issues of functionality and cost can be explored. What this research has revealed is the benefits that would arise if a new data-based handbook for primary health care facilities was available, but written through the eyes of the patient rather than from the perspective of the health service provider. Thus, new standards could be quantified and dimensioned for:

- patient control of their environment in treatment rooms, waiting rooms and other spaces
- design of furnishings, fixtures and fittings
- flexibility in the layout of equipment within a space
- flexibility of use of a space
- environmental design standards and performance specifications
- compliance with access for the disabled
- transportation links (on foot, cycle, car, or public transport)
- functionality
- landscaping
- building materials
- cost limits.

A nineteenth-century approach to well-being for town dwellers was the Victorian Park which was conceived as a green lung to improve the public health of the urban workforce. Allowed to fall into disrepair during the twentieth century they are being restored, once again, and their original qualities being rediscovered.

Table 12.1 A framework of issues for doctors and architects to discuss together when developing a brief for a healthy living centre – to compare, contrast and challenge each other about ideas when establishing the criteria for a new building

	Issue	Architecture	Medicine
1	Functionality	Space standards, initial cost effectiveness, data sheets	Flexibility, meeting future working patterns
1	Multi-agency	Planning flexibility, long life, loose fit	Choice of agencies, services to be offered
1	Accessibility/convenience	Transport linkages, pedestrian routes, parking, disabled access	Patient adjacency, alternative locations
1/2	Exemplar design models	Environmental performance standards	Good practice models, standard room plans
1/3	Site/location/land acquisition	Urban context, planning constraints, value for money	Convenience, visibility of building, availability
2	Brief – the ethos of building	Architectural language, style, patient comfort, therapeutic benefits	Personal rapport with patients, relationships, working environment, sense of well-being
2	Community	Quality of the place, welcoming, comfortable	Friendliness, reassurance, accessible
3	Finance – procurement method, costs	Contractual arrangements, PFI, LIFT, design criteria, project management, programming	PCG's/PCT's, ability to influence funding, budgets, access to finance
3	Sustainability	Energy consumption, life cycle costs	Recycle facilities, medical efficiency
3	Standardisation	Standard components within unique design, choice of materials	Routine procedures, clinic compatability with other surgery operating systems

Healthy living centres should be seen as a future resource (in the twenty-first century) for good advice. A patient-centred facility in the community where help can be found about diet, fitness, health checks, social services, and a range of other activities to encourage a sense of well-being in the place where we live.

Although not exhaustive, these items are typical of the main thrust of a design brief which needs to be analysed by looking at patient convenience, effectiveness and efficiency. The practical performance of a building is obviously important and it must work efficiently, – i.e. there must be a basic level of design competence of technical matters but they must contribute to achieving the design quality issues set out in the ethos.

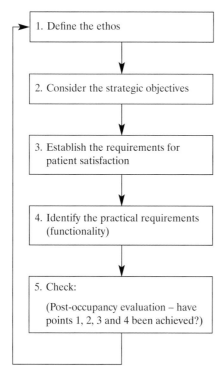

Figure 12.1 Assembling a brief.

The loop is completed by ensuring that post-occupancy evaluations are undertaken to measure the success (or otherwise) of meeting the aspirations for the building which were set out in the ethos statement.

The end of this book provides an opportunity to set out four key guides to providing better healthy living centres in the future:

- Doctors and architects must work together and develop common briefs for the next generation of primary health care buildings. They must be written for the benefit of patients.

- The buildings must be designed to create a framework for the social interaction of the community which they serve. They must be socially inclusive, flexible, caring and accessible.
- Well-designed primary health care buildings will become the focal point for the next generation of health buildings and will influence the shape and operation of larger and specialist facilities.
- Primary care buildings will become the catalyst to encourage greater harmony between health policies around the world. Sustainable construction methods will develop and at the same time provide shelter for holistic medical protocols to flourish.

Finally, I hope that the collation of ideas and examples in this book will encourage everybody involved with the design and provision of primary health care buildings to think about the briefing process. The broad strategic goal of good health for everyone starts with the ethos of care at primary health level. All the practical details which flow from that philosophy will develop and grow as the environmental and therapeutic benefits are researched and refined through the search for design quality in our buildings of the future.

Postscript

As this book goes to press the rate of change in the delivery of primary health care services in the UK is accelerating in a way that could not have been envisaged a few years ago. In particular, the importance of design quality is recognised by the government. The spring 2002 budget has introduced a commitment to spend an additional £40 billion on a series of reforms to improve the NHS. It will see a 46% increase in real terms on current spending by 2008 and effectively double the NHS budget of 1997. Much of this additional expenditure will be focused on the primary health care sector. For example:

- By 2008 there are 'likely to be' net increases of at least 15,000 more GPs and consultants, 30,000 more therapists and scientists and 35,000 more nurses, midwives and health visitors.
- Primary care trusts (PCTs) will be free to purchase care from the most appropriate provider – be they public, private or voluntary.
- PCTs will be required to publish prospectuses, accounting to local residents for their spending decisions, the range and quality of services, and explaining the increase in choices that patients will have.

The prime minister has said that 75% of total NHS funding will be with PCTs, although a significant percentage of this expenditure will be required to be spent on meeting statutory standards of care and the provision of health services.

NHS Estates are also moving rapidly towards embracing the benefits of good design. The PCT of NHS Estates has recognised that ideas have moved on considerably in the past few years and they are working towards further design guidance for primary care premises. They now view primary care as going far beyond traditional general medical services.

An annual 'Building Better Health Care Awards' competition includes a primary care category. At last year's event Lord Hunt, design champion for the NHS, emphasised his concern with good design and said:

'We have a strong record in health on promoting design quality. We recognise that how a building looks and how it feels to work in have a major impact on patients, staff and visitors. Well-designed buildings are welcoming, safe and effective. Good design lifts the spirit, helps patients to recover, and inspires staff to give of their best.'

This theme has been repeated in speeches he has given at several events during the early part of 2002. Likewise, CABE is building relationships ever more strongly with the government and has reached a funding agreement with NHS Estates which will see it working directly with NHS Trusts. This collaboration will include working together on five primary care projects and three one stop shop primary care centres. This will be watched with particular interest as the current NHS Plan includes the stated aim of realising 500 one stop centres around the country all offering a range of services beyond traditional GP surgeries such as dentists, opticians, pharmacies and social workers. CABE says it will launch a national design competition to establish design quality benchmarks for such centres, a process that will involve a number of real sites, preferably with an identified client and budget (*RIBA Practice Bulletin*, 10 May 2002).

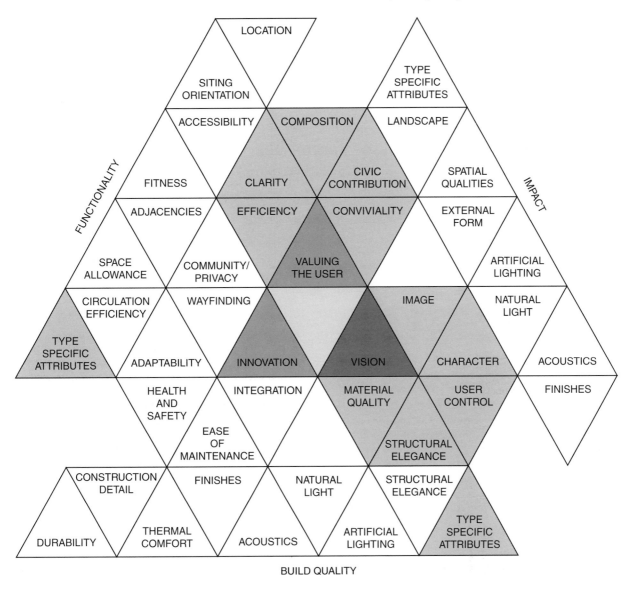

Figure 12.2

The government is also recognising the importance of consumerism, which mirrors the patient centred ideals of the NHS Plan. These concepts will apply not only to hospital design, but also to patient friendly environments in primary care centres. Perhaps the nomenclature 'waiting room' will be banished to be replaced by 'reception area'. Doctors will increasingly become aware that they are providing a service to customers who, however indirectly, are paying for their health treatment.

The LIFT programme, which attempts to address many of these issues, by the introduction of private finance at a local level continues to show teething troubles. The first wave of projects under this initiative is proving to be a testing time for the establishment of procedures and policies and may result in delays in procurement. Part of this process encourages the establishment of design benchmarking where CABE have a central role. Working with CABE the CIC is developing a set of Design Quality Indicators to be used as an evaluation tool. Currently at the test bed stage it is likely to be 2003 before this work is finally in the public realm. However the pilot project is producing innovative thinking and setting new standards to judge the quantitative and qualitative issues of design quality. Based on a matrix of responses firmness, commodity and delight become functionality, build quality and impact.

Figure 12.2, originated by Sunand Pasad from work carried out by the SPRU (The Science Policy Research Unit) is one of a series of illustrations which explore the relationships between functionality, build quality and impact. In particular it brings together three levels f quality – basic (generally quantitative), added value (the factors identified in the hexagons) and excellent (the centre, where all three quality fields overlap).

Ultimately, all of us as individuals (and patients) will determine the future shape of primary health care services in the UK. The impact these forces will have on the extent by which governments influence future health policy will depend on the power of consumerism, the demand for health services, and the competitive market forces of the private health sector. We can anticipate that a concern for higher design standards will inexorably become more important in this process. Perhaps the biggest challenge to architects is for them to design innovative solutions that rise to the high expectations now being looked for in health buildings.

References

Anon. (2000a). Only half way to health. *The Sunday Times*, 30 July.

Anon. (2000b). Better health. *The Financial Times*, 21 June.

Anon. (2000c). Unhealthy ambitions. *The Times*, 15 May.

Anon. (2000d). Radical medicine. *The Sunday Times*, 25 June.

Bailey, J., Glendinning, C. and Gould, H. (1997). *Better Buildings for Better Services: Innovative Developments in Primary Care*. Oxford: Radcliffe Medical Press.

Barrick, A. (2000). *Building*, 20 April, p. 9.

Blyth, A. and Worthington, J. (2001). *Managing the Brief for Better Design*. London: E & FN Spon.

Boyce-Tillman, J. (2000). The Rhythm of Life, *Classic fm*, Vol. 66, August, pp. 48–51.

Bristow, G. *et al.* (2000). Calling on mobiles. *Hospital Development*, February, p. 11

British Academy (2001). *The Quality of Life in the European Union: A Social Research Agenda*. www.britac.ac.uk

Bush-Brown, A. (1996). The healing environment. In Valins, M.S. and Slater, D. (eds) *Futurecare: New directions in Planning Health and Care Environments*. Oxford: Blackwell Science.

Calman, K.C. (1998). *The Potential for Health: How to Improve the Nation's Health*. Oxford: Oxford University Press.

Cammock, R. (1981). *Primary Health Care Buildings: Health Centres, Neighbourhood Clinics and Group Practice Surgeries: A Briefing and Design Guide for Architects and Their Clients*. London: The Architectural Press.

Chisholm, J. (1992). *Making Sense of the Cost Rent Scheme: The Business Side of General Practice*. Oxford: Radcliffe Medical Press.

Cole, J. (1995). Finance-over function. *Hospital Development*, May, Vol. 26, issue 5, p. 9.

Cole, J. (2000). Capturing design quality. Paper presented at 'Architects for Health' Seminar, on 17 February 2000, Reform Club, London.

Commission for Architecture in the Built Environment (2001). *The Value of Urban Design*. London: Thomas Telford.

Construction Industry Council. *Can We Measure the Quality of Design in Buildings?*

Coonan, R. (1996). *Time for Design: Good practice in Building, Landscape, and Urban Design*. London: English Partnerships.

Corner, J. (2001). *Between You and Me – Closing the Gap Between People and Health Care*. Monograph of the Ninth HM Queen Elizabeth the Queen Mother Fellowship. London, The Nuffield Trust.

Cox, S. and Hamilton, A. (1995). *Architects Job Book*, 6th edition. London: RIBA Publications.

Critchlow, K. and Allen, J. (1995). *The Whole Question of Health*. London: The Prince of Wales' Institute of Architecture.

Department for Culture, Media and Sport (2000). *Better Public Buildings – A Proud Legacy for the Future*. London: Department for Culture, Media and Sport.

Department of Environment, Transport and the Regions (1999). *Housing Quality Indicators*. London: HMSO

Department of Environment, Transport and the Regions (2000). *By Design – Urban Design in the Planning System: Towards Better Practice*. London: Thomas Telford.

Department of Environment, Transport and the Regions (2000). *KPI Report for The Minister for Construction*. London: HMSO

Department of Health (1996). *Choice and Opportunity. Primary Care: The Future*. London: The Stationery Office.

Downie, R.S. (ed.) (1994). *The Healing Arts: An Oxford Illustrated Anthology*. Oxford: Oxford University Press.

Downie, R.S. and MacNaughton, J. (2000). *Clinical Judgement, Evidence in Practice*. Oxford: Oxford University Press

Duffy, F. (1992). *The Changing Workplace*. London: Phaidon Press.

Duffy, F. (1997). *The New Office*. London: Contran Octopus.

Duffy, F. *et al.* (1993). *The Responsible Workplace*. London: Butterworth-Heinemann.

English Partnerships (1998). *Time for Design: Good Practice in Building, Landscape and Urban Design*. London: English Partnerships.

Fairley, J. (1997). Someone should DO something. *The Mail on Sunday*, 28 December.

Foque, R. (1999). *Healing Environments: New Typologies for Health Care Architecture*. The Architects for Health Open

Lecture for 1999. Held at the Royal Institute of British Architects, London.

Francis, S. (2000). Capturing design quality. Paper presented at 'Architects for Health' Seminar, on 17 February, Reform Club, London.

Francis, S. *et al.* (1999). *50 Years of Ideas in Health Care Buildings*. London: The Nuffield Trust.

Fuller, S. (1977). *Science*. Buckingham: Open University Press.

Gallup, J.W. (1999). *Wellness Centers*. New York: John Wiley.

Gibson, B. (ed.) (1999). *Human Rights and the Courts*. Winchester: Waterside Press..

Gledhill, R. (2000a). Therapy is replacing religion says Carey. *The Times* 1 August.

Gledhill, R. (2000b). Carey attacks 'arrogance' of surgeons. *The Times*, 19 October, p. 9.

Gombrich, E.H. (1964). *The Story of Art*. London: Phaidon Press.

Haldane, D. and Loppert, S. (eds) (1999). *The Arts in Health Care: Learning from Experience*. London: The King's Fund.

Hall-Dendy, A. (1997). Banking on design quality in PFI. *Hospital Development*, February, Vol. 28, issue 2, p. 8.

Hardman, R. (2000). We're doomed if we ignore nature says Prince. *The Daily Telegraph*, 17 May.

Harvey, D. (1997). The nature of enquiry and explanation in the social sciences: a neoclassical view. Lecture notes, University of Newcastle upon Tyne, November.

Hawkes, N. (2000). Surgeries will gain from £1bn enterprise fund. *The Times*, 7 December.

Healey, P. (2001). Researching people, place and urban governance: a city planning perspective. Talk for RAND Corporation Workshop. 'Population, health and the environment' theme. 11–13 January, Santa Monica, California.

Horam, J. (1997). Horam gets tough on designers and builders at PFI conference. News item. *Hospital Development*, March, Vol. 28, issue 3, p. 10.

Hosking, S. and Haggard, L. (1999). *Healing the Hospital Environment*. London: E & FN Spon.

Howie, J.G.R., Heaney, D.J. and Maxwell, M. (1997). *Measuring quality in general practice. Pilot study of a needs process and outcome measure*. Occasional Paper No 75 Royal College of General Practitioners.

Howie, J.G.R., Heaney, D., Maxwell, M. and Walker, J.J. (1998). *A comparison of the Patient Enablement Instrument (PEI) against two established satisfaction scales as an outcome measure of primary care consultations*. Family Practice; 15: 165-171.

Hunt, W.D. Jr. (ed.), (1960). *Hospital, Clinics and Health Centers, An Architectural Record Book*. McGraw-Hill. pp. 204–206.

Jacobs, J. (1961). *The Death and Life of Great American Cities*. London: Penguin Books.

Jencks, C. (1995). *The Architecture of the Jumping Universe*. London: Academy Group.

Jones, A. (2000). 'Capturing design quality' paper presented at 'Architects for Health' Seminar, on 17 February, Reform Club, London.

Jones, R.V.H., Bolden, K.J., Pereira Gray, D.J. and Hall, M.S. (1978). *Running a Practice*, London: Croom Helm.

Kantrowitz, M and Associates (1993). *Design Evaluation of Six Primary Care Facilities for the Purpose of Informing Future Design Decisions*. Martinez, CA: The Center for Health Design.

Kirklin, D. and Richardson, R. (eds) (2001). *Medical Humanities: A Practical Introduction*. London: Royal College of Physicians of London.

Kirtley, G. (2000). Briefing healthcare facilities – a resume. Notes from correspondence, 29 May.

Kuffner, D.J. (1996). Patient-focused design. In Valins, M.S. and Slater, D. eds, *Futurecare: New Directions in Planning Health and Care Environments*. Oxford: Blackwell Science.

Lacey, R. and Danziger, D. (1999). *The Year 1000*. London: Little Brown.

Laing, A. *et al.* (1998). *New Environments for Working*. London: Construction Research Communications.

Lawson, B. (1997). *Design in Mind*. Oxford: Architectural Press.

Lawson, B. (1997). *How Designers Think: The Design Process Dennystified*. Oxford: Architectural Press.

Leather, P. (2001). *A Comparative Study of the Impact of Environmental Design upon Hospital Staff and Patients (Draft Report)*. University of Nottingham (Institute of Work Health and Organisations).

Long, K. and Lewis, J. (2000). Doubts over PFI hospitals. *Building Design*, 22 September.

Loppert, S. (1999). The art of the possible. In: Haldene, D. and Loppert, S. (eds) *The Arts in Health Care: Learning from Experience*. London: King's Fund.

MacNaughton, R. J. (1996). Numbers scales and qualitative research. *Lancet* Vol. 347, pp.1099–1100.

MacRae, S. (2000). *Patient Centred Healthcare: An interview with Susan MacRae*. www.Best4Health.org.

Malkin, J. (1982). *The Design of Medical and Dental Facilities*. Van Nostrand Reinhold.

Malkin, J. (1992). *Hospital Interioir Architecture*. New York: John Wiley.

Martin, M. (2000). What is architecture? Lecture notes, University of Newcastle upon Tyne, September.

Maxwell, G. (1997). In search of design values. *Hospital Development*, March, Vol. 28, issue 3, p. 13.

Medical Architectural Research Unit (1996). *Designing Primary Healthcare Premises: A Resource*. North West Regional Health Authority.

Menin, S.C. (1997). *Relating the Past: Sibeluis, Aalto and the Profound Logos*. PhD thesis, Faculty of Law, Environment and Social Sciences, Newcastle upon Tyne.

Morgan, J. (2000). Charles wants minorities to aid architects. *The Sunday Times*, 3 September.

Morris, N. (1997). Niche Opportunity. *Health Service Journal*, 27 February, pp. 9–10.

National Health Service (1996). *Statement of Fees and Allowances*. London: HMSO.

National Health Service (1997). *Primary Care Bill*. 27 February. London: The Stationery Office.

National Health Service (1998). *Our Healthier Nation*. Cm 3852, February. London: The Stationery Office.

National Health Service (2000). Plan. Cm 4818-I, July. London: The Stationery Office.

National Primary Care Research and Development Centre (1995). *Prospectus 1995–1997*, University of Manchester.

NHS Estates (1991). *Health Building Note 46, general medical practice premises for the provision of primary health care services*. London: HMSO.

NHS Estates (1994). *Better by Design: Pursuit of Excellence in Healthcare Buildings*. London: HMSO.

NHS Estates (1994). *Environments for Quality Care: Health Buildings in the Community*. London: HMSO.

NHS Estates (1995). *Health Building Note 36, Local Healthcare Facilities*. London: HMSO.

NHS Estates (1999). *Improving the Quality of Design of Healthcare Buildings*. Report, 15 December 1999.

NHS Estates (2000). *Procure 21, Building Better Health*. Leeds: NHS Estates.

Noble, A. (1999). Needs of clients and patients in hopsital buildings. In: Haldane, D. and Loppert, S. (eds), *The Arts in Health Care: Learning from Experience*. London: King's Fund.

North West Regional Health Authority (1996). *Designing Primary Healthcare Premises: A Resource Prepared for North West Regional Health Authority/NHS Executive North West by Maru, Health buildings Research and Policy Centre*. Liverpool: North West Regional Health Authority.

Nugent, R. (1995). Shaping the future: new horizons. *Hospital Development*, July/August, Vol. 26, issue 7, 11–12.

O'Marberry, S. (ed.) (1997). *Health Design*. New York: John Wiley.

O'Neill, D. (2000). Whom do we serve? www.healthdesign.org.

Orr, R. (1991). In: O'Marberry, S. ed., *Innovations in Healthcare Design*. New York: Van Nostrand Reinhold, 1995.

Palumbo, Lord (1995). *Design Quality in Higher Education Buildings: Keynote Address*. London: Thomas Telford.

Parker, J. (1997). Urban landscapes. *Hospital Development*, March, Vol. 28, issue 3, 21–24.

Pena, W. with Parshall, S. and Kelly, K. (1987). *Problem Seeking – An Architectural Programming Primer*. Washington, DC: AIA Press.

Persaud, R. (2000). Ultra sounds. *Classic fm*, Vol. 66, August, pp. 56–59.

Pevsner, N. (1960). *Pioneers of Modern Design*. London: Penguin Books.

Picker Institute (1998). Working paper: *Consumer Perceptions of the Healthcare Environment – An Investigation to Determine What Matters*. Martinez, CA: Center for Health Design.

Rasmussen, S.E. (1959). *Experiencing Architecture*. London: Chapman and Hall.

Read, H. (1949). *The Meaning of Art*. London: Penguin Books.

Richardson, V. (2001). Architects workload survey. *RIBA Journal*, April.

Robertson, P. (1996). *Music in Mind*. London: Channel 4 Television.

Robertson, P. (2000a). In sound health. *Classic fm*, Vol. 66, August, pp. 55–59.

Robertson, P. (2000b). *The Second International Conference on Health and Design, Integrating Design and Care in Hospital Planning for the New Millennium*. 18–22 June, Stockholm.

Rogers, L. and Prescott, M. (2000). GP surgeries will be hospitals to cut waiting lists. *The Sunday Times*, 23 July.

Rogerson, P. (1996). Faith healing. *Hospital Development*, January, Vol. 27, issue 1, p. 10.

Roland, M., Holden, J. and Campbell, S. (1998). *Quality Assessment for General Practice: Supporting Clinical Governance in Primary Care Groups*. National Primary Care Research & Development Centre, University of Manchester.

Rouse, J. (2000). Why surveyors haven't got a clue. *Building*, 24 November.

Royal Fine Art Commission (1996). *Design Quality in Higher Education Buildings*. London: Thomas Telford.

Royal Institute of British Architects (1995). *Strategic Study of the Profession; Phases 3 & 4: The Way Forward*. London: RIBA.

Royal Institute of British Architects (1997). *Future Premises for Primary Health Care: Report on a Symposium (2 April 1996) and a Workshop (3 December 1996) organised by the RIBA Health Buildings Design Quality Forum*. London: RIBA/NHS Estates.

Rubin, H.R. *et al.* (1998). *An Investigation to Determine whether the Built Environment Affects Patients' Medical Outcomes*. Martinez, CA: Center for Health Design.

Scher, P. (1995). First fruit: the Orchards Health and Family Centre. *Hospital Development*, May, Vol. 26, issue 5, pp. 21-25.

Scher, P. (1996). *Patient-focused Architecture for Health Care*. Manchester: Faculty of Art and Design, Manchester Metropolitan University.

Scher, P. (1997). Letter from Norway: 'human centred' design. *Hospital Development*, October, Vol. 28, issue 9, p. 5.

Scher, P. (2000). The London Haven. *Hospital Development*, May.

Scher, P. and Senior, P. (1999). *The Exeter Evaluation*. Manchester: Arts for Health.

Scottish Executive (2000). *The Development of a Policy on Architecture for Scotland*.

Scrunton, R. (1996). *An Intelligent Person's Guide to Philosophy*. London: Gerald Duckworth.

Senior, P. (ed.) (1999). *The Culture, Health and the Arts World Symposium*, April, The Manchester Metropolitan University.

Senior, P. and Croall, J. (1993). *Helping to Heal, The Arts in Health Care*. London: Calouste Gulbenkian Foundation.

Shepley, M.M. (1997) Design evaluation. In: O'Marberry, S. ed., *Healthcare Design*. New York: John Wiley, p. 73.

Stanger, G. (1998). Royal Victoria Infirmary, Newcastle upon Tyne. Ophthalmology Department, Arts Lottery Project.

Steel, J. (1999). Arts and storytelling with young people in hospitals. In: Haldene, D. and Loppert, S. eds, *The Arts in Health Care: Learning from Experience*. London: King's Fund.

Thomson, W.A.R. (1964). *The Doctor's Surgery: A Practical Guide to the Planning of General Practice,* London: The Practitioners.

Toynbee, R. (1972). *A Study of History*. London: Oxford University Press and Thames and Hudson.

Treasury Taskforce (1999). *How to achieve design quality in PFI projects,* Private Finance, Technical note no 7. http://www.treasury-projects-taskforce.gov.uk and later in 2000 at http://www.ogc.gov.uk

Ulrich, R. S. (1984). View through a window may influence recovery from surgery. *Science* 224: 420–421.

Valins, M. (1993). *Primary Health Care Centres.* Harlow: Longman.

Valins, M.S. and Slater, D (1996). *Futurecare: New Directions in Planning Health and Care Environments,* Oxford: Blackwell Science.

Vesey, G. and Foulkes, P. (1990). *Dictionary of Philosophy.* Glasgow: Collins.

Wales, HRH Prince of (1989). *A Vision of Britain*. London: Doubleday.

Wales, HRH Prince of (2000). We must go with the grain of nature. *The Times*, 18 May.

Weaver, M. (2000). Delight detector. *Building Design*, 24 November, p. 1.

Wells-Thorpe, J. (2000). Design for enhanced recovery. Lecture given at conference, Integrating Design and Care in Hospital Planning for the New Millennium, Stockholm, June 2000.

Weston, R. (1995). *Alvar Aalto*. London: Phaidon Press.

Wilkin, D., Butler, T. and Coulter, A. (1997). New models of primary care: developing the future, a development and research programme, primary care discussion paper 2, National Primary Care Research and Development Centre. University of Manchester.

Wilson, C. St. J. (1992). *Architectural Reflections: Studies in the Philosophy and Practice of Architecture*. Oxford: Butterworth-Heinemann.

Winston, R. (2000). Modern medicine is bad for your health. *The Sunday Times*, 1 October, p. 9.

Wittkower, R. (1962). *Architectural Principles in the Age of Humanism*. London: Alec Tiranti.

World Health Organisation (1978). *Alma-Ata, 1978: Primary Health Care, 'Health for All' series, No. 1.* Geneva: World Health Organisation.

World Health Organisation (1979). *Formulating Strategies for Health For All By the Year 2000, 'Health for All' series, No. 1.* Geneva: World Health Organisation.

Wright, M. (1998). The best medicine. *The Sunday Times*, 19 April.

Wylde, M. and Valins, M.S. (1996). The impact of technology. In: Valins, M.S. and Slater, D. eds, *Futurecare: New Directions in Planning Health and Care Environments*. Oxford: Blackwell Science.

Yorke, P. (1995). A view from the estates office. *Design Quality in High Education Buildings*. Royal Fine Art Commission Seminar, 21 November. London: Thomas Telford.

Index